Pictorial Guide to the Planets

Pictorial Guide

Joseph H. Jackson &

Third Edition

to the Planets
John H. Baumert

HARPER & ROW, PUBLISHERS, New York

Cambridge, Hagerstown, Philadelphia, San Francisco

London, Mexico City, São Paulo, Sydney

1817

To Jane and Tom and
To Jean, John, and Jeffrey

Illustration credits will be found on page 242.

Title page photograph: As Viking 2 approached Mars in 1976, it recorded a white water-ice cloud (left) stretching from the volcano Ascraeus Mons to the frost-covered Argyre Basin (right). Between these features is the Valles Marineris (top), an extensive canyon system many times larger than earth's Grand Canyon.

PICTORIAL GUIDE TO THE PLANETS (*Third Edition*). Copyright © 1973, 1965 by Joseph H. Jackson. Copyright © 1981 by Joseph H. Jackson and John H. Baumert. All rights reserved. Printed in the United States of America. No part of this book may be used or reproduced in any manner whatsoever without written permission except in the case of brief quotations embodied in critical articles and reviews. For information address Harper & Row, Publishers, Inc., 10 East 53rd Street, New York, N.Y. 10022. Published simultaneously in Canada by Fitzhenry & Whiteside Limited, Toronto.

Designer: Charlotte Staub

Library of Congress Cataloging in Publication Data

Jackson, Joseph Hollister.
   Pictorial guide to the planets.

   Includes index.
   1. Planets. I. Baumert, John H., joint author.
II. Title.
QB601.J3   1981   523.4   80-7897
ISBN 0-06-014869-1

81 82 83 84 85 10 9 8 7 6 5 4 3 2 1

Contents

Color photographs follow page 150.

Five hundred years ago, near the beginning of the Renaissance, European civilization stood on the threshold of discovery. The plucky caravels of Prince Henry the Navigator were being urged for a variety of reasons—economic, political, and for the love of adventure—down the west coast of Africa, around the Cape of Good Hope, and on toward the Indian subcontinent. An extraordinary account of distant travel, published a century before by a Venetian nobleman named Marco Polo, was being reread. Sailing ships had reached a stage in design sophistication where extended voyages on the open seas seemed possible. Then, in the course of a single century, came the establishment of an eastward sea route to India, the apparent discovery of a westward route to the South Seas, the realization that a new continent had been discovered, a preliminary exploration, and the initial steps at colonization of the New World. What a ring those words had then! The New World! A distant land, populated by strange men, where your fortune could be made, and your life begun again.

The Age of Discovery was partly a cause and partly an effect of the great cultural outburst that has led to the values and achievements of our own times. The many who stayed behind acquired a legacy from the deeds and thoughts of those few who sailed beyond the western seas to the New World. The exploration of the Americas provided a sense of perspective. There were other plants and animals in the New World, other peoples, other societies, other ways of life. In a devastating social criticism of contemporary European society, Voltaire imagined a Huron Indian brought to France, and viewed the social landscape through his eyes. The opening of the New World brought out much of the best, and some of the worst, in human beings; it provided an escape from stagnation and the prospect of a second chance. On the whole, the results have been salutary, and perhaps essential for the evolution of our civilization.

But today, the exploration of the earth's surface has been completed. For the joys of discovery and the lure of the frontier we must turn to the oceans and the skies. More than one new world now awaits exploration. There are eight other planets and forty-three satellites in our solar system—and tens of thousands of smaller bodies. We are alive at the first moment in history when man steps forth beyond the ancient confines of the planet of his birth. Beyond lie other worlds.

The moon is a somber, airless, desolate place. But because of the absence of atmosphere and water, its surface is largely unweathered. Thus, clues to the origin and evolution of the solar system may reward the first lunar explorers.

Venus is hot and arid. Because of its dense cloud layer, no one has ever directly viewed its surface—our information comes from infrared and microwave observations and a few surface photographs. Why is Venus so hot? Where did all the water go?

Mars is perhaps the most earthlike planet in the solar system, a glorious world with enormous volcanoes, ancient river valleys, massive dust storms. The evidence for life is at best ambiguous. What is the history of this sister world?

As different as the earth, the moon, Mars, and Venus are from each other, Jupiter is another kind of place entirely. We cannot see beneath its brightly colored, banded and belted clouds. But the atmosphere abounds in hydrogen and helium. Organic molecules must be present.

We do not know how far below the clouds the surface lies. Worse yet, we do not even know whether Jupiter has a surface, in the ordinary sense. The range of pressures that operate there is outside ordinary terrestrial experience.

And on it goes. Each world has its own kind of differentness, its unique problems and challenges. But we shall seek them out. The step we make now is irrevocable. The eight other planets, forty-three moons, and miscellaneous debris that Drs. Jackson and Baumert introduce on these pages will occupy us for centuries: Langrenus, Pandorae Fretum, Sinus Aestuum, Tithonius Lacus, Io, Enceladus: . . . The strange names of those distant places will come readily to our children's lips. There may our grandchildren be born. But even centuries hence, when every planet, moon, and asteroid has been trod, when all that is habitable has been colonized, planetary exploration need not cease. For beyond this provincial solar system, light-years distant in the immensity of space, beckon, vast and imponderable, a hundred billion stars.

CARL SAGAN
*Director, Laboratory for Planetary Studies,
Cornell University, Ithaca, New York*

Acknowledgments

The first close-up pictures of the lunar surface from Ranger 7 were barely inserted in the first edition of this book as it went to press in 1965. In 1980, close-up pictures of Jupiter and Saturn taken by Pioneer and Voyager spacecraft have been included in this third edition. In those 15 brief earth years, our view of the solar system has expanded by nearly a billion miles through the combined new instruments and vehicles developed by astronomers and space scientists. In this book we have tried to compress and integrate the most significant features of the vast solar and planetary knowledge thus won.

Among the many scientists who generously donated ideas and illustrations, we wish especially to express appreciation for the contributions of the late Dinsmore Alter of the Griffith Observatory; Audouin Dollfus of the Observatoire de Paris; Brian Mason of the American Museum of Natural History; Peter Millman of the National Research Council of Canada; Elizabeth Roemer of Flagstaff Station, U. S. Naval Observatory; E. K. Bigg, Commonwealth Scientific and Industrial Research Organisation, Australia; George C. Atamian, Talcott Mountain Science Center, Avon, Connecticut; Robert S. Dietz, Atlantic Oceanographic and Meteorological Laboratories, Miami; George R. Carruthers, U. S. Naval Research Laboratory; Clyde T. Holliday, The Johns Hopkins University; Steve Fentress, Jet Propulsion Laboratory; David F. Webb, American Science and Engineering, Inc.; Stephen Larson, Lunar and Planetary Laboratory; Robert M. MacQueen, High Altitude Observatory; Edwin F. Erickson, Ames Research Center; Larry D. Travis, Institute for Space Studies; Werner M. Neupert, Goddard Space Flight Center; Howard L. DeMastus, Sacramento Peak Observatory; Robert G. Knollenberg, Particle Measuring Systems, Inc.; and Farouk El-Baz, National Air and Space Museum.

Observatories that supplied photographs to round out this pictorial guide include especially the Dominion Astrophysical Observatory (Victoria, B.C.), the Lick Observatory, the Lowell Observatory, the Meudon and Pic-du-Midi observatories (France), the Hale observatories, and the Mount Stromlo and Siding Spring observatories (Australia). Other individuals and organizations who contributed in various ways include the Astronomical Society of the Pacific, the Commission for Physical Study of the Planets and Satellites of the International Astronomical Union, and B. J. Levin of the O. Schmidt Institute of Physics of the Earth (Moscow); the United States Air Force, Army, and Navy; the Atomic Energy Commission; the Coast and Geodetic Survey; the National Academy of Sciences; the National Research Council; the National Aeronautics and Space Administration; the National Weather Service, National Oceanic and Atmospheric Administration; Lawrence Radiation Laboratory; U. S. Geological Survey; J. B. Kendrick of Thompson Ramo Wooldridge Technology Laboratories; and William H. Pickering, Jet Propulsion Laboratory. Many publishers have cooperated, in particular Houghton Mifflin Company, Boston, as have such periodicals as *Astronautics & Aeronautics*, the *Astronomical Journal*, the *Astrophysical Journal*, the *Journal of Geophysical Research*, the *Journal of the Royal Astronomical Society of Canada*, *New Scientist*, *Science*, *Nature* and *Nature Physical Science*.

It is our good fortune to live in an era during which sound knowledge and vivid pictures of our solar system are gathered day by day by scientists eager to share them without reserve, as they have with us.

Joseph H. Jackson
John H. Baumert

Chapter I

Countdown to the Planets

"For now we see through a glass, darkly; but then face to face: now I know in part; but then shall I know even as also I am known."

I Corinthians 13:12

During the past 20 years a great transformation akin to that of which Paul thus wrote has taken place in our view of the solar system.

For three and a half centuries, astronomers had scrutinized the dim images of the planets and their moons in the mirrors of their telescopes. The mirrors grew larger and the images brighter decade by decade. Yet these faraway bodies were still seen "through a glass, darkly," for their light reflected from the sun flickered down faintly to us through the vapors and dust of the earth's atmosphere.

Then on October 4, 1957, a new era in solar system astronomy began. Man was no longer forced to study the planets, comets, and asteroids (minor planets) from the bottom of his atmospheric ocean. He could at last see from above the atmosphere and no longer be subject to its meteorological whims and disturbances.

Man has progressed from his first feeble attempts to launch satellites into earth orbit and to "hit" the moon, just as a hunter would shoot a duck, to manned exploration of the moon and unmanned exploration of the planets. Spacecraft have flown past Jupiter, Saturn, Mercury, Venus, and Mars, and have landed on the last two. Another is penetrating the outskirts of the solar system beyond Saturn. Now much of our system has been viewed "face to face."

With the advent of the space age, whole families of rockets and space vehicles have been created. The main thrust of these vehicles has been, quite naturally, the study of the third planet from the sun, the earth.

Orbiting satellites and space vehicles have revealed much about the size and shape of our planet and its gravitational and magnetic fields. The Van Allen belts of energetic particles have been discovered circling the earth within the streamlined geomagnetic cavity. The great ball of hydrogen around the earth has been photographed from the moon.

Now dozens of specialized earth satellites add daily to our knowledge. Navigation satellites enable ships and aircraft to pinpoint their positions. Weather satellites warn us of approaching storms and soon may help us understand changes in climate. Environmental satellites probe and analyze the earth's continents and oceans, measure crops and forests, and detect the presence of minerals, the expansion of deserts, or the receding of glaciers and ice packs. And communication satellites flash pictures of historic events as well as weather conditions and educational and entertainment programs around the globe.

The earth has not been the only body in the solar system to be scrutinized by spacecraft. The planned landing of men on the moon provided the impetus to map the moon. Astronauts have walked on its surface and have returned with hundreds of kilograms of moon rocks for study. Spacecraft have flown by Mercury, revealing many craters and long, faulted ridges. Astronomers were surprised to learn that Mars was heavily cratered. Mars had other surprises: volcanoes, larger than those on earth, and a canyon, mightier than the Grand Canyon. Venus has displayed a rocky surface bathed in an atmosphere of carbon dioxide and sulfuric acid; Jupiter has revealed its intense radiation belts stretching hundreds of kilometers above its surface.

Space science is often called a distinct new field but the great demands of space exploration on all the established scientific and engi-

1

neering disciplines require that they work together and infuse a spirit of creativity and discovery. Once the only prober of the skies, astronomy is now but one among many sciences studying the planets and satellites.

The interdisciplinary demands of space science are demonstrated in the recent Viking studies of Mars. The Viking Orbiters first photographed the surface to enable selection of safe landing sites; they also mapped Mars's water vapor and heat and checked its size, gravity, mass, density, spin axis, and spin rate more precisely. Ejected from the Orbiters, the Viking Landers, like that pictured, established full-fledged scientific laboratories on the Red Planet. Cameras revealed the geology of Martian landforms, a seismometer checked for Mars's quakes, biology experiments searched for signs of life, and a weather boom recorded air temperature and pressure and wind velocity. The earth sciences are rapidly becoming planetary sciences.

Solar-system astronomy is also enjoying a renaissance among ground-based astronomers. The technology developed for satellites has been used to make new discoveries in our solar system from the surface of the earth. New interest in asteroids has led to the discovery of an asteroid with a satellite. An object named Chiron has been discovered orbiting the sun between Saturn and Uranus. Additional excitement in solar-system astronomy has been generated by the discovery of rings around Uranus and Jupiter and a moon of Pluto.

Discoveries about our solar system are continually being made both from the ground and from spacecraft. Our knowledge of the other objects in the system has increased dramatically in the past two decades. The cameras and instruments photograph and investigate various planetary surfaces and atmospheres, but ultimately they give man a more adequate perspective about his home, the earth.

Investigations for a variety of sciences carried by Viking Martian Lander.

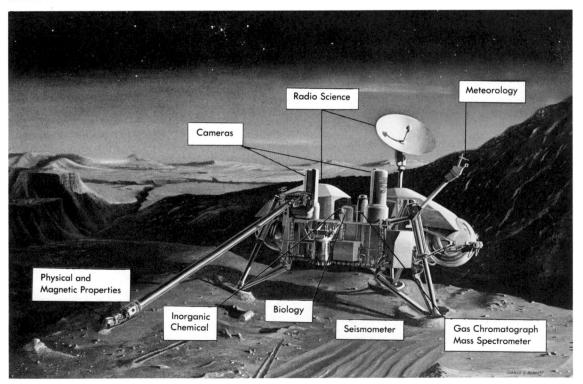

By day the dazzling sun moves slowly across the sky, and the shadows the sun casts have been used for thousands of years to measure the hours with sundials. At night the moon moves overhead, and its phases as it waxes from crescent to full moon and wanes to crescent again have been used to measure the passing months and seasons. Additional countless scintillating points of light—the planets and stars—fill the night sky. How far away are all these lights—sun, moon, stars, and planets? Where is the earth located in relation to them? In reality, are they moving as they appear to be, or is the earth moving, or are they all moving?

Appearance and Reality

Until the space age, all that was known about that sum and substance of everything called the universe, and about our place and motion in it, came from observations of these lights in the sky with instruments that have become more precise by leaps and bounds. But this is not all—radical shifts have also been required in the interpretation of these observations. "Things are not always what they seem to be" has been as good a maxim for astronomers as for magicians. A clear distinction between appearance and reality, what things appear to be as opposed to what they really are, has proved necessary time after time in working out the position of the earth in the universe and in explaining many features of that one infinitesimal bit of the universe called the solar system.

If you stop at a traffic light with another car alongside, your car may suddenly appear to be rolling ahead, even though your foot is pressed hard on the brake. Only when you look at the road between the cars or at the buildings in the background do you realize it is the other car, not your own, that is moving. The illusion was caused by seeing the other car move without an adequate reference system, like the road, to which both cars could be related. Lacking such a background, common to both the observer and the observed object, the observer cannot know whether an observed body, he himself, or both, are moving.

Until a few centuries ago, the earth was quite naturally taken as the stationary point in a reference system to which all motion on the earth, or above it in the skies, was referred. This simple way of viewing things seems naïve to us now, but an examination of the realities behind certain appearances of the motions of the moon and of the planet Mars will show how easily these motions can be misinterpreted.

To any observer here on earth, the moon rises, a huge sphere, over the eastern horizon, swings upward across the sky, and sets in the west. But the reality is entirely different.

The moon's apparent motion from east to west is largely caused by the earth's rotation, which carries the observer along with it. This fact is well known now, but it is still striking to the observer, who must adjust his manually operated telescope every half minute or so to keep the moon in his eyepiece. He realizes how rapidly the earth must be spinning with him. But this actual rotation of the earth could only be inferred in many indirect ways until the earth itself could be observed from a distance in space. Then the earth's real spinning could be shown, as in the photographs of the earth made by a Surveyor spacecraft on the moon.

Chapter II

Our Position in the Universe

"The world, the race, the soul—
in space and time the universe,
All bound as befitting each—
all surely going somewhere."
Whitman

Surveyor 7 photographs from the moon made over a period of hours (from top to bottom) prove that the earth turns.

3

Actually, the moon is also moving. It revolves around the earth in exactly the opposite direction, from west to east. In the first photograph of our "double planet," made by the Voyager 1 spacecraft, the moon (at the top of the photograph) is moving toward the left, while the earth moves toward the right in its trip around the sun. Voyager was 11.5 million kilometers (km), or 7.5 million miles (mi), from the earth when this picture was snapped, and the moon a mere 385,000 km (240,000 mi) from the earth. In the meantime, the earth is spinning from west to east (left to right) on its axis, and the moon spins in the same way, although much more slowly.

The moon takes 27 days, 7 hours, 43 minutes, and 11.5 seconds to complete its 2.4-million-km (1.5-million-mi) circumnavigation of the earth. The full circle through which the moon passes is divided by convention into 360 degrees, of which the moon passes through only a 13-degree arc each day, as shown in the diagram. This actual daily inching of the moon from west to east explains why it rises about an hour later each night.

The moon's size is also misleading—it appears almost equal to the sun's in the sky. The moon looks this way because at its distance the moon's average apparent diameter in the sky makes an angle of 31 minutes (just over 0.5 degree of arc) for an observer on earth, while the sun's average apparent diameter covers an angle of 32 minutes. In actuality, at its much greater distance the sun's diameter is over 400 times that of the moon, although they appear to cover about the same arc in the sky.

So the earth actually rotates from west to east, making the moon appear to move from east to west, even though it actually revolves in the opposite direction. It is our own vision that creates the moon illusion, in which the moon appears larger near the horizon than high in the sky. Almost every visual impression an observer has of the moon, including its size compared with the sun, turns out to be an appearance that must be penetrated to discover the reality behind it.

Like the moon, the planet Mars appears to rise in the east and set in the west, because of the earth's rotation on its axis from west to east. But like the sun and moon, Mars and the other known planets were found by ancient observers to move or "wander" through the fixed patterns of the stars. With the common-sense system of reference of a stationary earth, these early astronomers interpreted this to mean that each of these heavenly bodies revolved around the earth in its own transparent celestial sphere. On this basis, Ptolemy explained the motions of the sun, moon, and planets. Not until long after the death of Nicolaus Copernicus (1543), the Polish astronomer who resolved this celestial riddle, was the actual movement of the earth in concert with the other planets around the sun finally acknowledged. Even the early American colonists accepted the Ptolemaic doctrine. It was taught at Harvard until 1656.

Mars provides an excellent example of how deceptive relative motion can be. Over a period of time, the Red Planet moves from west to east through the stars along the ecliptic. The ecliptic (around which the constellations of the zodiac are found) is the track the sun appears to follow through the sky in the course of the year because of the revolution of the earth about the sun. But at a certain point in Mars's course each year, if it is watched for a week or two, the planet appears

Earth (below) and moon (above) first photographed together by Voyager 1 spacecraft as it left the earth on its long trek past the outer planets, Jupiter, Saturn, and beyond.

to come to a stop in relation to the stars, move backward for a time, stop again, and then return to its progression from west to east. When this apparent retrograde, or backward, action is plotted, it forms a loop in the sky. What is the reality behind this apparently weird behavior?

An observer looking down on the solar system from above would see that the planets revolve in a counterclockwise direction around the sun, as shown for earth and Mars in the diagram. Closer to the sun, and hurtling more rapidly around it than Mars, the earth completes its revolution in about 365 days, while Mars requires 687 earth days. As the earth catches up with Mars in its neighboring orbit, Mars appears to hesitate in its course. As the earth passes it, Mars seems to turn back to trace the path shown in the diagram before continuing its way along the ecliptic. The ancients had observed Mars's seeming retrograde motion, and Ptolemy was forced to add small circles on his larger ones to explain it in earth-stationary terms. Copernicus, who held the view that the planets orbit the sun at different velocities in the same counterclockwise direction, provided the simpler real explanation. Mars only appears to hover and rear backward among the stars because of the earth's changing relationship to it.

Such deceptive appearances abound in the solar system and, in fact, in the observed universe. One by one, the realities behind them are discovered and explained, but other appearances keep turning up to take their place.

Motion of the Earth

Bit by bit the motion of the earth at any given time has been found to be the resolution or combination of many different motions. Imagine the resolution of your own motions as you walk north down the aisle toward the back of an aircraft flying south in a crosswind from the west, as the pilot banks the plane to keep on course and angles up sharply to gain altitude but the plane drops as it enters an air pocket.

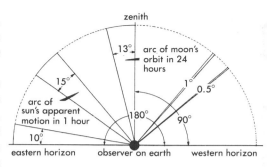

Apparent motion and size in the sky as measured by arcs and their corresponding angles for the observer. The sun's apparent motion through the sky is 15° in an hour, passing through an arc of 15° in the sky or forming an angle of 15° for the observer from the beginning to the end of the hour. This is also called an "angular motion" or an "angular distance" of 15°. Each degree is divided by convention into 60 minutes ('), and each minute into 60 seconds ("). Half a degree (0.5° or 30') is about equal to the arc in the sky of the average apparent diameter of the sun and the moon.

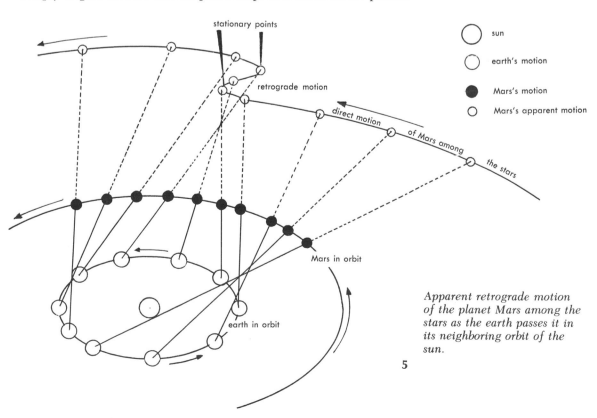

Apparent retrograde motion of the planet Mars among the stars as the earth passes it in its neighboring orbit of the sun.

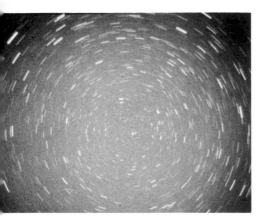

Apparent motion of the stars in arcs centered near the North Star reveal the rotation of the earth on its axis pointing toward the center, the North Celestial Pole. The film was exposed for 20 minutes to obtain these circular arcs. The brightest object near the center was made by the North Star.

The motions of the planets, sun, and moon along the ecliptic (from right to left or west to east) for the month of June 1980 reveal how they change their positions in relation to the fixed stars. The nearby members of the solar system thus move yearly through the far-distant stars in the constellations of the zodiac.

Only during the twentieth century has the analogous complex behavior of the earth been analyzed and our position in the universe pinpointed. This is a continued story, however, as astronomers keep revising old estimates of our motion and discovering new features of it.

At the end of the handle of the Little Dipper, the North Star, Polaris, appears to be fixed in the night sky of the Northern Hemisphere. The other stars seem to sweep from east to west in arcs of circles, the centers of which are near the North Star. Photographic trails like those shown are made by the stars during an exposure of several hours, with the tiny arc of the North Star near the midpoint. The stars in the southern polar region make similar arcs, although no brilliant star like Polaris marks the South Pole in the sky.

Although the stars appear to move in this manner, they are called fixed because to the sight they are so nearly stationary in relation to each other. Their actual motion in the patterns (like the constellations) they form in the sky is so infinitesimal at their great distances that it can be verified only over years of time. But members of the solar system—the planets, sun, and moon—change their positions constantly in relation to one another and to the fixed stars. The marked relative motions of the planets, sun, and moon over just one month against the background of the constellations of the zodiac are shown in the drawing. Note how much farther nearby planets, like Mercury and Venus, move than planets at great distances, such as Saturn and Uranus.

The apparent sweep of the stars in circles around the North Star results from our own actual motion on the surface of the earth as it rotates. The speed of our motion varies with geographic location. At the equator, where the earth's circumference is about 40,000 km (25,000

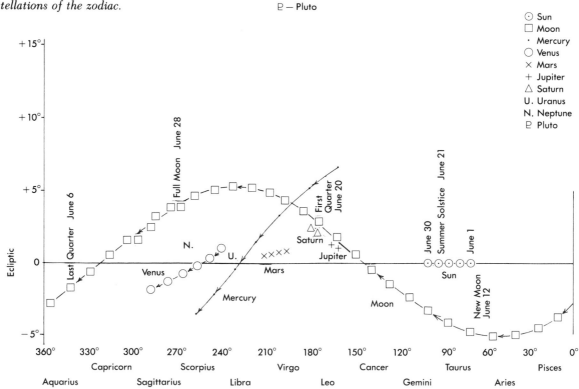

mi), any location must move at about 1,670 km (1,040 mi) an hour, or 0.5 km (0.3 mi) per second, to complete the full circle in 24 hours. Since the circumference shortens toward the poles, any place's speed with the earth's rotation decreases accordingly. A mere kilometer (0.6 mile) from either pole, the speed of rotation has diminished to a crawl of .25 km (.16 mi) an hour, and the distance traveled to only 6 km (4 mi) a day.

Again, the appearance of the sun's motion relative to the earth is deceptive. The sun seems to move with the rotation of the earth, rising in the east and setting in the west. But then, like the planets in the diagram of motion in a month, the sun appears to move in relation to the stars day by day throughout the year from west to east along the ecliptic, the imaginary great circle formed on the celestial sphere by the sun because of the earth's actual revolution around the sun.

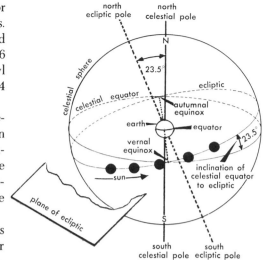

Elements of the celestial sphere.

The celestial sphere is an imaginary sphere of infinite radius with its center at the earth, used by astronomers as their frame of reference for the location of all celestial bodies. The ecliptic and other basic astronomical concepts are shown in the celestial-sphere diagram. The earth's axis of rotation extended indefinitely locates the north and south celestial poles on the celestial sphere. The celestial equator midway between the celestial poles is an extension of the earth's equator. But the apparent path of the sun through the year defines the line and the plane of the ecliptic, which is tipped or inclined at an angle of 23.5° to the celestial equator. Thus the north and south ecliptic poles on the celestial sphere are tipped at the same angle from the celestial poles, as indicated in the diagram.

The two points at which the line of the ecliptic crosses the celestial equator are called the vernal and autumnal equinoxes. Astronomers locate celestial bodies in the sky on the sphere just as places are located on the orb of the earth by latitude and longitude. The angle of a celestial body north or south of the celestial equator is called its declination (similar to latitude), and the angle east of the vernal equinox along the celestial equator is called its right ascension (similar to longitude). Declination is expressed in degrees, and right ascension in hours, minutes, and seconds, running from 1 hour to 24 hours around the celestial equator.

If an observer were looking down on the sun and earth from above the solar system, he would see that the earth really moves along the plane of the ecliptic in a counterclockwise direction, making the sun appear to move along the ecliptic. Since the earth's actual motion around the sun is a little less than 1° of arc a day (360° in a year of 365 days), to the casual observer it is noticeable in the apparent motion of the sun only over a considerable period of time. But in dramatic contrast to its relatively slow spinning, the earth carries us all along with it at a whistling 106,000 km (66,000 mi) an hour, or about 30 km (18.5 mi) a second.

As if all these apparent and real motions were not dizzying enough, we go through a variety of other smaller motions as we live at or near the surface of our planet. The sun and moon exert unequal gravitational pulls on the slightly bulging equatorial region of the earth, and these forces make the earth wobble a little like a top as it spins. As a result, the earth's poles and correspondingly the celestial poles have been found to shift over the centuries. This motion is called precession.

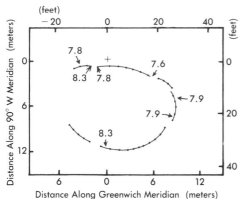

The dots trace the counterclockwise motion of the earth's North Pole in the Chandler wobble for one year. The numbers give the magnitude on the Richter scale of the largest earthquakes occurring during the same period, closely related to shifts in the wobble.

Part of our own Milky Way Galaxy, as we see it from inside, from where the sun is located in one of the galaxy's vast spiral arms. Black spots are dense dust in the Milky Way, through which light cannot penetrate but only infrared and radio waves. The brightest patch is toward the center of the galaxy in the constellation Sagittarius.

The pole actually traces a circle in the sky, completing a full turn in a period of some 25,800 years. A wiggle in this traced circle, called nutation, is caused by the unequal effect of the moon on the precession. Nutation has a period of only 19 years.

Still another motion of the earth's poles is called the Chandler wobble, after S. C. Chandler, a businessman of Cambridge, Massachusetts, who turned amateur scientist and discovered it in 1891. In this motion, the pole wobbles in an oval with a radius of only 6 to 8 meters (20 to 25 ft) over a period of about 14 months, and, of course, your own location moves in the same way. A part of the wobble that takes 12 months results from the shifting of the earth's atmosphere with the seasons. Perhaps the remainder is caused by earthquakes, for jerks in the motion often correspond with large earthquakes, as the diagram shows. But earthquakes may not be massive enough to excite the whole wobble. Precession of the earth's inner core or irregularities of the core-mantle boundary have also been proposed to explain this wobble.

Milky Way Galaxy

Our nightly view of the multitude of bright, twinkling stars in the sky around us leads to an incorrect picture of our star, the sun, surrounded by many nearby stars. Other stars shine, we imagine, just out beyond the planets in our solar system. But this appearance vanishes when the actual distances to the closest stars are known. The solar system diminishes to the merest speck, almost alone in space, like a solitary bit of dust glinting in the sunlight.

Distances between stars are so great that astronomers must measure them in terms of the yardsticks of light-years or parsecs. A light-year is simply the distance a ray of light will travel in one earth year at its fantastic speed of 300,000 km (186,300 mi) a second. (A parsec, or par-

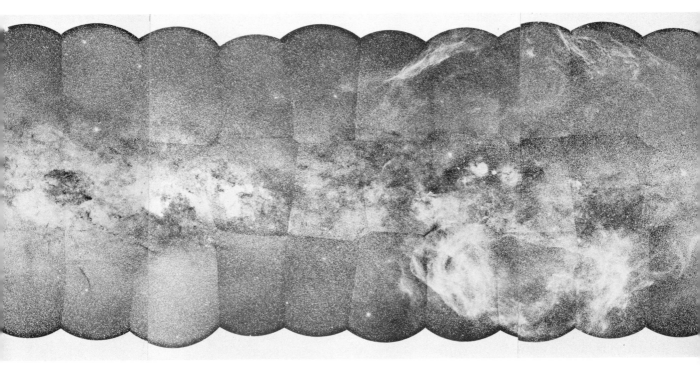

Our Position in the Universe

allax second, is a longer yardstick, amounting to 3.26 light-years.) The star nearest us (other than the sun), the triple system of Alpha Centauri, is about 4.3 light-years from the sun. Speeding about 10 trillion km (6 trillion mi) a year, the light from this system takes over 4 years to reach us, and the distances of most stars from us are much, much greater. Only 25 stars are known within a sphere having a radius of 14 light-years from the sun. On the other hand, some 10,000 stars shine within a radius of 100 light-years of the sun.

The motions of the nearby stars can only be called chaotic. Some are moving at different velocities toward the sun, some away from it, in terms of their radial velocities. Their proper motions, or transverse velocities across the sky, also vary greatly. However, by putting together the apparent motions of great numbers of neighboring and distant stars, clusters of stars, and clouds of gas and dust, astronomers have gradually begun to make sense of the sun's actual position and motion. Our home in the universe is that great system of stars, gas, and dust called the Milky Way Galaxy, part of which is pictured in the mosaic of many photographs.

Looking up at night, the stardust of the Milky Way seems to have spilled in a meandering stream across the sky, as shown in the sky map. The discovery early in the twentieth century that this band arching the sky is a galaxy and that our sun and its planets belong to this system of an estimated 140 billion stars was a great advance in itself. Our galaxy has been found to be shaped roughly like a disk with a somewhat thickened center and a number of long trailing spiral arms. Similar spiral galaxies are pictured, one in the constellation Coma Berenices (viewed edge on), and one in the constellation Pisces (viewed from above).

The flattened disk of our galaxy measures about 100,000 light-years in diameter and perhaps less than 1,000 light-years in thickness. Much

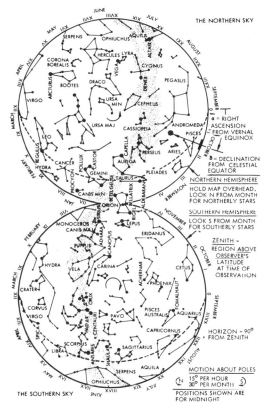

Arching path (gray) of the Milky Way across the stars and constellations in the skies of the Northern Hemisphere and the Southern Hemisphere. The dashed line is the ecliptic. By following the directions given for each hemisphere, this map can be used to locate the major constellations in the skies during any month of the year.

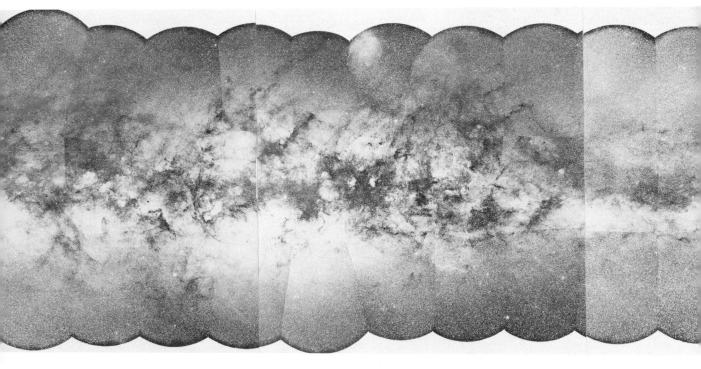

A spiral galaxy, NGC 4565, located in the constellation Coma Berenices, viewed edge on with a 2.1-meter (84-inch) telescope, just one of the many billions of galaxies in the universe.

Our Milky Way Galaxy seen from above might look somewhat like this galaxy, NGC 628, viewed with the 4-meter (158-inch) Mayall telescope.

of the galaxy is hidden from view by massive clouds of dust, so its shape, particularly that of its center, has only recently been determined. This mapping has been done with radio telescopes and infrared telescopes, since the long waves they collect penetrate dust clouds that visible light waves do not. The sun, with its planets, is situated at the edge of a spiral arm some 32,000 light-years from the galaxy's center and perhaps 18,000 light-years from its outer edge. The center is located in the direction of the constellation Sagittarius in the southern celestial sphere.

Analysis of the sun's motion in relation to many other stars indicates that it speeds at a whopping rate of about 225 km (140 mi) a second on a course around the center of the Milky Way Galaxy. Thus the earth's orbit of the sun becomes helical (as shown in the figure), as if the earth were moving up a spiral staircase with the sun rising with it up the center of the stairwell. This swift motion of the sun, at some 900,000 km (500,000 mi) an hour, carries us all in one complete revolution of the galaxy in about 250 million earth years. And this means, of course, that when it completes a revolution of the sun at the close of the year, on December 31, the earth does not return as we imagine it to the same place in space where it started on January 1 but to a location some 8 billion km (5 billion mi) from where it started.

The sun also appears to waver or move up and down at a speed of some 20 km (12 mi) a second, or 70,000 km (43,000 mi) an hour, in its orbital course in the galaxy. The sun's motion may be like that of a needle on a warped phonograph record that waves slowly up and down with the warp, or like carousel horses moving up and down as they revolve with the merry-go-round. As it makes one galactic circuit, the sun may go through 2 or 3 such oscillations within a span of some 500 light-years from the galactic plane of revolution, or this motion may be only a minor, unrepeated perturbation of the sun's course caused by a neighboring stream of stars.

Beyond the Galaxy

Astronomers probing our vicinity in intergalactic space have found the Milky Way Galaxy to be one of the Local Group, a set of galaxies also called the Local Cluster. It almost seems that the boxes within boxes enclosed in turn by boxes go on in an infinite series. The "local" galaxies vary in shape, from spirals like the Milky Way to elliptical, flattened elliptical, irregular, and dwarf galaxies. One member of the Local Group, the spiral Andromeda Galaxy, is visible to the naked eye in the Northern Hemisphere, as are the Magellanic Clouds in the Southern Hemisphere.

The distances of these "nearby" galaxies range from the 170,000 light-years of the Large Magellanic Cloud to the 2,400,000 light-years of a large irregular galaxy, IC 1613. The Large Magellanic Cloud, Small Magellanic Cloud, and the six dwarf galaxies, small in size and brightness, probably are satellites of the Milky Way Galaxy, orbiting around it somewhat as the planets orbit the sun. Similarly, the great Andromeda Galaxy has four small companion elliptical galaxies as satellites, and a recent survey in the vicinity of Andromeda turned up three new dwarf-galaxy companions. Although dwarfs are so small and dim that they cannot be detected at great distances, it has been suggested that they may outnumber all other types of galaxies com-

The scattered stars, clusters, and nebulae of the Large Magellanic Cloud, the nearest member of the Local Group of galaxies.

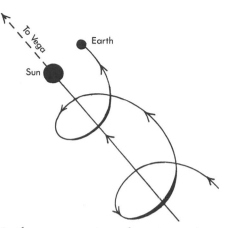

As the sun moves toward a point in the sky near the star Vega, the earth moves in a helical or springlike path, completing one loop of the spring each year.

bined, as they do in the Local Group. Observations of the universe would have been much easier had our solar system been a member of a dwarf galaxy.

Recent radio studies by Australian astronomers have revealed a long line of eddying hydrogen clouds trailing the orbit of the Magellanic Clouds in the Southern Hemisphere, as pictured in the diagram. Like the wake behind a boat or the eddies downstream of a pier in a river, the Magellanic Clouds may have formed this "contrail" as they passed some 500 million years ago through hydrogen in the halo of the Milky Way, or the Magellanic Clouds themselves may have expelled the gas to form the clouds eddying behind them.

Our Milky Way is near one edge of the Local Group. Regardless of our sun's motion in orbiting the Milky Way Galaxy, a swift solar motion in the Local Group of some 300 km (185 mi) a second, or about 1 million km (600,000 mi) an hour, has been proposed. Beyond this, motion through the microwave background radiation remaining throughout space from the original big bang has been observed recently. Although these observations need to be checked, they indicate that the Milky Way Galaxy and the whole Local Group may be moving at an astounding rate of 2 million km (1.3 million mi) an hour through this microwave radiation!

On the surface of the earth, then, our actual motion is a constantly varying resolution of many motions: the rotation of the earth on its axis, the wobbling of the axis with precession and the Chandler Wobble, the earth's revolution of the sun, and the sun's motions in the Milky Way Galaxy. The Milky Way's motion in the Local Group and against the microwave background require further precise observations. Nevertheless, in the twentieth century, astronomers have achieved a fairly definite picture of the actual position and motions of the earth and the solar system within the vast reaches of the universe.

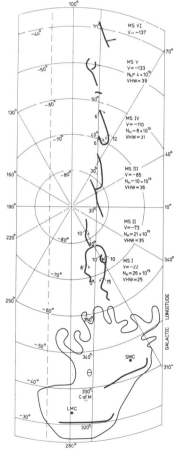

Turbulent hydrogen clouds in the wake of the Large Magellanic Cloud and the Small Magellanic Cloud (LMC and SMC). Radio observations show the ridges (black lines) of hydrogen in the clouds as well as rolling, swirling motions within them.

Chapter III
The Solar System

". . . What if the Sun Be Center to the World and other Starrs By his attractive Vertue and their own Incited, dance about him various rounds?"

Milton

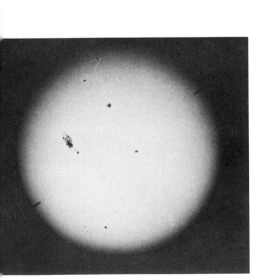

The whole disk of the sun photographed in white light. The dark areas are sunspots, regions in the photosphere that are cooler than their surroundings. Limb darkening is also evident. Light from the edge, or limb, of the sun comes from the cooler, upper part of the photosphere and does not appear as bright as the center of the disk.

Unlike a starry constellation, the solar system cannot be viewed in its entirety on a clear night. Of the myriads of luminous bodies visible in the heavens, only a couple of handfuls have been identified as bodies that must travel endlessly around the sun under the thrall of its powerful gravitational attraction. The sun is the largest object in the solar system. We are dazzled daily by its brilliance. The sun is the only star whose surface we are able to study with relatively simple equipment and techniques. The planets are the next larger bodies of the solar system, appearing as disks when viewed through telescopes. Only five planets—Mercury, Venus, Mars, Jupiter, and Saturn—are clearly visible to the unaided eye. The ancients called these brilliant bodies the wanderers, because they did not stay put in the regular wheeling pattern of the stars through the sky. Moving in orbit around some of the planets are natural satellites, such as the earth's moon; it is possible to discern the disks of a few other natural satellites with proper telescopic aid. Asteroids and meteoroids (small pieces of interplanetary debris) also travel about the sun in their own set paths. Often the latter enter the earth's atmosphere and become "shooting stars." The least massive, but very impressive comets are also subject to the gravitational pull of the sun. The solar system, in fact, appears to be imbedded in a huge cometary cloud.

The Sun

Despite the fact that we believe the sun is unique, it is not an unusual star. It is a typical yellow-dwarf star (designated G2 V), a member of a very numerous class of stars and believed to be middle-aged. It is unique in that Sol is the only star definitely known to have planets.

The sun dominates the orbiting movements of the earth and the other planets, and they receive almost all of their light and heat from it. Life on earth would be impossible without it, but present forms of life would also be impossible if the atmosphere and magnetosphere did not shield us from some of the sun's more intense radiations. While 95 percent of its emissions are in the visible and near-visible range of wavelengths in the spectrum and are fairly constant, the sun also emits varying quantities of all other types of electromagnetic radiations, particularly ultraviolet, x-ray, and radio waves, as well as streams of high-energy particles with which no radiation equipment on earth can compete.

The sun is a great spherical mass of hydrogen and helium atoms, with traces of the other natural elements, many free electrons, and a scattering of molecules. Its diameter of 1,390,000 km (869,000 mi) dwarfs that of the earth (12,756 km or 7,926 mi) and even that of the largest planet, Jupiter (143,200 km or 88,980 mi). Since the sun consists largely of lighter atoms, it is no wonder that it has a mean density only 1.41 times that of water. The earth's mean density is 5.52 times that of water. However, despite the sun's density it is so massive that what weighs 10 kilograms at the earth's surface would weigh 280 kilograms on the sun's surface.

The source of the sun's energy lies deep within its interior. There, controlled thermonuclear fusion converts hydrogen into helium. Scientists on earth are attempting to construct power plants that would duplicate this process in order to ease the earth's energy problem. Each second the sun converts 4 million metric tons of hydrogen into energy.

This is sufficient energy to satisfy the requirements of the world for 1 million years. The details of the fusion process have recently been questioned. By-products of the process are neutrinos, energetic particles that are extremely difficult to detect. However, an experiment involving 100,000 gallons of dry-cleaning fluid in a gold mine 1.6 km (1 mi) under the earth's surface have been detecting these elusive particles. But the number detected does not agree with the number predicted. Considerable work, both experimental and theoretical, must be done to resolve this discrepancy.

Like the earth and the other planets, the sun's rotation is direct, but it spins flexibly, like a mass of gases rather than a solid, with a period of about 25 days at its equator (moving from west to east some 14° each day) and 31 days in the higher latitudes toward its poles, so its average period is called 27 days. Is the rotation of the sun constant? Recent work has revealed that the equatorial rotation speed of the sun increased by 5 percent from 1967 to 1975.

The sun is perfectly spherical within a thousandth of a percent, not elliptical like the planets. Its equator is inclined at an angle of 7 degrees, 15 minutes to the plane of the ecliptic. Perhaps at one time it rotated much faster, but gave up most of its spinning momentum to its family of planets. The sun has a general dipole magnetic field, much stronger than that of the earth, and many other magnetic fields and disturbances, with 1, 2, or several poles scattered over its surface.

The sun has a complex atmosphere. The lowest layer is the photosphere, which defines the sun we see on a bright, clear day. It is perhaps 300 to 500 km (200 to 300 mi) thick and at a temperature of 5,800° K (absolute temperature) (10,000° F). Above the photosphere is the transparent chromosphere, a region with a distinct red color (due to the glowing hydrogen gas) at times of total solar eclipse. The chromosphere is a transitional region about 10,000 km (6,000 mi) between the photosphere and the corona above it.

The chromosphere is filled with thousands of luminous jets or spikes, called spicules, perhaps 1,000 km (600 mi) across, which shoot up at high speeds, pause, and then fade out or retract, all within about 8 minutes. Although the amount of gases present decreases the farther from the photosphere, the temperature rises! At the boundary between the chromosphere and the corona, the temperature has reached 100,000° K.

The outermost feature of the sun's atmosphere, the corona, streams out above the chromosphere. The corona consists of a transparent, very low density, high-temperature plasma (a gas comprised of free electrons and atomic nuclei) perhaps as hot as 2 million°K. Normally the corona is invisible, since its luminosity is about half that of the full moon, and the light from below overwhelms it. But during a total solar eclipse, the corona appears as a pearly-white, scalloped halo around the sun, visible out to several solar diameters. The actual appearance of the corona changes with time. When there are few sunspots in the photosphere, the corona appears smooth and very uniform; at the times when there are many sunspots, the corona breaks down into fans and streamers, as seen in the photograph.

Skylab observations have revealed the existence of coronal holes, regions less dense and cooler than the surrounding areas. These holes are believed to be the sources of the solar wind, consisting largely of

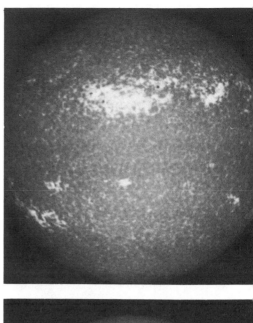

The sun takes on different appearances when viewed in light of different colors. The picture at the top, taken in the violet light of calcium, reveals plage areas (white) in the atmosphere of the sun. The image of the sun taken in red light (bottom) of hydrogen also shows these areas but with more detail. Dark wormlike features in the bottom photograph are prominences, gases extending from the photosphere to the corona. The bright area just to the left center on the red-light photograph is a solar flare, an eruption of gases in the atmosphere of the sun. Both photographs were taken on May 28, 1978.

Above left: Spicules in the sun transport energy from the photosphere to the chromosphere. Photographed here in the red light of hydrogen, they resemble dark blades of grass in a lawn.

Above right: The solar corona during the total solar eclipse of June 30, 1973. A special filter reveals the delicate detail in the corona.

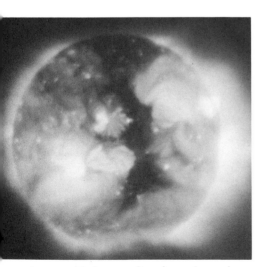

A coronal hole extending from the sun's North Pole (top) southward across the equator is evident in this x-ray image of the sun recorded on June 1, 1973, from Skylab. Such holes are regions of the corona that are cooler and have less material than their surroundings. The large, bright features running east to west (left to right) across the middle of the photograph are hot, dense regions that overlie sunspots in the photosphere.

atomic particles like protons and electrons. The solar wind probably spreads through the entire solar system and has been observed at least as far as Saturn by the Pioneer 11 and Voyager spacecraft.

As seen from the earth, the sun serenely radiates its life-sustaining warmth. But the sun is very active: Certain events occur in minutes, others over many days.

Considerable activity occurs in the photosphere. The entire surface undulates like a waterbed, with a period of 5 minutes. Longer oscillations, of 160 minutes, have also been recorded. Furthermore, the photosphere consists of discrete cells called solar granules. These granules give the entire surface the appearance of a hooked rug. About 1,000 km (600 mi) or more in diameter and lasting about 8 minutes, the granules are believed to be the tops of rising convection currents transmitting heat out of the interior. Larger units of matter, with diameters of 32,000 km (20,000 mi) and 20-hour lifetimes, are known as supergranules. With the spicules, the granules give the sun a constantly changing appearance.

The black-etched sunspots are located in the photosphere. They may be round, elliptical, or irregular in shape, with a dark center or umbra edged by a grayish ring or penumbra. They appear dark only because their temperature (4,200° to 5,700°K) is below that of the photosphere around them. Starting as tiny pores in activity centers on the sun, where very strong magnetic fields are usually to be found, they grow in a few days to full spots ranging in size from 800 to over 80,000 km (500 to 50,000 mi) in diameter. Then they decay, lasting from a few hours to a week or longer, sometimes several months. Groups of many spots sometimes make irregular splotches on the sun's disk. Solar flares often occur in the activity centers, rising at great velocities from the sun's surface. They may reach the earth with their showers of proton particles in from 1 hour to 5 hours. A day or two later, they may cause a sudden decrease in the intensity of cosmic-ray radiation and severe storms in the earth's magnetic field.

Sunspot frequency runs in cycles, reflecting general periods of quiet and activity on the sun. This solar cycle averages 11.1 years, but has been known to range between 7 and 17 years, and the period is not yet predictable. At a period of "quiet sun," or sunspot minimum, a few spots from the old spot cycle remain within 5° to 10° of the sun's equator, and a few of the new cycle begin to appear at high latitudes of 25° to 35° north or south of the solar equator. With the increase toward a sunspot maximum (1980–81), the spots spread throughout the sunspot zone between 35° north and south of the equator, usually passing the peak of activity about 5 years after the minimum, and then decreasing gradually over 6 years toward the sluggish activity of quiet sun again. The magnetic polarities of sunspots are reversed in each 11-year period, so the full cycle of activity may be 22 years, though 88 and 178 years have also been suggested.

An interesting phenomenon occurred from A.D. 1645 to 1715, when hardly any sunspots were recorded. This period is known as the Maunder Minimum. Coinciding with the decrease in sunspots, the average temperature on the earth fell, and particularly severe winters occurred in Europe. Other unusual activity has occurred: the Spörer Minimum from A.D. 1460 to 1550, and the Grand Maximum, a period of remarkable activity, from A.D. 1100 to 1250. These periods of unusual behavior must be intimately related to processes occurring deep within the solar interior. Possibly the sun is now again entering a period of prolonged sunspot minimum. The last minimum lasted 2 years longer than expected, for an 11-year cycle; the sun's equatorial rotation speed has increased 5 percent, just as it did prior to the Maunder Minimum; and recent winters in the Northern Hemisphere have been severe. The sun, however, appears to have broken out of its minimum, at least temporarily, and has passed through an active period with a large number of sunspots and intense flares.

Senior Members of the Solar System

New planets or satellites may, of course, be discovered tomorrow, but at this moment the known solar system consists principally of 9 planets and a swarm of at least 43 satellites. Our own natural satellite, the moon, is included in this total, but not the artificial satellites and planetoids that man himself has placed in orbit around the earth and sun.

In order of their distance from the sun, the first planet is little, silvery Mercury, flitting closest to the sun's fiery breath. Then comes cloudy Venus, nearly the earth's twin in terms of size, if in no other characteristic. Farther out from the sun than the double earth-moon system swings the ruddy planet Mars, slightly more than half the size of the earth and two times the size of the moon. Beyond Mars circle the minute planets called asteroids. These smallish space debris bridge the gap between Mars and Jupiter. Past the asteroid belt giant Jupiter looms white and belted, and beyond it the ringed, yellow Saturn, considered by many to be the most beautiful telescopic object in the heavens. Uranus, with its nearly invisible rings, lies between Saturn and Neptune. Uranus and Neptune are so distant that they appear as faint stars, but through a sizable telescope both planets show bulky greenish spheres. Finally, farthest out and last discovered, bobs tiny Pluto, which may well be a moon detached from Neptune in some long-ago dramatic shift in orbit. Although the average distance of Pluto from the sun is greater than that of Neptune, early in 1979 Pluto actually came closer to the sun than Neptune. This is due to a large departure

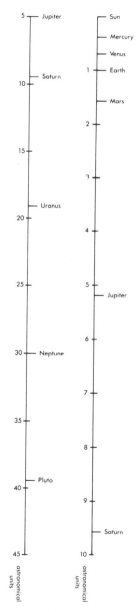

The scale of the solar system. Note that the left scale is four times that of the right scale.

15

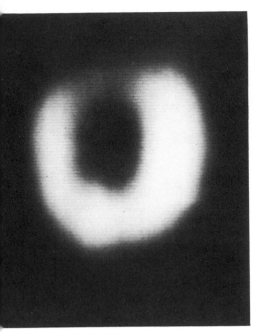

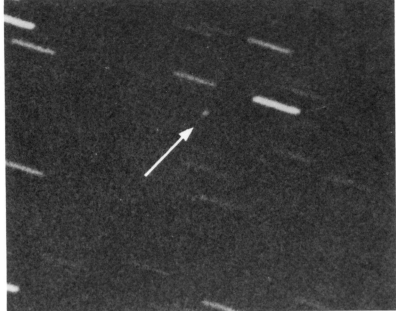

The nine rings of Uranus as recorded in infrared light. This computer-generated photograph was obtained by simultaneously observing Uranus and its rings at two different wavelengths: one at which Uranus was brighter than the rings and one at which it was darker. By subtracting one observation from the other, only the image of the rings remained. Due to the technique used in "photographing" the rings, they are not seen individually but as a halo about Uranus. First results indicate the rings probably consist of stony or dark material rather than ices. It has been suggested that these rings represent gases spread along the orbits of individual satellites circling Uranus rather than rings similar to those about Saturn.

Above right: The discovery photograph of Leda, the thirteenth satellite of Jupiter. Indicated by the arrow, this tiny satellite, with a diameter of only 8 km (5 mi), was discovered by Charles T. Kowal in 1974. Since the telescope was set to track on Jupiter, the background stars appear as bright streaks.

from circularity in the orbit of Pluto. In the year 2000 Pluto will once again assume its role as the most distant planet.

No one definitely knows how the satellites got into orbit around their planets, but the satellites are there. Enthusiastic reports of satellites around Mercury and Venus have never been confirmed. In fact, satellites do not thrive around the planets near the sun. Our earth has its solitary moon, unusually large in proportion to our planet's size; the earth and moon can be called a double-planet system.

Two pinpoint satellites moving swiftly in tight orbits around Mars were discovered at the U. S. Naval Observatory in Washington, D.C., in 1877, and were named Deimos and Phobos, after the 2 attendants of the war god Mars. Jupiter holds the record, with its 16 known satellites. The first 4 were discovered by Galileo in 1610; the sixteenth was identified in 1980. Out beyond the marvelous disk of rings encircling its equator, Saturn has at least 16 satellites. One of these, Titan, has an atmosphere. Uranus has 5 satellites, and Neptune has 2. One of Uranus's satellites was discovered as recently as 1948, one of Neptune's in 1949. Pluto, Lord of the Underworld, dumfounded the astronomical world in 1978 when a satellite only 2 to 3 times smaller than its parent was found orbiting it. Like the earth-moon system, Pluto and its satellite, named Charon, form a double-planet system. Do satellites have satellites? To date nobody has seen one except for the artificial lunar orbiters that have photographed most of the moon's surface. But the asteroid Herculina, with a diameter of only 175 km (about 109 mi), may have a satellite with a diameter of 46 km (about 29 mi).

The relative brightness of the planets, satellites, and stars is measured on a scale of visual magnitude, like a meterstick but with units in brightness, or light intensity, rather than centimeters. Between each magnitude is a brightness-intensity ratio of about 2.5; first magnitude is 2.5 times brighter than second magnitude, and so on. Magnitude developed in an odd manner, and as a result brightness decreases with decreasing negative magnitude (-5, -4) to 0 magnitude, and then decreases with increasing positive magnitude (+1, +2). Stars or planets down to about the first 6 positive magnitudes are visible to the sharp, unaided eye. Bodies with magnitudes dimmer than +6 (those with higher positive magnitudes) can only be seen with telescopes.

The moon and the planets out as far as Saturn appear very bright in the sky, shining with the light they reflect from the sun. Under even very favorable viewing conditions, Uranus, the next planet out beyond Saturn, with an apparent visual magnitude of +5.5 when it is at opposition (that is, seen in the sky opposite the sun), is so dim that to see it unaided one must know exactly where to look for it. Uranus was accidently discovered on March 13, 1781, by English astronomer Sir William Herschel. Thought for a year to be a comet, it was finally correctly identified.

Neptune, with an apparent visual magnitude at opposition of +7.85, cannot be seen without a telescope. Its discovery was an international affair. Independently, at about the same time, John C. Adams of Cambridge, England, and Urbain J. J. Leverrier of Paris predicted its approximate position on the basis of small variations, called perturbations, in the orbit of Uranus. Neptune was seen and identified in this position on September 23, 1846, by German astronomer Johann G. Galle. For 84 years thereafter it was generally believed that the planetary count was in. But in 1930, Clyde W. Tombaugh at the Lowell Observatory at Flagstaff, Arizona, discovered Pluto. A sizable telescope is required to view this small planet, which has a magnitude of +14.9 at opposition.

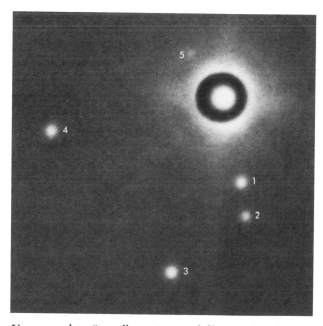

Uranus and its 5 satellites. A special filter was used to reduce the brightness of Uranus relative to that of the satellites. Uranus is the image in the center of the black circle (produced by the filter). The white ring surrounding the filter image is more of the over-exposed image of Uranus. The satellites are Ariel (1), Umbriel (2), Titania (3), Oberon (4), and Miranda (5).

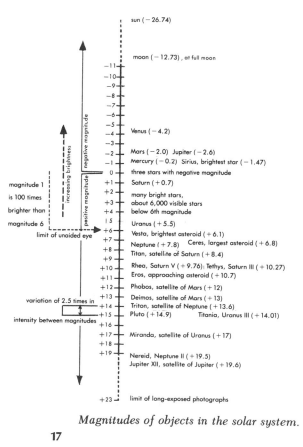

Magnitudes of objects in the solar system.

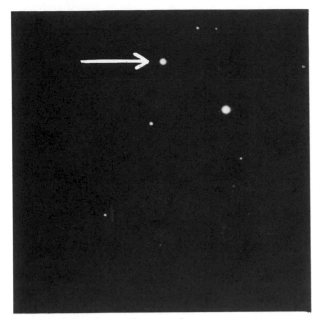

Motion of the planet Pluto in relation to the "fixed" stars. The photograph on the right was taken with the 5-meter (200-inch) Hale reflector 24 hours after that on the left.

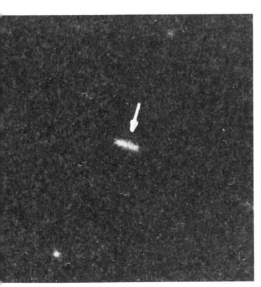

The unusual asteroid Chiron (arrow) as discovered by C. Kowal in 1977. Chiron circles the sun once every 50.7 years. Chiron's unusual orbit places it inside that of Saturn when it is closest to the sun and almost out to the distance of Uranus when farthest from the sun.

Search for New Members

The discovery of Pluto reawakened interest in searching the skies for new planets and satellites. On two or three successive nights, photographs are taken of the same tiny overlapping regions of sky, producing a night-to-night series of negative plates. The areas studied are either along the path of the ecliptic, where planets might be situated, or in the space around a planet governed by its gravitational attraction rather than that of the sun, where satellites might be found. The negative plates for two evenings are then viewed side by side in a blink microscope, dot by dot, to see if any of the celestial objects photographed have moved from one night to the next. If one has, its image appears on the viewing of the first plate, disappears on the viewing of the second, reappears with the first plate, and so on, producing the blinking effect for which the instrument is named. Pluto was discovered with a device of this kind.

In the combing of the heavens many nibbles or planetary suspects have to be tracked down. These usually turn out to be small asteroids or dim variable stars, whose light has diminished below the threshold of visibility on one of the plates. Due to the faintness of any suspected new planet, its discovery would be difficult and require many hours of time and effort. More likely is the serendipitous detection of a new body, like that discovered by Charles T. Kowal in 1977. When first observed, this asteroidlike body had a brightness of +18 and was situated in the constellation of Aries. Further observations revealed that Chiron, as it was named, is not a typical asteroid. Its distance of 2.5 billion km (1.5 billion mi) from the sun places it between the orbits of Saturn and Uranus, far from the normal asteroid belt.

New and faint satellites continue to be discovered orbiting different planets. The thirteenth satellite of Jupiter, Leda, was spotted by Kowal in 1974; this was followed by his announcement in 1975 of another possible satellite of Jupiter. The existence of this satellite has yet to be confirmed. Searches of Voyager 1 and Voyager 2 photographs have led to the discovery of 3 new satellites orbiting Jupiter and at least 4 new satellites of Saturn. Pluto's satellite was discovered on June 22,

1978, by James W. Christy of the U. S. Naval Observatory. This object, called Charon by Christy, is so close to Pluto that under the best of conditions it appears only as an elongation of Pluto along the north–south direction as seen in the photograph. Table 2 presents in summary fashion some basic facts about all known planetary satellites.

Planetary Orbits

With the development of geometry in Greece and for centuries thereafter, celestial bodies and their movements were analyzed only in terms of the sphere and the circle. These forms were "perfect," and it was thought that whatever lay in the heavens, associated with the gods, must manifest perfection. But observations of the natural world soon demonstrate that it is always much more complex than simple, abstract, human concepts. Our own creations, like roads, buildings, and furniture, do accord with the straight lines, circles, and spheres of human geometry. Such forms are rarely approached in the natural world.

What struck early astronomers as straight lines, perfect squares, or other geometric figures on the moon's surface have been resolved into natural components—the wasted rims of old craters, abrupt shifts in contour, or rills slashed deep into the surface. The moon and planets themselves are not perfect spheres, but oblate spheroids, or ellipsoids, bulging out at their equators, but still beautiful to see. And as Johannes Kepler, the great German astronomer, finally and reluctantly concluded, the planets move in elliptical, not circular orbits.

These orbits are like squashed or flattened circles. The characteristics of an ellipse are identified in the drawing. A mathematical definition of an ellipse is that the length of any line from one focus (A) to the curve of the ellipse and back to the other focus (B) is constant. In the drawing the length of ACB is the same as AC′B. The large axis passing through the foci is known as the major axis; half of this is the semimajor axis, which dictates the size of an ellipse. In planetary orbits the semimajor axis also represents the mean, or average, distance of the planet from the sun.

The shape of an orbit is determined by its eccentricity, which is the ratio of the distance between the foci and the major axis. When the foci are placed on top of each other, this is a circle. As the distance between the foci becomes greater and greater, the ellipse becomes more and more flat. Except for Mercury and Pluto, the planets have orbits with small eccentricities. In fact, if the orbit of Mars were drawn to scale, it would be difficult for the casual observer to distinguish its orbit, with an eccentricity of 0.09, from that of a circle (eccentricity equal to 0). Information on the orbits of all the planets can be found in Table 1.

Although the eccentricity of the earth is small, minute changes of the quantity do occur. Every 100,000 years the earth's orbit goes from nearly circular to elliptical to nearly circular again. While this is occurring, the rotation axis of the earth is also undergoing slow changes. First, the earth's equator is attempting to line up with the earth's orbital plane. Due to gravitational effects of the sun, moon, and the other planets, this will never happen. Instead, the earth's rotation axis will continuously change its orientation in a "nodding" motion, with 40,000 years required to complete one nod. This nodding accentuates

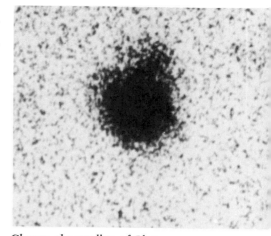

Charon, the satellite of Pluto, appears as a "bump" on the image of Pluto at approximately the 12:30 position. Charon orbits Pluto once every 6.4 days at a distance of approximately 20,000 km (12,000 mi).

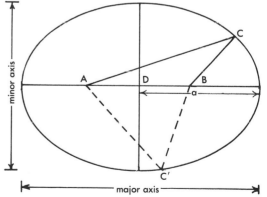

The elements of an ellipse. A and B are the foci of the ellipse, while D is the center. In the solar system the sun is at one focus, and the other is empty. The size of a planet's orbit is dictated by a, the semimajor axis, while the shape is determined by the eccentricity, defined as the distance DB (or DA) divided by the semimajor axis (a).

the effect of the seasons, since the pole facing the sun will experience a warm summer. At the opposite pole, the winter will be harsh and cold.

Second, just as a child's top or gyroscope describes a circle as it slows down, so does the rotation axis of the earth describe a circle in the sky. This precessional motion requires 26,000 years to complete one revolution.

The coupling of this precessional cycle with the nodding cycle and with the change in the earth's orbital eccentricity may be responsible, at least in part, for the recurring ice ages on the earth.

An ellipse is one of the family of curves known as conic sections. Newton showed that bodies in the solar system can move along any of these conics under the tug of the gravitational force of the sun. An ice-cream cone (without the ice cream), or some fairly stiff cone-shaped object can be cut in a number of ways. The shape of the edge of each of the slices cut will be a conic section: either a circle, an ellipse, a parabola, or a hyperbola, depending on the angle of the cut.

The majority of bodies in the solar system move in elliptical orbits whose eccentricities are so small that the orbits are nearly circular. Mercury and Pluto and certain satellites move in more elongated orbits. Many of the asteroids have very flattened orbits, and so do some of the meteoroids. Comets have the most unusual orbits, which may be either elliptical or parabolic. Periodic comets, like Halley's Comet, move about the sun in elliptical orbits. If a comet moves in a parabolic or open orbit, it comes plunging in to barely round the sun and then goes zooming off into cosmic space, never to return.

Elements of Orbits

Each member of the great astronomical triumvirate—Copernicus, Kepler, and Newton—contributed to the explanation for the swift and relentless coursing of the planets through the vast reaches of the solar system. Their principles reveal the foundations of celestial mechanics, which make it possible to calculate the orbits of distant planets or meteoroids plunging through the earth's atmosphere, to predict such events as eclipses, and to plan the orbits that space vehicles follow on their forays through interplanetary space.

Polish astronomer Nicolaus Copernicus blew the earth-centered scheme of thought sky-high in his work *On the Revolutions of Celestial Bodies* (1543). His insistence that the sun is the center of the entire system, with the planets and their satellites moving around it, was the beginning of the modern concept of the heavens, creating a ferment in men's minds.

Tycho Brahe, the famed Danish astronomer, designed many of his own instruments and was a stickler for precise observations, which were passed on after his death to Johannes Kepler, the German astronomer who had assisted him. Brahe thought, with Copernicus, that the five known planets spun around the sun, but held to the conviction that the sun and moon revolved around the earth, leaving it fixed as the center of the system.

In 1577, however, Brahe followed the path of a comet in the sky in his usual methodical manner. His notes show that he wondered whether this comet might have moved in an elongated, egg-shaped, rather than circular, course around the sun. In using these terms, Brahe very nearly described an ellipse. Unfortunately, it was simply a passing fancy on his part.

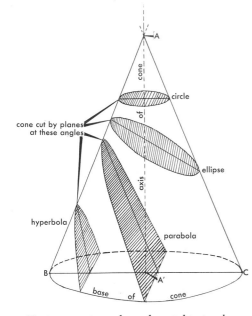

Various sections through a right circular cone, forming a circle, an ellipse, a parabola, and a hyperbola. Line AA' is the axis of the cone, formed by the rotation of the right triangle AA'C around the axis. The sides of the cone thus formed are AB and AC, representing its surface. A slice across the cone at right angles to its vertical axis AA' makes a circular section. Every point on its circumference is equally distant from its center on the vertical axis. An oblique slice across the cone produces an ellipse; the greater the angle from a right angle, the more eccentric the ellipse. A slice exactly parallel to one side of the cone, AB or AC makes a parabola, an open curve, not closed, as are the circle and ellipse. To round out the family of conic sections, a hyperbola is formed when the cut is at a greater angle to the base of the cone than the side of the cone, making another open curve.

So it remained for Johannes Kepler to discover laws strictly governing the orbits of the planets and to announce them in his book, *New Astronomy, or Celestial Physics* (1609). For year after frustrating year, he had tried to fit the accurate data left him by Brahe into circular planetary orbits. All at once, while working on the orbit of Mars, Kepler hit upon the solution. The planets, he conceived, move in elliptical, not perfectly circular, orbits. Then he formulated the three laws of motion that explained their movements.

Kepler's first principle, sometimes called the law of ellipses, states simply that orbits like those of the planets are some form of ellipse, with a central attracting body, like the sun, at the principal or primary focus, and nothing occupying the other focus.

Kepler's second generalization, called the law of equal areas, displays his remarkable insight. He stated that the line joining the sun and the planet, known as the radius vector (BD or BC in the diagram), sweeps over equal areas of the plane of the ellipse in equal times as the planet moves around in its orbit. In the diagram, the radius vector is shown sweeping over the shaded areas, each covered by the planet in its orbit in, say, 10 days, and each having an area equal to the others, though of very different shape. The orbiting body, then, must speed up as it goes through perihelion, the point nearest the sun, having a much longer arc of the ellipse to cover within 10 days. But the orbiting body slows down as it passes aphelion, the point farthest from the sun, covering a much shorter arc of the ellipse in a 10-day period as it sweeps an equal area.

The artificial satellites orbiting the earth speed up in the same way as they near the earth in their ellipses and slow down as they move out farther from the earth, although sometimes their orbits are so nearly circular that little change in velocity is noted. The comets in highly elliptical orbits (like Halley's Comet) vary greatly in orbital velocity. They speed very quickly, in a few days, through that portion of their orbits in the vicinity of the sun including their perihelion, and then take years for the remainder of their orbits, including aphelion, so far out from the sun that they are not observable even by the largest telescopes.

Kepler's third generalization is known as the harmonic law or law of squares. As formulated later by Sir Isaac Newton, it states that the squares of the time periods for the complete revolution of the orbiting planets around the sun are proportional to the cube of their average distances from the central attracting body, the sun. The average distance from the earth to the sun, about 150 million km (93 million mi), is called the astronomical unit (a.u.).

A little later, Newton integrated the ideas of Copernicus and Kepler, as well as those of Galileo and some of his own, into three sweeping laws of motion and the law of gravity, which he stated in 1687 in his *Mathematical Principles of Natural Philosophy (Principia Mathematica)*. With superlative insight, he grasped the universal law that governs the fall of all bodies here on earth and the continuous fall of the planets as they orbit the sun.

Newton's first law of motion states that every body, anywhere in the universe, here on earth, or in the heavens above, remains at rest, or in a state of uniform motion, unless it is acted on by some outside force. In space, friction is negligible, and the principal outer force is gravity. According to his second law, any body acted on by a force is acceler-

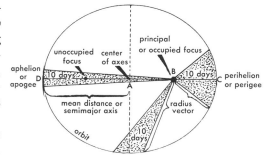

According to Kepler's first law, the sun is at one focus (B) of an ellipse. A consequence of the second law is that a planet will travel fastest near perihelion and slowest at aphelion. Satellites in earth orbit move in an identical way. In this case, the earth is at one focus of the ellipse. The point of closest approach to the earth is then called perigee, while apogee denotes the most distant point in the satellite's orbit from the earth.

ated in the direction of the force's action, in direct proportion to the force's strength and in inverse proportion to the mass of the body. Mass is the amount of matter or material in a body, as opposed to its weight, which in turn is the result of the gravitational pull of one mass on another. In his third law of motion, Newton stated that for every action there is an equal and opposite reaction. This third law is vital to the movement of missiles and spacecraft driven by rocket engines.

According to Newton's final or fourth law, that of gravitational attraction, every body in the universe attracts every other body with a force that varies directly with the product of their masses (such as the masses of the earth and the sun) and varies inversely with the square of the distance between them (such as the square of the astronomical unit in the case of the earth and the sun). The orbits of our artificial satellites and spacecraft are governed just as surely by this attraction as is the wheeling of the planets around the sun, and the attraction determines the actual routes taken by interplanetary probes as they speed through the earth's atmosphere and out into space.

The laws of Newton and Kepler are all that are necessary for a grasp of the nature of orbits. The revolving motion of the earth in its orbit follows all of these laws. The gravitational attractions of the sun, and to a lesser extent, the other planets and satellites, act on the earth, varying directly with the product of their masses and that of the earth, and varying inversely with the square of the distances between them. Against the earth's centrifugal motion, acting at right angles to the direction of the sun, is the centripetal force of the attraction of the sun, tending to make the earth fall directly toward it. These forces are just balanced at the earth's distance from the sun in the elliptical orbit actually followed by the earth and representing the resolution of all the forces acting on it.

The unit of gravity on the earth, commonly called a "g," is defined in terms of its effect—the acceleration it produces in a body falling freely toward the earth under its influence. This acceleration for a body in free fall is 9.8 meters (32 ft) a second. For a body falling from rest under the influence of 1 g, the velocity at the end of the first second of fall is 9.8 meters (32 ft) a second, at the end of the second it is 19.6 meters (64 ft) a second, and so on. At the end of 10 seconds, the body's speed will be 98 meters (320 ft) a second and it will have fallen 490 meters (1,600 ft). Astronauts endure a force of from 6 to 8 g's when they are accelerated into orbits in their capsules and again when the retrorockets are fired. These decelerate the capsules enough so they will not burn up as they re-enter the dense atmosphere and drop down to the earth.

The principles of Kepler and Newton outlined in the previous chapter hold for spacecraft as well as for the planets and natural satellites. The Mariner 10 mission is a brilliant application of these principles.

Launched from earth on November 3, 1973, the 475-kilogram (1,045-pound) spacecraft winged its way to an encounter with Venus on February 5, 1974. It was not to land or orbit cloudy Venus but to take thousands of photographs of the Cytherean (Venusian) clouds.

As Mariner 10 whipped by Venus at breakneck speed, the spacecraft's orbit was altered by the Cytherean gravity. A final orbit was found that placed Mercury and Mariner 10 at the same place at the same time every six months. Accordingly, Mariner 10 passed within 750 km (450 mi) of Mercury on March 29, 1974; 48,000 km (30,000 mi) on September 21, 1974; and 300 km (186 mi) on March 16, 1975. They continue to meet, but the now-exhausted fuel supply prevents scientists from positioning Mariner 10 properly for taking measurements.

More was learned about Mercury during this 1-year period than ever before. The orbital dynamics improved our knowledge of Mercury's mass. Like the moon, Mercury is covered with thousands of craters. Most craters appear to have been formed by meteoritic impact. Other features, including scarps or cliffs, hundreds of kilometers long, provide clues to Mercury's geologic past and to its interior structure.

Mariner 10 also detected about Mercury an atmosphere with a density only a few billionths that of the earth's atmosphere. Helium, one of the constituents of Mercury's atmosphere, must be continually replaced, since the gravitational field of Mercury is so weak that helium should escape in a very short time (less than a day). Another surprise was the discovery of a magnetic field near Mercury. Magnetic fields can be produced by the rapid rotation of a molten iron core inside a planet. Mercury's slow rotation (once every 59 days) appears to contradict this idea. The origin of Mercury's magnetic field (only about 1 percent the strength of the earth's magnetic field) remains an enigma.

Measurements of the distances of the planets from the sun, the details of their orbits, and their sizes, masses, and rotational periods are continually becoming more and more accurate. The structure of the solar system and the bodies composing it have been outlined in broad strokes. But the system's origin is a conundrum to which a dozen or more answers have been given, and no one yet knows which one is right.

Birth of the Planets

Remarkably steady and unvarying as the planets are in their rounds, no one believes that the present scheme of things has always existed. What came before? Explanations of the origin and development of the solar system and the universe, sometimes called cosmogonies, have been offered from time immemorial, in myths and legends, religions, dogmas, and scientific hypotheses.

Galileo, who in 1609 first used a telescope to observe the moon and the then-known planets, discussed a theory of the birth of the solar system in his *Dialogues* (1632 and 1638), which he credited to the Greek philosopher Plato. In his *Timaeus*, Plato had described how the world-

Chapter IV
The Planets and Their Satellites

". . . And measure every wand'ring planet's course,
Climbing after knowledge infinite."
Marlowe

The hemisphere of Mercury seen by Mariner 10 as it approached the closest planet to the sun early in 1974. This hemisphere is marked by large craters, basins, and plains.

soul or creator made the original bodies (which he identified as the sun, moon, Mercury, Venus, Mars, Saturn, and Jupiter) and brought time into being by setting them in motion. "Now all of the stars that were necessary to the creation of time had attained a motion suitable to them . . ." Plato wrote, "they revolved, some in a larger and some in a lesser orbit; those that had the lesser orbit revolving faster, and those that had the larger more slowly."

While this contains the germ of Galileo's theory, Galileo went beyond with his idea that the planets were originally all gathered in one place, out beyond Saturn, the most distant from the sun, and they then began to fall toward the sun with their "natural acceleration," later known as the force of gravity. When each reached its present velocity, the creator halted its straight fall toward the sun and changed it into the familiar uniform circular motion.

Plato and Galileo were correct in asserting greater planetary orbital velocities with lesser orbits, but with his law of gravitation Newton easily refuted Galileo's notion that the natural acceleration of gravity on the earth was the same throughout the solar system.

After Newton had hit the nail on the head with his universal laws of motion and gravitation, a rash of more or less scientific theories of the origin of the universe and of the solar system broke out. Immanuel Kant, the German philosopher, said that the universe originated out of a scattering of cosmic dust. This theory appeared in his highly ambitious *General History of Nature and Theory of the Heavens* (1775). The concept later came to be known as the nebular hypothesis, after being more scientifically formulated in 1796 by Pierre Simon, Marquis de Laplace, the French mathematician and astronomer.

At the very end of his *Explanation of the System of the World*, Laplace described the primitive atmosphere of the sun extending far out beyond the orbits of the later planets and resembling a nebula: a thin, hot, slowly rotating cloud of gases and particles.

Eventually the cloud cooled and condensed, with first one and then other equatorial, doughnut-shaped rings forming around the sun. These unstable, whirling rings were then clotted and compressed into planets—the outer planets first, then the inner ones—all revolving in the same direction around the sun at the center of the system. Laplace's theory won general acceptance for about a century; then increasing knowledge of the system led to a rapid succession of new theories in the twentieth century.

Laplace's nebular theory had refuted the notion of French naturalist Comte de Buffon (1707–88) that a comet had approached very close to the sun and torn out a stream of matter from it that was gathered at a distance into smaller and larger globes. Buffon thought that these globes then became opaque and solid by cooling, thus forming the planets and their satellites.

In the so-called planetesimal hypothesis, formulated early in the twentieth century, a star or stars were substituted for Buffon's much too insubstantial comet. Passing close to the sun, such a star pulled out bulging masses or filaments of hot materials from the sun, leaving clumps of debris revolving around it. The planets were formed from these clumps by gradual accretion. In a later variation of this same idea, Sir James H. Jeans's tidal hypothesis (1928), a passing or colliding star drew out from the sun a long cigar-shaped prong, conceived as thicker in the middle than at either end, explaining the formation of the giant, gaseous midplanets like Jupiter and Saturn. But none of these hypotheses satisfactorily explained the solar system's great circling movement, or angular momentum, with the sun rotating and the planets revolving about it.

Collision theories like Jeans's, moreover, made the birth of the solar system seem a very fortuitous and unusual occurrence, because it is most unlikely that stars will approach close to one another in the vast voids of interstellar space. During the 1940s and 1950s such theories began to be replaced by ideas harking back to the old nebular hypothesis of Laplace. In the contemporary view, the solar system condensed in a cool state from some original source of cosmic dust, the sun in the center being or becoming a radiant star because of its increasing mass and density, which initiated the fierce torch of nuclear fusion reactions within the sun.

On the basis of the infrared emission observed from the infrared source MWC 349, some astronomers believe that they are observing a planetary system in the process of formation. The planets in our solar system may have formed out of a preplanetary disk of material much like this accretion disk envisioned to be circling MWC 349.

Most modern theories assume that the sun and the planets formed from a large cloud or nebula of gas and dust, as shown in the photograph. Left to itself the nebula would probably not form a solar system. But if the nebula can be made to contract, gravity will force the material into a protosun.

But how does the contraction begin? Some theoreticians believe the solar system formed when the nebula passed through a spiral arm of the Milky Way; this is supported by the fact that our solar system is indeed situated on the edge of a spiral arm in our galaxy. Others believe that a disturbance or shock wave from a supernova explosion was the impetus for the formation of the solar system. As the disturbance from this catastrophic explosion of a massive star passed through the solar nebula, the pressure would have decreased and gravity become dominant, thus starting the collapse of the nebula.

The primitive cloud became disk-shaped, some think, and the planets and satellites are assumed to have formed from great whirlpools in it. Others believe that the planets agglomerated from denser nuclei of gas and dust, which gradually formed into larger bodies by attracting the clouds of debris along their courses—meteoroids, comets, larger asteroids, or even infant planets. In the inner portion of the disk-shaped cloud, the denser planets formed from the heavier, less volatile elements, while the huge outer planets formed from the lighter, gaseous elements driven farther out from the sun.

These present-day theories contend that the planets were formed in a cold state. They were conceived and incubated in a refrigerator, not in an oven. Later they were heated by the disintegration of radioactive elements within them, the radiation of the sun, and the explosive shocks of smaller bodies plunging into them. Gigantic infalls of debris plastering the planets' surfaces, cataclysmic explosions caused by collision with larger bodies, and clouds of dust and hurtling bodies blasted loose by their impact may sketch the lurid early history of the planets.

The pocked, jagged, and blasted surfaces of the moon, Mercury, and to a lesser degree Mars, are thought to show the scars of the earlier history of the solar system, unhealed by the effects of oceans and an atmosphere. Some believe the moon may be a small, primitive protoplanet that fell under the control of the earth late in the formation of the system. Others believe that the earth and moon formed separately and at the same time as a double-planet system. The old notion that the moon was torn from the earth while both were still in a plastic state, leaving a vast hole, the remnants of which are the deep trenches in the Pacific Ocean, is now given little credence, for lunar materials and those of earth's upper mantle and crust do not correspond.

Another hypothesis shows promise because it integrates the development of the sun with that of the planets. A contracting nebula of material rotated very fast, as do most stars. Soon the inner core reached the mass and density necessary for nuclear fusion reactions. In fusion, helium is created from hydrogen through a multistage cycle, losing mass and releasing excessive energy. This formed the radiant sun. In this process the sun became unstable when it had shrunk to a diameter about equal to the present orbit of Mercury; from it a disk of gas sloughed off and expanded, although still coupled by magnetic fields to the sun. From this disk the protoplanets condensed, acquiring most of the angular momentum of the sun and solar system. As the planets

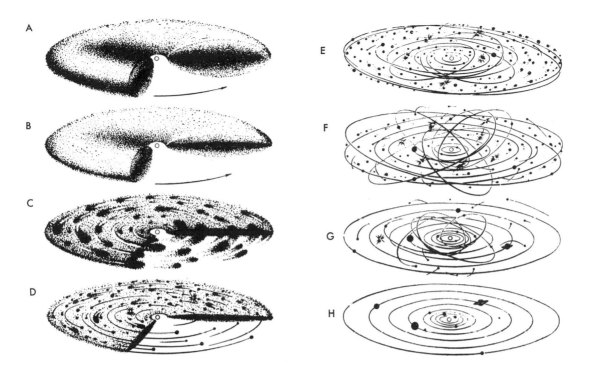

coalesced around the sun, they moved farther away, shaping up into the present solar system.

Meteoroids that plunge into the earth's atmosphere and are large enough to survive a fiery journey to its surface are beginning to furnish some clues to the history of the solar system. These small bodies are assumed to have formed at the same time as the rest of the solar system. They should reveal the composition of the primitive solar system. Unfortunately, most meteorites are altered by weathering processes once they have landed on the earth. Antarctica has surprisingly come to the rescue of astronomers. Any meteorite falling into the Antarctic is largely shielded from normal weathering by the low temperatures and the snow cover. Several hundred meteorites have been recovered by joint United States–Japanese expeditions. Among the discoveries was a golfball-size carbonaceous chondrite, a rare type of meteorite. Preliminary analysis of this chondrite showed it to be rich in water and carbon, which indicates that it may have formed in a relatively cool region.

Scale of the Planetary System

Some idea of the relative sizes and distances of the planets can be obtained by reducing them all to a very small scale. Suppose earth is scaled down from its near 12,800-km (8,000-mi) diameter to a sphere 30 cm (12 inches) in diameter, about the size of a basketball. What happens to the other planets on this same scale? The planet Mercury becomes a ball 11.4 cm (4.5 inches) in diameter. Venus is almost the size of the earth—28 cm (11.5 inches) across. The moon, surprisingly, is 8 cm (3.25 inches) in diameter, and Mars is about 16 cm (6.4 inches) across, slightly more than half the diameter of the earth and about twice that of the moon.

Coming to the blown-up gas giants, on this same scale Jupiter is about the width of the average room, 3.4 meters (11.25 ft) in diameter; Saturn is nearly as large, at 2.8 meters (9.5 ft). Then the size decreases

One form of the nebular theory of the formation of the solar system, developed from that of Soviet mathematician O. J. Schmidt. Left: The formation of asteroidal bodies from a gas and dust cloud around the sun. Dust collecting into a disk, A and B; disintegration of the disk into agglomerations, which turn into asteroidal bodies, C and D. Right: the formation of planets from a swarm of asteroidal bodies. Increase in eccentricity and inclination of orbits as a result of mutual gravitational perturbations, E; accretion of asteroidal bodies and their fragments to form planets, F and G; the planetary system today, H.

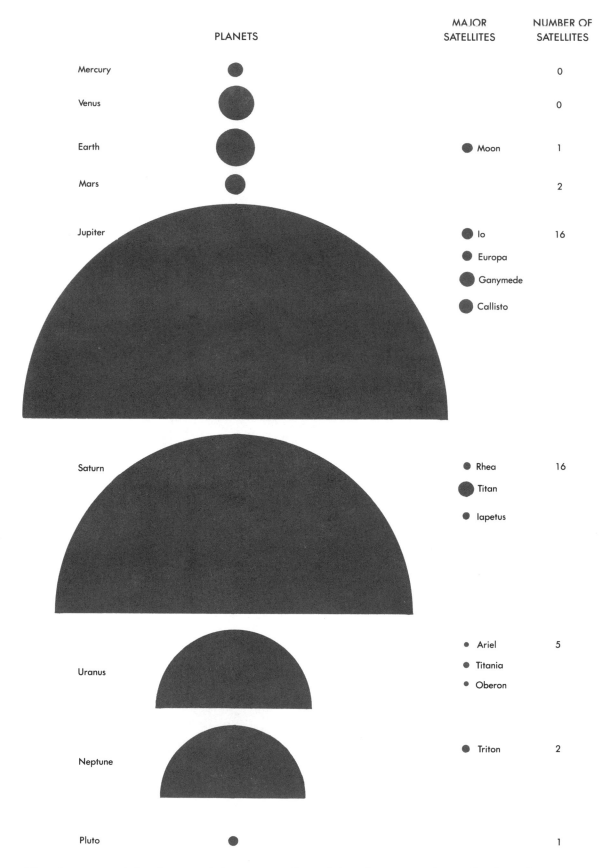

PLANETS

MAJOR SATELLITES

NUMBER OF SATELLITES

Mercury — 0

Venus — 0

Earth — Moon — 1

Mars — 2

Jupiter — Io, Europa, Ganymede, Callisto — 16

Saturn — Rhea, Titan, Iapetus — 16

Uranus — Ariel, Titania, Oberon — 5

Neptune — Triton — 2

Pluto — 1

The relative sizes of the planets and the major satellites of the solar system. If a satellite has a diameter less than 1,276 km (790 mi) it is not drawn, but it is included in the number of satellites for that planet along the right side of the figure. On the same scale the sun would have a diameter of 109 cm (43 inches).

sharply to Uranus and Neptune, large beach balls 1.21 and 1.16 meters (4.0 and 3.9 ft), respectively, in diameter, down to Pluto, with a diameter of only about 6.3 cm (2.5 inches). The sun itself is an enormous balloon 33 meters (108 ft) in diameter.

Using exactly the same scale, and expressing the distances of the planets from the sun in miles, Mercury is placed about 1.4 km (0.9 mi) from the sun. The earth is about 3.5 km (2.25 mi) and Mars over 5.4 km (3 mi) away. Across the asteroid belt, Jupiter is 18.3 km (11.6 mi) distant from the sun. Pluto wanders almost lost in the vastnesses of space at about 139 km (87 mi) from the 33-m (108-ft)-wide sun!

Revolution of the Planets

The planets, from Mercury to Saturn, have come under the scrutiny of spacecraft. Information and close-up pictures are appearing more frequently in newspapers and magazines. Basic facts about orbits, sizes, and rotation rates of the planets are given in Table 1. Although the data in the table are continually refined, the changes in most cases will be small.

The orbits of the planets are elliptical and follow the principles of orbital motion and gravitation. They are most stable in their rounds and are spaced out quite neatly from the sun. Bode's law, named for German astronomer Johann E. Bode (1747–1826), who popularized it, is a geometric progression that fits their distances quite well, though it is irregular for Mercury at the start and breaks down for the outer planets, Neptune and Pluto, undiscovered when the law was formulated.

Frequently the distances of the planets from the sun and other distances in the solar system are given in terms of astronomical units (a.u.), the "yard" of the solar system. For the planets, these represent the mean distances from the center of the sun to the centers of the planets, in comparison with that of the earth, which is by definition 1 a.u. from the sun. In Table 1, 1 a.u. has been taken as 149,597,870 km (92,958,000 mi), the value adopted by astronomers in 1976.

Although the planets move about the sun at different speeds, they move in the same direction. If an observer were conveniently located high above the North Pole of the sun, the planets would move in a direct or counterclockwise direction.

Sizes and Shapes of the Planets

The planets are conveniently divided into two major groupings: the terrestrial planets (those most like the earth) and the Jovian planets (those most like Jupiter).

The Jovian planets (Jupiter, Saturn, Uranus, and Neptune) are the larger planets and have mean densities similar to that of the sun. The smaller, terrestrial planets (Mercury, Venus, earth, and Mars) are more dense and are closer to the sun than the Jovian planets. It is not definite to what group Pluto belongs.

The earth is the largest of the terrestrial planets. It outranks all of the other inner planets in diameter, volume, sheer mass or amount of substance, and the density of its composition. However, compared with the outer giants, it is small, even though it does have the highest average density of all the planets, great and small.

Mercury, with a volume only 6 percent that of the earth and a di-

The earth as photographed by the Apollo 11 astronauts from a distance of 181,000 km (113,000 mi). North Africa and the Arabian Peninsula are visible in the middle of the photograph between extensive clouds.

Venus as viewed by Pioneer Venus on February 10, 1979, from an altitude of 65,000 km (40,000 mi). The extensive cloud cover is evident in this ultraviolet-light photograph. The clouds rotate from east to west (right to left), completing a circuit of Venus in about 6 days.

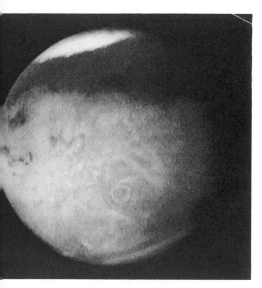

Far-encounter photograph of Mars made by the Mariner 7 spacecraft in 1969 from 448,000 km (280,000 mi). The southern polar cap (top) stands out with its ragged edge. The light circle just below center is the volcano Olympus Mons.

Voyager 1 took this photograph of Jupiter on February 1, 1979, from a distance of 32.7 million km (20 million mi). Features as small as 600 km (375 mi) are recognizable. The Great Red Spot is evident in the lower, middle portion of the photograph. One of the major goals of the Voyager missions was to understand the forms and motions in the complex Jovian atmosphere.

ameter of roughly 4,850 km (3,013 mi), is the smallest of the terrestrial planets. At 6,790 km (4,219 mi) in diameter, Mars is less than halfway between the moon and the earth in size, and Mars has only 15 percent of the earth's volume. Venus is nearly the size of the earth (it once was believed to be larger), with an estimated diameter of 12,140 km (7,543 mi) and roughly 88 percent of the volume of the earth.

Because they are nearer the sun than the earth, Mercury and Venus can occasionally be viewed as small, dark, round spots gliding from east to west and making solar transits across the brilliant face of the sun's disk. These solar transits occur when the orbits of the planets bring them directly between the earth and the sun. Prior to the Mariner flybys of Venus and Mercury, these solar transits provided a chance to correct the calculated orbits and diameters of Venus and Mercury and to study their atmosphere. However, Mariner and Pioneer missions to Venus and Mercury have permitted astronomers not only to improve their values for the orbits and diameters of these 2 inner planets, but also to study the atmospheres of Venus and Mercury in much more detail.

The Jovian planets dwarf the terrestrial planets. Uranus and Neptune have equatorial diameters of 51,800 and 49,500 km (32,190 and 30,760 mi), respectively. But even these planetary sizes pale next to those of Saturn and Jupiter. Saturn measures in with an equatorial diameter of 120,000 km (74,560 mi), while mighty Jupiter has the measuring-tape-busting size of 143,200 km (88,980 mi), over 11 times the size of the earth and nearly 30 times the size of Mercury.

The Jovian planets differ from the terrestrial planets not only in size but also in composition. The terrestrials are composed of material with high melting points, while the Jovian planets are comprised mainly of hydrogen and helium. It is possible that the Jovian planets have solid surfaces like the earth, but this is not certain. The compositions and the sizes of the Jovian planets combine to give the low average densities to these objects. In fact, if a bathtub large enough could be built and filled with water, Saturn would float!

Seen through a telescope, the disks of the Jovian planets actually seem to be slightly flattened at the poles and bulging at the equators. The motion of the axial rotation of the planets is faster at their equators, and the centrifugal forces are stronger there, so they naturally tend to slump in this direction. Flattening, or the index of oblateness, is arrived at by subtracting the polar diameter from the equatorial diameter and dividing the result by the equatorial diameter. The index is indicative of the inner construction and structure of the planets (Table 1).

If the oblateness of a planet, like Mercury and Venus, is 0, this means that the planet is spherical. The polar radius of the earth is 22 km (about 13 mi) shorter than the equatorial radius, for an oblateness index of 0.003. The radius of the moon pointing toward the earth is estimated to be about 1 km (0.6 mi) longer than its polar radius. This implies that the moon is very nearly a perfect sphere, with equatorial diameter no more than a couple of kilometers greater than its polar diameter.

The gas giants, Jupiter, Saturn, Uranus, and Neptune, show particularly high oblateness; that is why they look a bit mashed down in a telescope. Although the edge, or limb, of Jupiter's disk is not too sharp in the photograph of the planet on page 30, you can note Jupiter's oblateness if you measure its equatorial diameter (across) and compare this with its polar diameter (up and down).

The density of an object—that is, its mass per unit volume—tells a great deal about its nature. The moon's density, 0.6 relative to an earth density taken as 1.0, is by all odds the lowest of any body in the inner solar system, although Mars comes close, with its relative density of 0.72. Scientists were long puzzled over what materials could compose the moon, so light in comparison with the earth. Since lunar rocks have been brought back to earth by Apollo astronauts, study has revealed that the rocks on or near the surface are mostly of lighter kinds, such as basalts or anorthosites. Also, the moon may entirely lack or have only a very small nickel-iron or iron core, such as the earth is supposed to have.

Planetary Rotation

Since the surface of Mars can be seen (although indistinctly) under good viewing conditions from the earth, the tilt of Mars's equator to its solar orbit, or of its polar axis to its orbit, and its period of rotation are known (Table 1).

As if some giant playing with tops had given them exactly the same kind of spin, the inclination of the axes of the earth and Mars coincide within 1°. The Mariner flybys of Mars have shown that its axis inclination determined from earth had been accurate within half a degree. Consequently, Mars and the earth have many other features in common. The path of the sun moves north and south of their equators annually, the polar regions of both are frigid and never entirely thaw, and their seasons change in similar cycles. The Martian days and nights are very like ours—the planet takes only 41 minutes longer to complete a full rotation. In certain respects, people would feel right at home on Mars; in others, the Red Planet would be a completely alien world. If they were unable to create a terrestrial environment around them, with a plastic dome, or living quarters under the surface, human beings would be promptly asphyxiated in the Martian air, which consists largely of carbon dioxide, and pass into a deep freeze at night, even in Mars's most tropical areas.

The periods of rotations of Mercury and Venus and the inclinations of their equators to their orbital planes have long been subjects of controversy, and only their rotation periods are now well known.

For many years, astronomers thought that Mercury rotated on its axis once in 24 hours. They observed dim features apparently coming into nearly the same position where they had seen them the day before. Later observers believed that Mercury turned only once around on its axis in 88 days, with each revolution of the sun. With such rotation, like that of the moon in its orbit of the earth, Mercury would always keep the same face toward the sun, with one half blowtorch hot and the other half always dark and cold.

Finally, it was suggested by radar data from radio signals bounced back to earth from Mercury that its period of rotation is 59 days, just two thirds of its swift revolution of the sun. This was then proved by careful scrutiny of previous photographs of Mercury's surface features.

Dozens of early observers concluded that Venus's period of rotation was about 24 hours, like that of the earth. Then late in the nineteenth

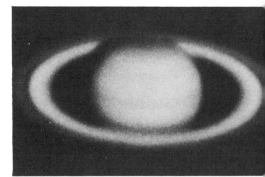

The subtle markings in Saturn's atmosphere are evident in this excellent photograph of the solar system's second largest planet. The famous rings of Saturn are tilted at their maximum angle to earth, revealing their beauty. The dark lane separating these two rings is known as Cassini's division. Pioneer 11 discovered additional rings and Voyager 1 found each ring composed of many tiny rings.

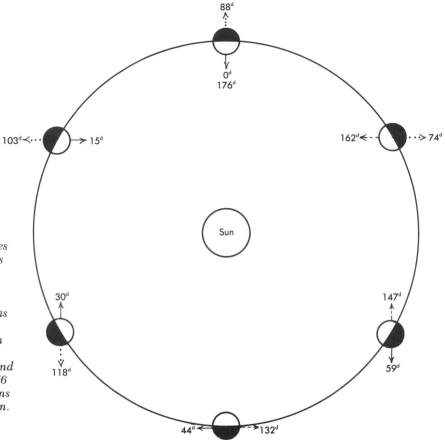

Mercury rotates 3 times for every 2 times it revolves around the sun. After 59 days Mercury has completed 1 rotation (denoted by the solid arrow) but has completed only two-thirds of its path about the sun. After 88 days Mercury has completed its sidereal period but is only one-half way through its second rotation (dotted arrow). After 118 days Mercury starts its third rotation (dashed arrow) and has completed 1.33 revolutions. After 176 days Mercury has completed 2 revolutions about the sun as well as its third rotation. Mercury has returned to its original configuration.

century, Italian observer Giovanni V. Schiaparelli, of Martian *canali* fame, attributed to Venus a synchronous or captured rotation of about 225 days, coinciding with its year; others set the rate at 30 days, and some estimates ranged down from this to 24 hours.

During the 1960s, however, radio-echo or radar analysis finally came into its own. Venus's rotation proved to be retrograde, or backward, from east to west, the only planet with such a spin. And its rotation had a period of about 244 days, longer by far than the planet's year!

The Jovian planets all rotate faster than the terrestrial planets. Jupiter spins fastest, with a period of only 9 hours, 50 minutes, and 30 seconds of earth time. Workers on Jupiter have little free time if they work an 8-hour day like their counterparts in the United States.

Uranus exhibits a unique rotation. Its axis of rotation lies nearly in the plane of its orbit. Although it rotates about once every 15 to 24 hours, it keeps one pole pointed to the sun for 21 years! Of course, the opposite pole is experiencing a 21-year night while the other is basking in the solar warmth.

The Moon and Natural Satellites

There are 43 confirmed natural satellites in the solar system. Only Mercury and Venus travel alone about the sun. These satellites range in size from Titan (5,720 km or 3,550 mi) to small objects like Phobos and Deimos, which are only tens of kilometers across. The diameters, as well as other basic data, for all the satellites are given in Table 2.

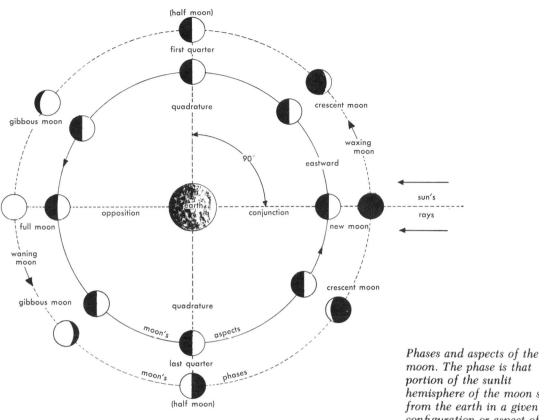

Phases and aspects of the moon. The phase is that portion of the sunlit hemisphere of the moon seen from the earth in a given configuration or aspect of the sun, earth, and moon.

The Jovian satellites Ganymede and Callisto would be considered planets if they did not orbit Jupiter. Whether these natural satellites formed alongside their parent planets or were captured later is an un-answered question, although several of Jupiter's smaller satellites are probably captured asteroids.

Moving out from the sun, the first natural satellite encountered is the moon of the earth. At its average distance of 385,000 km (239,000 mi) from the earth, the moon takes 27 days, 7 hours, and 43 minutes on its terrestrial round and rotates on its axis in the same time. Thus the moon always keeps the same face toward the earth as it moves around it. But the moon's far side, away from the earth, its not always dark and cold. The moon has a hemisphere of sunlight sweeping around it from east to west, as does the earth. Since the moon passes from one conjunction to the next (new moon to new moon) in about 29.5 days, any point on its surface endures a 14-day day and a 14-day night, alternating frying and freezing. Since the moon is not inclined on its axis to the ecliptic nearly as much as the earth, certain points on high ground near its poles may be continuously lighted by the sun, a feature that may prove useful in obtaining constant power from solar radiation.

Although the moon keeps the same face toward the earth, about 59 percent of the moon's surface can be seen over a period of time be-cause of certain "librations," or variations in the whirling earth-moon system. Those additional sectors at the edge of the moon's face that are rarely seen have been painstakingly studied and mapped. Forty-one

33

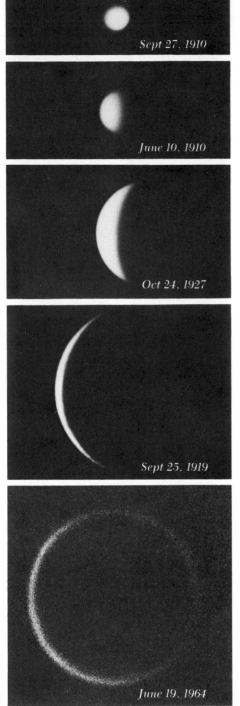

Sept 27, 1910

June 10, 1910

Oct 24, 1927

Sept 25, 1919

June 19, 1964

Like the moon, Venus exhibits phases as seen from the earth. The photograph on top shows a nearly full phase. Moving down is a quarter phase and 2 different crescent phases. The bottom photograph is the nearly new phase. Due to the thickness of the Cytherean atmosphere sunlight is extensively refracted, giving Venus a "halo" appearance. Also evident in this series of photographs are the varying sizes of Venus as seen from the earth. At new phase Venus is closest to the earth, while at full phase Venus is on the other side of the sun and shows its smallest diameter.

percent of its surface is observable whenever lighted by the sun, and up to another 18 percent can be seen on occasion because of the variations. But none of the remaining 41 percent was ever viewed until the Russians photographed a part of it from a space vehicle. Launched on October 4, 1959, the "automatic interplanetary station" Lunar 3 telemetered back to earth the first crude photographs of about 70 percent of the moon's far side.

Most of the moon has been photographed by the Lunar Orbiters. The primary mission of these satellites was to select landing sites on the moon for the American astronauts. The first three Orbiters photographed 29 percent of the moon's surface, while Lunar Orbiter 4 photographed the lunar poles, 80 percent of the moon's near side, and 90 percent of its far side. The last of the Orbiters, Lunar Orbiter 5, filled in gaps. Not only did it photograph the entire near side of the moon covered by Lunar Orbiter 4, but it also photographed 95 percent of its far side.

The moon and the planets, most notably Mercury and Venus, pass through the familiar phases. Their visible shapes, known as their apparent figures, change as increasing or decreasing proportions of their hemisphere lit by the sun are seen from the earth, depending on the relative positions of the sun, the body, and the earth. The dark portion of the moon with the terminator, or line dividing day from night, is not the shadow of the earth across the moon. Rather, the terminator is the edge of the sunlit hemisphere of the moon, and the dark portion beyond it is the part of the hemisphere turned toward the earth and unlit by the sun. This dark portion is sometimes lit very dimly by "earthshine," the sunlight reflected onto the moon from the earth and reflected back again.

The next satellites encountered are Phobos and Deimos, Mars's two streaking satellites. These peanut-sized satellites of Mars race around it only 6,000 km (3,200 mi) and 20,100 km (12,500 mi), respectively, away from the surface, closer than the orbits of some of the earth's artificial satellites. In fact, Soviet astrophysicist Josef Shklovskii and American astronomer Carl Sagan once suggested that Phobos and Deimos may just be the products of some ancient Martian civilization. Photographs beamed back to earth by the Mariner 9 spacecraft have laid such notions to rest by revealing them to be small, pockmarked asteroidlike bodies. Nor are they spherical. Deimos measures 15 by 12 by 11 km (9 by 7.5 by 7 mi), while Phobos is 27 by 21 by 19 km (17 by 13 by 12 mi).

Phobos revolves around Mars in less than a third of Mars's own rotation period; from the planet, it would appear to rise in the west and swing across the sky to set in the east 3 times a day. The period of revolution of Deimos is also relatively fast, taking only about 30 hours compared to Mars's 24.5 hours, so that Deimos rises in the planet's east and sets in its west, as does our moon. Appearing to move very slowly westward as seen from Mars's surface, Deimos goes through the entire cycle of phases twice between each rising and setting, in a period of nearly 3 earth days.

The 2 satellites of Mars are similar and yet unlike each other in several ways. They both revolve about Mars with their long axes pointed directly toward the mother planet, and both have black-gray surfaces similar to the asteroid Ceres. These two facts lead many astronomers to believe that Phobos and Deimos have a common origin.

The Planets and Their Satellites

The surfaces of these 2 satellites, however, are quite different. As seen in the photographs, the surface of Phobos is lined with many long parallel grooves and appears quite rugged, while the surface of Deimos is relatively smooth. Despite their appearances, the number of craters on both satellites is surprisingly identical. The craters on Deimos are partially filled with fine light-colored material, which gives Deimos its smooth appearance. Under high resolution the grooves, 100 to 200 meters (330 to 550 ft) wide and 20 to 30 meters (66 to 100 ft) deep, are seen to be chains of adjacent pits rather than one continuous groove. The arrangement of the grooves on Phobos strongly suggests that they are related to its 10-km (6-mi)-wide crater Stickney. Why Deimos is covered with loose fill and Phobos isn't remains an unanswered question.

If the satellites of Mars are unusual, those of Jupiter are even more remarkable. Jupiter has sixteen satellites. A seventeenth has been reported but this observation still requires confirmation. These satellites, ranging in size from a few kilometers to larger than the planet Mercury, orbit Jupiter at distances from 127,950 km (79,970 mi) to 23,700,000 km (14,700,000 mi). The last satellite discovered, 1979J3, was confirmed in 1980, while the first four were discovered when Galileo turned his telescope skyward in 1610.

These Galilean satellites have recently provided much excitement among astronomers as the results of the Voyager 1 and 2 missions became available. Hints about these satellites' true natures had been previously obtained from earth-based observations. These had indicated that water frost existed on the surface of Europa, Ganymede, and Callisto, while Io is enveloped in a cloud of gaseous sodium. At certain times in Io's journey around Jupiter the sodium condenses and a sodium snowstorm occurs.

The cameras of Voyager 1 and 2 have shown Io to be even more unusual. The color photograph of the Galilean satellites (color pages) shows that Io resembles an enormous cheese pizza pie; the equatorial regions are bright orange-red (the pizza sauce) speckled by whitish patches (the mozzarella cheese). The surface of Io is dominated by volcanic features. More than 100 calderalike depressions have been detected. (A caldera is a depression at the top of a volcano that forms when the chamber, now empty of lava, cannot support the weight of the volcano cone and collapses.) Eight volcanic eruptions have been recorded on Io, two of which are shown in the photograph. Plumes from these volcanoes have been seen as high as 260 km (160 mi) above Io's limb or edge. Smooth plains stretch between the volcanic features, while isolated rugged mountains approximately 10 km (6 mi) high are seen more often in the polar regions. No impact craters larger than 1 to 2 km (0.6 to 1.2 mi) in diameter were detected. Those that are believed to have existed have more than likely been filled in by lava flows. Scientists believe that the surface of Io is no older than a million years.

Ganymede is the largest of the Galilean satellites and is larger than the planet Mercury. Superficially Ganymede's surface resembles the earth's moon with its rayed impact craters. Unlike the moon, all traces of the impact have been destroyed; all that remains are broad circular features. The surface of Ganymede is divided into two types of terrain: the cratered and the grooved.

Craters are everywhere. They are generally very shallow, 10 to 50

Viking Orbiter 1 recorded this image of Deimos from a distance of only 3,300 km (2,050 mi). The illuminated portion measures about 12 by 8 km (7.5 by 5 mi). Craters as small as 100 meters (330 ft) across can be detected. The two largest craters measure 1.3 km (0.8 mi) and 1 km (0.62 mi) in diameter.

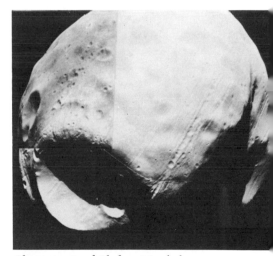

Photomosaic of Phobos, Mars's larger satellite, made from a series of photographs taken by Viking Orbiter 1 from a distance of 612 km (380 mi) on October 19, 1978. Resembling a gaping mouth, the crater Stickney is the dominant feature at the bottom. Stickney is 10 km (6.2 mi) across. Linear grooves coming from and passing through Stickney appear to be surface fractures caused by the impact that formed this crater.

This dramatic photograph of Io revealed that active volcanoes exist not only on earth but also on other bodies in the solar system. Two volcanoes are seen here: The plume of one appears along the limb or edge of Io at the lower right, while the second is the bright spot (right middle) seen along the terminator, the day-night boundary.

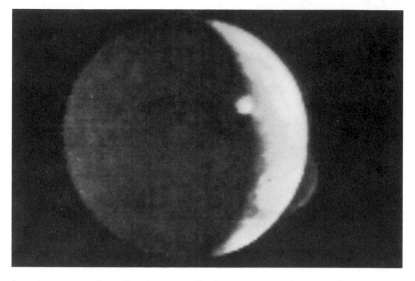

km (6 to 30 mi) in diameter, with sharp rims and convex floors. This shape is rarely observed on terrestrial planets and could be produced on Ganymede by the impact of an object onto an icy mantle. Scientists believe that water comprises 50 percent of the weight of Ganymede.

The surface of Ganymede is also marked by grooves that resemble dune-buggy tracks in the desert. These grooves form systems that range from 10 to 1,000 km (6 to 600 mi) long and 10 to 100 km (6 to 60 mi) wide. An individual groove may be 5 to 15 km (3 to 9 mi) wide and a few hundred meters (yards) deep.

Callisto is the most heavily cratered of the Galilean satellites and probably the most heavily cratered object in the solar system. Its surface is characterized by large impact structures. One of its more striking features is a bright circular patch shown in the photograph some 300 km (190 mi) in diameter and surrounded by 8 to 10 ridges that extend some 1,500 km (950 mi) from the center. This feature is similar to the large circular impact basins seen on the moon and Mercury. However, the ice crust of Callisto probably accounts for the flatness of this feature and the unusual spacing of the surrounding rings, two properties not observed in the basins on the moon or Mercury. Because of the extensive cratering of the surfaces of Callisto and Ganymede, scientists believe that they are at least 4 billion years old.

Scientists were not able to see much detail on the surface of Europa, since the Voyager 1 spacecraft remained relatively far from it. Voyager 2 confirms that Europa is different from the other Galilean satellites, though. There are no obvious basin structures or rays from impact craters, as on Ganymede and Callisto. The most striking feature seen by Voyager 1 is a pattern of intersecting linear features, 50 to 200 km (30 to 125 mi) wide and thousands of kilometers long. Voyager 2 photographs have revealed these features to be shallow cracks in an icy surface rather than deep canyons. Few craters are seen on Europa. The density of Europa suggests that 20 percent of this satellite is water. A shell of water ice as thick as 100 km (60 mi) has been postulated to exist on this satellite.

Amalthea, the fifth satellite of Jupiter, was also photographed by Voyager 1. It has been found to be ten times larger than Phobos, measuring 265 by 140 km (165 by 87 mi), with a very red color marked by several small bright spots.

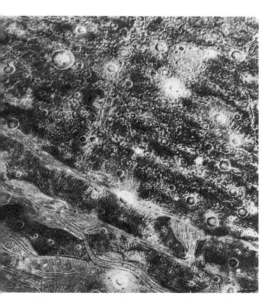

The two types of terrain on Ganymede are apparent in this photograph taken by Voyager 2 when it was 120,000 km (74,500 mi) from Jupiter's satellite. Parallel grooves resembling dune-buggy tracks are seen in the lower part of the photograph, while craters are everywhere. Craters on Ganymede are smoother than those on earth's moon.

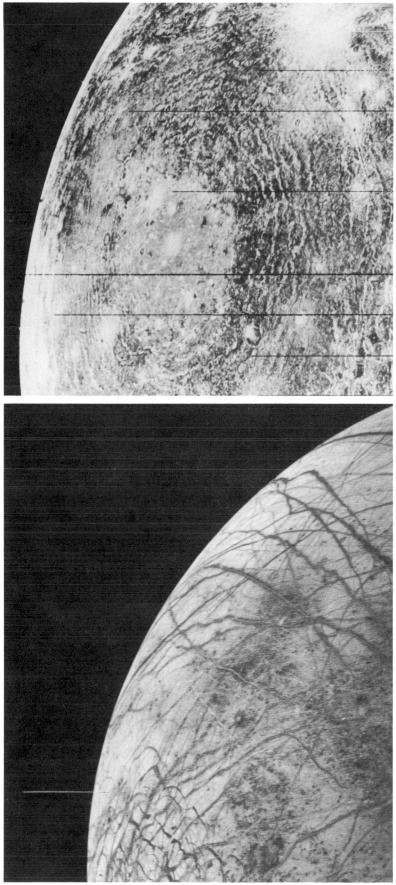

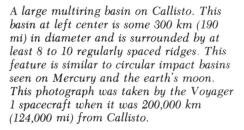

A large multiring basin on Callisto. This basin at left center is some 300 km (190 mi) in diameter and is surrounded by at least 8 to 10 regularly spaced ridges. This feature is similar to circular impact basins seen on Mercury and the earth's moon. This photograph was taken by the Voyager 1 spacecraft when it was 200,000 km (124,000 mi) from Callisto.

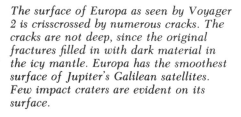

The surface of Europa as seen by Voyager 2 is crisscrossed by numerous cracks. The cracks are not deep, since the original fractures filled in with dark material in the icy mantle. Europa has the smoothest surface of Jupiter's Galilean satellites. Few impact craters are evident on its surface.

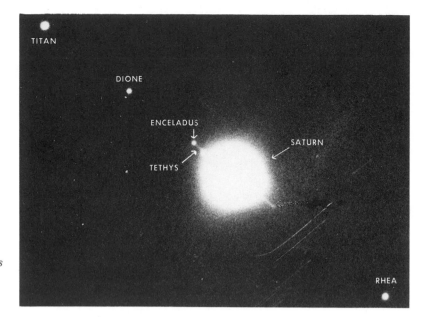

Five of Saturn's satellites are seen in this photograph. When it was made in 1966 the rings of Saturn were edge-on as viewed from earth.

In addition to its spectacular rings, Saturn has at least 16 satellites. They range in size from 80 km (50 mi) to planet-sized. Titan, Saturn's largest satellite, is larger than Mercury and nearly the size of Mars. The remarkable feature of Titan is its extensive atmosphere, which has been shown by Voyager 1 data to be mostly nitrogen with a small percentage of methane. The atmospheric pressure at the surface is half again as great as that of the earth's. Titan's surface temperature is estimated to be a chilly 92°K (−294°F)!

Little is known about the remaining satellites in the solar system. Uranus has five, Neptune two, and Pluto one. Triton, the largest satellite of Neptune, is three fourths the size of Mercury. Triton is massive enough and cold enough to retain an atmosphere but none has been discovered.

The 2 satellites of Neptune—Triton and Nereid. An exposure of 10 minutes was made on June 25, 1962, with the 3-meter (120-inch) Lick Observatory reflector. Triton's orbit is so nearly circular that its eccentricity has not yet been determined. Nereid orbits Neptune at a mean distance of 5.6 million km (3.5 million mi) with direct motion, in a period of 360 days.

The discovery of Pluto's satellite, Charon, has permitted astronomers to determine more accurately the physical characteristics of Pluto. Charon circles once every 6.4 days some 20,000 km (12,000 mi) above Pluto and has a diameter of about 850 km (530 mi). Pluto and the earth are similar in that their moons are about one quarter the size of the parent planet.

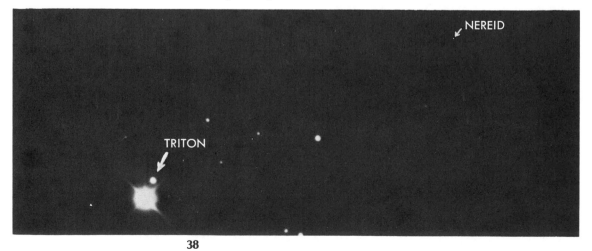

The age of the Milky Way Galaxy, in which the solar system and our earth were born and nurtured, has been set at from 10 billion to 20 billion years based on three separate lines of evidence: two galactic, one subterrestrial.

Our universe began in a mammoth explosion, or "Big Bang," it is generally believed. In the beginning there were no stars or galaxies, just matter in the form of elementary particles and energy. Some 10 million to 100 million years after the Big Bang our Milky Way Galaxy and the other galaxies formed. As a result of the original cosmic explosion, the distances between the galaxies in the universe continue to increase as they participate in the expansion of the universe. By measuring the rate of this expansion and assuming that the expansion has been proceeding at the same rate since the beginning, astronomers can run the clock backward, so to speak, and determine when the expansion began—that is, when the universe exploded. The age of the universe determined in this way is about 19 billion years.

After galaxies formed, stars began to form within them. If the ages of individual stars are determined, we know that the galaxy is at least that old. The oldest stars known in the Milky Way are found in compact groupings of stars known as globular clusters. The ages of these oldest stars are between 9 billion and 18 billion years.

The last line of evidence derives from the extent of the radioactive decay of rhenium 187 to osmium 187, as measured in samples of ores found deep within the crust of the earth itself. These heavy chemical elements of the earth were not made in the earth but in the first, massive stars formed in the Milky Way galaxy. These stars were relatively short-lived and ended their evolution in violent supernova explosions. The sun, a second- and possibly third-generation star, and the rest of the solar system formed out of hydrogen laced with these heavy elements. The age determined from this slow-ticking clock ranges from 10 billion to 20 billion years.

The texture of the earth's surface has been compared with that of a dried prune or wrinkled apple, full of spots, pits, and fissures, and obviously very old, with a long and rugged history. Fossil organisms discovered in a flinty-iron deposit near Lake Superior, Ontario, probably are 2 billion years old, and it is surmised that life may have existed on earth for 4 billion years. On the basis of radioactive decay, the earth itself has been roughly estimated to be between 4.5 billion and 5 billion years of age, young in relation to its parent galaxy, old in relation to the fleeting 2-million-year period during which man has evolved.

The Apollo expeditions to the moon have forced man to view the earth not just as his home but also as one of nine planets circling the majestic sun. We have landed on the moon, Mars, and Venus, have photographed their surfaces, as well as that of Mercury, and most importantly, have viewed the whole great earth from space. Earth has become another subject to be studied by astrogeologists.

At the same time, vessels and instruments have been designed that can withstand the gigantic pressures of the ocean depths and probe their secrets. With ultrasensitive recording devices, more and more has been discovered about what lies far beneath our planet's thin crust. The broad outlines of knowledge of the planet earth, from its very center to the outer limits of its atmosphere, have been blocked out over a couple of centuries. But such is the acceleration of scientific ad-

Chapter V
Planet Earth

*"...This Earth, a spot, a graine,
An Atom, with the Firmament
compar'd...."*

Milton

vance that in the last decade a great proportion of these facts have had to be revised.

All this knowledge of our own planet forms the backdrop against which the other planets will be investigated. In turn, whatever new information is obtained by space exploration about the moon and the other planets, under the extremely different conditions of each, will reshape our explanations of the earth itself, its origin, and its history.

The Great Globe Itself

The size and shape of the planet earth, the exact location of places on it, and the variations in terrestrial gravitation and magnetism are the province of geodesy. The earth's basic shape or figure has long been known to be spherical. With more accurate measurements, a little flattening at the poles was found: The polar diameter was calculated as about 42.8 km (26.5 mi) shorter than the equatorial diameter. This flattening or oblateness comes from a "slumping" toward the equator caused by the rotation of the earth on its axis. It is very small, 0.34 percent or 1/297 of the 12,756 km (7,926 mi) of the earth's equatorial diameter. The earth's figure is like that of an ellipse rotated on its minor axis, or diameter of least length, to form an ellipsoid. The greater diameter of the earth at the equator is called the equatorial bulge. The differential pulling and hauling of the gravitation of the sun and moon on this bulge produce polar precession, the slight wobbling of the earth as it spins on its axis.

The variations of the earth's surface are familiar: the flatness of its plains, plateaus, and oceans, the roughness of its mountains, valleys, and deep-cut gorges. But these variations—8,848 meters (29,028 ft) above sea level and 11,035 meters (36,204 ft) below it—are not extreme viewed in relation to the full sweep of the earth's surface. The distance from the lowest to the highest point of the earth is about 0.3 percent of the earth's radius. For Mars this is about 1 percent. The largest feature on Mars is the mammoth volcano Olympus Mons. Its base stretches 700 km (430 mi), and its cone is 21 km (13 mi) above the surrounding plain. Olympus Mons is more than 2.5 times the height of Mount Everest.

The earth's variations in elevation above and below sea level are similar to those standing out so clearly on the surface of the moon. The moon, however, is smoother than its stark shadows make it look. And Venus, judging by the radar echoes, has a generally smoother surface than the moon, although the same echoes have shown craters, a massive canyon, and large volcanoes up to 10 km (6 mi) in height. Mariner 10 revealed that the surface of Mercury is similar, but not identical, in many ways to the moon. The major difference on Mercury is the existence of prominent scarps, or line of steep cliffs, up to 3 km (1.8 mi) high and running for hundreds of kilometers.

Mercury, Venus, Mars, and the moon, then, are all rocky bodies like the earth, battered by impacts from space and smoothed more or less by the various forces acting on their surfaces. Hidden under their thick atmospheres, the surface contours of the giant planets have yet to be determined. Both the Russians and the Americans have reported the bouncing of radar signals from Jupiter, but little interpretation has been possible.

To map the continually varying surface of the earth accurately, obtaining the exact locations, elevations, and distances of points all over the globe, the basic shape of this surface must be known precisely. To provide a uniform and standard international reference system, geodicists have adopted the so-called international spheroid. This spheroid, a theoretical construct, is a perfectly regular ellipsoid, the minor axis of which is parallel to the axis of rotation of the earth, with values assigned to its major axis and its oblateness or eccentricity that fairly closely approximate those of the earth itself.

To make the center and the axes of this standard ellipsoid coincide with the center and the axes of the earth, another theoretical construct, the geoid, has been developed. The geoid is the surface coinciding with the mean sea level in oceans, everywhere at right angles to the gravitational field. While the geoid is warped and twisted by varying gravitational forces at different places on the earth and affected by the heavy land masses of the continents, it holds fairly closely to the basic reference spheroid, not varying from it normally by more than a few hundred meters.

Artificial satellites in orbit around the earth already have extended geodetic knowledge. The gravitational field of the earth's equatorial bulge pulls a satellite observably out of line each time it crosses the equator, causing the plane of its orbit to move slowly clockwise along the equator at a rate that depends on the size of the bulge. Measurements of this orbital perturbation indicate that the flattening ratio of the earth's geoid is $1/298.2 \pm 0.2$, rather than the adopted value of $1/297.00$. The earth is slightly less flattened than had been thought. It has been calculated that the flattening ratio would be $1/299.8$ if the earth were relatively fluid in its interior, because of the high temperatures and pressures deep down inside it. So the observations of many satellites have shown that the interior of the earth must have less plasticity and more mechanical strength than had been predicted.

On the basis of many thousands of satellite tracking photographs by powerful telescopic cameras situated around the world, revealing the swervings of the satellites in their orbits, a map of the earth has been

The gravity field of the earth as measured by its effect on the orbits of artificial earth satellites. Numbers on contour lines are (+) high gravity and (−) low gravity in milligals (a gal is a small gravitational unit). Heavy lines indicate compression of the crust, double lines indicate crustal tension, and dashed lines show ocean basins at the 3,000-fathom depth.

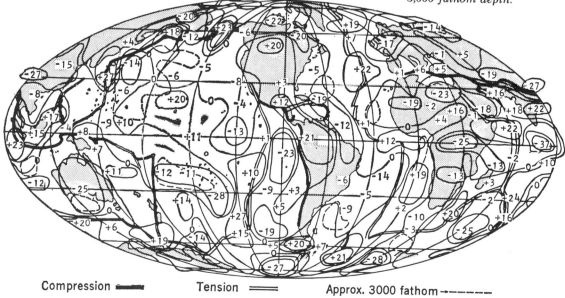

Compression ▬▬ Tension ══ Approx. 3000 fathom ▬-▬-▬

The earth as viewed by a camera aboard a sounding rocket some 110 km (70 mi) above the American Southwest. The black area (lower right) is a lake, and dusky areas (lower middle) are forests. Note the earth's curvature over the Pacific Ocean (upper left).

made showing very precise computer-derived contours of the geoid, or geopotential surface of the earth. The gravitational bulges and indentations around the earth make it appear quite misshapen.

The bumps and hollows stand for areas in which the density of the earth is large or small, resulting in a greater or a smaller pull of gravity toward the center of the earth. These areas were later found to be related to the action of the plates of crust on which the continents ride. Along the edges of these plates a rift system was found, running along the deep bottoms of the earth's oceans. Along the tensional rises in the rift system, where new crust is rising from below and adding to the edges of the plates, the gravitation is high. Along the compressional trenches, where old crust of the plates is sinking deeper down into the earth, the gravitation is low. So discoveries of rises and trenches along the ocean bottoms were related to variations in the earth gravitation revealed by the swerving of satellites orbiting the earth.

Views of the Earth

We all know what our own planet looks like from space. But the earliest such photographs showed only a part of the great curve of the earth, beneath which swept views of large areas of it never before seen entire.

The first photographs from great heights were made by cameras carried up in high-altitude balloons to heights of 24 to 32 km (15 to 20 mi) and later lofted in sounding rockets as high as 480 km (300 mi). Made in black and white by V-2 and U. S. Navy Aerobee rockets, they revealed how details begin to merge at such heights, how the view changes with the season, and the reflectivity of various surface materials. The actual colors seen from such heights are pastels, ranging from red-brown to blue-green.

The astronauts have described the earth to the inhabitants below from altitudes of 160 to 256 km (100 to 160 mi) and from the moon. They reported recognizing cities, different types of clouds, cloud fronts, and weather patterns. John Glenn identified the Gulf Stream in the Atlantic Ocean by its different color from the surrounding waters. Their visual observations were supplemental to their photographic observations. One view of earth, taken by the Apollo astronauts, is shown in the color section. The Apollo 17 crew on their way to the moon marveled at their view of the full earth. The polar icecap of Antarctica is visible at the bottom of the photograph, as well as nearly the entire coastline of Africa (middle to top). The Malagasy Republic lies off the eastern (right) coast of Africa. Asia can be glimpsed to the right of the Arabian Peninsula (top). Extensive cloud cover blankets a large portion of the Southern Hemisphere. A different view of the earth (color section), made from the Landsat satellite in 1979, displays the vast complexity of the Grand Canyon of the Colorado.

The early photographs of the earth provided man a better view of his home, but they cannot compare with the details seen in photographs taken by second- and later-generation satellites. These newer satellites are designed to provide man with a better understanding of his weather and environment. Most Americans see photographs of the United States, like that pictured, on their evening televised weather reports. The study of such photographs have made weather predictions more accurate, believe it or not.

42

The Himalayas in the India-Nepal-Tibet border area photographed by astronaut Gordon Cooper from a height of 160 km (100 mi).

43

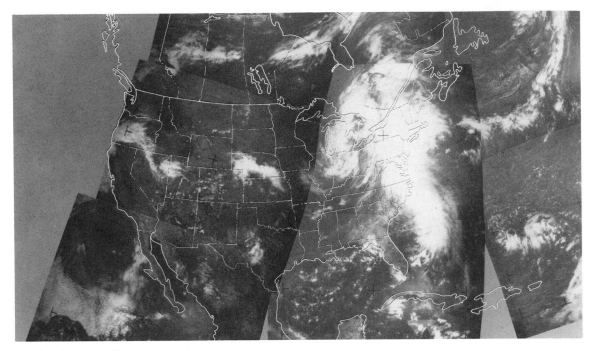

Earth-orbiting satellites extended human views of the earth. A few photos made this view of the cloud cover over the United States on one day. Weather satellites in higher orbit now cover the entire United States in one photograph. Such pictures are routinely seen in televised weather reports.

Different types of detectors are carried on the various satellites. The Landsat series of satellites have as their primary detectors sensing devices that observe narrow sections of the earth in green, red, and near-infrared light. The numerical data beamed to earth are then converted into pictures by computer. Not only are the pictures beautiful to look at, but they also provide information on the geology of the terrain, as evidenced in the October 1976 Landsat photograph of the Grand Canyon of Colorado in the color section. The main part of Grand Canyon National Park is in the middle of the photograph with Marble Canyon running north-south (right middle). The Painted Desert is on the right. The different colors represent different types of terrain and vegetation. The Landsat photographs have indicated likely areas to contain oil, water, and diseased plants. These photographs further help countries to manage their wetlands, survey the amount of snow cover, and manage the growth of their agricultural products. Landsat is designed to identify features with a resolution of 80 to 100 meters (260 to 330 ft), but bridges and roads with widths of about 10 meters (30 ft) have been detected.

Before the advent of earth-orbiting artificial satellites from which photographs could be returned to earth, the appearance of earth from space had to be determined indirectly. Ancient observers noticed that occasionally the dark portion of the moon (not at the moment illuminated by the sun) could be dimly seen, particularly at the new-moon and crescent-moon phases. The dark areas seemed to glow, so they thought the moon was phosphorescent like the sea, or perhaps translucent, allowing a little light to filter through it. Kepler finally gave the correct explanation for this moonglow: It was light from the sun, he said, reflected on the moon by the earth, and then back to earth. Analysis of this doubly reflected light, called earthlight, earthshine, or ashen light, indicated how the earth must look from a distance.

Astronomers found that the earthlight was predominantly bluish

44

light, rather than bluish-green or olive-green as had been believed. They correctly inferred that the earth would look mainly blue or bluish-white from a great distance, as opposed to Mars's predominantly reddish light and Venus's yellowish-white light. The photometer, by which light from unknown sources is compared with light from standard sources, showed the earthlight to consist largely of the blue wavelengths. Its color appears to vary, both at random and with the seasons, becoming bluer as its intensity increases.

Now we know that, as astronomers predicted, the bluish earth appears more bluish-white or gray when its cloud cover is heavy. Where the clouds are scattered, the dim outlines of bluish to blue-black oceans, and brownish to red-brown continents and islands, are traceable. The closer an observer is to the earth, the more variation is noted in its colors.

The reflectivity of the earth (called its albedo) has been studied by means of the earthlight. (The albedo is the proportion of light a body reflects of the total light striking it.) The earth's mean albedo is about 0.39 on a scale in which a perfect reflector of light would be 1.0 and a perfect absorber of light (black body) would be 0.0. The mean-residual albedos of the planets are compared with that of the earth in Table 3, along with their solar constants, the amount of radiation per unit area arriving at the planets from the sun. Substantial confirmation of the figure 0.39 for the earth's mean albedo has been found in direct measurements of the average proportion of light from the sun reflected by the earth's surface and its atmosphere together, with instruments on earth-orbiting satellites. The earthlight has been correctly interpreted. The magnitudes of the earth, moon, and the other planets are also compared in Table 3. The type of magnitude described in Chapter 3 is the measure of the apparent visual brightness of celestial bodies viewed from the earth. The magnitudes given in the table are the unit magnitude (the planet's brightness at the same unit distance from the earth and the sun) and the opposition magnitude (their brightness when the earth stands on the straight line extended from the sun to the other planet).

Earth's Surface

On globes of the earth, the possibility that South America may have fitted snugly against Africa is at once apparent. That these two continents had once been united with the others in one supercontinent, called Pangaea, was proved during the 1960s.

The ridge or rift system running through the oceans of the earth revealed the prior existence of Pangaea, its breakup, and the drifting apart of the continents, gradually spreading around the earth. First, it was discovered from the magnetization of rocks that the magnetic field of the earth had gone through many reversals in the past over millions of years, with the North Pole becoming the South Pole, and vice versa. Then the magnetic reversals turned up in long, narrow bands running along both sides of the newly mapped ridges in the ocean bottoms. Also, volcanoes and earthquakes were most frequently located along the lines of the ridge system.

These discoveries implied that melted rock was pouring up along these cracks in the earth's crust, pushing apart the plates of crust along the ridges and forming wider and wider oceans, like the North and

The continents as they had started to drift apart about 135 million years ago as the ridge system opened and the oceans expanded. Arrows indicate direction of drift and arrow length relative speed of drift. Note India drifting rapidly toward Asia, and Australia breaking from Antarctica.

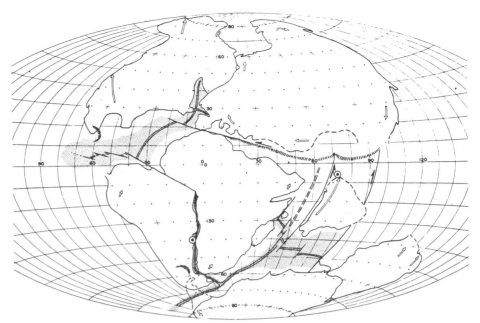

The earth's plates are outlined by earthquake centers and volcanoes (dots). As plates move away from each other great rifts form; mountain chains form as plates "crash" into each other.

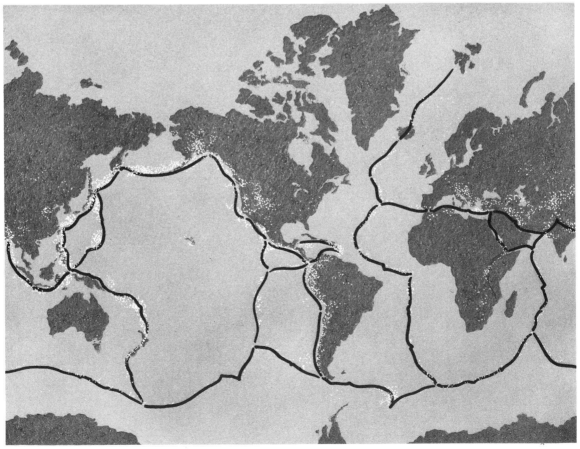

South Atlantic. This spreading of the oceans made the continents on the plates drift apart. This theory was confirmed when deep-sea drilling into the bottom showed that the rocks grew older and older the farther they were from the ridge.

At other places, the ocean bottom revealed deep trenches. Along these trenches and along certain volcanic-island arcs like those in the South Pacific and Japan, it is believed that the earth's crust is being gobbled up. Here the crust is plunging down into the earth's interior to make up for the crust being added along ridges elsewhere. So the con-

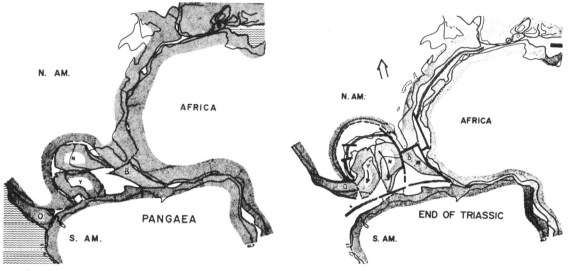

Panel #1:

The drawings show how the Gulf of Mexico and the Caribbean Sea may have formed, under the continental-drift theory. Two hundred million years ago (above), continents were one, called Pangaea. Y stands for Yucatan, N for Nicaragua-Honduras, O for Oaxaca, and B for Bahamas.

Panel #2:

After 20 million years, North America moved (arrow), opening the Atlantic; Y and N moved to leave the Gulf of Mexico as a small ocean basin. The Bahamas plate moved northeast, but South America stayed where it was, joined to Africa. Oaxaca has slipped east.

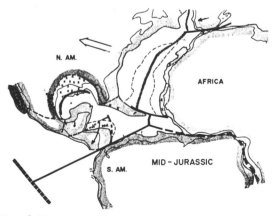

Panel #3:

In another 30 million years, as North America moved west, the Atlantic Ocean had widened, and Central America was nearly formed, with Yucatan and Nicaragua in place. The Gulf of Mexico was formed, and the Caribbean was opening up. Salt deposits (x) formed in the Gulf Basin.

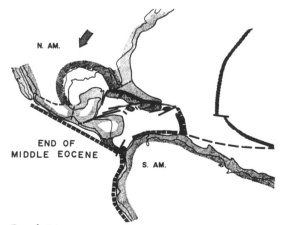

Panel #4:

About 45 million years ago, South America had split from Africa, and the Atlantic Ocean widened to give essentially the present positions. Volcanoes had built up the Panama Isthmus.

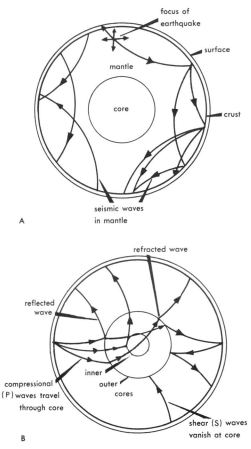

A

B

(A) Representative paths of seismic waves through the mantle of the earth; (B) waves reflected or refracted by the earth's core or absorbed in it. The compressional waves are longitudinal, and the shear waves are transverse; they react differently at the earth's core, as shown in (B).

tinents and oceans of the earth have not been permanent features. Instead they have changed with these events going on in the crust and under it, moving continents a few centimeters a year.

In order to measure continental drift accurately, LAGEOS—the LAser GEOdynamic Satellite—was launched in 1976. This satellite carries no transmitters or instruments, only 426 reflectors. The satellite is designed so that ground stations, eventually 2 on each of the earth's plates, can measure the travel time from themselves to the satellite and back by "bouncing" laser pulses off LAGEOS. These times will enable scientists to measure the distance between ground stations—and any changes in their distances over a long period of time—to within 2 or 3 centimeters over thousands of kilometers (about 1 inch over thousands of miles). LAGEOS has such a stable orbit 5,900 km (3,700 mi) above the earth's surface that it is expected to orbit the earth for about 10 million years.

Earth's Interior

The mass, or quantity of matter, of the earth totals the almost incomprehensible figure of about 6×10^{21} tons. This has been determined in the laboratory by comparing the gravitational attraction of a large sphere for a tiny sphere with the gravitational attraction of the earth for one of these spheres.

The mean or average density of the earth (its mass per unit volume) has been calculated to be 5.52 grams per cubic centimeter. A cubic inch of average earth stuff equals about 0.2 pound (⅕ pound). By comparison, a cubic inch of average moon stuff weighs about 0.12 pound (⅛ pound). The same amount of Martian material weighs about 0.17 pound (1/6 pound) and that of Saturn only 0.025 pound (1/40 pound). The comparative volumes, masses, and densities of the planets are given in Table 1.

The mean density of the earth seems very great compared with familiar substances. It is about 5.5 times that of water, 2 times that of aluminum, .67 that of iron, .50 that of lead, and .33 that of gold. It is almost twice as great as the mean density of the rocks underlying the continents and about 70 percent greater than that of the heaviest of the common igneous rocks at the surface. What can lie beneath the surface of our globe to make its mean density so high?

Something about the nature of the earth beneath its crust has been inferred from the action of seismic waves as they pass under the surface and through the earth. The back-and-forth oscillation of some earthquake waves in long periods of from 1 minute to 6 minutes has been interpreted as indicating that the whole earth rings, somewhat like a struck bell, with heavy earthquakes.

Some evidence about the earth's interior comes, too, from observations of the strength and variation of the earth's magnetic field, variation in the gravitational field at the surface, and heat-flow measurements. The study of both natural earthquake waves and vibrations caused by man-made explosions, including nuclear detonations, indicates that the earth is not completely uniform inside, but consists of a series of concentric spherical shells or layers.

The crinkled and jumbled outer layer of the earth, appropriately called the oceanic and continental crust, runs down to an average depth of 20 km (12 mi), ranging between 10 and 40 km (6 and 25 mi).

Planet Earth

This layer makes an insignificant contribution to the mass of the earth and only composes 1 percent of the earth's volume. The mantle of the earth, the next layer beneath the crust, is roughly 2,900 km (1,800 mi) thick. Traditionally the mantle is divided into 2 parts, the upper mantle extending to 700 km (453 mi) below the earth's surface, and the lower mantle stretching from the upper mantle to the core, 2,900 km (1,800 mi) below the surface. The mantle comprises 83 percent of the earth's volume and 68 percent of its mass. It is also the source of most of the earth's internal energy as well as the forces responsible for sea-floor spreading, continental drift, orogeny (mountain building), and major earthquakes.

Despite the chemical differences between the crust and the mantle, the boundary between layers called the lithosphere and the asthenosphere may be more important to the theory of plate tectonics. This theory proposes that the outermost skin of the earth, the lithosphere, consists of 6 or 7 rigid plates that float about on the partially molten asthenosphere. The motion of the plates is responsible for continental drift, sea-floor spreading, and the earth's seismic activity. The lithosphere is relatively strong and thought to be about 70 km (44 mi) deep. The boundary between the lithosphere and the asthenosphere is not as clearly defined as the crust-mantle boundary. The lithosphere may extend to as deep as 100 km (62 mi). The asthenosphere stretches from the lithosphere to a depth of 300 to 400 km (180 to 250 mi). Since the material in the asthenosphere is mushy it is very near the melting

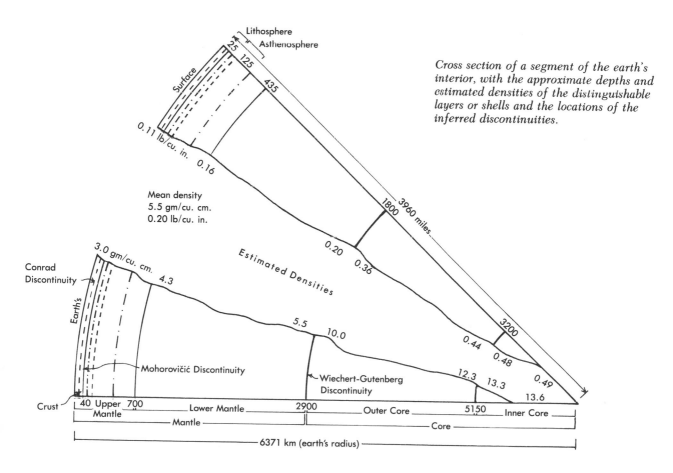

Cross section of a segment of the earth's interior, with the approximate depths and estimated densities of the distinguishable layers or shells and the locations of the inferred discontinuities.

point and provides the cushion upon which the plates of the lithosphere ride.

Beneath the mantle is the core, that part of the earth running from about 2,900 km (1800 mi) down to the center, a huge sphere with a diameter of about 6,960 km (4,320 mi), a little larger than the planet Mars and almost exactly twice the size of the moon. The outer core probably is in a liquid state, and the inner core, solid. The great density of the earth is explained by assuming that its core consists largely of iron or nickel-iron, with traces of other elements.

The crust of the earth averages about 20 km (12 mi) in thickness, though continental crusts are thought to be much thicker (up to 40 km or 25 mi) than the crust under the oceans. A skin of sedimentary rocks such as sandstone, and light silicic metamorphic rocks like granite, compose the upper surface of the crust, down to a depth of perhaps 10 km (6 mi). Beneath this, the material may be largely basalt, a dark-colored, fine-grained volcanic rock, or a heavier, dark "mafic" rock containing magnesium and iron. This material runs down for 8 to 16 km (5 to 10 mi) or more, depending on the thickness of the crust, and the temperature increases with depth, perhaps up to 1,100°C (2,000°F) at 40 km (25 mi) down.

Between the earth's crust and the mantle lies the Mohorovičić discontinuity, named for Yugoslavian seismologist Andrija Mohorovičić, who inferred its presence in 1909 from observations of an earthquake's seismic waves. This discontinuity is a boundary below which earthquake and other seismic waves begin to behave very differently than in the crust, indicating a change in the materials composing the interior, or perhaps a change in crystal structure or phase. (Water changes phase, for example, when it becomes ice or vapor under different temperature-pressure conditions). The seismic waves accelerate from an average rate of 6.9 km (4.3 mi) a second above this boundary to about 7.8 km (4.9 mi) a second below it.

Changes in seismic velocities imply that additional discontinuities occur in the mantle at depths of 200 km (125 mi) and 700 km (435 mi). From the Mohorovičić discontinuity to the 200-km (125-mi) depth there is a gradual increase in the velocity of the seismic waves, as well as in the rock density. Between 200 and 700 km (125 and 435 mi) there is a rapid increase in both velocity and density, while the velocity and density increase slowly but regularly from 700 km (435 mi) to the core.

The Wiechert-Gutenberg discontinuity marks the boundary between the mantle and the core of the earth. The compressional or primary waves travel more slowly below this point, while the shear or secondary waves vanish at this discontinuity. Compressional waves oscillate or compress back and forth in the direction of the wave motion, while the shear waves oscillate or vibrate at right angles (transversely) to the direction of the wave motion and are sometimes called the shaking waves. This indicates the beginning of some different phase of the material, probably a liquid core. The position of the Gutenberg discontinuity has been measured very accurately at 2,900 km (1,800 mi) beneath the surface and marks a sharp change in the density from 5.5 grams per cubic centimeter (0.20 pound per cubic inch) to about 10 grams per cubic centimeter (0.36 pound per cubic inch).

With the crust, the upper mantle is the site of earthquakes and is thought to be in a state of slow-motion turbulence. The mantle may consist primarily of olivine, a magnesium-iron silicate, or it may be peridotite, classed as an igneous rock. Its density and the velocity at which sound waves travel through it are similar to those of the mantle. The exact composition of the mantle is difficult to determine because of its remoteness. Indeed, less is known about the mantle than about the surface of the moon, since soil samples and rocks of the latter have been brought to earth by astronauts. What is really needed is to have sample chunks of the mantle to examine in the laboratory.

Scientists believe small samples of the lower crust or upper mantle have been found near or on the surface. In Italy, for example, the thrusting in the forming of the southern Alps may have shaved up a chip of the mantle, which curled up to the surface. Here the basalt of the lower crust exposed over a distance of 5 to 10 km (3 to 6 mi) changes suddenly with a discontinuity to the peridotite that may well be a chip from the mantle.

The older view of the earth's interior was that it consisted of an iron core beneath a basaltic mantle; the core was believed to be liquefied, containing small amounts of nickel or cobalt mixed with the iron, or possibly silicon. This theory, it was believed, best explained the earth's high mean density and the formation of its magnetic field. In addition, it related the earth's interior to the composition of the iron type of meteorites, which consist largely of such nickel-iron and may be remnants of a small disintegrated primitive planet or planets.

The liquid core of the earth may be moving or swirling slightly, for the magnetic poles move about the surface of the earth. Accordingly, the needle of a compass, while always pointing to magnetic north, will point in different directions relative to true north. For example, in London, England, in 1580 the compass pointed 11° to the east of true north; in 1660 it pointed due north; in 1820, 24° to the west; in 1970, 7° to the west. The South Magnetic Pole moves at a faster rate than the North Magnetic Pole, which creeps along at the rate of 8 km (5 mi) a year. This may be about as fast as cold molasses pours, but it is relatively rapid on a geological time scale.

How did the earth develop its current structure? It is generally believed that 4.5 billion years ago the earth gradually grew by the condensation and accretion of particles in the solar nebula described in the preceding chapter. As the earth grew it began to heat up as the result of gravitational collapse of its mass, meteoritic impact, and the heat from the radioactive decay of uranium, thorium, and potassium. The interior reached such high temperatures and pressures that it melted, which resulted in the "iron catastrophe," a complete restructuring of the earth. Molten drops of iron and other heavy elements sank to the center of the earth to form the core. The lighter elements floated to the surface with further differentiation along the way, thus forming the mantle and the crust.

An alternate theory proposes that the earth's current structure results from the fact that the heavy elements, especially iron, crystallized first in the condensing solar nebula. Since the lighter elements were still in a gaseous form, the accreting earth would have an iron-rich core. As the lighter elements crystallized, they were accreted on the outside of the core, forming the mantle. The lightest gases crystallized last and as the particles were added to the earth, they formed its crust.

Interior of Other Planets

The observations, models, and theories of the interior of our own planet have been applied by analogy to the other terrestrial planets—Mercury, Venus, and Mars. These are presumed to have compositions and structures somewhat similar to that of the earth, since their mean densities (running from 4 to 5.4 grams per cubic cm or 0.14 to 0.19+ pound per cubic inch) are close to that of the earth (5.5 grams per cubic cm or 0.20 pound per cubic inch), and their sizes do not vary tremendously from that of the earth. Perhaps the greatest surprise was the discovery of a magnetic field about Mercury 0.01 (1/100) the strength of the earth's. Mariner 10 observations have also shown that Mercury's surface composition probably consists of silicates, like the moon. These two results imply that a silicate mantle surrounds a nickel-iron core, a core whose radius is three fourths that of the planet!

Jupiter, Saturn, Uranus, and Neptune, the Jovian planets, or gas giants, have very low mean densities, running from 0.7 gram to 1.7 grams per cubic cm (0.03 to 0.06 pound per cubic inch). A density of 2.8 grams per cubic cm (0.10 pound per cubic inch) is just about the point that divides the terrestrial from the Jovian planets. This places the moon, with a density of 3.34 grams per cubic cm (0.12 pound per cubic inch) almost on the borderline, though slightly closer to the rocky bodies like the earth. The plethora of varied theories about the moon's inner composition reflect this borderline-density position. The density of Pluto (1.5 grams per cubic cm or 0.05 pound per cubic inch) would place it with the Jovian planets, although its size is more like that of the terrestrial planets.

On the basis of density, the heaviest satellites of Jupiter, Io (Jupiter I) and Europa (Jupiter II), as well as Titan, Saturn's largest satellite (Saturn VI), may fall into either classification, like the moon, as may a number of other satellites. However, Ganymede (Jupiter III) and Callisto (Jupiter IV) and inner satellites of Saturn, Mimas (Saturn I), Enceladus (Saturn II), and Tethys (Saturn III), are light enough to fall into the Jovian planet class.

With the exception of Jupiter, little is known about the interiors of the outer planets. Neptune, the densest of the Jovian planets, probably has the greatest concentration of heavier materials. Its rocky core, perhaps 16,000 km (10,000 mi) in diameter, is probably surrounded by ices 8,000 km (5,000 mi) thick. It was recently suggested that Uranus's interior may consist of a solid, rocky core with a 10,000-km (6,200-mi) radius beneath a liquid mantle of hydrogen. Saturn's rocky core, with a 10,000-km (6,200-mi) radius is surrounded by a 5,000-km (3,000-mi)-thick shell of ice and an 8,000-km (5,000-mi)-thick shell of metallic hydrogen. This in turn is surrounded by molecules containing hydrogen.

The Pioneer 10 and 11 spacecraft have provided clues to the interior of Jupiter. Like the other outer planets, Jupiter is believed to have formed initially by the accretion of rocky material and ice followed by the accretion of gas. Jupiter, however, accumulated gas sooner than the others and has a smaller iron-silicate core than Saturn, Uranus, and Neptune. From the core of Jupiter to a distance of 46,000 km (28,600 mi) from the center is a layer of liquid metallic hydrogen. In this state, hydrogen is an electric conductor. The electric currents in this layer of the interior may be the sources of Jupiter's magnetic field. Liquid mo-

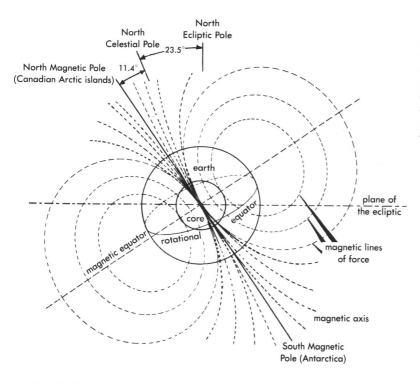

North Celestial Pole
North Ecliptic Pole
23.5°
North Magnetic Pole (Canadian Arctic islands) 11.4°
earth
plane of the ecliptic
core
equator
magnetic lines of force
rotational
magnetic equator
magnetic axis
South Magnetic Pole (Antarctica)

Cross section of the lines of force of the earth's dipole magnetic field. The North and South Magnetic, Celestial, and Ecliptic Poles are distinct from each other. (See also the diagram of the geomagnetic cavity, in Chapter 6, within which the magnetic field is probably largely contained.)

lecular hydrogen stretches from the metallic hydrogen layer to just 1,000 km (620 mi) below the cloud tops. In the upper part of Jupiter, the liquid hydrogen is converted into gaseous hydrogen. In this layer, liquid water as well as ice and ammonia crystals may exist.

Models for the interiors of Jupiter and Saturn are difficult to make, since Jupiter radiates 2.7 times the solar radiation it receives, while the outward heat flux from Saturn is about twice as great as the incoming solar radiation (see Table 3). The source of this internal heat remains a mystery.

Earth's Magnetic Field

A compass needle swinging toward the North Magnetic Pole demonstrates the existence of the earth's magnetic field positively. But the magnetic phenomena of the earth are, in fact, extremely complex, and their large-scale investigation is only beginning.

The measured intensity of the general terrestrial dipole (two-poled) magnetic field is very small compared with that of natural or artificially created magnets. The gauss is a measure of the magnetic field strength, named after German scientist Karl Friedrich Gauss, a pioneer investigator of the earth's magnetism. A gamma is 0.00001 (1/100,000) gauss. At the Geomagnetic North and South Poles, the intensity of the magnetic field is about 0.63 gauss or 63,000 gammas. At the geomagnetic equator, which does not correspond to the rotational equator, the intensity is more than halved, to about 0.31 gauss. The surface magnetic field ranges from a high of about 0.725 to a low of about 0.245 gauss, averaging around 0.5 gauss or 50,000 gammas.

The form of the earth's magnetic field is about like that of any uniformly magnetized sphere. Within this doughnut-shaped (toroidal) form, however, the earth's field shows large short-term fluctuations. The great variations probably result from excess magnetic materials, such as magnetite or other mineral deposits in the crust of the earth. One of these spots is at Kursk, in the U.S.S.R. near Moscow. It has an intensity of 1 gauss, much larger than that of the main field and even reversing the direction of the lines of force on occasion. The earth may have other minor magnetic poles in addition to its two major ones, forming a multipolar field. The shape of the outer portions of the lines of force of the earth's magnetic field may vary extremely from the doughnut shape, dependent on conditions in the geomagnetic cavity and space, becoming lopsided, with the side opposite the sun tapering off into a tail.

The strength of the earth's magnetic field has been found to wax and wane (from studies of rock magnetization, which have also indicated the reversals in the field). About three such reversals per million years have taken place in recent geologic times. It is possible that the movements of the earth's magnetic poles are related to this field reversal. It has been theorized that when the magnetic poles move close enough to the earth's poles of rotation, or geographic poles, within about half a degree, the currents in the core that create the field are reduced, and this reduces its strength to nearly zero and causes its reversal. In this connection, it has been determined that the sun's magnetic poles reverse in 11-year periods.

The most widely accepted explanation of the earth's magnetism is the theory that the field is generated by the movement of material conducting electric currents in the fluid or plastic core of the earth, causing the core to operate as a self-exciting dynamo and create the magnetic field. The field could hardly be generated in the crust, because magnetic changes do not appear to be correlated with the crust's geology, or in the mantle, which, although turbulent, does not seem mobile enough either to generate the field or to cause the magnetic variations discovered. A fluid or liquid core, with electric currents generating the field proper and swinging or surging enough in relation to the earth's surface to carry along with it the lines of magnetic force and flow of current, appears to be the most plausible explanation at the moment.

Distant Magnetic Fields

Evidence that the moon once had a magnetic field has been found in remnant magnetization of lunar rocks returned to earth and by a satellite orbiting the moon. Whether such a lunar field came from a small core or from an external field is not settled.

Mercury's magnetic field is a dipole field like the earth's, with the magnetic poles nearly aligned with Mercury's rotation poles. The magnetosphere of Mercury is not as extensive as that of the earth. The distance from the center of the earth to the leading edge of its magnetosphere is more than 10 planetary radii, while for Mercury it is only 1.6 planetary radii. Charged particles in Mercury's magnetosphere more readily hit the planet's surface. Accordingly, Mercury has no Van Allen radiation belt. The source of this magnetic field is not known but its existence implies that there is an extensive nickel-iron core within Mercury.

Venus has also surprised astronomers about its magnetic field (or rather its apparent lack of one). For years, Venus was believed to be earth's twin. Venus's size and density are very similiar to earth's (see Table 1). If the earth had a magnetic field, why not Venus? Some even believed that Venus possessed a magnetic field stronger than earth's.

54

At periods of inferior conjunction, when Venus lay nearly on a line between the earth and the sun, the streams of electrified solar particles (solar plasma or wind) reaching the earth appeared to be affected. It was thought that an intense magnetic field on Venus might explain these effects. But in 1962, when Mariner 2 carried a magnetometer past Venus at a distance of 34,890 km (21,650 mi), there was no indication of a magnetic field, though the instrument was sensitive to a 0.5-gamma variation or a field strength 100,000 times weaker than that of the earth. Venus's field was tentatively concluded to be at most no more than 0.1 (1/10) to 0.05 (1/20) of that of the earth, or so weak that it was pressed in by the solar wind to a very limited region close to the planet.

Additional observations of Venus by spacecraft reveal that if it has a magnetic field it is at least 10,000 times weaker than the earth's. It is believed that the earth's field is due to the rotation of earth and its core. It is possible that no magnetic field exists (or at least is extremely weak) on Venus because Venus rotates slowly, nearly 250 times slower than the earth.

If the planet Jupiter were human, it could be accused of having an inflated ego. It has to be first in everything: It is the largest planet, it has as many satellites as any other planet, it rotates the fastest, and so on. Continuing in this tradition, Jupiter has the strongest magnetic field and the most extensive magnetosphere known of any planet in the solar system.

The structure of Jupiter's magnetic field is complex. Away from the planet, the field is dipolar like the earth's. However, the direction of the field is reversed from that of the earth—that is, a terrestrial compass would point to the South Magnetic Pole on Jupiter rather than the North Magnetic Pole, as on earth. Like the earth's field, the axis of this dipolar field is inclined about 12 degrees to the planet's rotation axis. Close to Jupiter's cloud tops, the field strength ranges from 3 to 14 gauss (as compared to 0.3 to 0.8 gauss at the earth's surface) and the field becomes extremely complex. Pioneer 11 measurements indicate that magnetic fields with 4 or even 8 poles may exist.

The magnetosphere of Jupiter is also large. Its shape is similar to that of the earth, but it is much more extensive. For the earth, the boundary between the magnetosphere and the solar wind, called the magnetopause, is found at approximately 75,000 km (46,500 mi). In the case of Jupiter, this boundary may be 750,000 km (465,000 mi). Sizable belts of trapped radiation similiar to the Van Allen belts around the earth are found within the magnetosphere.

In 1979 Pioneer 11 measured a dipole magnetic field for Saturn. The strength of the field measured 0.2 gauss, some 5 times less than predicted. The polarity of the field is like that of Jupiter; that is, it is opposite the polarity of the earth. Saturn has presented astronomers with another problem, however. Unlike the earth and Jupiter, Saturn's magnetic poles are tilted only about one degree to Saturn's rotational poles. This implies that the origin of Saturn's magnetic field must be different from that of the earth and Jupiter.

Essentially nothing is known about the existence of magnetic fields for the remaining outer planets. Although the magnetometers on Mariner flybys of Mars were working, they did not report a magnetic field on the Red Planet.

Chapter VI
Earth's Atmosphere

"This most excellent canopy, the air."
Shakespeare

A teardrop-shaped mass of gases that weighs less than one millionth of the earth's mass, the atmosphere comprises all that lies between the earth and interplanetary space. A necessary condition for nearly all living things, and the conveyer of climate and of the weather, the atmosphere is one of the most significant features of the human environment. What goes on in the chaos of these great billowing and streaming masses of gases, of particles mixing in them, of plasmas, of gravitational and magnetic fields, and of turbulent showers of radiation and massive shock waves composing the atmosphere?

A great deal has been learned about the atmosphere largely because of the drive into space. Balloons have soared into the atmosphere's lower levels, rockets have penetrated higher, and earth satellites have collected reel upon reel of data as they orbited through its upper levels. These developments have forced complete revisions of what was solid textbook doctrine only a few years ago and have given birth to a new discipline, aeronomy, the science of the physics and chemistry of the atmosphere's upper levels.

Atmospheric Regions

The atmosphere has been mapped out vertically in a number of concentric spherical regions or shells, somewhat like the strata in rocks. Such regions are only roughly demarcated, as much to indicate the type of investigation as actual significant atmospheric variations, but they have proved valuable. Many of these atmospheric layers or spheres are recent discoveries. The suffix "sphere" denotes each of these regions, as in the term troposphere, the lowest level of the atmosphere, which runs up to 8 to 12 km (25,000 to 39,000 ft) above the surface of the earth. The roughly defined upper boundary or borderline of each region is denoted by the suffix "pause." The tropopause is the shifting upper limit of the troposphere, at an elevation of 8 to 17 km (5 to 11 mi). In the past the customary atmospheric scale was in terms of feet of elevation; now it is in terms of miles, and our knowledge of what goes on up there has increased by about the same ratio.

The main regions of the atmosphere and the principal elements composing it are shown in the diagram. The basic thermal classification of the atmosphere distinguishes the troposphere, stratosphere, mesosphere, thermosphere, and exosphere—distinctions based on variations in temperature with height. Classified according to composition, the main regions of the atmosphere are called the homosphere, the lower region in which the composition remains constant and the gases are fairly well mixed, and the heterosphere, in which the composition begins to change markedly through molecular dissociation and recombination, diffusion, and photoionization. Classified according to dominant processes, several regions of the atmosphere are significant, such as the ionosphere, characterized by changes in intensity of ionization, and the chemosphere, where chemical reactions are dominant. In the ozonosphere, ozone (O_3), vital for most life on earth, plays a major role; in the magnetosphere, the earth's magnetic field is the dominant force.

Thermal Regions—Troposphere and Stratosphere

Making up the cellophane-thin skin called the earth's lower atmosphere, the troposphere and stratosphere are the regions most directly affecting our lives. Most weather is made in the troposphere, but the

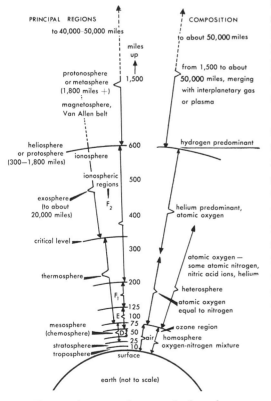

Principal regions distinguished in the earth's atmosphere and its major constituents.

clouds that abound in it are few and far between in the stratosphere. The dividing line between them, the tropopause, varies in elevation from about 16 to 17 km (10 to 11 mi) at the equator, decreasing to 8 km (5 mi) at high latitudes, and varying from between 8 and 15 km (5 and 9 mi) in the North and South Temperate Zones.

During the 1930s, the stratosphere was considered a windless, cold place of dead calm and quiet. The discovery of jet streams at the tropopause and in the lower stratosphere came as a surprise. These ribbons of wind 9 to 13 km (6 to 8 mi) up may be as much as 500 km (300 mi) wide, but only 1.5 to 3 km (1 or 2 mi) thick; they have normal velocities of 56 km (35 mi) an hour in the summer and about 150 km (90 mi) an hour in the winter, but they occasionally whip along at 160 to 320 km (100 to 200 mi) an hour. Aircraft often fly in the stratosphere because of the slighter resistance of its thinner air, and can take advantage of these jet streams to speed them even more quickly on their way.

The temperature decreases with height up through the troposphere, plummeting down steadily from a mean of about 10°C (50°F) at the earth's surface to a low of between -45° and -60°C (-50° and -75°F). The cold remains quite constant up through the stratosphere, which reaches an altitude of 50 km (30 mi), although the temperature begins to rise in its upper levels. With greater altitude, the west winds that are found in the lower stratosphere diminish, and easterlies take over at very high levels.

The bulk of the earth's atmosphere is concentrated near its surface in the troposphere and stratosphere. At an altitude of 5.4 km (3.4 mi or 18,000 ft), about half of the total mass of the atmosphere is below. About 95 percent of the atmosphere's mass is below the 24-km (15-mi or 80,000-ft) level. Conditions at the top of the dents that the earth's crinkled surface makes in the atmosphere attest to this fact. Atop Mount Everest, for example, at 8,848 meters (29,028 ft), the air is already getting very thin, and even well-acclimated climbers require extra oxygen to avoid altitude sickness. Even at elevations of 1,500 to 2,300 meters (5,000 to 7,500 ft), distance runners at track meets are badly slowed by the lack of normal concentration of oxygen in the air.

Composition of the Lower Atmosphere

The blend of gases that makes up the air of the lower atmosphere has been thoroughly analyzed, and the proportions of each gas in the mixture are known with great accuracy. Air consists of a mixture of so-called permanent gases, which remain at nearly the same proportions up through the troposphere and stratosphere. The major variable components are water vapor, carbon dioxide, and ozone; the proportion of each keeps shifting.

The principal gases, nitrogen and oxygen, together constitute about 99 percent of the atmosphere near the earth; argon accounts for almost another 1 percent. Other gases, such as neon, helium, methane, krypton, nitrous oxide, hydrogen, and xenon, are present in extremely limited quantities. Oxygen becomes dissociated into atomic oxygen, which with greater elevation makes up a greater and greater proportion of the total atmosphere, until at a height of about 480 km (300 mi) above the surface the atmosphere is composed almost entirely of oxygen atoms along with helium and hydrogen.

Many other gases and particles can be found in the air in very small

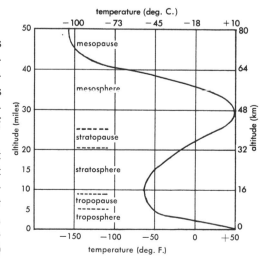

Temperature variation in the lower part of the earth's atmosphere up through the thermal regions to the mesopause.

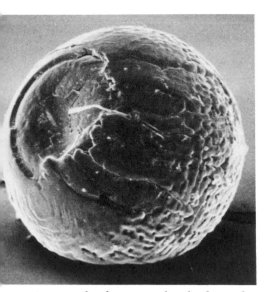

An example of an iron spherule obtained from red clay in the Atlantic Ocean. The appearance of such particles suggests that they are micrometeorites that have entered the earth's atmosphere and gradually drifted to the earth's surface. This particular sample is 70 micrometers (0.0028 inch) in diameter.

and varying proportions, either taken up from the earth's surface, or, occasionally, produced by chemical processes in the air itself. These include carbon monoxide, (CO), sulfur dioxide (SO_2), ammonia (NH_3), and nitrogen dioxide (NO_2) among the gases; compounds, mainly from the oceans, such as sodium, magnesium, calcium, and potassium salts; very fine soil particles such as quartz, mica, calcium carbonate, and feldspar; radioactive isotopes such as iodine 131 and strontium 90, the products of nuclear explosions; and some fine particles of dust that have sifted down from cosmic space or from meteors consumed in the atmosphere.

Once in a while great quantities of fine dust or ash are belched out with large volcanic eruptions, like the blasting of Krakatoa on Java in 1883 or the eruption of the Agung volcano on the island of Bali in 1963. The dust is not limited to the region of the eruption. Volcanic dust and ash were detected as far as the eastern coast of the United States from the relatively minor eruption of Mount St. Helens in the state of Washington during the spring of 1980. Volcanic dust circulates about the earth's troposphere in a period of 2 to 6 weeks. The length of time dust persists depends on the original amount available and on the heights reached in the troposphere and stratosphere. Colorado experienced optical effects of dust from the Krakatoa eruption three years later. Dust from the Agung eruption is believed responsible for the brilliant golden sunrises and sunsets that year as well as for the very dark lunar eclipse that occurred on December 30, 1963. For many observers the moon virtually disappeared. It has been established that Agung dumped 15 million metric tons of dust into the earth's atmosphere, ten times the amount of man-made particulates.

Oxygen—one fifth of the atmosphere—is what sustains the lives of animals and men. While there are anaerobic bacteria that do not require oxygen, and organisms of this kind may have been the predominant form of life under primitive terrestrial conditions, the metabolism of more complex life is based on oxygen. Plants, on the other hand, use carbon dioxide in the atmosphere for their metabolism and produce most, if not all, of the atmospheric oxygen, which was probably not part of the primitive earth atmosphere.

The carbon dioxide in the atmosphere comes from several sources: from natural processes, like the gases emitted by volcanoes, and as a product of animal metabolism and decomposition and of such oxidizing processes as fires and internal-combustion engines. It has been estimated that if industrial consumption of the earth's fossil fuel continues to grow at current rates, the amount of carbon dioxide in the atmosphere will double in 50 years. A large-scale increase would wreak havoc at the earth's surface by creating a "greenhouse" effect—absorbing and then trapping solar radiation and warming the terrestrial climate. Some models indicate that the average global temperature would rise about 1.5° to 3°C (about 3° to 6°F). Other models indicate that the temperature would rise about 2°C (4°F) at the equator but more than 10°C (18°F) near the poles. These models are very simple and ignore such factors as the extent of snow and ice cover and the reactions of the oceans and the clouds.

Evidence for warming is contradictory. The temperature in the Southern Hemisphere may have increased by about 1°C (2°F) since 1940, despite the fact that 1976 was the coldest year at the South Pole since records began being kept there in 1957. Furthermore, temperatures have dropped in the Northern Hemisphere since 1940 despite the increase in carbon-dioxide content. For the moment, the earth's variable water vapor absorbs nearly six times as much of the radiant energy from the sun as all the other gases combined, as well as accounting for nearly all the absorption by gases of the radiation emerging from within the earth, so water vapor has the major role in determining the weather.

The ozone in the atmosphere is largely concentrated in the region 16 to 48 km (10 to 30 mi) above the earth. This is fortunate, for one thing, because of ozone's penetrating and rather nasty odor, which can sometimes be whiffed near a short circuit, after lightning has struck nearby, or around electrical machinery in operation. While some ozone can be identified at the earth's surface, it becomes more concentrated with increasing height and it is most dense at 22 to 24 km (13 to 14 mi) above the equator and at 10 to 13 km (6 to 8 mi) up in the high latitudes. Stratospheric winds move it from equatorial regions toward the North and South Temperate Zones, where it moves into the troposphere through gaps in the tropopause related to jet streams.

The ozone layer is extremely important to man. Made of three oxygen atoms, an ozone molecule absorbs ultraviolet radiation. The majority of the sun's ultraviolet light striking the top of the earth's atmosphere is absorbed in its ozone layer. The minute amount leaking through to the earth's surface has been responsible for many a painful sunburn. Some believe that an increase in the amount of ultraviolet radiation impinging on the surface of the earth, caused by lowering the amount of ozone in the atmosphere, would result in a rise in the incidence of skin cancer.

In 1978 the United States government banned the manufacturing of chlorofluorocarbons within its boundaries. It was feared that these aerosols float into the ozone layer and destroy the ozone molecules. It has not been precisely determined whether such man-made pollutants deplete the ozone more than natural effects. A satellite named SAGE—Stratosphere Aerosol and Gas Experiment—has been launched to study the amount of ozone and other gases in the terrestrial atmosphere. It does this by observing the sun at four different regions of the spectrum each time it enters and leaves the earth's shadow. Eventually, SAGE should tell us precisely what is happening to the ozone layer.

Solar Constant and Heat Balance

High-altitude balloon, sounding-rocket, and satellite observations have made possible a more precise determination of the total radiation from the sun on a unit area of the earth. Called the solar constant, this unit measure of the heat available to the earth has an average intensity of about 2 calories per square centimeter per minute when the solar radiation is at normal incidence (that is, at right angles) to the atmosphere and directly above it, at the earth's average distance of 1 astronomical unit from the sun (Table 3). While recent determinations of the solar constant have varied from 1.93 to 2.00 calories per unit area per unit time, the unit figure, like that of the a.u. itself, is rapidly becoming more exact. The constant represents a tremendous flood of radiant heat being received over the entire hemisphere of the earth exposed to the sun. This solar energy generates the monumental forces involved in the earth's weather; in comparison with these forces, thermonuclear explosions are popguns.

Insolation is that portion of the solar radiation not reflected, scattered, or absorbed in its passage through the atmosphere—it actually reaches the earth's surface. Under average conditions, about 35 percent of the solar radiation is reflected and back-scattered in the atmosphere, and about 17 percent is absorbed by water vapor, by other gases, and by dust, so that only 48 percent finally warms the surface. These average proportions vary greatly with time of day and season, latitude, and type of surface and cloud condition. With overcast skies, perhaps only 35 percent of the solar radiation finally reaches the ground; with average cloudiness (52 percent) over the earth's disk, the insolation is about 50 percent.

Is the solar constant really constant? We know that solar flares and sunspots produce significant variations in the x-ray radiation from the sun, with increases running from 10 to several hundred times the normal intensity. It has not yet been proved that such variations affect the

The ESSA 5 weather satellite recorded these 8 hurricanes and tropical storms (T/S) around the earth's Northern Hemisphere on September 14, 1967. Continents are traced lightly on the mosaic of photographs. Beulah, shown here south of Cuba, was the hurricane that eventually destroyed a billion dollars' worth of property.

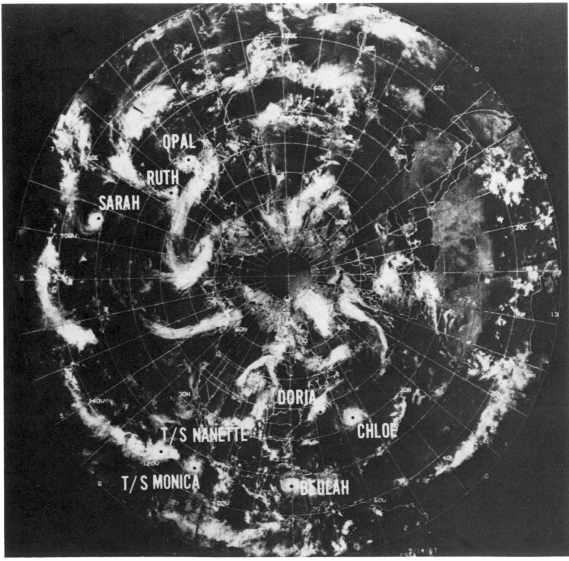

solar constant. Although questions have been raised, it appears that the solar constant is remarkably stable, at least on the time scale of years. Recent studies have placed the variations in the solar constant to be less than 0.75 percent. The very steadiness of the constant helps to provide the stable environment in which life on earth thrives.

Over a period of a few years, at least, a very steady balance also is maintained between the thermal radiation received by the earth from the sun and the earth's own radiation back into space. If the equilibrium did not exist, the earth would be heating up or cooling down slowly—which does not seem to be the case. The complex movements of thermal radiation into and from the earth's surface somehow maintain this balance.

The sun's radiation filtering down through the stratosphere and the troposphere, warming large masses of air and ocean and land surfaces, creates the earth's weather. The rotating earth and its atmosphere act like a huge heat engine, transforming radiant (or heat) energy into kinetic energy (the energy of motion) by heating its working fluid, the atmosphere, at a high pressure and cooling it at a low pressure. In this process the heat is transported from the hot source (that part of the atmosphere most heated by the sun's radiation) to the coolest atmosphere—the "cold sink," as it is called. For the earth, the hot source consists of the equatorial regions, and the cold sinks are the polar regions; the heat is carried by winds (kinetic energy) from the equator toward the poles, and cold from the poles toward the equator.

Large-scale atmospheric conditions, visualized in mathematical models and satellite photographs of cloud cover, are helping meteorologists to forecast weather. Global coverage, particularly over oceans and sparsely inhabited mountainous regions and deserts, had never been achieved by ground-based weather stations. Satellite data have meant a great immediate step forward in meteorology. Photographs, like that from the ESSA 5 weather satellite, have proved invaluable for the detection and tracking of hurricanes and tropical storms.

In addition, the weather satellites have carried sensitive infrared (heat) detectors to measure the intensity of the radiation transmitted or reflected up through the atmosphere from the earth. This varies greatly with changes in temperature, water-vapor density, and the extent and height of the cloud coverage. As the techniques are developed, the maps based on these measurements will become most significant in the long-range forecasting of the weather and the understanding of its causes, for they will reveal the complex, over-all heat-transfer processes taking place in the earth's atmosphere, which can now be only roughly diagrammed.

Solar-Terrestrial Relations

The number of sunspots visible in photographs of the sun is known to vary with an 11-year period. There is also a 22-year periodicity called the Hale magnetic cycle, and the Wolf-Gleissberg cycle, with a period of roughly 80 years. The latter is related to the variation in the number of sunspots at the solar maximum during each solar cycle, while the former refers to the variation in the polarity of the leading sunspot within a sunspot group. Since these solar variations occur, scientists have attempted to link them to variations in the earth's climate. In the past 100 years over 1,000 papers have been written on solar-terrestrial relations.

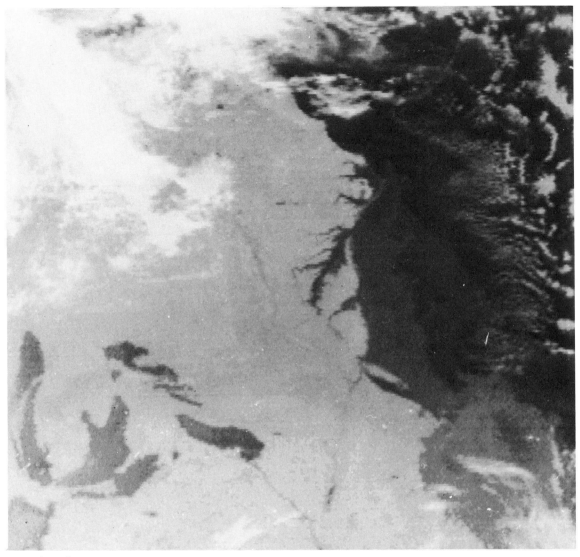

An infrared TV camera on a satellite at a height of 1,400 km (900 mi) above the earth takes the temperature of the earth's surface during October in this photograph. The cloud tops (white) are cold, and the land of the eastern United States (light gray) cool, while the Great Lakes are warmer (gray). Lighter shades in Canada show the land cooler there than in the United States. The Atlantic Ocean is warm (almost black) where the Gulf Stream runs from the south, but the Atlantic is cooler along the East Coast.

Many sun-weather correlations have been discussed. In addition to those mentioned are minor climate changes that occur with periods of 200, 400, and 800 years, and a Little Ice Age cycle that occurs every 2,500 years. There are also annual and semiannual variations in geomagnetic and auroral activity. These are directly related to the earth's changing distance from the sun during the course of the year and the amount of solar energy falling on the earth. Weather variations on time scales of 27 days (related to the sun's rotation period), and 8 days (related to the earth's passage through regions of differing magnetic polarity in the solar wind) have been discussed, as well as the 1- to 2-day-long geomagnetic storms resulting from solar flares.

Of the many suggested sun-weather correlations 3 appear to be firmly established. The solar wind is made of charged particles streaming out from the sun. Regions have been discovered in the solar wind that have a single dominant magnetic polarity, pointed toward or away from the sun. These regions, or sectors, are marked by precise boundaries. Both rotate with the sun. At any particular time 2 or 4 sectors exist. One day after the earth crosses a sector boundary the amount of large-scale rotation in the atmosphere of the Northern Hemisphere decreases. The specific index used measures the intensity and extent of low-pressure areas, which are usually associated with "bad weather." The effect is noted only during the winter months, however.

The second solar-terrestrial weather connection is between the 22-year Hale magnetic cycle and droughts in the western United States. Using tree-ring data from 1700 to 1962, scientists were able to determine that droughts occurred with nearly a 22-year cycle and that the drought cycle and solar cycle were in step. Furthermore, the extent of the drought is modified by the strength of the sunspot cycle. During a weak sunspot cycle—a cycle with fewer total sunspots—the maximum drought area coincides with sunspot minimum. The minimum area occurs 2 to 3 years after sunspot minimum for a particularly strong cycle. Probably the drought is not actually caused, but just modified by the solar activity.

Perhaps the most interesting solar-terrestrial relation was discovered by John A. Eddy of the National Center for Atmospheric Research. He has convincingly shown that the Maunder Minimum was related to solar activity, or rather the lack of it. From A.D. 1645 to 1715 Europe was wracked by unseasonal cold and severe winters. During this same interval, the Maunder Minimum, sunspots were essentially absent on the face of the sun, just as auroras appeared to be absent in the earth's atmosphere. Additional support for the correlation is the amount of carbon-14 in tree rings. This isotope is formed when nitrogen-14 in the earth's atmosphere interacts with cosmic rays, energetic particles traveling in interstellar and interplanetary space. The number of cosmic rays incident on the earth is in turn related to solar activity. When the number of sunspots is low, more cosmic rays can strike the earth's atmosphere and form carbon-14. Carbon combines with 2 oxygen atoms to make carbon dioxide, which is absorbed by earth's plants and trees. Thus rings formed at times of diminished solar activity should have more carbon-14 than those formed when the sun is active. Such is the case. The rings formed at the time of the Maunder Minimum do show an enhanced carbon-14 content. They also show that higher amounts of carbon-14 were present during the Spörer Minimum (A.D. 1460–1550), another period when Europe was experiencing unusually cold weather. The opposite was true during the Grand Maximum, or Medieval Climatic Optimum, in the twelfth century. During this period the earth warmed up and the amount of carbon-14 present was low.

Exactly how solar variations cause or modify the earth's weather is not understood, although connections between the sun and earth's weather are evident.

The Maunder Minimum and the Spörer Minimum occurred during a period called the Little Ice Age. What about other ice ages, which occurred about 100,000, 41,000, and 23,000 years ago? Variations occur in the shape of the earth's orbit, in the angle between the earth's

The amount of carbon-14 present in the earth's atmosphere depends on solar activity. When the sun is active, less carbon-14 is produced in the atmosphere than at times when the sun is relatively quiescent. The amount of carbon-14 present can be traced back in time by studying tree rings, since the carbon is assimilated by the trees in the carbon dioxide they absorb. The shaded areas in the figure indicate times when the relative carbon-14 deviations exceeded 10 parts per million. These areas define the unusual behavior of the solar cycle during the Grand Maximum (A.D. 1100 to 1250), the Spörer Minimum (A.D. 1460 to 1550), and the Maunder Minimum (A.D. 1645 to 1715). One indicator of solar activity is the number of sunspots (R). Historical records show that naked-eye sunspots (denoted by black dots above) were reported during the Grand Maximum but none (with one possible exception) during the Spörer and Maunder Minima.

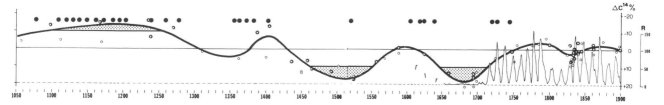

rotational axis and its orbital plane, and in the direction of the earth's North Pole. Since the variations occur on approximately the same time scale as these ice ages, some believe these ice ages result from these slow motions of the earth. Another ice age occurred about 250 million years ago. Scientists have pointed out that this is also the time required for the earth to complete one revolution about the Milky Way Galaxy.

Rainfall and the Moon

Farmers have always known somehow that a relationship exists between the weather and the moon, and farmers' almanacs have supported this tradition. One of the old and now shattered myths of scientists has been that there was no such relationship. Like many categorical statements, this one has eventually had to be retracted. The data on the relationship between the earth's weather and the moon have been available all along to anyone who cared to examine routine U. S. Weather Bureau reports on the dates and places of maximum 24-hour precipitation per calendar month.

The data showed very clearly, with high statistical significance, that in North America there is a strong tendency for the extreme precipitation to fall near the middle of the first and third weeks after new moon, especially on the third to fifth days after new moon and full moon. In the same way, the weeks after first quarter and third quarter were lacking in such heavy precipitation, the low point falling about 3 days prior to full moon and new moon.

While day-to-day rainfall cannot be reliably predicted from the moon's phases, the discovery of this relationship does open up new vistas for atmospheric research. What kind of underlying mechanism could produce such a relationship? It might be a common factor related to both the heavy precipitation and the lunar phases. A solution of this mystery may well lead to a more satisfactory understanding of how our over-all atmosphere operates, particularly in its outer reaches, and have profound effects on the long-range forecasting of the weather.

Mesosphere and Airglow

Oddly enough, little is known about the mesosphere, the region immediately above the stratosphere. Ranging up from the stratopause at 32 to 40 km (20 to 25 mi), the mesosphere extends to an elevation of 80 to 120 km (50 to 75 mi). The heavier meteors reach down into it, and their trails have been studied there with radar. The temperature rises quite rapidly up through its lower portion, where many chemical reactions take place. At about 48 km (30 mi) up, the temperature is roughly comparable to that at the earth's surface. Then the temperature about-faces and drops rapidly again, down to around −100°C (−150°F), far lower than stratospheric temperatures.

The mesosphere is a borderline region, hard to investigate because its constituents are, on the one hand, too rarefied to support high-altitude balloons, and, on the other, too dense for orbiting satellites to remain any length of time without their orbits decaying. The mesosphere's radiation is almost too feeble to be studied from the earth, as it is drowned out by other radiation originating lower down in the atmosphere. Most of our knowledge of the mesosphere is coming from the sounding rockets, which can flash swiftly through it, and from the significant spectroscopic studies of the airglow.

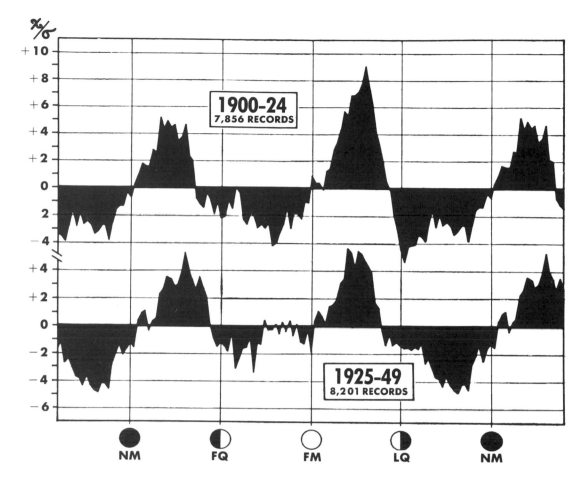

The chemosphere falls within the mesosphere, and here many chemical reactions take place, stirred in the very thin soup of this region. These chemical processes involve atomic (O) and molecular (O_2) oxygen, ozone, hydroxyl radicals (OH), and sodium compounds; during the day they mop up masses of penetrating solar energy such as ultraviolet rays. Then these chemical reactions are reversed, particularly at night, and various forms of radiation are emitted. One manifestation is the so-called airglow.

The ultraviolet light or x-ray radiation from the sun breaks down the ozone (O_3) into its atomic-oxygen and molecular-oxygen components; these recombine at night, and the excited electrons involved emit the airglow, forming ozone again by recombination. The ozone may also combine with molecular hydrogen (H_2) to form molecular oxygen and hydroxyl, which emits an infrared glow at night when the process occurs; a good proportion of the night airglow in the infrared region of the spectrum may derive from the hydroxyl reaction. A photochemical cycle of nitrogen oxides is believed to give the visible emissions in the green region of the spectrum.

At a height of about 80 km (50 mi), near the top of the mesosphere and in the lower levels of the ionosphere, the strange and beautiful streamers or waves of the noctilucent clouds appear. Prevalent during the summer in the northern latitudes, they have been investigated in joint Swedish-American experiments using sounding rockets to trap samples in the region of the clouds. Such samples were obtained from rockets sent up from Kronogard, in northern Sweden near the Arctic Circle.

Changes in maximum precipitation in the United States with phases of the moon, divided into 2 separate 25-year series for comparison. The changes are treated in terms of variations (+ or −) from standard measure of 10-unit moving totals of synodic decimals for 16,057 record dates of maximum precipitation in the calendar month of 1,544 U.S. weather stations, for the years 1900 to 1949.

The noctilucent clouds drift mostly toward the west, and sometimes toward the southwest. Their form continually changes, as if the motions of the atmosphere at this level were very irregular. They travel with a mean velocity of about 48 km (30 mi) an hour, with occasional velocities of up to 96 km (60 mi) an hour.

The origin of noctilucent clouds is believed to be related to the influx of cosmic dust upon the earth. These small particles—less than 1 millionth meter (about 4 hundred-thousandths inch) in size—serve as centers on which supercooled water vapor forms ice at the temperature minimum of the mesopause. The ice-laden particles grow in size and form the noctilucent clouds. They are visible long before sunrise and long after sunset, since the 80-km (50-mi) level is still illuminated by the sun although the surface underneath is buried in darkness.

Samples from noctilucent clouds show a large increase in the number of particles within a cloud. One rocket penetrating a noctilucent cloud collected about 10 million particles per square inch—many times more than a rocket that did not penetrate such a cloud. This result is comparable to known variations in the number of dust particles falling onto the earth. It appears that noctilucent clouds form when large numbers of dust particles enter the earth's atmosphere.

Upper Atmospheric Regions

Above the mesosphere lies the thermosphere, a region of the atmosphere ranging from about 80 km (50 mi) up to between 400 and 480 km (250 and 300 mi) in elevation, where the exosphere sets in. The thermosphere is appropriately named, since it is a mighty hot place, in which the temperature rises with increasing elevation until it levels off at an average of about 1,230°C (2,250°F). Over the solar cycle the temperature of the upper thermosphere may vary between a minimum of about 370°C (700°F) and a steady maximum of 1,230°C (2,250°F), with occasional brief excursions to about 1,370°C (2,500°F). This high-level heating of the atmosphere has not yet been satisfactorily explained. It may have something to do with extreme ultraviolet solar radiation.

Atomic oxygen is the principal constituent of the thermosphere, with small and diminishing proportions of the heavier atomic nitrogen and nitric-oxide ions, and increasing proportions of helium. Gas diffusion, dissociation, ionization, and recombination are the principal processes taking place. The thermosphere is close to the critical level where atmosphere may be lost to space. The mean free path of travel without a collision of neutral (unionized) particles of gas is long enough so that some of the gases may begin to escape entirely into interplanetary space; they may be replaced by gases flooding in from space, principally hydrogen.

A region of helium appears in the thermosphere and exosphere at an elevation of about 320 km (200 mi), running up to about 960 km (600 mi). This then gives way to a region of tenuous hydrogen, the lightest gas and the simplest element. It is believed that this atomic hydrogen is generated by the dissociation of water vapor and methane at heights down to 80 km (50 mi) in the mesosphere and diffuses upward from there, though the upper levels may be supplied in part from space. The hydrogen gas runs far out, getting thinner and thinner, for at least 80,000 km (50,000 mi) and perhaps more, then tapers off, merging with the interplanetary gas. The helium region is sometimes

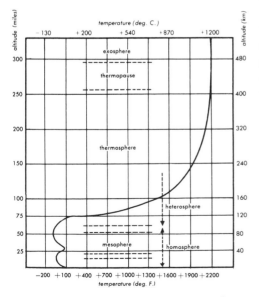

Temperature variations in the atmosphere up through to the exosphere.

referred to as the heliosphere or protosphere, and the hydrogen region as the protonosphere or metasphere; this whole tenuous mist of gas around the earth is appropriately called the geocorona.

Ionosphere

The ionosphere is a deep region of the atmosphere distinguished by the fact that the particles in it are largely ionized, or charged. It overlaps many of the thermal regions so far described, and may, in fact, be conceived as encompassing the ionization features of the whole atmosphere, rather than existing as a distinct region. It contains ions (positively charged atoms that have lost outer electrons) and free electrons of negative charge. This ionization is produced by the powerful solar and galactic or cosmic ionizing radiation entering the atmosphere from space and penetrating to great depths in it.

The ionosphere begins with what are termed the C and D regions, which are transient; with the C below and the D above, it ranges between about 48 and 80 km (30 and 50 mi) up in the mesosphere. Then come the E and F regions, and the helium- and hydrogen-ion regions above. The concentration of ions increases with altitude, although the particle density decreases.

Many features of the ionosphere have been studied with earth satellites. Much information on the ionization regions and the density of the atmosphere at various levels has also been obtained by the use of radio sounders, such as the huge 22-acre antenna system of the United States Bureau of Standards, jointly run by the United States and Peru on a site at Jicamarca, near Lima, Peru. At this location near the equator the horizontal character of the earth's magnetic field overhead keeps the electrified components of the atmosphere also horizontal, so that they reflect a great enough proportion of the radio pulses from the antenna to reveal the density of ionized fields from a low level right on up into the magnetosphere.

Geomagnetic Cavity

The discovery of the Van Allen belt region, related to the earth's magnetic field, was probably the most significant discovery yet made about the earth's immediate environment by means of artificial satellites. It was predicted by American physicist S. Fred Singer in 1956, and was discovered in 1958 by James A. Van Allen of the State University of Iowa by means of an analysis of the Geiger-counter data transmitted from the instruments of the Explorer 1 satellite correlated with data from sounding rockets. Since then, many other satellites have furnished mountains of information about these belts and the magnetosphere that encloses them.

As shown in cross section in the diagram, the earth's magnetic field consists of a huge doughnut-shaped ring of magnetic lines of force fanning out from the magnetic poles, its effective strength running out at least some 10 to 14 earth radii (64,000 to 96,000 km or 40,000 to 60,000 mi) from the earth into space. The magnetosphere is the name of this region where the atmospheric plasma is strongly affected by the earth's magnetic field; it encompasses both the ionosphere and the exosphere. The shape of the magnetosphere is similar to that of a comet. On the sunward side of the earth, the magnetopause, the boundary between the solar wind and the earth's magnetic field, is circular and is located relatively close (10 to 15 earth radii) to the earth's

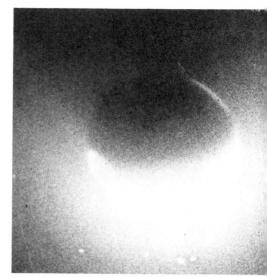

First ultraviolet photograph of earth made from lunar surface by Apollo 16 astronauts shows hydrogen ball or corona around the earth out to about 80,000 km (50,000 mi).

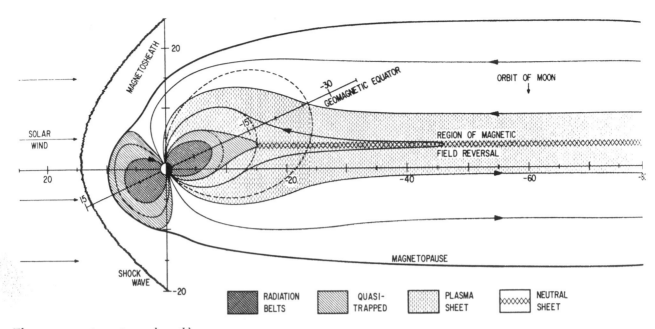

RADIATION BELTS   QUASI-TRAPPED   PLASMA SHEET   NEUTRAL SHEET

The geomagnetic cavity and earth's magnetosphere are contained within the magnetopause in this summary cross section of the earth's immediate environment in space inferred from reports from many spacecraft. The scale is in earth radii. The earth may lose some of its hydrogen and helium from its upper atmosphere through its geomagnetic tail, which extends far out beyond the moon, millions of miles into space.

surface. As the magnetopause encircles the earth it is stretched out like the tail of a comet, pointing directly away from the sun. At its outer limits this geomagnetic cavity is battered into weird shapes by the solar wind. The shape of the magnetosphere is continually changing even though its gross properties do not. The solar wind plays a role in the instantaneous shape of the magnetosphere. As the solar wind changes, so does the magnetosphere.

The Van Allen region consists of somewhat artificially distinguished belts of positively charged protons and negatively charged electrons in the inner portion of the magnetosphere. These protons and electrons have been trapped by the earth's magnetic lines of force and spiral back and forth between mirror points around the magnetic poles, with energies ranging from what is called "soft" radiation to very "hard" or intense radiation. The Van Allen belts extend from a height of about 1,120 km (700 mi) above the earth at the magnetic equator out to perhaps 32,000 km (20,000 mi). At their horns, where they curve in closer to the earth's surface at its magnetic poles, they may approach within heights of 320 to 480 km (200 to 300 mi), and other areas have been found where they may dip down as close if not closer to the surface.

These belts constitute plasmas, involved in the transfer of energy from the sun down through the ionosphere to the earth, particularly when the great solar flares cause such effects on earth as magnetic storms, auroras, and blacking-out of radio communications. The relation of the belts to the ionosphere is not completely understood. It seems possible that the protons and electrons trapped in the belts may sometimes be shaken out at the tips near the poles and cause the auroras, which occur most frequently in what are called the auroral zones around the earth's North and South Poles. Not only do the energetic solar particles produce the auroras, but they also alter the radiation-to-heat conversion in the mesosphere, stratosphere, and upper troposphere. As the effects of these particles trickle down through the atmosphere, there is the possibility that they even affect the earth's weather.

68

Not so long ago the space beyond the earth and its atmosphere was thought to be black, cold, inactive, and empty, an all-pervasive void characterized by three dimensions and little else. Space was conceived in the mathematical manner, as a kind of receptacle having length, breadth, and depth, but no contents; it was that which surrounded or existed between material things. Mathematical concepts are fine for measuring, relating, and explaining, but they do not exist in nature as such any more than do straight lines or points. This concept of space as a complete void mirrored human imagination and ignorance more than it expressed any knowledge.

In the twentieth century, and particularly in the past decade, scientists have contrived to turn space inside out. It has proved to be fairly bursting with activity—a jungle rampant with all kinds of gases, particles, dust, large and small bodies, and a multitude of fields and waves. Through it all only the first exploratory trails have been hacked.

Space Regions

When confronted with a blooming, blinking chaos, about which little is known, usually the first steps are to sort out similar things, make preliminary classes, and begin to describe and analyze. Something like this has happened as information about space has come flooding in and its complexity has been grasped.

A number of regions have been distinguished within space, so that each can be studied and characterized in its own right. Near space extends from the earth's atmosphere out around its immediate vicinity, and more is known about it than any other sector of space. Instrumented rockets, earth satellites, and space vehicles have probed it and checked it out. The point at which near space is assumed to begin above the earth depends on the feature being investigated. Even 32 km (20 mi) above the surface, 99 percent of the gases in the material atmosphere lie below. At 160 km (100 mi) up in orbit, though still within the ionosphere, an astronaut sees the stars brilliantly steady against a dark, velvety background. If he opened a port in his capsule, he would experience most of the untoward effects of space. At about 24,000 to 32,000 km (15,000 to 20,000 mi) up—another cutoff point for near space—the hydrogen and helium gases peter out to about the consistency of interplanetary gas, perhaps 10,000 particles per cubic centimeter (roughly 60,000 particles per cubic inch). Near space may also be conceived as ending at the boundary of the geomagnetic cavity where the solar wind meets the earth's magnetic field, and a region of turbulence has been discovered 80,000 to 96,000 km (50,000 to 60,000 mi) out from the earth. Within this huge sphere many fascinating materials and effects have already been investigated.

In relation to the moon, the earth's gravitational field is dominant out to about 352,000 km (220,000 mi), or to within 32,000 km (20,000 mi) of the lunar surface, and this may also be thought of as the limit of near space. At this "null point," the gravitational fields of the earth and the moon are balanced in strength, though both fields actually extend beyond this to infinity, growing weaker and weaker as the inverse square of the distance. A body at exactly this point, which varies with the motions of earth and moon, would not fall toward either body until moved in one direction or the other by the shifting forces. A sphere around the whole earth-moon system, the center of gravity of

Chapter VII
Interplanetary Space

"The wreck of matter and the crush of worlds."

Addison

which (the barycenter) is under the surface of the earth itself, is called cislunar space. The gravitational forces of the sun and the earth-moon system are balanced at about 6.4 million km (4 million mi) from the earth, and this sphere of 6.4-million-km (4-million-mi) radius around the earth is often called "terrestrial space."

Numerous spacecraft have been given a velocity of more than 11.2 km a second (7.1 mi a second) in addition to the earth's own velocity of 29.6 km a second (18.5 mi a second). This velocity, known as the earth's escape velocity, is sufficient to drive them out of the earth's effective gravitational field into that of the sun, which becomes more powerful at the 6.4-million-km (4-million-mi) limit of terrestrial space. As these spacecraft move toward their mission objectives, they speed along under the sun's gravitational influence in interplanetary space, becoming satellites in solar orbit. If they pass fairly close to the target planet, the orbit will be changed or perturbed by that planet's gravitational field.

The first such artificial planet was the Russian Luna 1, launched toward the moon on January 2, 1959; the next were the American Pioneer 4 space probe and its fourth stage, launched as a lunar probe on March 3, 1959. These tiny, silent bodies in solar orbit, sometimes called planetoids, became man's first additions to the architecture of the solar system. Recent additions are the Pioneer and Voyager missions to Jupiter.

On March 2, 1972, Pioneer 10 was successfully launched from Cape Kennedy toward colossal Jupiter. This spacecraft was truly a pioneer,

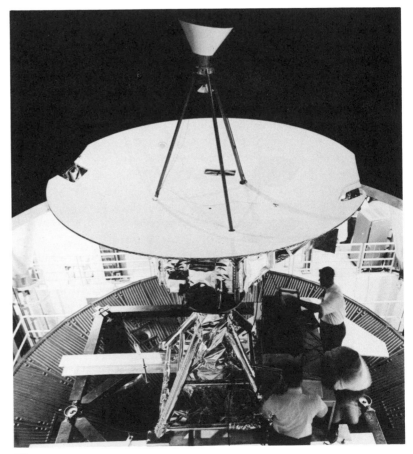

The dish antenna of the Pioneer 11 (also known as the Pioneer Saturn) spacecraft dominates this view as the spacecraft is being prepared for tests. This antenna beamed the 8-watt radio signal to earth as the Pioneer 11 made its historic visit to Saturn.

since it achieved many space "firsts." It was the first to travel beyond Mars, at which point Mariner 9 had stopped in orbit to reveal many Martian wonders. Pioneer 10 was also the first to traverse successfully the zone in which the minor planets, or asteroids, are thickest. On December 4, 1973, Pioneer 10 came to within 130,000 km (81,000 mi) of Jupiter. The strong gravitational pull of Jupiter (it is approximately 2.6 times that of the earth) increased the speed of Pioneer to an incredible 132,000 km (82,000 mi) an hour. This is so fast that Pioneer 10 was tossed right out of the solar system into interstellar space. Moving at a speed of approximately 2 astronomical units each year, Pioneer 10 was 20 a.u. from the sun by 1980. This is farther from the sun than the planet Uranus. In about 100,000 years Pioneer 10 will be about 3 light-years distant, or three fourths of the distance to the nearest star to our sun.

Pioneer 10 carries an aluminum plaque etched with a message for any intelligent beings who might intercept it. The message depicts our solar system, the path of the space probe, male and female human beings, and the location of our solar system in relation to 14 pulsars and the center of the Milky Way Galaxy, so that any intelligent and scientific being could find us.

Like Pioneer 10, Pioneer 11 was launched toward Jupiter on April 6, 1973. This probe, however, followed a different path to Jupiter, and the probe's orbit was perturbed differently by Jupiter. The orbit of Pioneer 11 was planned so that the spacecraft approached Jupiter on a polar route. This enabled scientists to investigate a part of the Jovian atmosphere that cannot be seen from earth. Pioneer 11 came to within 42,760 km (26,575 mi) of the tops of the Jovian clouds. Accordingly, it traveled faster and its orbit was perturbed more than that of Pioneer

PIONEER 10 AND PIONEER SATURN OUTBOUND TRAJECTORIES

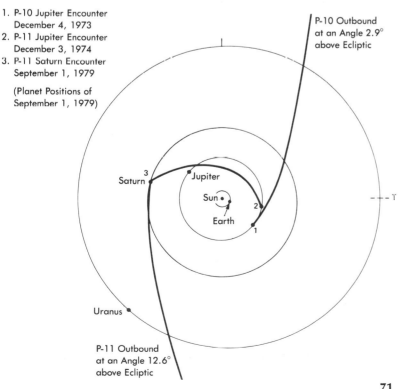

1. P-10 Jupiter Encounter
December 4, 1973
2. P-11 Jupiter Encounter
December 3, 1974
3. P-11 Saturn Encounter
September 1, 1979

(Planet Positions of
September 1, 1979)

P-10 Outbound
at an Angle 2.9°
above Ecliptic

Saturn 3   Jupiter
Sun
Earth
2
1

Uranus

P-11 Outbound
at an Angle 12.6°
above Ecliptic

The orbits of Pioneer 10 and Pioneer 11 after their encounter with Jupiter. Pioneer 10 was launched on March 2, 1972; Pioneer 11 on April 5, 1973. Jupiter's strong gravitational pull was employed to redirect Pioneer 11 to the opposite side of the solar system and its encounter with Saturn. These spacecraft are the first 2 man-made vehicles to leave the solar system.

10. Pioneer 11's orbit was changed so that it would pass by Saturn in September 1979. The orbits of both Pioneer 10 and 11 through interplanetary space are shown in the figure.

Interplanetary space is the space between the major bodies in the solar system, the planets and the sun. The radiations from the sun and their reflections from the planets must cross this space in reaching the earth. This region is far from empty. Protons and other charged particles stream from the sun in the solar wind. Dust also exists in this apparent void. Interplanetary space is very cluttered, and the dust and gas found therein must be considered in the design of any space vehicle, whether manned or unmanned.

The outer reaches of interplanetary space have often been thought to be at the farthest known planet, Pluto, some 39 a.u. (5.9 billion km or 3.6 billion mi) from the sun. Actually, the sun's gravitational influence extends much farther, out to perhaps 150,000 to 200,000 a.u. from the sun, where myriads of refrigerated comets may roam, and where, on occasion, the gravitational influence of nearby stars may become greater than that of the sun. Sometimes these stars may so perturb the courses of comets that they plunge in a highly elliptical orbit toward the sun, becoming visible from the earth as they dart in to round the sun.

Beyond interplanetary or solar space lies interstellar space, which stretches out between our star, the sun, and the other stars. The 9 nearest known stars are 4 to 10 light-years (40 to 100 trillion km or 25 to 60 trillion mi) away. The more distant stars of our galaxy are up to 100,000 light-years away. Yet this is all part of galactic space within the Milky Way. Out beyond the galaxy lies intergalactic space; it, too, may contain much more than the vast emptiness previously assigned to it.

Electromagnetic Spectrum

The most evident signals from beyond the earth arrive in the form of light and heat, so naturally light and heat waves, or radiations, were studied in the first investigations of what lies in space. As physics and astronomy amassed more and more information about events on earth, in the solar system, and beyond, it became apparent (about 1870) that light and heat were only tiny segments of a broad range of radiating waves of various kinds. With the gradual analysis and integration of this array of waves, called the electromagnetic spectrum, came many of the historic discoveries of science. As it took shape, gaps in the spectrum were filled in gradually and the spectrum was greatly extended at both ends.

The electromagnetic spectrum encompasses all waves emanating from molecular and atomic processes. Scientists speak of different types of waves, but each wave represents a specific amount of electromagnetic energy. Different energies have different names. The shortest-wavelength photons (a photon can be thought of as an energy packet) have the greatest energy and are called gamma rays. Radio waves are the longest and have the least energy. The sequence gamma rays, x-rays, ultraviolet, visible, infrared, and radio waves is arranged in order of decreasing energy and increasing wavelength.

Since the range in wavelength of the entire electromagnetic spectrum is so immense and since knowledge of it has been gained in fits

72

Interplanetary Space

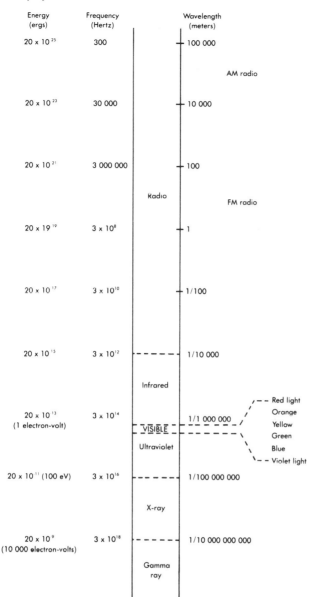

Energy (ergs)	Frequency (Hertz)		Wavelength (meters)	
20×10^{25}	300		100 000	
				AM radio
20×10^{23}	30 000		10 000	
20×10^{21}	3 000 000		100	
		Radio		FM radio
20×19^{19}	3×10^{8}		1	
20×10^{17}	3×10^{10}		1/100	
20×10^{15}	3×10^{12}		1/10 000	
		Infrared		Red light
				Orange
20×10^{13} (1 electron-volt)	3×10^{14}		1/1 000 000	Yellow
		VISIBLE		Green
		Ultraviolet		Blue
				Violet light
20×10^{11} (100 eV)	3×10^{16}		1/100 000 000	
		X-ray		
20×10^{9} (10 000 electron-volts)	3×10^{18}		1/10 000 000 000	
		Gamma ray		

The electromagnetic spectrum. The light that man sees with his eyes is a small fraction of the entire spectrum. The boundaries dividing the various sections are somewhat arbitrary.

and starts, scientists have come to use different units in measuring various parts of it, or even different units for the same parts, which is sometimes confusing. Ultraviolet and visible light is most often measured in angstrom or micrometer units, while centimeters or meters may be used for the longer radio waves. An angstrom is one hundred-millionth cm, and a micrometer is one ten-thousandth cm. For the larger units, conversion charts that aid in translating metric units into the customary United States system are easily found. Length, area, volume, capacity, weight, temperature, pressure, density, power, heat, and other measurements can be easily converted with these charts from metric units used by scientists into the more familiar units of everyday life. Thus 1 meter is 39.37 inches, 1 km is about 0.6 mi, 1 ft is slightly over 0.3 meter, 1 yard is about 0.9 meter, and 1 mi is a little more than 1.6 km. Scientists use the metric system exclusively throughout the world.

Radio astronomers often use the frequency of radiation instead of the wavelength. Hence the 21-cm line of neutral hydrogen is also known as the 1,420 MHz (megahertz) line.

All electromagnetic waves can also be described in energy units known as ergs. One erg of energy is produced when a mosquito with a 5-milligram (about 2-ten-thousandths-ounce) mass flies into a wall with a speed of 20 cm a second (about 0.5 mi an hour). For comparison the energy emitted by the sun is 4 billion trillion trillion ergs a second (4 followed by 33 zeroes).

Although the gamma rays and x-rays can be expressed in ergs, they are often measured in thousands of electron-volts. An electron-volt, which is the energy an electron acquires as it falls through a potential difference of one volt, is even smaller than an erg, since about 600 billion electron-volts are equivalent to 1 erg.

Fortunately for mankind, the earth's atmosphere absorbs or reflects a great many of the waves and particles rolling in toward it from space. Less than 1 percent of the ultraviolet light falling on the top of the atmosphere filters through to the earth's surface. And yet it is this minute amount of ultraviolet radiation that has caused many painful sunburns.

Certain wavelengths are able to pass through the earth's atmosphere relatively unimpeded. These wavelength regions are known as "windows." Such a window occurs for wavelengths from about 4,000 to 7,000 angstroms, known as visible light. Traditional or optical astronomy has been limited to this region of the electromagnetic spectrum. Other windows occur in the infrared. Thus visible light and heat (infrared radiation) were the earliest known radiations and gave astronomers their first view of the universe.

In the past few decades the entire electromagnetic spectrum has been utilized by astronomers. Radio astronomy made tremendous advances in the decades of the fifties and the sixties. If our eyes were sensitive to radio waves rather than visible light, the night sky would look very different. With eyes sensitive to radio waves we would not see the familiar stars and the patterns they form. Our friendly stars would be replaced chiefly by bright features corresponding to galaxies that we normally do not see without telescopic aid.

The decade of the seventies has seen strides in ultraviolet, x-ray, and gamma-ray astronomy technology. To observe in these parts of the spectrum it is necessary to use satellites, since the earth's atmosphere absorbs these radiations. Familiar objects like the sun look very different when viewed in these different spectral regions, as illustrated in the photograph.

X-ray and ultraviolet observations from the Orbiting Solar Observatory series of satellites have improved our knowledge of the sun. Other satellites, including the Orbiting Astronomical Observatory and the High Energy Astronomical Observatory, are concentrating on observing objects outside our solar system. The far infrared is used in observations made aboard the Kuiper Flying Observatory and an especially modified U-2 airplane.

As each new region is opened, new phenomena are observed. These include the observations of cool, nearly dark celestial objects of which there had been preliminary hints, and the mysterious quasistellar radio sources (quasars) that may mark the far boundaries of the known universe.

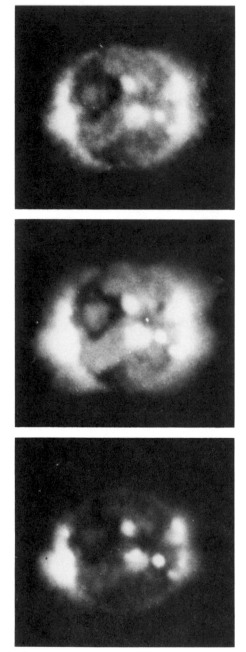

Three ultraviolet images of the sun as recorded by the Goddard Extreme Ultraviolet Spectroheliograph flown on the Orbiting Solar Observatory 7 spacecraft. Each view is taken in the light of a different iron ion. The top photograph shows the regions of the corona where Fe XIV is concentrated, the center Fe XV, and the bottom photograph Fe XVI. Since the higher ionization stages represent higher temperature, the photographs also represent an increase in coronal temperature from 1.8 million °K in the top photograph to 2.5 million °K in the bottom photograph. The bright regions tend to occur over active regions lower in the sun's atmosphere.

Gases in Space

The tenuous outermost sphere of the earth's atmosphere, largely composed of hydrogen gas, begins to shade off into the consistency of interplanetary space at a distance of about 32,000 km (20,000 mi) from the earth's surface. While there are undoubtedly a great variety of the atoms of other elements in interplanetary and interstellar space, spectroscopic studies have shown that the basic constituent is hydrogen. Other atoms and molecules identified in space are calcium, sodium, potassium, iodine, titanium, and cyanogen (CN) and hydrocarbon (CH) ions.

The hydrogen atoms are probably very thinly scattered through interplanetary space, forming what is called a low-density plasma. It is estimated that there are probably only 1,000 to 2,000 particles (largely hydrogen) per cubic centimeter in space at 2,960 km (1,850 mi) elevation, from 10 to 1,000 hydrogen protons and electrons (separated by ionization) per cubic cm in interplanetary space, and perhaps fewer than 1 per cubic cm in interstellar space beyond. How empty is this? By comparison, a few years ago the most highly exhausted vacuums that had been produced here on earth still contained about 1 million particles per cubic cm.

Prior to 1968 astronomers believed that only atoms or very simple molecules could survive the rigors of interstellar space. Cosmic rays and ultraviolet radiation were expected to break apart any polyatomic molecules. In 1968 ammonia (NH_3) and water (H_2O) were discovered. Since then numerous, and in some cases complex, molecules have been detected. The molecules may build up or be accumulated on grains of interstellar dust. Approximately 50 molecules are now known to exist in interstellar space. A few molecules have also been discovered in other galaxies.

Particularly interesting is the number of organic molecules found in the harsh interstellar environment. The three molecules formaldehyde (H_2CO), hydrogen cyanide (HCN), and cyanoacetylene (HC_3N) are especially important in the formation of amino acids, which are necessary for the creation of life. It would appear that interstellar space houses the building blocks for life. Given the proper conditions, it is possible that life has formed elsewhere in the universe.

Magnetic Fields

The relationship between the relatively stable magnetic field (magnetosphere) around the earth, extending out to perhaps 64,000 km (40,000 mi) at the earth's equator, and the activities going on in interplanetary space beyond are shown in the diagram of the geomagnetic cavity and tail in Chapter 6.

Jupiter has an even more impressive magnetosphere, which expands and contracts with changing conditions in the solar wind. The magnetopause, a boundary where the pressure of the magnetic field of Jupiter and the solar wind are equal, was measured by Pioneer 10 and Pioneer 11 to be as close as 50 Jupiter radii and as far as 100 Jupiter radii from the planet. This is not a discrepancy in the results but reflects the ever-changing conditions in interplanetary space. Like the earth, Jupiter has a dipole magnetic field with a strength ranging from 3 to 14 gauss.

Astronomers have proposed that a heliosphere, similar to earth's

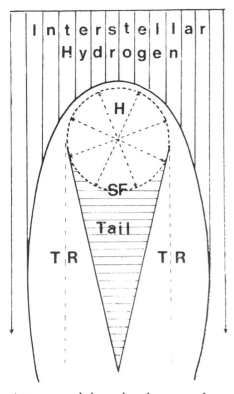

Astronomers believe that the corona forms a heliosphere (H) around the sun, with a shock front (SF), a turbulent region (TR), and a tail as the sun races through the free hydrogen in space.

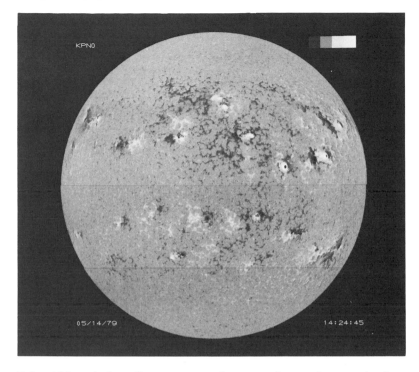

A magnetogram of the sun provides an instant picture of the magnetic field of the sun. The white and black areas represent regions of magnetic activity; white represents areas of positive polarity, black represents negative polarity.

light. Although these flares are most frequent during the periods of intense sunspot activity, which follow a mean 11-year cycle ranging from 7 to 17 years, they can occur at any time.

Solar flares, or bursts of solar cosmic-radiation particles, are known to be mostly protons, with energies ranging widely, from less than 10 Mev (million electron volts) up to almost 50 Bev (billion electron volts). Low-energy solar-flare events, with particles up to 400 Mev, and medium-energy events, with particles up to several Bev, occurred from 5 to 13 times a year over the period from 1935 to 1959. High-energy events were relatively rare; their bursts of solar cosmic radiation up to 20 to 50 Bev occurred only once or twice every 4 or 5 years. The flares appear to originate in active, disturbed, and turbulent regions of the sun.

The sun's own complex system of magnetic fields must play a role in these solar flares, which have such spectacular effects on the earth. Special instruments called magnetoscopes have been developed for observing the magnetic sun. These are basically spectroscopes that have been fed the sun's light by large telescopes, such as the special tower telescope at Mount Wilson Observatory in California and the 152-cm (60-inch) telescope at the Kitt Peak National Observatory, Arizona. Spectral lines are split by magnetic fields. In a typical solar magnetogram, like that in the photograph, astronomers get an instant picture of the magnetic activity on the sun. Different colors represent different polarity, while the shades from black to white indicate the intensity of the magnetic field.

It is known that extremely strong (up to 1,000 gauss) magnetic fields exist in the vicinity of the active areas of the sun where the solar flares occur, and may have something to do with the origin of the solar flares. According to one theory, magnetic fields of great strength collapse and produce a turbulence on the solar surface that results in the flare. Another theory states that changes in the magnetic fields on the sun cancel each other out and cause the release of enough heat to start a thermonuclear reaction at the surface, involving the fusion of hydrogen atoms and helium atoms and resulting in tremendous explosions that eject the materials composing the flare and create the radiations that accompany it. Theories of this kind cannot be confirmed with the scanty evidence at hand. However, solar flares appear to form in bright patches or plages in the sun's outer envelope (the chromosphere) above the photosphere, in which the sunspots originate.

With a solar flare, which may last from several minutes to a few hours, a mass of charged particles is flung out from the sun's surface and spurts into interplanetary space. The photograph shows the intense flare that appeared on the sun on April 28, 1978. Flare material, consisting of a variety of particles and radiations, is believed to drag a strong magnetic field with it, drawing out the magnetic lines of force like loops of taffy and creating a magnetic field enveloping the earth but still rooted in the site of the flare on the sun's surface. With these flares a magnetic storm occurs on the earth, but the cosmic-ray intensities from interstellar space decrease; they must be deflected by the magnetic field accompanying the flare. The earth also experiences auroras and radio blackouts. The cosmic-ray intensity, chiefly of the lower-intensity rays, decreases by about 5 percent.

Many statistical studies of the correlation between solar flares and various features of the sun are done for purposes of their reliable prediction. Typical flare indicators tentatively tried in such predictions are large and complex sunspot groups, complex magnetic fields in such groups with many poles of opposite sign, very bright plages, frequent radio bursts from the sun, hot spots in the corona, the presence of many small flares in active regions, and certain types of prominences.

Reports from a solar observatory orbiting the earth have shown that the sun has polar caps cooler and less active than its other regions. The sun was blotted out by a disk just as the moon covers the earth during a solar eclipse. In this way the sun's hot atmosphere, or solar corona, can be studied. This corona appears as a beautiful halo around the sun during total solar eclipses. The corona's temperature over the caps is about 1.8 million degrees, as opposed to the average coronal temperature of 3.6 million degrees. Temperatures above active regions of the sun may rise to 8 million degrees and to 70 million degrees above flares. During the active periods at the solar-cycle maxima, the sun's corona runs even higher temperatures.

Cosmic Rays

With its solar flares the sun produces some of the low-energy cosmic rays that bombard the earth, but it is believed that the sun's contribution is only a small part of the whole. Cosmic rays consist of very high-energy protons (hydrogen nuclei), alpha particles (helium nuclei), and the nuclei of heavier elements (up to zirconium at least, with an atomic weight of 92 and possibly to heavier elements), with some high-energy electrons. The energy of the particles ranges from 1 Mev up to 100 billion billion electron volts. Solar flares, producing particles with energies ranging up to 20 to 30 Bev, do not begin to approach the energies of some cosmic rays that arrive from other sources.

The particles in the cosmic radiation from the sun seem to consist al-

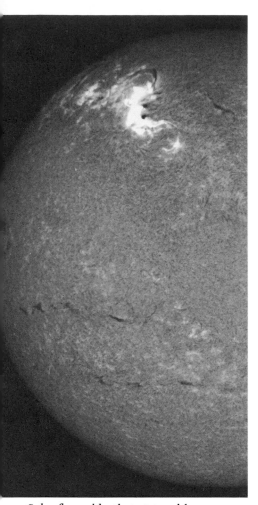

Solar flares, like that pictured here, contribute material to the interplanetary medium. Not only are copious amounts of electromagnetic energy released in these violent events, but also large amounts of protons, electrons, and other cosmic rays. The flare pictured here occurred on April 28, 1978. This flare had an intensity of 4 on a scale of 1 to 4, making it a flare of major importance.

most entirely of protons, with only a very minute proportion of alpha particles. Typical cosmic rays, however, contain about 13 percent alpha particles, so the sun does not appear to be their primary source. Cosmic radiation from the sun decreases during periods of the quiet sun, while the cosmic-ray bombardment from interstellar space rises, perhaps because the interplanetary solar magnetic field is then weaker, and more of the cosmic rays can penetrate to earth's vicinity.

Except for the cosmic rays produced in the sun, the origin of these particles is not well determined. In an effort to explain the high energies observed in cosmic rays, Enrico Fermi suggested that clouds of magnetized plasma present in interstellar space repeatedly scatter the cosmic rays. A more likely scenario is that they originate in regions of violent events, such as supernova explosions.

A supernova is the catastrophic demise of a massive star. In this cosmic explosion a large amount of energy is released in a relatively short period of time. In addition to blowing away most of the material originally contained in the star, it is believed that cosmic rays are produced. The end product of such an explosion is a supernova remnant, such as the Crab Nebula shown in the photograph, and a neutron star.

A neutron star is a very small object with a diameter of about 10 km (6 mi). Since about twice the amount of material found in our sun is crammed into the neutron star, the density of the material is enormously high, on the order of a million billion grams packed into each cubic centimeter. Neutron stars rotate very rapidly. If the rotation axis of a neutron star is properly aligned, observers on earth see it as a pulsar, the radiation being emitted in a series of pulses. In visible light the pulsar would blink on and off much like a neon sign. Calculations show that pulsars can generate very powerful cosmic rays.

Other likely sources of cosmic rays are centers of galaxies and quasistellar objects. The density of material in these regions is unusually high. Furthermore, radio and infrared observations indicate that violent activity does occur there. Whether the radiation is the result of explosions between clouds of gas and dust is not known, but some believe that such explosions can be a source of the energy emitted by these objects and of cosmic rays.

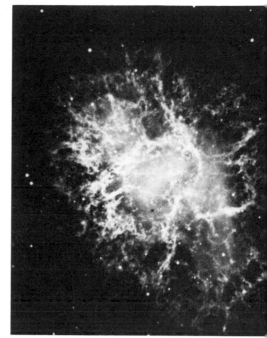

The Crab Nebula in Taurus resulted from a great supernova explosion observed in A.D. 1054.

Zodiacal Light

Tons upon tons of dust in fine, microscopic particles like those that glint in sunlight sift down gradually to the surface of the earth through its atmosphere. A small proportion of this comes from the earth itself, swept into the upper atmosphere by winds and rising convection currents, having been blown up into the air by volcanic eruptions. But most of this dust comes from outside the earth's atmosphere. Earth-satellite data have shown that the dust immediately around the earth, evidently trapped within the earth's gravitational and magnetic fields, has a considerable nickel-iron content similar to that of meteorites, from which it may have been ground in innumerable collisions.

Before the space around the earth and the moon had been thoroughly explored by earth- and moon-orbiting satellites, it was feared that there might be a giant dust ball around the earth, cluttered with large particles and chunks, which would be very dangerous for spacecraft rapidly plunging through them. The unknown is always feared. And reports from the first probes into near space tended to strengthen

79

The zodiacal light appears as a faint cone of light extending into the sky along the plane of the ecliptic after sunset and before sunrise, as shown in the inset.

this fear, with estimates of a dust-particle flux in near space 100 times greater than that in interplanetary space.

More orbiting and probing spacecraft soon settled this fear, however, with more comprehensive samples. Spacecraft have not been damaged in near space, nor have spaceships bearing astronauts been holed by flying natural missiles, although accidents have happened from internal breakdowns.

The dust and small particles are there, however. The existence of the interplanetary dust had been suspected for almost 300 years, ever since Jean-Dominique Cassini, director of the Paris Observatory, had studied the phenomenon known as zodiacal light in 1683 and attributed it to fine particles of dust in space.

The zodiacal light is a dim cone or pyramid of light, usually barely visible over the normal nightglow in the sky. It appears in the west about an hour after the sun sets and can be seen in the east an hour before the sun rises, probably often contributing to the lightening effect in the sky known as false dawn. Seen under favorable conditions, the zodiacal light is about as bright as the band of the Milky Way. The cone's base is on the horizon, and its apex is almost along the path of the ecliptic, normally fading out toward the observer's zenith, though some visual photographic and photoelectric observations have traced it right across the sky along the band of the zodiac, from which it derives its name.

On the side of the earth opposite the position of the sun occurs an even dimmer phenomenon, called the counterglow, or Gegenschein. This is a dim patch, 8° to 10° deep and 5° to 7° wide, occasionally visible in the night sky. After its discovery two theories were developed to explain its existence: a phase-angle effect on sunlight that has been reflected from interplanetary dust particles, or a kind of tail of the earth, pushed out away from the sun by its radiation, consisting of such atmospheric atoms as hydrogen or other particles, and reflecting light from the sun. Experiments aboard the Pioneer 10 spacecraft have confirmed the interplanetary hypothesis by observing the Gegenschein far from the earth.

The zodiacal light does not show a parallax (differing angles of observation varying with the location of the observer on the earth), so there has been no direct evidence as to where it occurs. Over the centuries, and even in recent years, there has been much speculation as to the nature of this cone of light. Some have viewed it as an extension of the solar corona, the bright glare of light visible around the sun during total solar eclipses, resulting from the scattering of sunlight by electrons from the sun. Others have believed it was a phenomenon in the upper atmosphere of the earth, but the Pioneer 10 spacecraft has now shown this to be false. Still others have agreed with Cassini that it represented the sunlight scattered by a lens- or discus-shaped cloud of interplanetary dust more or less centered about the sun and extending out at least past the earth. The basic question concerns what scatters the sunlight. Results from the Pioneer 10 mission have shown that the asteroid belt contributes little to the zodiacal light, and there appears to be virtually no contribution from beyond 3 a.u.

Free electrons in the ionized solar atmosphere are believed to cause the great solar corona by the scattering of sunlight; this view is supported by the fact that the light of the corona is polarized. But the corona, even as seen and photographed from high in the stratosphere during solar eclipses, cannot be seen to extend out beyond 10° to 13° from the limb of the sun. This may represent in part the limitations of the photographic plates or the effect of light scattering in the earth's atmosphere. On the other hand, the zodiacal light seems to start at about 18° to 20° from the sun, and is not visible until the sun is that far below the horizon. It is difficult, therefore, to see how it can be solely an outward extension of the solar corona, the intensity of which diminishes rather sharply toward its outer edge. Furthermore, the symmetrical disk of the zodiacal light is not exactly in line with the plane of the ecliptic, but more in line with that of the plane of Jupiter's orbit, which has an inclination to the ecliptic of 1.3°. So the zodiacal light seems more likely to be reflections of some sort from interplanetary space, where the gravitational effects of Jupiter's sphere appear to affect it, than reflections in the atmosphere of the earth, though the latter may play some minor role in its creation.

The spectrum of zodiacal light more closely resembles the absorption spectrum of the sun, with its dark Fraunhofer lines, than the continuous spectrum of the solar corona. Electron scattering of the light probably makes only a minor contribution to it, and tiny dust particles in inner-planetary space are probably the major cause of it, reflecting and scattering it into the faint, cone-shaped blur in the sky.

Interplanetary Dust

Beyond its probable appearance and effects in zodiacal light, the interplanetary dust has been intensively investigated in recent years because of the effects it might have on satellites at a great distance from the earth and on unmanned or manned spacecraft. The larger particles might pit and hole the shells of space vehicles, while the smaller ones might etch or erode the skins; both could be very dangerous for human occupants, particularly on longer trips, and might quickly disable the instruments or the operations of manned or unmanned craft themselves.

The interplanetary dust, including that found in the generalized-disk area of the zodiacal light, probably originates primarily from comets as they come to the sun at perihelion. The cometary nuclei are heated by solar radiation, giving off the dust particles as well as larger particles and gases and producing the comae and tails, which are boiling, buffeted, and turbulent, and lose many particles. These are dispersed as interplanetary dust by means of such forces as light pressure, solar-radiation drag, the gravitational fields of planets, and collisions among themselves. Asteroids and meteoroids probably produce only a small proportion of the total interplanetary dust. The possibility must not be overlooked that some of the dust particles may be formed by accumulation from the atoms and molecules in space, as well as by the breaking down of larger bodies.

Planets and satellites gradually collect the dust, and much of it may be drawn in toward the sun itself. Current estimates as to how much dust the earth collects from space vary widely—from 1,000 to 10,000 or more tons a day, and 3 to 5 million tons a year. Once the dust has entered the ionosphere level of the earth's atmosphere, it may take a month or more to drift to the surface. Most of the interplanetary dust near the earth is very fine.

The tiny particles of interplanetary dust entering the earth's atmosphere may serve as the nuclei around which water vapor can condense, or condensation nuclei, as these are called. This dust may then explain how the noctilucent clouds form at such great heights (see Chapter 6). The effects of lunar gravitation on this dust in the upper atmosphere have also been suggested as the explanations of lunar-phase rainfall. Some scientists believe that most of it must be concentrated clouds of dust blasted into cislunar space when meteoroids crash into the moon. Laboratory studies have been made of rock and sand particles sprayed out in a jet reaction when high-velocity projectiles strike. When meteoroids strike the moon, some of the surface material may be sprayed up at greater than escape velocity, most of it going into orbit around the sun, but part of it, up to a ton or more of lunar dust a day, falling into the earth's gravitational field and being attracted toward it, or being collected again by the moon. Some of this dust shifting down to earth, then, may well be material from the surface of the moon.

A "Venus flytrap" rocket experiment (named for the flower that captures flies by closing its petals) has provided some indication of the nature of this dust. A rocket was sent up by the U. S. Air Force Cambridge Research Laboratories with sections that opened when it reached an altitude of 88 km (55 mi), stayed open as the rocket soared to a maximum height of 166 km (104 mi) and started to fall back, and closed again when the rocket reached 115 km (72 mi) altitude on the way down. While the sections were open—for a total of 4 minutes— cosmic-dust particles were collected on plates within coated with a thin metallic film that indicated the nature of the particles grazing them. Most of the particles were smaller than 1 micrometer (0.000039 inch) in diameter. The greatest proportion (72 percent) were irregular in shape, but some of them were almost round (16 percent), and others were "fluffy" or smashed particles (12 percent). Some of the particles were found to be clumped together.

While the concentration of these tiny dust particles is still far from accurately known, it has been found that they do not furnish too great an obstacle for space vehicles. The dust in interplanetary space should not be so dense, in terms of its average concentration, that it will greatly erode the surfaces of vehicles passing through it, if the surfaces are fairly hard and thick. Actually, the effect should be greater near the earth and in cislunar space than out in the farther reaches of space. This does not include the more sizable meteoroids, small and large, that may be found in space.

Space has provided designers of satellites and space vehicles with a variety of other knotty problems as well. Space contains no air to carry away by convection currents the heat generated by motors and other operating equipment in the vehicles. All of the heat must be radiated directly away from the hot surfaces, or from specifically designed antenna radiators, which may require a great deal of extra weight and take up much-needed space in the satellites. Polished aluminum exposed in space to solar radiation heats up to about 300°C (575°F), as hot as most baking ovens, since aluminum is a surprisingly poor radiator of heat. A thin layer of silicon monoxide has been found to improve its heat-radiating capacity. The heat balance of Mariner 2 was not judged correctly, and its batteries began to heat up alarmingly as it came closer to the sun in its approach to Venus; fortunately, the batteries still functioned.

The high vacuum of interplanetary space, containing only 10 to 1,000 particles per cubic cm, creates other design problems. The grease on bearings evaporates or sublimates into space very quickly. The coefficient of friction of these bearings increases because in space they lack two things present in a normal atmosphere: a thin coating of adsorbed gases and moisture from the atmosphere, and a layer of oxide, both of which serve to form a shield keeping the metal surfaces from immediate contact. But gases, moisture, and oxides evaporate into space, leaving clean, raw metal surfaces, between which cohesion and cold welding may take place when they contact each other. They may weld tightly together even at temperatures as low as 10° to 24°C (50° to 75°F). Even graphite does not serve well as a lubricant in space. Consequently, units with rapidly moving parts and bearings often have to be completely enclosed in pressurized containers. Bearings have been developed of a solid lubricant, molybdenum disulphide, sintered or merged directly with the bearing metal. These and similar new products may eventually provide a solution for lubrication problems in space.

The x-ray, gamma-ray, and cosmic radiation in space, and the intense radiation of the trapped protons and electrons in the Van Allen belts have crippled some radiation-sensitive devices, particularly electrical equipment, in space. Solar cells that generate electricity using sunlight have proved sensitive to the heavier Van Allen radiation. Many new designs are being developed to overcome this and give the cells a longer effective life. Transistors and other semiconducting devices have had to be placed in contained vacuums, since any gases around them are ionized by radiation.

Chapter VIII
Asteroids, Meteors, and Comets

*"Atoms or systems into ruin hurled,
And now a bubble burst, and now a world."*

Pope

When the solar system was first formed, some of the ingredients must have been left over, for bits and pieces are still scattered helter-skelter through it, nearly 5 billion years after its birth. The result is by no means as neat and orderly as a perfectionist would desire. Over and beyond swirling masses of interplanetary gas and dust, there are thousands of so-called minor planets, or asteroids, and countless meteoroids and comets, large and small.

Minor Planets

At any time, day or night, a great asteroid 15 to 30 km (10 to 20 mi) in diameter might suddenly darken the sky or black out the stars and crash into the earth unannounced, causing untold destruction over a wide area several hundred kilometers around its point of impact and leaving a great smoking crater, perhaps 80 km (50 mi) across, blasted deep into the crust of the earth. Such a catastrophe is only an extremely slim possibility, however; it is much more likely that small asteroids passing near the earth will be put to use as space stations. Certainly they would make good ones—protecting men dug in under their surfaces from injurious solar radiations, furnishing plenty of room for observatories and research laboratories, and providing cheap and almost inexhaustible sources of nickel iron for the industries of earth, the moon, and even of Mars, if and when it can be colonized.

The asteroids are rocky, subminiature bodies, in orbit around the sun like the nine major planets.

The first four asteroids discovered (see Table 4) were the largest: Ceres (1) (the number assigned to the asteroid), with a diameter of about 1,025 km (640 mi); Pallas (2), 608 km (380 mi); Vesta (4), 538 km (340 mi); and Juno (3), 247 km (150 mi). Besides these, probably a handful of asteroids are more than 50 km (30 mi) wide, and there are many no more than a few kilometers in diameter. They are such small bodies that Vesta, with a variable visual magnitude of about 6.1, is the only one occasionally barely visible to the unaided eye; the rest can be sighted only through telescopes. Only a dozen or so are seen to have disks when viewed with the largest telescopes; the rest are simply points of light. As they move in orbits around the sun, they make trails on photographic plates in telescopes set to track the stars. This is the way most of them have been found—that is, by chance—and often no one has bothered to work out their exact positions and orbits. Only recently have systematic searches of the solar system begun that seek asteroids.

The four largest asteroids were identified between 1801 and 1807 (see Table 4). No more were added to the list until 1845. Since then, asteroid discoveries have been fairly continual, becoming more numerous each decade. By 1890 about 300 had been identified. On a sampling basis, not by direct counting, it has been estimated that there may be an over-all total of 125,000 asteroids up to the nineteenth magnitude, but the majority are so diminutive that all put together, their mass cannot be 0.17 (1/6) that of the earth and is probably less than the total mass of the moon. Roughly 3,000 of these tiny, glinting celestial objects have been identified as asteroids by their behavior. About 1,800 have had their orbits calculated, and have been given numbers and sometimes names and entered in asteroid registers. But they are such faint, fast-moving bodies that the 5 or more good observations

84

needed to determine their orbits reliably have just not been made in most instances.

The courses of most asteroids lie in the great gap between the orbits of Mars and Jupiter. One asteroid, Chiron (1977 UB), discovered in 1977, with an estimated diameter of between 160 and 640 km (100 and 400 mi), has the longest known period of any of the asteroids—50.68 earth years, an eccentricity in orbit of 0.379, and an orbital inclination of 6.9° to the ecliptic. In its tilted journey around the sun it comes closer to the sun than Saturn and sweeps nearly out to the distance of Uranus.

The average inclination of asteroid orbits to the plane of the ecliptic (the imaginary plane formed by the earth's orbit) is 10°, and only a few of the orbits lie very close to it. Several asteroid inclinations run up as high as 20° or more from the ecliptic. The asteroid designated 1973 NA has the largest known inclination of any of the asteroids: 68°. Since in the main they are farther out from the sun than the earth and Mars, with some exceptions the periods of the asteroids range between 4 and 6 years.

Only the four largest asteroids show definite enough disks for their diameters to be measured. The diameters of a number of others have been inferred: Given a known distance from the earth in their calculated orbits and assuming an average asteroid reflectivity or albedo, their magnitude is measured and the size of the body that would produce that brightness under those conditions is calculated. Since the albedos of asteroids may vary considerably, this is only a rough approximation. Mercury and the moon have low albedos of 0.056 and 0.067, respectively; those of the asteroids Ceres and Pallas are very similar (0.06 and 0.07, respectively). Juno and Vesta have greater reflectivity; that of Juno is 0.12 and that of Vesta is 0.26, compared with Mars's albedo of 0.16.

Most of the asteroids are thought to be irregular masses of rock mixed with some iron and other metals; the smaller ones are probably odd-shaped fragments and splinters rather than neat spheres. These minor bodies definitely have the characteristics of the small inner, rocky planets, not those of the gas giants. Studies of the polarization of the light reflected from asteroids plus its spectral analysis reveal that the surface composition of asteroids falls into two general categories. The first class contains asteroids that are relatively bright and reddish; this results from the silicates and metals that dominate their surface. These asteroids lack large quantities of light-absorbing minerals. The second class are dark and have essentially no color, which results from large amounts of carbon on the asteroid surface.

With their small masses, the minor planets have very little gravitational effect. On Ceres (diameter of 1,025 km or 640 mi), weight would be only 0.025 (1/40) that on the surface of the earth. An average car would be easy to lift on Ceres, since the car would weigh under 45 kilograms (100 pounds), though one would not want to carry it very far. On an asteroid with a diameter of 16 km (10 mi) things would weigh only 0.000625 (1/1,600) what they would on the earth. With such negligible gravitational fields, the minor planets could not hold atmospheres.

The light from many of the asteroids varies in brightness, often in a regular manner. Although they may be luminescent, reacting to the

Variation in the track of the Sputnik 3 carrier case passing near Vega (bright star above the trace) on July 1, 1958; the satellite's periodic fading from view and then brightening was probably caused by the tumbling of the cylindrical case. The light from some asteroids may vary for similar reasons. A timing device cuts the track of the satellite at regular intervals, and the stars made arcs on the plate because the telescope followed the satellite.

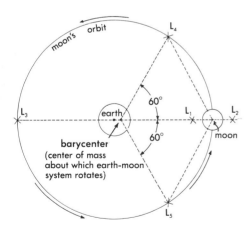

Lagrangian libration points in the earth-moon system. All in the plane of the moon's orbit, these points are indicated by the x's at L_1, L_2, and L_3 on the line passing through the centers of the earth and the moon, and L_4 and L_5 in the moon's orbit, preceding and following it by 60 degrees. Both L_4 and L_5 form equilateral triangles, with the earth and the moon at the other two apexes of the triangle.

solar radiation with which they are pelted, they can have no light sources of their own. Their light pulsation must be caused by their own motion. Eros (433), which sometimes comes within 24 million km (15 million mi) of the earth, has a period of rotation of 5 hours, 16 minutes, during which the brightness of its reflected light shows two maxima and two minima. The generally accepted explanation is that it has an oblong shape, roughly that of a brick, and rotates on an axis perpendicular to its greatest length. The light variations would be due to the angle at which its rotation was visible from the earth; just the ends and sides, also part of the top and bottom, or only the top or bottom might be seen. Some of the artificial earth satellites have developed similar odd motions, such as tumbling from end to end about an axis.

Although the gravity of an asteroid may be too weak to retain an atmosphere, it is strong enough to keep an object in orbit about it. On June 7, 1978, the asteroid Herculina, which has a diameter of 220 km (about 140 mi), occulted the star SAO (Smithsonian Astrophysical Observatory) 120774. Not only did the star "disappear" for 21 seconds, but also other events occurred that can be interpreted only by a smaller body orbiting the asteroid. In this particular case, this minor satellite, as it is called, is about 50 km (31 mi) in diameter and about 1,000 km (620 mi) from its parent asteroid.

Seven other asteroids may also have minor satellites. Among them is Pallas, the second asteroid discovered. It is interesting that the two expert double-star observers, W. H. van den Bos and W. S. Finsen, reported that they saw Pallas as two objects in 1926.

In addition to the majority of asteroids found between the orbits of Mars and Jupiter, there are two asteroid swarms that precede and follow Jupiter on its trek about the sun. In 1772 French mathematician and astronomer Joseph Louis Lagrange found that there are five stable positions within a system, like those of the earth and the moon or the sun and a planet, in which two bodies revolve about a common center of gravity. These Lagrangian points, referred to as L_1, L_2, L_3, L_4, and L_5, have the same orientation in all systems, as shown in the figure for the earth-moon system. Calculations show, however, that the L_1, L_2, and L_3 points (called collinear points, since all are on the same line that intersects the two bodies) would be quite unstable in comparison with the L_4, and L_5 positions.

In 1906, the asteroid Achilles (588) was discovered in the Lagrangian position L_4, preceding Jupiter in its orbit. Achilles has a period of 11.98 earth years, very similar to that of Jupiter's 11.862 years, but with a greater inclination of 10.30° to the ecliptic than Jupiter's 1.3°.

This discovery was followed by others, so that nearly 1,000 asteroids have been put into two "camps" on either side of Jupiter. As more Trojans (as these asteroids are called) were discovered, a convention was established to name these asteroids after the heroes of the Greek and Trojan War. An additional convention placed all the Greeks at the eastern Lagrangian point (L_4) and the Trojans at the western Lagrangian point (L_5). This convention wasn't established, however, until a Greek "spy" had been placed in the Trojan camp and a Trojan "spy" in the Greek camp. Two Trojans, Achilles and Priamus, are shown in the photographs.

The Trojan orbits generally have small eccentricities and a variety of inclinations to the ecliptic. They tend to wander about the Lagran-

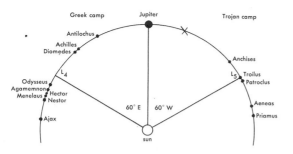

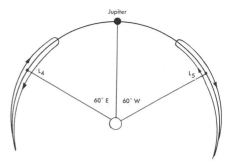

gian positions, principally because of the gravitational effects of Saturn out beyond them. They oscillate around the apex of the 60° triangle formed among them, the sun, and Jupiter (see diagram), but still remain in fairly stable orbits. Probably some escape entirely from, and others are captured in, these Lagrangian positions mainly by the effects of Saturn, or possibly of other asteroids passing in the vicinity. Some of the Trojans are rather large; the Trojan Hektor measures 100 km (62 mi) by 300 km (188 mi). Typically, though, they are dimmer than +12 magnitude, so they are not visible to the naked eye. Studies have revealed that the Trojans are darker than most asteroids, which may indicate a different chemical composition. The Trojans possibly represent material left over from the formation of Jupiter, or interplanetary material pulled into their position by the gravitational influence of Jupiter.

There may be several families or natural groups of asteroids. Calculations into the past from their present orbits, weighing in the various major perturbations that have affected them, reveal that they may have a common origin. One investigator concluded that nearly 200 asteroids appear to fall into 5 such families. Another, working on the orbits of a greater number of asteroids, found the same families, and possibly 24 more closely related groups. Could such families, however vague the relationships of the members, indicate a common origin in space?

Two remarkable sets of asteroids are the Apollo and Amor groups. An asteroid is placed in the Apollo group if its perihelion distance from the sun is less than an arbitrary 1.0 a.u., and into the Amor if less than about 1.3 a.u. The Apollo/Amor boundary has little, if any, significance, since two Amors—Quetzalcoatl and Betulia—have perihelion distances that vary from less than to greater than 1 astronomical unit. These groups of objects have rather eccentric orbits; the majority move well out beyond Mars at their aphelia and pass within the earth's orbit as they zip around the sun. Since they cross earth's orbit, a collision between an Apollo asteroid and the earth is possible. In 1937 Hermes, with a 1-km (0.6-mi) diameter, passed within 800,000 km (500,000 mi) of the earth. This is only twice the distance from the earth to the moon. If Hermes and the earth had collided, the energy released would have been equivalent to 10,000 10-megaton hydrogen bombs and left an impact crater about 20 km (12 mi) in diameter. Another close approach occurred in 1936, when Adonis (1936 CA) passed within 1,440,000 km (900,000 mi) of the earth. Apollo itself missed the earth by 3 million km (1.9 million mi) in 1932. Although these distances sound enormous, on an astronomical scale these asteroids were all but brushing the earth.

Is the earth likely to collide with one of these wandering asteroids?

Position of the Trojan asteroids (left) on June 20, 1960, in the Greek camp east of and preceding Jupiter in the L_4 Lagrangian position, and west of and following Jupiter in the Trojan camp in the L_5 position. The "x" west of Jupiter indicates the closest that Anchises approaches the planet. The fairly large oscillation of Trojan asteroids (right) about the L_4 and L_5 positions is produced in part by perturbations caused by Saturn and other planets, and in part because the Trojans are not exactly in the same plane as Jupiter's orbit. Some of Jupiter's outer satellites may be Trojan asteroids it has captured.

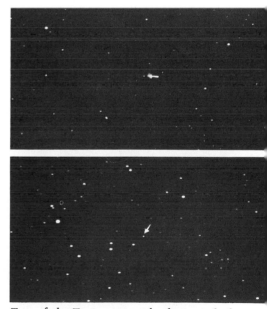

Two of the Trojan asteroids photographed with the 102-cm (40-inch) reflector of the U. S. Naval Observatory. Achilles (588) (top) was the first Trojan asteroid discovered, located in the Greek camp east of Jupiter, near the L_4 Lagrangian position in its orbit. Priamus (884) (bottom) is in the Trojan camp west of Jupiter, following it by about 60° in the L_5 position. Achilles (estimated diameter, 56 km or 35 mi) was photographed on November 9 and Priamus (diameter, 45 km or 28 mi) on June 22, 1963, with 10- and 30-minute exposures, respectively.

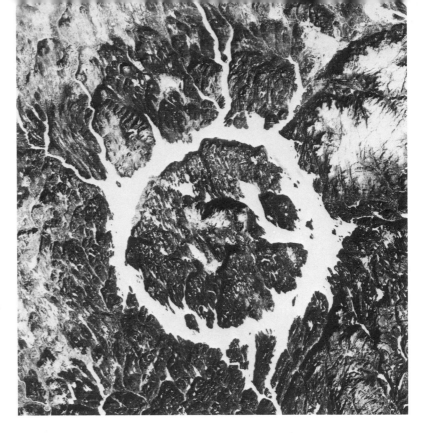

The ring structure of the Manicouagan Reservoir in northeastern Canada. This feature, some 70 km (43.5 mi) in diameter, forms the central region of a larger (150-km or 93-mi radius) area formed by the impact of an asteroid some 210 million years ago. This feature is believed to be the terrestrial analog for the 200-km (125-mi)-diameter ring structures on Mercury and Mars and for the 400-to-500-km (250-to-312-mi) basins on the moon.

The possibility has inspired some excellent fiction, but in truth it is very remote. Only once a century might an object like Hermes pass the earth within the lunar distance. A collision might occur once every 250,000 years. Filled by the waters of Lake Manicouagan, a giant crater in northeastern Quebec may be the result of a collision between the earth and an Apollo asteroid. The crater, measuring about 65 km (41 mi) across, had to be formed by an asteroid with a 3-km (2-mi) diameter. Skylab photographs revealed that an area as far as 150 km (93 mi) from the center has been disturbed by this impact some 210 million years ago. Some of the alleged terrestrial meteor craters (Table 6), as well as certain lunar seas, may have been produced by the impact of large asteroids in the past.

One obvious and popular way to explain the origin of the asteroids is to say that they are the remnants of a small planet or primitive protoplanet that was in orbit between Mars and Jupiter hundreds of millions or billions of years ago. Then this planet broke up in some cosmic catastrophe and was gradually fragmented and pulverized by further collisions into the small bodies we call asteroids.

The shattered-planet hypothesis is now viewed with skepticism by scientists. The pulverized-planet theory implies that the asteroids as well as the meteoroids were created from this destroyed planet. Data from meteorites, however, imply that the parent bodies of meteorites were of asteroid, not planet, size. Furthermore, a large amount of energy is required to rip a planet apart and disperse its fragments against their mutual gravitational pull. There is no plausible source for such large amounts of energy. Finally, only a small amount of material would have been accreted into the asteroid belt when the solar system formed 4.6 billion years ago. It is unlikely that any sizable planet would have formed at that location due to Jupiter's gravitational influence.

Just because the shattered-planet hypothesis is not a viable model for the origin of the asteroids does not imply that the asteroids formed from the material that never became a planet. As stated above, the amount of material available in the asteroid belt was small at the formation of the solar system. Much of this material eventually combined with the planets themselves.

The Apollo group may have an origin different from that of the other asteroids. Perhaps the Apollo group represent nuclei of short-period comets that have lost their volatile elements. The orbital similarity between Comet Encke and the Apollo object 1978 SB, and the decline in activity of Comet Encke in recent times support this idea.

Although the origins of asteroids remain a mystery, these small bodies may prove useful to humanity in the future. They may become a valuable mineral resource as our terrestrial resources dwindle, especially since there may be 400,000 asteroids larger than 1 km (0.6 mi). If these asteroids are rich in badly needed minerals, they can be mined. A first step toward mining would be the retrieval of soil samples from an asteroid to actually determine their composition. A likely candidate for a space mission is the asteroid 1977 HB. Little fuel would be required to launch a spacecraft into an orbit similar to that of 1977 HB and also to match its velocity.

Meteors and Meteorites

On the afternoon of March 8, 1976, the sky above Kirin City in northeastern China exploded and blazed with the fragments of a giant fireball passing through the earth's atmosphere. More than 100 remnants of this body have been retrieved from a 500-square-km (about 193-square-mi) area. The last remnant to strike reportedly dug a crater 3.3 meters (3.33 yards) deep and 2 meters (2.2 yards) wide. The largest piece recovered weighed a whopping 8,600 kilograms (18,920 pounds). This is the largest chunk ever observed to fall on the earth. Two other pieces weighed more than 440 kilograms (970 pounds).

An amazing number of meteors hit the earth—at which time they become meteorites—in a 24-hour period, yet no one has ever been killed by one as far as is known. Only one human injury has been definitely recorded when, on November 30, 1954, "stars fell on Alabama." A small stony meteoritic fragment weighing about 4 kilograms (9 pounds) crashed through the roof of a house in Sylacauga, Alabama, where Mrs. E. H. Hodges was resting on a sofa after lunch. The fragment ricocheted off a radio and struck her on the upper thigh, causing a slight bruise.

Called meteoroids in space, meteors as they penetrate the earth's atmosphere, and meteorites if they strike the earth, very few of these stony, stony-iron, or iron bodies are ever recovered. For the most part, they land in the oceans, at the poles, or in such sparsely inhabited regions as forests and deserts. The bright but transitory streaks they make in the sky, which give them the name shooting stars, are due to friction with the atmosphere. The streaks are usually described as white, and sometimes as greenish, reddish, or yellowish. Very large and brilliant meteors are called fireballs, and when, rarely, these fireballs explode, they may be known as bolides. The term meteoroid, or meteoric body, is reserved for any fairly small object in space, smaller than an asteroid and considerably larger than an atom or molecule, be-

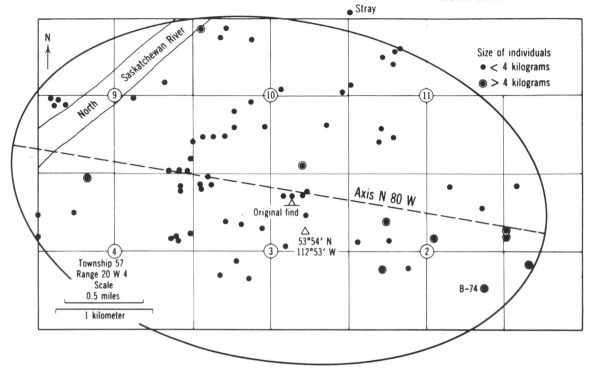

Elliptical distribution of the individual stones recovered from the Bruderheim (Alberta) meteorite of March 4, 1960. The fragments of the gray chondrite showered down from the west in a nearly west–east line, the larger chunks heavier than 4 kilograms (9 pounds) being carried farther than the smaller ones by their momentum.

fore it enters the earth's atmosphere, which only a very small proportion of them ever do. Meteoroids in space are nonluminous and thus not detectable by optical telescopes, but eventually some may be picked up by radar telescopes.

Here is the history of a relatively rare phenomenon: a daylight fireball. On August 10, 1972, this object was observed over a long path stretching from some 1,500 km (935 mi) from south of Provo, Utah, to south of Edmonton, Alberta, Canada. The meteor traversed this path in 101 seconds for an average speed of 15 km (about 9 mi) a second. Near midtrajectory over Montana sonic booms were heard. This meteor was unusual in that it not only skipped off the earth's atmosphere back into space, but it was also observed by an astronomer who is interested in the study of meteors!

Luigi G. Jacchia of the Center for Astrophysics observed the phenomenon from Wyoming and studied it carefully upon his return to Cambridge, Massachusetts. Assuming the meteor is a typical one, Dr. Jacchia estimated from its brightness that it had a mass of 4,000 tons and a diameter of 13 meters (about 42 ft). Fortunately, this object returned to interplanetary space, since it would have impacted with the energy of a large hydrogen bomb if it had struck the earth.

When meteorites do impact the earth, fragments are usually scattered over an ellipse-shaped area. The figure illustrates a typical impact area. Fragments from the Bruderheim meteorite scattered over an elliptical area approximately 5.3 km (3.3 mi) long by 3.2 km (2 mi) wide. Some 188 sizable chunks were collected, weighing a total of 304 kilograms (670 pounds). The Bruderheim meteorite was a chondrite, one type of stony meteorite, gray in color, with a low iron content.

Meteoritics, as the science of meteors is called, has made great headway during the twentieth century, first by means of visual, photographic, and spectroscopic observational techniques, and then with radar. Amateur meteor observers around the world cooperate in the work. On a clear night an average of about 10 meteors an hour can be seen streaking across the sky in a single location. When there is a meteor shower, the number greatly increases. A star map is reproduced, designed by Peter M. Millman of the National Research Council of Canada. This is used to accurately plot and record the paths and magnitudes of visually observed meteors. The paths of many meteors spotted over a period of about 5 hours on a single night are plotted on the map.

It has been estimated that about 24 million visible meteors pass through the atmosphere of the entire earth in 24 hours. Observations with telescopes up to the tenth visual magnitude indicate that 8 billion meteors must plunge into the earth's atmosphere a day. Added to this are the much more numerous micrometeorites, objects with a diameter of less than 1 millimeter (0.03937 inch), and cosmic debris and dust (see Chapter 7).

Meteors plotted (numbered arrows) by an observer at Springhill Meteor Observatory near Ottawa in 5 hours on the night of August 14–15, 1963, with their estimated magnitudes (20 indicates +2 magnitude, 25 indicates +2.5 magnitude, etc.). The radiant of most of the meteors was in the northern part of the constellation Perseus, the date falling near the end of the Perseid shower. A few sporadic meteors not related to the shower appear. The whole group of 8 observers saw 500 meteors on this night, explaining the range of numbers.

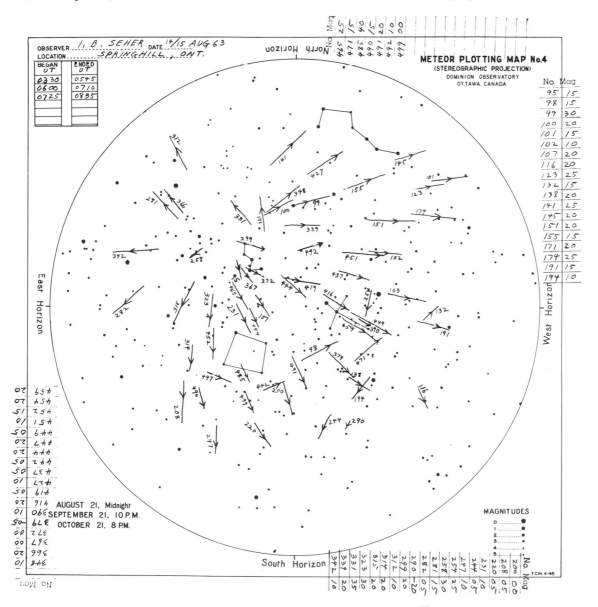

Only very rough estimates have been made of the mass that the earth must accumulate each day as a result of this infall from interplanetary space. The greatest meteorites that gouge out craters in the earth's crust may add from 0.5 up to 1 ton a day; fireballs, visual meteorites, and the dimmer telescopic and radio meteorites add from 1 ton to 10 tons daily. The largest share by far must come from micrometeorites and interplanetary dust, depositing some 1,000 to 10,000 tons of cosmic debris on the earth each day. It has been calculated that all this must add from 5 to 10 pounds a year to each square mile of the earth's surface. We can stop hoping that smoke control will eliminate all the dust and grit with which housewives do battle, for some of it has sifted down from the far reaches of interplanetary space, leaving the very stuff of the universe on our doorsteps.

Meteors penetrating the earth's atmosphere often belong to meteor streams or meteor showers. A meteor stream is a group of meteoric bodies in space with nearly identical orbits around the sun. A meteor shower is a number of meteors with approximately the same trajectories actually entering the earth's atmosphere. Sporadic meteors, not linked with any recognized showers, greatly outnumber the shower meteors, though the latter sometimes come so thick and fast that they put on a much more spectacular scene, very like the grand finale of a fireworks display. The meteor radiant is that point where the path of the meteors intersects the celestial sphere. A spray of meteors appears to come in a shower from the radiant, arching out from it as the ribs of an opened umbrella curve out from the center.

The more prominent nighttime meteor showers of both Northern and Southern Hemispheres are listed in Table 5. Although there are variations, most of these appear consistently each year as the earth in its orbit intersects the meteor stream producing the showers. Occasionally yearly showers exhibit unusual activity. The Leonids, which is not a particularly strong meteor shower, provided a celestial spectacular in 1966 when observers at Kitt Peak National Observatory saw the Leonids fall at the astounding rate of 60,000 meteors an hour for a 40-minute period! Sizable daytime showers occur quite often, but usually they are observable only by radio techniques. Sometimes the Leonids have been brilliant enough to be seen in the daylight.

Many meteor streams follow closely in the orbits of comets. Thus the Southern Taurid stream is in the orbit of Encke's comet, and the Draconids are associated with the periodic comet Giacobini-Zinner. On the other hand, there are meteor showers unrelated to any present or previously known comets. A recent estimate is that perhaps 90 percent of visually observable meteorites are of cometary origin. Most meteoritic orbits, however, have low inclinations to the ecliptic, with no apparent relation to the asteroids.

Opinions have clashed over the question of whether some meteors have hyperbolic orbits and velocities of their own over 41.85 km (26.159 mi) a second. If so, they are likely to have come from interstellar space. The tendency now is to consider nearly all meteors members of our solar system. One estimate is that interstellar meteors constitute no more than 1 percent of the total.

The calculated orbits of the bulk of meteors show that their motions are direct, though some are retrograde. Many of them come in from the direction toward which the earth is moving, and it is quite natural

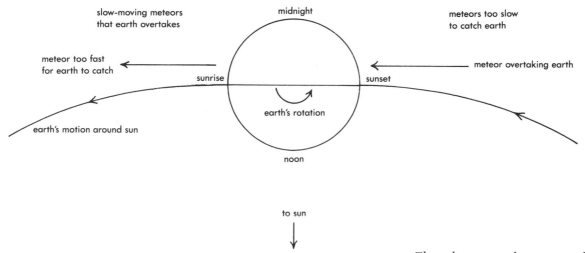

slow-moving meteors
that earth overtakes

midnight

meteors too slow
to catch earth

meteor too fast
for earth to catch

sunrise

sunset

meteor overtaking earth

earth's rotation

earth's motion around sun

noon

to sun

The only meteors that are seen from sunset to midnight are those that are traveling faster than the earth. They are capable of catching the earth and entering its atmosphere. From midnight to sunrise the earth sweeps up the slower-moving meteors. Since there are more slow-moving meteors, more meteors are seen in the second half of the night than in the first half.

that the earth should sweep up a greater concentration of meteors from this direction. Similarly, more meteors are observed between midnight and sunrise than between sunset and midnight, since the earth is turning into the slower-moving meteors. They usually become visible at heights from 120 km (75 mi) down to 90 km (55 mi) in the atmosphere; the brightest, flaunting their fiery and sometimes smoky trains, may plunge down to altitudes as low as 16 to 40 km (10 to 25 mi).

The actual velocities of meteors range all the way from about 11 km (7 mi) a second or less to 72 km (45 mi) a second. Meteoroids in space move in elliptical orbits about the sun, with velocities of less than the 42 km (26 mi) a second, which would be escape velocity from the solar system. The earth's own velocity in its orbit is 29.6 km (18.5 mi) a second. Thus meteors overtaking the earth have the earth's velocity subtracted and enter the atmosphere at 12 km (7.5 mi) a second or less; those meeting the earth have the earth's velocity added, so they may enter the atmosphere with velocities as high as 72 km (45 mi) a second. Meteorites of less than 1 ton in weight lose almost their own velocity in atmospheric passage and collide with the earth at velocities of only 0.10 to 0.20 km (0.06 to 0.124 mi) a second. Those with masses of 10 or more tons may retain a good share of their initial velocity on impact.

Meteorites have been classified and analyzed intensively for what they can reveal about the interplanetary space through which they have traveled. The major meteoritic groups that have been identified are the stony meteorites (aerolites), the iron meteorites (siderites), and the intermediate stony-iron meteorites (siderolites). The stony meteorites consist of siliceous minerals in the main (magnesium-iron silicates), and resemble rather soft, light rocks, somewhat like volcanic rock. They may be either chondrites or achondrites. Chondrites are stony meteorites with fibrous, banded, or glassy inclusions, called chondrules, in their mineral matrix. Achondrites consist basically of magnesium-iron silicates without much nickel iron and usually without chondrules. The stony irons are part mineral and part iron in composition (averaging half nickel iron and half silicates). Iron meteorites, composed of masses of nickel iron (averaging 90 percent iron and 10 percent nickel) with infrequent silicate inclusions, are very heavy. Some stony chondritic meteorites are called carbonaceous chondrites, since

Microphoto of a chondrule in a thin section of a meteorite. Chondrules are spheroidal bodies, usually about 1 mm (0.04 inch or 1/25 inch) in diameter, the origin of which is not completely known. They may have been produced by the heating of carbonaceous chondrites, by direct condensation from a cool dust cloud among the earliest bits of matter in the solar system, or by metamorphic processes on larger bodies, although none have been found in terrestrial rocks.

they contain amorphous carbon, graphite, and other carbon inclusions, notably complex hydrocarbons.

Among the over 2,000 meteorites actually recovered, the stony type predominates, with over 1,250; then come the irons with about 650; and, finally, the very scarce stony irons, of which only 74 are known. Of the total number of meteorites recovered, 913 were picked up or located after actually being observed falling. A greater number, 1,131, were discovered and identified merely by their characteristics.

Meteoroids are traveling at many kilometers a second when they crash into the earth's atmosphere, but meeting the resistance of the gases high in the atmosphere begins to slow them down. Their great energy of motion must be dissipated, and by the time they have reached a height of 120 to 80 km (75 to 50 mi) they are glowing in the sky because of the heat that has been produced. They become white-hot and their surfaces molten, streaming back from the direction of their travel, with drops flaming off and sometimes exploding or fragmenting and forming a number of wakes or trains in the sky. They lose fluid and vapors to the atmosphere in the process known as ablation, by which heat is rapidly carried away. The same ablation effects have been used to advantage in the design of spacecraft or missile nose cones, which must re-enter the atmosphere with as little destruction as possible. The intense heat produced by the friction of their passage through the air must run off or be shucked off, as it were, with the molten nose-cone material.

As they pass through the atmosphere the larger meteors produce loud booms, the result of shock waves formed by their supersonic speed of entry. Few meteors are large enough to survive the atmosphere. Those that reach the earth's surface have been so slowed down that they have lost most of their surface heat, have formed what is

Clearwater Lake Craters, near Hudson Bay, Canada, 22 and 32 km (14 and 20 mi) in diameter, may have been blasted out by a huge double meteorite.

called a fusion crust on their surfaces, and are barely warm, or may even be cold, to the touch. They cannot possibly start fires, as one might assume. The Hoba iron meteorite of southwestern Africa probably weighed 90,720 kilograms (100 tons) when it fell, and a number of others weighing from 9,072 to 27,216 kilograms (10 to 30 tons) are known. Meteorites of over 90,720 kilograms will probably never be found, since their impact would be so explosive that they would be entirely vaporized or fragmented. Meteor craters constitute the sole evidence that such massive bodies have fallen from the sky.

A dozen well-authenticated meteoritic craters have been identified on earth, and many others are candidates. Their locations and principal features are given in Table 6. Iron or stony meteorites and many meteoritic fragments have been found in or near most of the craters. The Siberian formations were made as recently as 1908 and 1947, perhaps by clusters of meteorites or small comets. Their effects on seismographs and other instruments were noted at these times, and the air blasts of the earlier event felled forests and killed herds of reindeer. All but the Barringer Crater were identified in the twentieth century, yet most are thousands of years old.

The so-called fossil craters probably range from millions to billions of years old. In 1961 Peter M. Millman of the National Research Council of Canada and others thoroughly investigated the site of the alleged meteor crater in Algonquin Provincial Park, Ontario, and certified it as a fossil crater. Called the Brent Meteor Crater, it is about 3.2 km (2 mi) in diameter, roughly circular, and dips down 0.8 km (over 0.5 mi) deep beneath the material that has filled it in. Paleozoic rocks found within it are evidence of its antiquity. Judged to be of the Precambrian Era, it must have been formed some 600 million to 900 million years ago.

Evidence other than meteoritic fragments has been adduced as proof of meteor craters and impact zones, particularly of the fossil variety, in which the meteoritic material as such may be entirely dissipated. Shatter cones have been found at a number of older, suspected meteor-crater sites, such as the Sierra Madera circular structure near the W. J. McDonald Observatory near Fort Davis, Texas, or the huge Vredefort Ring in the Transvaal of South Africa, southwest of Johannesburg; the Vredefort Ring has a diameter of some 224 km (140 mi). Another type of evidence, the mineral coesite, has been found in the rock at the Ashanti Crater, Lake Bosumtwi, in Ghana, and in the Ries Kessel Basin, 27 km (17 mi) in diameter, located in southern Germany. Are these definite proofs of meteorites?

Shatter cones are conical chunks of rock with grooves or fissures (striations) radiating from their apexes. They vary in length from less than an inch up to many feet, and have been found in many kinds of rock, particularly in limestone and sandstone. They appear to be shock-wave products, and have been produced experimentally by firing small pellets at a velocity of 5.5 km (18,000 ft) a second into limestone. Some think they may be the product of great volcanic stresses; others, that massive shearing forces such as those involved in the production of geological faults may have formed them. That they are solely the result of the heavy impact of meteorites has not yet been proved.

The mineral coesite was first discovered in 1953 in the laboratory of the Norton Company in Worcester, Massachusetts, by Loring Coes, Jr., and was named after him. Coesite, a superdense form (or polymorph) of silica (SiO_2), was produced by Coes at pressures exceeding 21,100 kilograms per square cm (300,000 pounds per square inch), pressures that meteorites striking the earth could initiate. Coesite has, in fact, been found in small quantities at a number of sites, including the well-known Barringer Meteor Crater, near Flagstaff, Arizona; at the Holleford Crater in Ontario, Canada; at the less authenticated Ries Kessel Basin in Germany; and at the Wabar Crater in Saudi Arabia. Most remarkably, coesite was identified at the Teapot Ess Crater at the Yucca Flats, Nevada, nuclear-test site, produced by the tremendous pressures from an underground nuclear explosion. The high pressures at which coesite was created in the laboratory occur at depths greater than 64 km (40 mi) under the earth's surface, but it is possible that greater upheaval nearer the surface might produce such pressures, as well as meteorite impacts. Together with shatter cones, the presence of coesite may document, in part, the proposition that "a meteorite was here," but neither proves it.

What is the origin of meteorites? Despite the fact that German physicist E. F. F. Chaldni in the last decade of the eighteenth century suggested that the meteorites were solid particles falling to earth from interplanetary space, French scientists firmly believed they originated in the earth's atmosphere. Even Thomas Jefferson, who himself had a good grasp of the world around him, is reported to have remarked that it was easier for him to believe that a Yankee could lie than that stones fall from the sky.

No one seriously doubts today that meteorites have an extraterrestrial origin. But exactly what is that origin? Laplace (1827) suggested that they originate in volcanic eruptions on the moon; Olbers (1840) proposed that they represent fragments of disintegrated planets that also gave us asteroids; Schiaparelli (1910) believed them to be cometary remnants.

Current evidence indicates that the meteorites arose in one or more bodies no larger than the asteroid Ceres (1,025 km or 640 mi in diameter). However, the diversities of chemical compositions indicate that not all are due to fragmentation of these parent bodies. Minerals and chondrules found in carbonaceous chondrites hint that these minerals and chondrules are particles that have condensed out of the same material that formed the sun and the planets.

A possible scenario unfolds: The solar nebula forms. Within the nebula the chondrules form before the sun and the planets. This is followed by the condensation of the parent bodies of the meteorites and the planets. Each parent body probably consists of a crude layer configuration, with each layer containing a mixture of material. The chondrites are representatives of an outer layer, while the stony irons, achondrites, and some iron material come from a deeper layer. The cores of the parent bodies produce the irons.

The cause of the breakup of the parent body is not known. A popular belief is that these bodies experienced numerous collisions. Since the parent body was chemically differentiated, the different collisions produced the different types of meteorites. An alternate hypothesis suggests that the smaller parent bodies disintegrated due to internal pressure as the parent body suffered abrupt outgassing.

Clues to the origin of meteorites may be found in the analysis of meteorites discovered in the ice of Antarctica. A recent expedition discovered 309 meteorites in the Antarctic, including 2 carbonaceous chondrites and a large 660-kilogram (1,450-pound) iron. It is believed that the icy Antarctic environment preserves these meteorites from the contamination and erosion they endure in warmer climates. Since they are so well preserved, these meteorites should be more like those that remain in orbit about the sun.

Glassy Enigmas

An absorbing story of detection is unfolding from studies of the small, glassy stones called tektites, found strewn in fields around the earth. Tektites range in size from about 2 to 10 centimeters (1 inch to 4 inches), and are usually translucent yellowish-brown, but sometimes green. Silica-rich, containing 70 to 80 percent silica, they also have high proportions of alumina, potash, and lime, and small amounts of magnesia, iron oxides, and soda. They may be spheres, dumbbells, teardrops, disks, or buttons. Early theories attributed their origin to terrestrial mineral or earth-soil fusion caused by flashes of lightning or volcanic eruptions. Theories for their formation were eventually reduced to four: volcanic activity on the moon or earth, or meteoritic impact on the moon or earth. Tektites have not been seen falling, unfortunately, but they are to be found in Australia (australites), Indochina (indochinites), southern China, the Philippines (philippinites), Malaya (malaysianites), Thailand, Borneo, Java (javaites), Tasmania, the islands of Banka and Billiton (billitonites) in the Java Sea, the western African Republic of the Ivory Coast, Czechoslovakia (moldavites), and Georgia and Texas (bediasites) in the United States.

One single fragment of a pale brownish-green tektite was reported-

(A) An australite "button" tektite that shows evidence of 2 periods of melting. The flanged edge indicates high-velocity flight through the atmosphere in which, in the second melting, the ablating material from the front melted, ran back, and formed the flaring flange (x2.9). (B) Two bediasites from Texas (x1.8). (C) The hollowed side of a Georgia tektite. (D) A tektite from Brunei, Borneo, with a surface-flow pattern indicative of its internal structure.

ly found in a wash in the cliffs at Gay Head, Martha's Vineyard, Massachusetts, in 1960, below the only Miocene layer remaining on the New England coast. At least three groups of investigators have since combed the vicinity without finding any more. Perhaps some sailor off a whaling or coastwise ship dropped this memento of his voyages to the far corners of the earth, or to Georgia or Texas. Or perhaps this was a fragment separated by a detonation from other tektites as the parent body sped into our atmosphere.

Tektites have been dated by comparing the radioactive decay of the potassium 40 found in them to that of argon 40, the proportion of the radioactive elements in them roughly indicating their ages. The age of tektites in the United States has been set at about 34 million years, that of the tektites in Czechoslovakia at 15 million years, and those of the Australian–East Asian groups at about 750,000 years. But not enough clear-cut evidence has yet been marshaled to prove whether tektites originated in great meteoritic impacts on the moon or on the earth.

Only the Australian tektites appear to have been melted and then remelted. They might have been melted when splashed up from the moon and then remelted on passing through the earth's atmosphere; or they might have been melted when a huge meteorite impact on earth flung them up through the atmosphere at high velocities, and then remelted on their re-entry into the atmosphere after an orbit or part of an orbit of the earth.

On the one hand, tektite materials may have come originally from the earth, since they are related in chemical composition to igneous rocks, unlikely to occur on the surface of the moon, and not akin to the composition of meteorites. The analysis of certain tektites from Thailand, for example, has revealed the presence of mineral grains in some layers, most likely formed from earth materials. On the other hand, nickel-iron spherules have been found in a Philippines tektite; these spherules are closely related to, if not a kind of, meteoritic material. And, while they have been challenged, various calculations have led investigators to believe that the speed (11 to 13 km or 7 to 8 mi a second) and angle of entry of the Australian tektites into the atmosphere indicate the moon as their most probable place of origin. Tektites may have come, in one instance, from the Cyrillic meteor shower of 1913, which orbited the earth in a nearly circular fashion and may have consisted of debris from meteor impacts on the moon.

A recent suggestion is that tektites are actually formed in volcanic activity on the moon. If they originated at distances greater than that of the moon, their distribution on earth would be more uniform. Formation by the impact of a meteor on the lunar surface is ruled out for

two reasons: Ejecta from the impact would not reach the necessary velocity to escape from the moon, and the composition of tektites is different from the lunar surface (but not, perhaps, from the lunar mantle). Terrestrial volcanism as the source of tektites is also eliminated.
Glasses from earth's volcanoes have a different chemical composition
from tektites, nor can terrestrial volcanoes account for tektite distribution on the earth's surface. If tektites formed during the impact of a
meteorite on the earth's surface, where are the impact craters? It has
been estimated that a crater 300 km (186 mi) in diameter and 40 km
(25 mi) deep had to be formed at the time of meteorite impact to account for the Australian, North American, and Ivory Coast fields. No
such craters, which would be hard to conceal, have been detected.
Counterarguments exist, however, that convince some scientists that
tektites formed on the earth. Included in these arguments is the fact
that the ages and chemical compositions of the lunar samples returned
to earth by Apollo astronauts are different from those of tektites.

Comets

Comets may be great luminous bodies with long, streaming tails, clearly visible in the sky, or they may be tiny specks or smudged blurs
when reflected in even the largest telescopes. Men may be filled with
wonder at their loveliness or struck with terror of the doom comets are
believed to portend. They suddenly emerge from the darkness at the
fringes of the solar system and streak in toward the sun from almost
any direction. Their orbits may be entirely changed by the mighty
pull of Jupiter, or the incandescence of the sun may rupture them.
Their tails change direction and shape in the sky, and they vanish into
the depths of space. Some are periodic, coming back year after year;
others may be seen only once, perhaps never to appear again, to return
thousands of years hence. Few generalizations can be made about
comets; they seem to behave as randomly or as irrationally as frantic
moths attracted to a light.

Sizable comets near the sun have a distinguishable head and tail.
The head consists of a bright, hazy mass called the coma (from the
Latin for "hair"), and usually a bright, more or less central condensation or nucleus. The nucleus is believed to be a kind of loosely gathered body of metallic grains and frozen gases, perhaps averaging 0.75
km (.50 mi) in diameter.

Comets shine by reflected sunlight, not by their own radiance, becoming brighter as they approach the sun. The average diameter of a
comet has been estimated at about 112,000 km (70,000 mi), largest at
about 1.4 a.u. from the sun, decreasing in diameter as perihelion is approached, and decreasing again when out beyond 1.4 a.u. The tail,
which grows as the comet approaches the sun and may extend for millions of kilometers, becomes orientated away from the sun, just as a
flag flutters away from the wind, except that cometary tails are influenced by streams of solar particles and radiation.

On September 1, 1961, Milton L. Humason, of the Mount Palomar
Observatory, California, discovered Comet Humason (1961e), the fifth
comet discovered or rediscovered that year. At that time it was a very
dim, diffuse comet, of the fourteenth magnitude, with no tail, moving
in toward the sun very slowly from a great distance, in an orbit with
an estimated period of 2,000 years. When it had reached a point be-

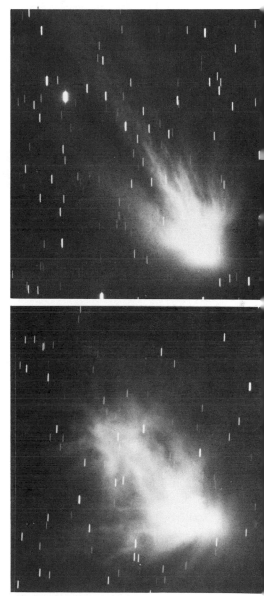

*Marked changes in the coma and tail of
Comet Humason (1961e), photographed on
July 9 and August 8, 1962, with the 1-
meter (40-inch) Naval Observatory
reflector. Discovered on September 1,
1961, by Milton L. Humason of the
Mount Palomar Observatory, the comet
was still at a distance of some 400 million
km (250 million mi) from the sun,
between the orbits of Mars and Jupiter,
when these "explosive" effects occurred.*

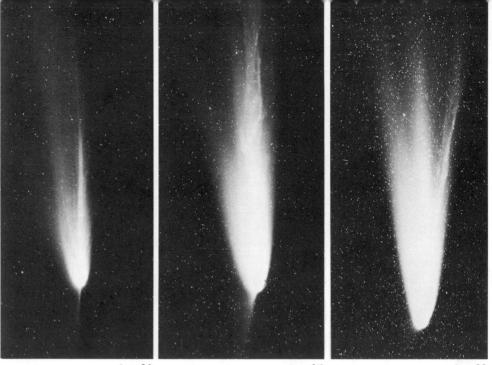

Apr 26   Apr 27   Apr 30

Photographed with the 1.2-meter (48-inch) Schmidt telescope of Mount Palomar in 1957, Comet Arend-Roland's (1957III) odd "spike" points toward the sun, changing rapidly in form and fading from April 26 to April 27 and 30.

tween the orbits of Jupiter and Mars, in July and August 1962, it had developed an irregular tail about 14 million km (9 million mi) long, with an area judged to cover about 20 times the size of the full moon in the sky. Suddenly the comet collided with something, either solar particles or a radiation storm caused by a solar flare or a stream of gas or dust particles in space. Or possibly it had been affected by internal explosions. Whatever disaster befell it, its parts disintegrated and its tail rapidly changed form and volume, demonstrating the extremes of metamorphosis that comets can undergo.

On the average, 5 or 6 comets are discovered or rediscovered each year, although in 1947 there were 14; two thirds, or about 4 out of 6, are usually new. They are named for their discoverer or discoverers and are identified by the year of discovery, followed by letters giving the order of discovery in that year—1956a, 1956b, and so forth. If they prove to be periodic when their orbits are calculated, they are identified by the year of their passage through perihelion about the sun (which may differ from the year of their discovery), and their order among the other comets in perihelion during that year is given in Roman numerals. Thus the first periodic comet passing perihelion in 1964 was known as 1964I, the second as 1964II, and so on.

Comet Arend-Roland (1957III), discovered by Sylvain Arend and Georges Roland at Uccle, Belgium, on November 8, 1956, developed an odd spike directed toward the sun in April 1957. At first this appeared fairly broad, then it became sharp and pencil-like (April 26), and then faint and stubby (April 29)—all within a week's time. One suggestion was that it was actually very thin but fan-shaped, and when the earth crossed the plane of the comet's orbit it was seen edgewise as a pencil-thin (less than 16,000 km or 10,000 mi) jet directed toward the sun, even though it was millions of kilometers wide.

Whether any comets have definitely parabolic orbits with a velocity that will take them out of the solar system never to return is an open question. Many comets have nearly parabolic orbits, with an eccentricity very close to 1, in that portion of their orbits that can be observed near the sun. But comets have very little mass and can be strongly affected in their orbits by the sun, by huge Jupiter, and even by Saturn and other planets. In addition, the orbits of comets are hard to determine, since they are pulled tightly through perihelion near the sun; the exact positions of such large, diffuse bodies as these comets are difficult to pin down. However, most, if not all, comets are thought to be in elliptical orbits over the long run, but the wavering paths of these orbits near Jupiter and the sun make calculations difficult.

Some comets have such great ellipticity in their courses that it will be thousands or even hundreds of thousands of years before they will return to the sun's vicinity, for they lose much of their velocity, and must move very slowly, near and through their aphelia. Other comets have periods not exceeding a few to a few hundred years; the Schwassmann-Wachmann 1 Comet (1925II) is an example. Revolving in a 16-year orbit entirely within the space between Jupiter and Saturn, it is visible in telescopes even at aphelion, when farthest from the sun. Occasionally it flares up to become 100 times as bright as usual—comets are known to do odd and inexplicable things of this sort. The sequence of photographs shows the changes in its appearance among October 12, 1961; October 18, when it had become much brighter and extensive; and November 3, when diffuse material is visible in a kind of haze around its small, central, bright area. Periodic Comet Encke, a faint comet normally, now and then increases suddenly in brightness for causes unknown. Such increases occurred in 1957 and again in 1960.

Perhaps the best-documented splitting of a comet nucleus is that of Comet West (1976VI). Discovered by Richard M. West at the European Southern Observatory headquarters on November 5, 1975, Comet West reached perihelion on February 25, 1976. The photograph shows the beauty of this spectacular comet. The sequence of drawings from March 8 to March 25 reveals the breakup of the cometary nucleus into four components. On March 8 component B could be seen above and to the right (northwest) of component A. By March 12, 4 components were seen. Component C was directly north (to the right in the se-

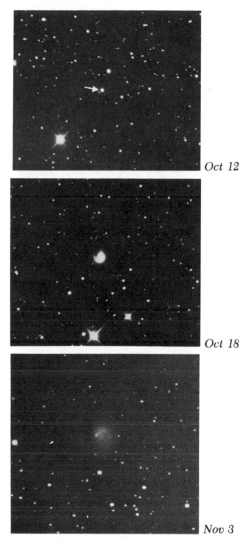

Oct 12

Oct 18

Nov 3

One of the strange "outbursts" of periodic comet Schwassmann-Wachmann 1 (1925II), photographed with 30-minute exposures on October 12, October 18, and November 3, 1961. The envelope expanded with a linear velocity of about 320 km (200 mi) an hour. Although the comet generally appears stellar or nearly so, as on October 12, it experiences such eruptions, which are not related to its distance from the sun, on the average of once or twice a year. The brightness may increase as much as 5 magnitudes in a single day, the light becoming 100 times more intense.

Comet West (1976VI) as photographed on March 8, 1976, with a 30-cm (12-inch) Schmidt telescope. This comet, discovered on November 5, 1975, by Richard M. West, reached perihelion on February 25, 1976, and has been one of the more spectacular comets of recent history.

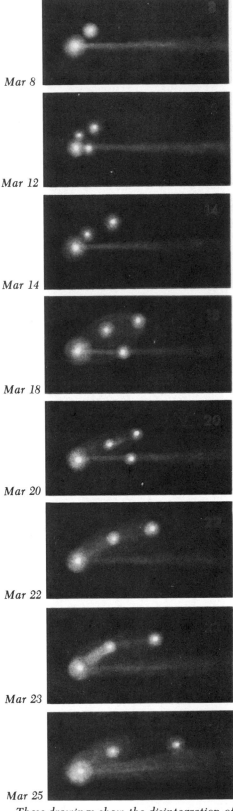

Mar 8

Mar 12

Mar 14

Mar 18

Mar 20

Mar 22

Mar 23

Mar 25

These drawings show the disintegration of the nucleus of Comet West into four distinct components from March 8 to March 25, 1976. The brightnesses of the components changed from night to night with conditions in the nucleus.

quence), and component D to the west-northwest of A. The brightnesses of the various components fluctuated due to the changing conditions in the nucleus. Component C started to fade rapidly on March 18. Although it was still detectable on photographic plates as late as March 28, component C had disappeared for visual observers a week earlier.

The first periodic comet identified (1682) was Halley's Comet, named for its discoverer, Edmund Halley, an English astronomer contemporary with Isaac Newton. It has reappeared about every 75 years. It returned in 1759, again in 1835, and last passed perihelion in 1910. In 1948, at aphelion, it was invisible, far out beyond Neptune, and is now moving back slowly in its retrograde orbit toward the sun. One of the most brilliant and impressive of comets, with an enormously long tail, it is expected to reappear in May 1986.

When Halley's Comet approached the sun in 1910, the earth passed into or very close to its tail, and a good many people prepared to meet their Maker. However, nothing very much happened. Its tenuous tail may have caused very small variations in illumination in the earth's atmosphere, but they were not seen in the bright moonlight conditions at the time. When Halley's Comet then passed directly between the earth and the sun, the most meticulous observations with the best telescopes of the time revealed no trace of it against the sun's disk. Comets have been known to dim the light from bright stars slightly when they pass in front of them, as seen from the earth, so they are not completely transparent.

Theories about the nature and origin of these cosmic blowtorches are not easy to construct. Their behavior is often strange and seemingly contradictory. Conditions in comets are so different from familiar terrestrial conditions that few analogies can be drawn. Perhaps the most widely accepted theory of the nature of comets is one proposed in 1950 by American astronomer Fred L. Whipple. Called an "icy-conglomerate model" of comets, it visualizes the cometary nucleus as a porous mass of very finely divided mineral particles, perhaps in loosely related matrices called dustballs, immersed in an ice of solidified gases. The outer portion of these masses is heated and vaporized as the comet nears the sun, giving rise to the jets, the expansion of the coma, and to the gases streaming behind it in the tail.

The principal molecules in the nuclei of comets, inferred from spectroscopic evidence, are ammonia, methane, and possibly acetylene, with water and small amounts of such metals as iron, nickel, and sodium. These may be held as an agglomeration of ices frozen solid at great distances from the sun—though hydrates have been suggested in another model, and free radicals in still another, formed and trapped by radiation, perhaps when the comet is distant from the sun in its orbit. As comets near the sun, various ions of these substances appear in the coma and tail, while the metal traces are identified when the comet comes very close to the sun.

A theory was developed from bits of evidence that comets probably have a halo or "atmosphere" of gas atoms around their heads. To check this theory, observations of two bright comets were made in 1970 from the U. S. Orbiting Astronomical Observatory (OAO 2) and the Orbiting Geophysical Observatory (OGO 5) satellites. Sure enough, spectroscopic and photometric instruments on these observatories reported the head halos around the comets that had been pre-

dicted, although they were invisible in naked-eye or optical-telescope viewing.

Analysis of the satellite data showed that the comets had great halos of hydrogen encircling their heads, extending out about 9.6 million km (6 million mi). Hydroxyl (OH) radicals were also found in these halos, so perhaps water molecules from the icy comet nuclei had been broken down in space into the hydrogen and hydroxyl particles. Perhaps 100 tons of comet nucleus per second vaporizes to produce these halos. These observations tend to confirm the icy-conglomerate model of comets.

Some of the dustballs in the nucleus may be ejected, or parts of the head may disintegrate and give rise to meteor streams or showers, meteoritic dust, and some of the smaller porous, stony meteors, as well as causing change in shape and brightness. Many meteor streams have been found to follow the orbits of comets. As the outer layers of the comet evaporate, the mineral particles collecting at the surface would be heated and might give rise to the explosive jets seen in the coma, and the gas streams of considerable velocity seen in the tails. Such jets might also explain why the nuclei of many comets rotate; in similar fashion spacecraft are rotated around their axes by small jets of stored nitrogen or hydrogen peroxide gases on their surfaces, in this case to maintain a stable position or to effect a change in attitude.

Many theories of the origin of comets have been proposed, but none is considered adequate or accepted by most scientists today. Earlier discredited theories held that comets had been expelled from the earth, the other planets, or the sun. It was thought that the sun's prominences might sometimes be ejected and become entirely detached from it. More recently, comets have been ascribed to masses of gas and dust about the outer rim of the gravitational field of the solar system, 100,000 to 200,000 a.u. from the sun; or to interstellar dust and gas clouds through which the sun may carry the solar system, scooping up some accretions of these materials to form the comets.

Scientists are eager to launch a space probe to pass through a comet's head. Technically this should be quite easy, since many comets cross the plane of the earth's ecliptic somewhere between the orbits of Venus and Mars, closer to the earth's orbit than either of these planets. Halley's Comet and Comet Encke are often cited as likely targets for such a mission. Despite budgetary constraints, a probe of Halley's Comet in 1986 is being planned for the valuable data it would provide not only about comets but also about the origin of the solar system.

Discovered in 1900 and definitely associated with the October Draconid meteor shower, periodic comet Giacobini-Zinner (1959VIII) is viewed on October 12, 1959, in photographs on the same scale in blue light (left) and yellow light (right) with exposures of 15 and 45 minutes, respectively. The blue-light photograph shows the distribution of material strongly emitting in blue light (by a process of fluorescence, activated by sunlight)—principally CN, C_3, and NH of the head, and CO^+ and other ionized molecules in the tail. The yellow-light photograph shows the distribution of a few neutral molecules of C_2, but the principal contribution is of small solid particles that simply reflect and scatter sunlight.

Chapter IX

Atmospheres of the Planets and Their Satellites

"There was the veil through which I might not see."
        Omar Khayyam

Earthlings are aware, either consciously or unconsciously, of the atmosphere enveloping Mother Earth. Little thought is given to the gases that provide the oxygen needed for mammals, the carbon dioxide for the flora, but we are always unhappy when it rains on our picnic, or when it doesn't rain to make the crops grow. What of the moon, the other planets, and their satellites? Do they even have atmospheres? The answer is that some planets and satellites have atmospheres and some don't. Also, each atmosphere is different. But how do astronomers learn about these different planetary and satellite atmospheres?

Detection of Atmospheres

The most direct way to detect an atmosphere is to get a telescope and look at the planet. Earth's clouds were obvious to the Apollo astronauts. A casual observer, a low-powered telescope, and a momentary viewing are all that is required to establish that the planets Venus, Jupiter, and Saturn are surrounded by those gaseous envelopes known as atmospheres. Mars's atmosphere too makes its presence obvious. At first glance the casual observer would claim that there is no atmosphere about the moon or Mercury.

One rough indicator of an atmosphere around a body is its reflectivity, or albedo (Table 3). The moon and Mercury have very low average albedos—Mercury 0.056 and the moon 0.067. Venus's albedo, in contrast, is 0.72, Mars's is 0.16; the earth's has been estimated at about 0.39, Jupiter's is 0.70, and Saturn's is 0.75. On the basis of albedo alone, the moon and Mercury are immediately set apart. It is a great temptation to attribute their low reflectivity to the absence of an atmosphere and thus clouds to reflect the light.

During an eclipse of the sun it would seem that any lunar atmosphere should appear as a delicate, luminous fringe along its edge. Peer as they will, however, astronomers have not seen this fringe—which proves only that the moon does not have a heavy atmosphere. A very thin one might well not appear against or near the glaring and mobile surface of the sun or its corona. The moon's edge (or limb, as it is called) as seen from earth simply appears dark, clear-cut, and scalloped with mountains under these circumstances. But as a test for an atmosphere this is much too crude and hardly conclusive.

A second method of checking out the moon's atmosphere is observing it as the lunar limb occults, or passes in front of, one of the brighter stars. When an occultation of a star by Venus or Mars is observed, the star dims perceptibly and quite rapidly as its light passes through thickening layers of the planets' atmospheres. Lunar observers report to the contrary that the point of light from the bright star remains steady and then is suddenly cut off as it passes behind the limb of the moon, "snapping out" as an electric light does when the switch is flicked.

The presence of even a very thin atmosphere, perhaps down to one ten-thousandth of the density of the earth's at sea level, should produce a twilight effect by scattering the sunlight falling on it. This effect should be noticeable in the extension of the sharp horns, or cusps, of the crescent moon along the limb of the moon beyond the terminator, the line dividing the lighted side of the moon from the dark side. It might also be observable in the scattering of light across the terminator itself into the dark side on the disk of the moon, when gases were present in the area. What has been discovered on this score?

Not at every crescent moon, but on rare occasions, several skilled observers have noted the twilight effect in the extension of the cusps of the moon. This effect may, however, be hard to distinguish from the well-known earthshine, the dim reflection by the moon of light from the earth. Earthshine should be visible across the face of the darkened moon as a widespread dim glow, not concentrated at the cusps or along the terminator of the moon, and astronomers who have seen the cusp extension maintain it is not earthshine. High mountains range around the South Pole of the moon, with sizable peaks also near the North Pole. It has been suggested that the glinting of the light from these peaks after the sun has set for the lower levels produces this extension of the cusps, rather than a lunar atmosphere or a haze produced by gas emission. A long lunar ridge or mountain will often glint in the sun's light while the lower levels are still in darkness. So the twilight technique is also not a very sensitive one for distinguishing effects of a lunar atmosphere.

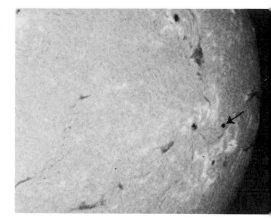

The planet Mercury (arrow) is the perfectly round black spot and the irregular patches are sunspots in this hydrogen-alpha photograph of Mercury's transit of the sun on May 9, 1970.

Distinct elongations of the horns of Venus's crescent occur frequently. The horns or cusps are often greatly extended in thin arcs, sometimes forming a complete narrow ring around the whole dark portion of the disk, proving that the Venusian atmosphere is considerable. The fuzziness or duskiness of the terminator line across the disk of Venus also reveals its atmosphere, demonstrating the scattering through the atmosphere of the light falling on the sunlit side of the disk toward the twilight and night side of the disk. Often the terminator appears much more fuzzy and less clear-cut than the limb, or lighted edge, of the disk of Venus.

Only the moon can eclipse the sun, and not all the planets show crescent phases. Occasionally Mercury and Venus pass between the earth and the sun. During such a transit they appear as tiny black dots crossing the disk of the blazing sun and look smaller than some sunspots. Early astronomers, hoping to find some hint of an atmosphere, concentrated on Mercury's transits, which occur every 5 to 10 years. Some of the early observers saw a light ring appearing around the dark disk of the planet when it passed in front of the sun. This gave rise to the belief that Mercury had a huge atmosphere, and this belief persisted for a long time. Other observers saw a gray or a dark-colored ring instead. It was finally concluded that the ring was an illusion caused by the extreme contrast of the black planet and the sun's flaming surface. Contemporary observation of Mercury in its transits shows no such misty ring. Photographs taken on May 11, 1937, as Mercury appeared to be passing through the corona only a few minutes of arc from the sun's limb, proved this conclusively.

The light coming from the planets and satellites provides clues to the composition of their atmospheres. Every chemical element and compound emits and absorbs light energy at wavelengths that are unique to that element or compound. The light coming from a planet is spread into its various colors and photographed through an instrument called a spectrograph. Some objects in the solar system shine by reflected sunlight, but the sun's contribution to the spectrum can be subtracted. The features remaining are unique to the planet. By measuring the position or wavelength of these features astronomers can determine the element responsible for the feature in the spectrum. Just as no two fingerprints are alike, no two elements produce the same spectral features.

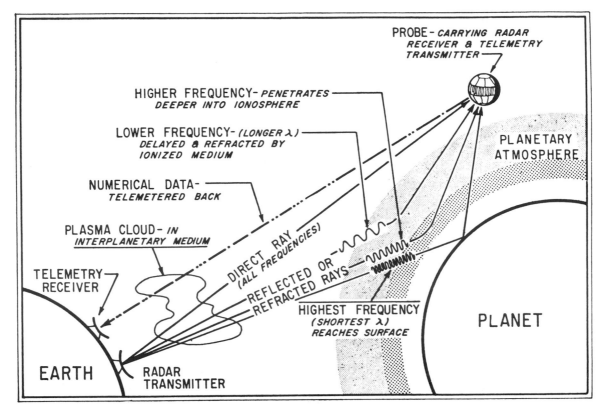

Bistatic radar astronomy technique for study of features of interplanetary space and of the atmospheres and surfaces of planets: retransmitting rays from earth that have passed through or been reflected by various media from a transmitter on a space probe back to a telemetry receiver on earth for analysis of the effects of their travel (λ=wavelength).

The space age has provided astronomers with a new technique, bistatic radar, to study planetary surfaces as well as planetary atmospheres. Bistatic radar involves a powerful radar transmitter as well as a large receiving antenna on the earth and a smaller receiver and retransmitter on a space vehicle or probe. The earth transmitter sends out radar pulses that go directly to the space probe as it flies by the moon or another planet and is also reflected from the other body and back to the space probe. The probe then directly retransmits both signals and they are picked up by the receiving antenna on earth. This process shows a clear difference between the signals that have only gone directly to the probe and those that have echoed from the other body, and so make it possible to cancel out the effect of interplanetary space on the signals. Bistatic radar systems can be used in detailed studies of planetary ionospheres, atmospheres, and surfaces, without landing on them or even approaching very close to them. Such systems can also be used in analyses of the solar corona, and the interplanetary medium itself, to say nothing of enabling the more precise measurement of interplanetary distances.

Why do some planets and satellites have atmospheres and others don't? Also, why do the various atmospheres have different compositions, since every object presumably had a common origin? Two properties dictate whether a planet has an atmosphere: its mass and its temperature. The mass of the planet determines the velocity that an object, whether it be a simple atom or a huge rocketship, must have to leave its gravitational influence. The escape velocity of the earth is 11.2 km (7 mi) a second, for Jupiter a whopping 61 km (38 mi) a second. The greater the mass of a planet, the greater is its escape velocity. The second property, temperature, dictates the average velocity at

106

which the atoms and molecules in the atmosphere move about. As with mass, the atmospheric constituents move faster with a higher temperature. The lighter constituents, like hydrogen, would be moving faster than the average value, while the heavier molecules would be moving slower. With time the light elements leave the planet. The net result is that a large, cool planet like Jupiter would be able to retain its original atmosphere, while Mercury, small and hot, should have lost its atmosphere. The earth also lost most of its original atmosphere, consisting of hydrogen and helium. Jupiter, though, still tightly grips its original material. The atmosphere currently enveloping the earth resulted from outgassing, chiefly from volcanic activity. Nitrogen and oxygen, being heavier than hydrogen, could not escape and constitute the bulk of the earth's atmosphere.

Veil Around Mercury

Mercury is small. Its diameter is 4,850 km (3,013 mi), a bit larger than the moon's and a little more than one third of the earth's. Yet its density is nearly as great as that of our own planet, which makes it considerably more compact than either the moon or Mars and probably slightly more dense than Venus.

One would expect such a dense body to have a high gravitational field, but because of Mercury's small size the escape velocity from its gravitational field is only 4.2 km (2.6 mi) per second, in contrast to the earth's 11.2 km (7.0 mi) per second. The acceleration of gravity is only 363 cm (11.9 ft) per second per second at Mercury's surface, compared with the earth's 982 cm (32 ft) per second per second. Thus atmospheric gases would not be so tightly bound in Mercury's gravitational field as they are in the earth's.

Physical conditions on Mercury bespeak very little, if any, atmosphere. With its small size and low gravitational attraction, gases on its surface must escape very quickly. Temperatures on Mercury's daytime side run high, almost 700° K (800° F), as measured by Mariner 10, while on its nightime side they drop to 100° K (−280° F). This is the greatest range in temperature known in the solar system.

In February 1961, at the Crimean Astrophysical Observatory, Soviet astronomer N. A. Kozyrev obtained 20 spectrograms of the light from Mercury when it was high in the sky during a total solar eclipse. He reported emission lines in these spectrograms, which he tentatively interpreted as caused by luminescence in an atmosphere on Mercury, attributing the lines to hydrogen gas, and suggesting they indicated an atmosphere 0.01 (1/100) as dense as that of the earth, of perhaps 7 to 8 millimeters mercury pressure at the surface. He believed Mercury might have an equilibrium atmosphere of hydrogen, steadily losing it by escape into space, with fresh hydrogen from the solar wind steadily replenishing it.

Mariner 10 observations have shown that such an equilibrium atmosphere exists, but not with the density postulated by Kozyrev. Such an atmosphere probably results from the interaction of Mercury's weak magnetic field and the solar wind. Although the field strength is only about 1 percent that of the earth's, it can still influence the motions of the solar-wind particles, perhaps trapping them briefly as a thin atmosphere. The atmosphere of Mercury consists of hydrogen and helium. The atmospheric pressure is about 10^{-15} that of the earth: This means there are approximately 10,000 particles in a cubic centimeter at the surface of Mercury, while the same cubic centimeter at the surface of the earth would contain 10 billion particles. Mercury is indeed surrounded by a thin veil!

The Tropics of Venus

As either the Morning Star or the Evening Star, gleaming brightly in the sky just before sunrise or after sunset, Venus is rather difficult to observe. The earth's atmosphere is ordinarily turbulent near the horizon, and while Venus's phase can be clearly identified by its shape, usually the planet appears to be nothing more than a blank, cottony surface, with such intense brightness that it causes trouble for the observer. Many of the best observations made of Venus have therefore been made during the daytime when the planet is high in the sky, protecting the telescope's objective with a shade. Great effort has gone into trying to penetrate Venus's mysteries by prolonged visual and photographic observation.

These observations reveal that Venus is swathed in a dense, almost opaque, yellowish-white atmosphere of clouds. The bright rim of this atmosphere has been viewed on those rare occasions when Venus makes a solar transit, and the atmosphere definitely affects the light from bright stars when Venus occults them.

Venus's atmosphere has certain features remarked on by most persistent observers. Dusky, dim shadings can be viewed across the disk; these have been photographed quite clearly. Bright areas may also appear and persist for some time. Venus has cusp caps that seem to wax and wane in intensity, and on rare occasions a strange "ashen light," somewhat like the earthshine reflected from the earth on the moon, has been viewed on Venus's darkened side.

Observations of Venus with more effective techniques (like studies with filtered light, studies of the polarization of the light, and by spectroscopic and radar instruments) reveal that considerable amounts of carbon dioxide compose part of the atmosphere of Venus, greatly exceeding the proportion of this gas in the earth's atmosphere. There have been spectroscopic indications of carbon monoxide in the Venus daytime atmosphere. It has also been asserted that there is water vapor there.

Venus had long been suggested as a sister planet to the earth. Venus's gross properties, size, mass, and density supported this belief. Nor did the detection of carbon dioxide, nitrogen, and water vapor in the Cytherean atmosphere contradict it. This belief was shattered on December 14, 1962, when American space probe Mariner 2 flew past Venus at a distance of 34,850 km (21,648 mi) from its surface. Mariner 2 was the first space vehicle ever to fly by another planet. Mariner 2's few, carefully selected instruments reported unexpected data that went far toward proving that the planet is unique in many ways. The data definitely imply that Venus is not a sister planet of the earth.

Two radiometers aboard Mariner 2 showed that they had picked up emissions from Venus's atmosphere and surface and further opened the lid of its Pandora's box of mysteries. They implied little water vapor in Venus's atmosphere, less than 0.001 (1/1000) of that in the earth's atmosphere. The extremely high temperatures of 533° to 698°K (500° to 800°F), inferred from radio-echo studies, were confirmed. The amount of carbon dioxide in the atmosphere is considerable, and no breaks in the cloud cover were found over the regions scanned by Mariner 2.

Since then numerous Russian and American space probes have flown by and flown through the Cytherean atmosphere. Venus came under considerable scrutiny in December 1979 when 2 Russian Venera and the American Pioneer Venus spacecraft photographed, probed, and sniffed the Venusian atmosphere.

The Pioneer Venus mission consisted of 5 probes and an orbiter. The probes passed through the atmosphere at different locations. The orbiter was placed in a polar orbit and was designed to operate for over 243 days. This allowed the study of Venus and its interaction with the solar wind through a rotation period as well as a revolution of the sun.

Early missions had shown that the clouds of Venus whipped around the planet every 4 to 6 days. Furthermore, a Y-shaped feature was observed by Mariner 10 that some astronomers thought may be a permanent feature. Pioneer photographs suggest otherwise. At times the Y is completely absent, at others there is a very loose Y. It is possible that the Y feature is not a single feature, but rather a combination of cloud patterns.

The clouds of Venus are divided into four distinct regions, as shown in the figure. Clouds are first encountered at about 66 km (41 mi) above the surface. This upper cloud region consists of sulfuric-acid particles approximately 1 micrometer (one-millionth meter) in radius. A fairly sharp transition occurs at 58 km (36 mi), marking the boundary between the upper and the middle cloud regions. The size of the particles increases in the middle cloud region, which may be sulfur crystals. The lower clouds in the region from 49 to 52 km (30 to 32 mi) above the surface have been called "real clouds," since little light can penetrate them, just as it is difficult for light to pass through earth's clouds. Sulfuric-acid particles 8 to 10 micrometers in diameter make up these clouds. The clouds end abruptly at 49 km (30 mi) and are replaced by a haze extending to 31 km (19 mi). This extremely thin haze has only about 1 particle in every cubic cm of space. Below this no particles were detected down to the surface. The clouds appear to have a structure more like stratus than cumulus clouds. Mist and drizzle may be produced within the clouds, but it is unlikely that heavy precipitation occurs. The Russians have reported that Venera 12 encountered "inclement weather" about 10 km (6 mi) above the surface and recorded fairly frequent electrical discharges (lightning) during the descent. The temperature at the cloud tops is 230°K (-45°F) and increases to 346°K (163°F) at the boundary between the middle and lower cloud regions. At the bottom of the lower cloud region the temperature has risen to a sizzling 493°K (428°F).

Although the clouds, with their sulfuric-acid droplets and sulfur crystals are the most obvious features of the lower atmosphere of Venus, they represent only a minute fraction of the atmosphere. Ninety percent of the atmosphere lies below the clouds. Carbon dioxide constitutes a little more than 96 percent of the volume of Venus's atmosphere; molecular nitrogen (N_2) adds another 3.5 percent. Traces of argon, neon, carbon monoxide, molecular oxygen (O_2), sulfur dioxide, and water have also been detected. Water makes up only a few tenths of a percent of the volume of Venus's atmosphere.

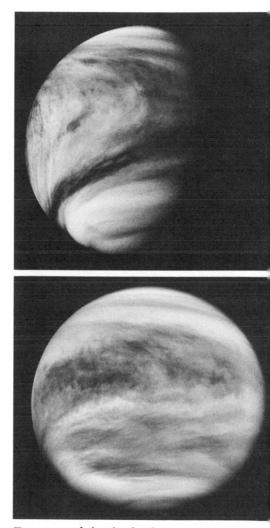

Two views of the clouds of Venus taken by Pioneer Venus show that the Y feature first observed by Mariner 10 may not be permanent. The top photograph, taken on January 14, 1979, shows the fork of the Y lying on its side with the bottom part out of view to the right. Nearly a month later, on February 12, the bottom photograph taken by Pioneer Venus shows no strong evidence for the Y feature. Both photographs were taken 65,000 km (40,000 mi) above Venus's surface.

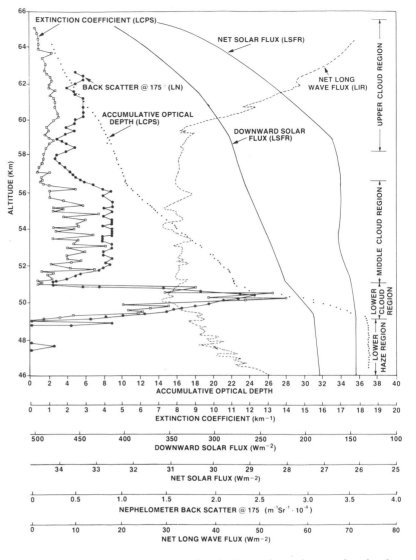

As the various probes from Pioneer Venus passed through the clouds of Venus, they recorded data to produce this profile of the Venusian cloud system. Among the quantities measured are the amount of sunlight passing through the clouds at long wavelengths, the total amount of solar radiation, particle size, and the amount of absorption. Along the right side of the figure 4 distinct cloud regions are denoted. The lower cloud region between 49 and 52 km (30 and 32 mi) can be considered as a "real cloud" region, as the amounts of absorption and scattering increase rapidly, as in terrestrial clouds.

The upper atmosphere can be divided into three distinct levels: the turbosphere, the exosphere, and the ionosphere. The turbopause, at a height of 145 km (90 mi), is the lower boundary of the turbosphere. It also marks a chemical separation of the atmosphere. Below it the composition is fairly homogeneous; above it the constituents separate into distinct layers. The exosphere begins at the exobase, 190 km (118 mi) above the surface. In this part of the atmosphere the atoms and molecules can obtain enough energy to escape the gravitational influence of Venus.

The magnetosphere shields the earth from the solar wind. Since Venus has no magnetic field, the ionosphere is buffeted by particles and radiation of the solar wind. The ionopause, marking the boundary between the ionosphere and the solar wind, is subject to the vagaries of the latter. The height of the ionopause above the surface depends on the velocity and strength of the solar wind. It has been detected at 250 km (155 mi) and 1,500 km (930 mi) above the surface.

One unanswered question is why Venus has an ionosphere at all. During daylight hours the sun's radiation can break molecules and atoms apart, forming ions and electrons in the ionosphere. During the night, however, they should recombine, since the sun is below the horizon. This occurs in the lower ionosphere of the earth. One earth night is not sufficient time to complete the recombination process, so the earth's ionosphere remains. But night lasts 8 weeks on Venus, more than enough time for the ionosphere to dissipate. Measurements indicate, however, the presence of an ionosphere throughout the night. Perhaps its existence is related to the 4-to-6-day cloud circulation.

Few people would agree today with Nobel Laureate Svante Arrhenius, who believed that Venus supported luxuriant vegetation. The surface temperature is a scorching 750°K (nearly 900°F). This high temperature probably results from an extreme greenhouse effect operating on Venus. The solar radiation is absorbed by the surface and is reradiated at long wavelengths. The carbon dioxide traps this radiation, which heats the surroundings.

The atmospheric pressure is also a staggering, bone-crushing 90 kilograms per square centimeter (1,280 pounds per square inch), 90 times the pressure on the earth's surface. Photographs of the Venusian surface taken by Venera 9 and 10 reveal a rocky desert. No bright blue sky exists on Venus. The majority of the incoming sunlight is absorbed in Venus's clouds. Venera 8 determined that only 1 percent of this sunlight reached the surface. The daytime illumination has been compared to a midday overcast on the earth. Venus is hardly a sister planet!

The Winds of Mars

Anyone who has observed the planet Mars even for a short time can assure you that it has an atmosphere. Clouds, mists, and hazes have been clearly observable from the earth. Frequent variations also reveal its presence. The atmosphere of Mars has been susceptible to the usual earth-based proofs. Photographs in red and infrared light penetrate deeply into its atmosphere, while plates taken in the violet or ultraviolet record the outer portions of the atmosphere. Spectroscopic and polarization observations placed limits on the amount of water vapor in the atmosphere. All earth-based data led to speculations, often incorrect, about the Martian atmosphere. Not until Mariner 9 in 1971 and the Viking missions in 1976 did definite answers about the Martian atmosphere become available.

The lower atmosphere of Mars is mostly carbon dioxide (95.3 percent); molecular nitrogen (2.7 percent) is the next most abundant constituent, followed by argon (1.6 percent), molecular oxygen (0.13 percent), carbon monoxide (0.07 percent), and varying minute amounts of water vapor. Traces of neon, krypton, xenon, and ozone have also been detected. The surface atmospheric pressure is roughly 6 millibars, about 0.005 (1/200th) that of the earth. The Viking cameras on the landers recorded a pinkish-yellow sky. The temperatures at the two Viking Lander sites ranged during the summer from around 187° K (−123° F) at night to 244° K (−20° F) in the afternoon. Winds during the summer were light, ranging from 2 to 7 meters per second (5 to 15 mi per hour).

As the landers dropped to the surface, the particle density and temperature were continuously monitered. The density changed fairly smoothly, as seen in the graph. The temperature showed variations, especially between 50 and 100 km (30 and 60 mi) due to the tidal winds, planetwide oscillations in the wind patterns. In this region alternate layers of sinking gas are compressionally heated, while the rising gases cool as they expand.

The Martian turbopause occurs at 120 km (75 mi). Below this the at-

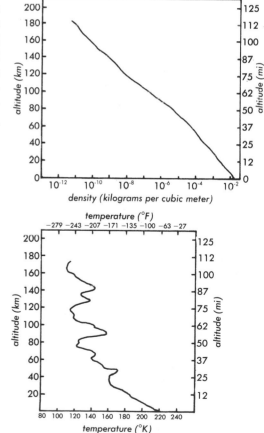

As the Viking 1 and 2 Landers passed through the thin Martian atmosphere they measured the particle density (top) and the temperature (bottom) at different altitudes.

mosphere is well mixed, giving a uniform composition, while above it the gases separate out; the lightest rise to the top and eventually escape into space. Mars has an F_1 ionosphere similar to one of the terrestrial ionospheric layers. The maximum number of ions, about 100,000 per cubic cm, occurs just below the 130 km (80 mi) level. Ninety percent of the ions are O_2^+, while CO_2^+ makes up the remaining 10 percent. The number of particles falls off steadily with altitude. At 300 km (186 mi) there are only about 100 particles per cubic cm. As the drawing indicates, the temperature fluctuates with altitude. At the surface, the temperature is about 220°K (−65°F). At 120 km (75 mi) the temperature has decreased to about 125°K (−235°F). Data indicate that the temperature may increase to 200°K (−100°F) or higher at 200 km (125 mi).

Analysis shows that 4 types of clouds exist in the Martian atmosphere. Convective clouds form when gas heated near the surface during the day rises into the atmosphere and cools as it expands. Clouds form into distinct puffs, uniformly shaped and evenly spaced, when the temperature reaches the saturation point.

When a stormy wind blows steadily across an obstacle, like a rise, atmospheric waves, similar to water waves, form on the protected side of the obstacle. If temperature and moisture conditions are right, clouds form at the crests of the waves. These wave clouds appear to hang motionless in the atmosphere.

The third type of cloud, an orographic cloud, forms when atmospheric gas is forced to move slowly and steadily up the slow rise of a large upland. The higher volcanic regions are typical sites of such clouds, which have frequently been observed. The clouds are probably composed principally of water ice condensed from the atmosphere while moving up the slopes of the volcanoes. The Martian volcanoes are often enveloped in clouds during spring and summer in the Northern Hemisphere.

Perhaps the most surprising observation of the orbiters was the number of low-lying areas exhibiting ground fog in the early morning. The fog is seen day after day in the same areas, implying that a new layer of frost is deposited each evening. As the warming sun vaporizes the frost each morning it rises into the chilly morning air, where it once again condenses, forming fog.

It is assumed that the majority of clouds consist of water ice. The diffuse edges of most of the Martian clouds support this belief. However, the Mariner and Viking spacecraft have photographed clouds with sharp edges. In the polar regions during winter and at high altitudes, the temperature is so low the carbon dioxide can condense into clouds of dry ice.

The winds recorded at the Viking Lander sites were light as expected for that region and time of year (the Northern Hemisphere in summer). Much stronger winds must exist, however, since great dust

This view of the horizon recorded by the cameras of Viking Orbiter 1 on July 11, 1976, shows clouds, or layers of haze, 25 to 40 km (15 to 25 mi) above the Martian surface. These clouds are believed to be crystals of carbon dioxide (dry ice).

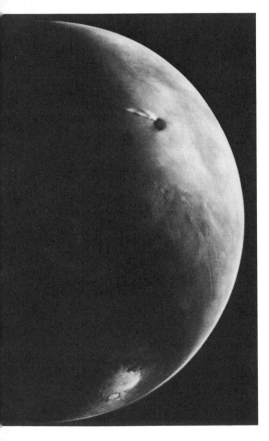

As Viking 2 approached Mars it snapped this picture from a distance of 419,000 km (260,355 mi). Near the top a white water-ice cloud stretches northwest from the volcano Ascraeus Mons. The gash below this volcano is the Valles Marineris, an extensive canyon system many times larger than earth's Grand Canyon. The Argyre Basin is the impact crater outlined at the bottom of the photograph. Near the South Pole of Mars, the crater is covered by frost and fogs as the Southern Hemisphere experiences winter.

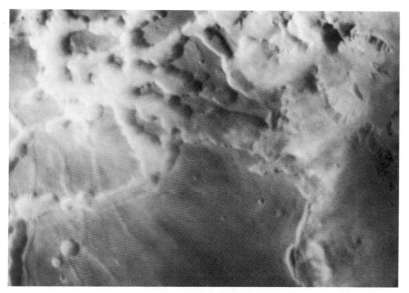

Fog fills Noctis Labyrinthus at sunrise. This Martian region, sometimes called the Chandelier, is at the west end of Valles Marineris. The fog indicates that water, although scarce by earthly standards, does exist in the Martian atmosphere.

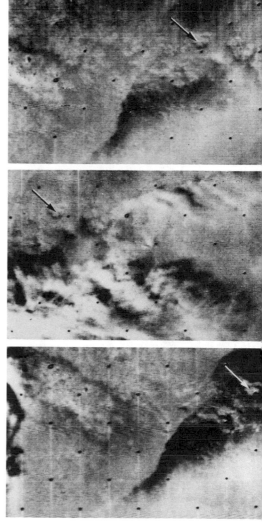

storms long have been observed from the earth. These massive storms usually occur early each Martian year when Mars is at perihelion. Such a storm usually begins suddenly in the Noachis region in the southern tropics. It is initially observed as a long white feature several thousand kilometers long. For the first few days the central dust cloud expands slowly, then rapidly, until it completely encircles the planet in several weeks. Branches of the storm form and stretch to higher and lower latitudes. Within a month the entire Southern Hemisphere is covered. Occasionally, the storm spreads into the Northern Hemisphere and completely obliterates any surface feature under a cloud of dust. Such a global storm greeted Mariner 9 in 1971.

Once in the atmosphere the small dust particles can remain suspended for weeks and months. As the winds subside, the dust eventually settles to the surface and the atmosphere again becomes transparent. Winds of only 6 to 7 meters a second (13 to 16 mi per hour) are required to lift grains of sand from terrestrial deserts. Because of the thin Martian atmosphere winds of at least 30 to 60 meters a second (67 to 135 mi per hour) are necessary to lift the sand grains on Mars.

The source of these winds remains a mystery. One theory suggests that within a limited area, like the Noachis region, the local surface winds and the global winds combine to reach a velocity sufficiently high to raise dust into the atmosphere. Then the atmosphere in this localized area further heats up due to the increased amount of dust in it. Dust particles can absorb sunlight and heat the surrounding atmospheric gases quite efficiently. If the atmosphere contains a sufficient amount of dust, the global tidal winds can grow in intensity and become nearly strong enough to raise the dust themselves. As the dust spreads by the winds, so does the heated area of atmosphere. By repeating this process, the storm continues to develop and spreads over a larger and larger area.

Recently the cameras of the Viking 1 Orbiter recorded the first two

The winds of Mars may be responsible for the markings seen on Mars from the earth. This sequence of 3 photographs shows the changes that occurred in the Euxinus Lacus region above the Martian equator. The arrows point to the same crater in each photograph. The top photograph shows normal conditions in the area, with a dark marking in the center. The middle photograph, taken 24 hours later, shows a large dust storm, 480 km (300 mi) wide, sweeping from west (left) to east (right) across the region. The bottom photograph, taken 2 weeks later, shows that the dark marking in the top photograph has become blacker and much larger! A new dust storm is appearing (left) on the bottom photograph. The winds in the first dust storm may have uncovered a dark area of lighter-colored dust, causing the enhancement of the dark marking. Perhaps the alternate covering and uncovering of a dark surface by wind-blown, light-colored dust cause the changes in the dark markings on Mars.

A large storm observed near the polar front on Mars on August 9, 1978, by Viking Orbiter 1. A polar front is a temperature boundary separating the cold air at the pole from the warmer air to the south. This storm resembles the cyclones near the polar front on earth. Its counterclockwise circulation is consistent with winds expected in a low pressure situation as a cyclone. The frost-filled crater Korolev, approximately 92 km (58 mi) in diameter, is the white oval-shaped feature above and to the right of the cyclone. The remaining white patches are part of the north polar remnant ice cap. The clouds forming the cyclone are believed to be water ice.

cyclones observed on Mars. Mariner 9 had earlier hinted that pressure systems associated with cyclones may exist during late winter over the northern polar region. The two cyclones were observed in the Northern Hemisphere during the summer. One, located almost at the edge of the northern polar cap, had the characteristic spiral-cloud pattern of a cyclone. It appeared to be 4 km (2.5 mi) above the ground with wind speeds of 31.5 meters a second (70 mi an hour) in the cloud and about 12.6 meters a second (28 mi an hour) near the surface. The second, farther to the south, was estimated to be 6 to 7 km (about 4 mi) above the surface with wind speeds of 23.1 meters a second (52 mi an hour) in the cloud and 9.2 meters a second (20 mi an hour) near the ground. Probably both systems were composed of water ice crystals.

One of the primary missions of Viking was to search for water. None has been found flowing on the surface, although it may have at one time. Water vapor was known to exist on Mars because of the existence of clouds. The Mars Atmospheric Water Detector (MAWD) aboard the Viking Orbiters was designed to study the amount of water vapor in the atmosphere. For the period just after a solstice to the following equinox the results indicate that the total amount of water vapor present in the atmosphere is constant but the amount over any particular area changes with time. Strong latitudinal (north and south) dependence also occurs. The maximum amount of water vapor occurs over the northern polar ice during the summer. As fall approaches, the maximum shifts to lower latitudes, but the maximum at the lower latitudes never attains the polar value.

One way of measuring the amount of water vapor in the atmosphere is by converting the amount of water vapor in a column stretching from the surface to the top of the atmosphere into a liquid equivalent. The result is the "precipitable centimeter," the depth of the water if it precipitated. The earth's atmosphere normally contains 2 to 3 precipitable centimeters of water. The Viking orbiters determined Martian values ranging from less than 10^{-4} precipitable centimeter in high southern latitudes in midwinter to 10^{-2} precipitable centimeter over dark material in the northern circumpolar region. The residual summer ice cap at the North Pole was also found to be dirty-water ice, not frozen carbon dioxide (dry ice).

Daily variations in Martian water-vapor content were also investigated. Regional effects were detected. These may result from other influences, such as dust and condensate particles. The large daily variations seen from earth may result from an observational effect. Among the questions yet to be answered are what mechanisms control the seasonal redistribution of water vapor. Does the water vapor migrate during the course of the year from the Northern Hemisphere to the Southern Hemisphere and back, and most importantly, are there major subsurface reservoirs of water ice other than those at the poles?

Venus, Earth, and Mars: A Comparison

It is hoped that study of the atmospheres of Venus and of Mars will help man better understand the earth's. The atmosphere of Mars is similar to earth's in chemistry and pressure. The length of the Martian day and the tilt of Mars's rotation axis are also similar to the earth's. The wind patterns should also be similar to the earth's. The rapid rotation of the Venusian clouds should provide clues to the circulation of large air masses.

Atmospheres of the Planets and Their Satellites

The atmospheric compositions of Venus, earth, and Mars are compared in the pie-charts. At first glance, the earth seems to be grossly different from the other two. But if all the carbon dioxide trapped in carbonates in the earth's oceans and crust were added, the amount of carbon dioxide on the earth and on Venus would be the same.

Among the many surprises greeting scientists were the relatively large amounts of helium, neon, and argon-36 in Venus's atmosphere. These gases are rare in the earth's atmosphere but are common in the universe. Having formed out of the solar nebula, the earth had these elements in its primordial atmosphere. As the earth heated, it lost these gases into interplanetary space. Earth's present atmosphere is the result of outgassing, primarily through volcanic activity. It is believed that Venus and Mars had similar histories. This is supported in part by the presence of volcanoes on both bodies.

On earth the dominant form of argon is argon-40, created by the radioactive decay of potassium-40. For every atom of argon-36 there are approximately 300 argon-40 atoms. This ratio is even higher on Mars. Nearly equal amounts of argon-36 and argon-40 exist on Venus. For every 85 argon-36 atoms there are 100 argon-40 atoms. The ratios of nitrogen-15 to nitrogen-14, and carbon-12 to carbon-13, as well as the ratio of neon-20 to argon-32 are similar on all three planets. The value of this ratio, 0.5, is definitely terrestrial and differs greatly from the solar value of 31. The implication of these measurements is that the terrestrial and Martian atmospheres evolved as expected. Venus, however, evolved differently. The relatively large numbers of noble gases (those that don't combine with others) imply that Venus either retained some of its primordial atmosphere, or it formed from material different from earth and Mars.

Jupiter Kaleidoscope

From the earth, Jupiter's light is on the whole more yellowish than the sun's. Jupiter has yellow zones with a series of gray belts parallel to its equator. Some of the darker gray has a brownish cast, and traces of pink or blue can be seen occasionally. Some very white zones stand out in contrast to the yellowness. And there is the Great Red Spot, discovered by Giovanni Cassini in 1665. The names adopted for Jupiter's zones and belts are shown in the chart. Some are labeled in the photograph.

The light zones and dark belts around Jupiter must trace currents in its atmosphere that are maintained by its rapid, 10-hour rotation. While the belts are semipermanent, their position, size, and form vary, and sometimes the variations occur very rapidly.

The Pioneer missions to Jupiter revealed that the light zones are colder, and therefore higher in the atmosphere, than the dark belts. Temperature measurements indicate that the zones are regions of rising gas and the belts are regions of descending gas. The average temperature for Jupiter is 128°K (−229°F). Furthermore, the temperature is fairly uniform. The night-side and day-side temperatures are identical. Variations on the order of 2°K (about 4°F) were found between the belts and the zones. Additional variations occur in the upper troposphere and the lower stratosphere.

The Great Red Spot in Jupiter's South Tropical Zone has maintained its elliptical shape over the years, but it has moved up and down in latitude and wandered in longitude. Its width is fairly constant at

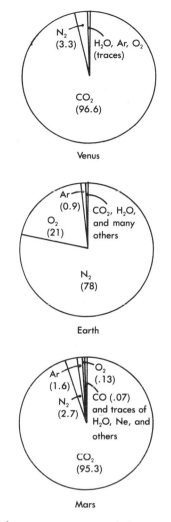

The relative compositions of the earth, Mars, and Venus are represented in these pie diagrams. Carbon dioxide comprises the main constituent of the atmospheres of Venus and Mars (96.6 and 95.3 percent, respectively), while the earth's main atmospheric ingredient is molecular nitrogen at 78 percent.

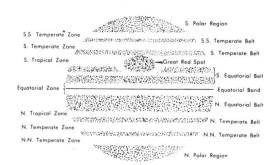

Chart of Jupiter's dark belts and lighter zones with the names that have come to be used for them, and the position of the Great Red Spot. North is at the bottom.

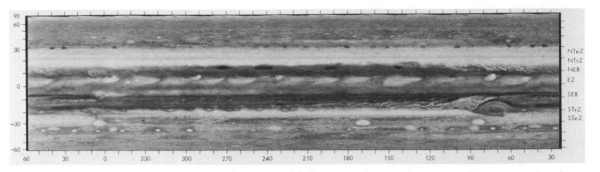

Jupiter's zones and belts are evident in this image of Jupiter produced by combining 10 images taken on February 1, 1979. The abbreviations on the right edge of the photograph identify the major belts (dark features) and zones (light features): NTeZ, North Temperate Zone; NTrZ, North Tropical Zone; NEB, North Equatorial Belt; EZ, Equatorial Zone; SEB, South Equatorial Belt; STrZ, South Tropical Zone; and STeZ, South Temperate Zone. North is at the top.

about 14,000 km (8,700 mi), but its length varies from 30,000 to 40,000 km (18,600 to 24,800 mi). This feature is large enough to contain a dozen earths.

The Great Red Spot is similar to a hurricane on the earth. The rotation in this feature is anticyclonic (counterclockwise in the South). The driving force maintaining this spot is not understood, but evidence indicates that material is rising within it and spirals out from the center. A number of white oval and other anticyclonic spots similar to the Great Red Spot are known to exist at midlatitudes. Unlike the Great Red Spot, however, these are transient features. This presents a new problem for theorists: Why do these features come and go while the Great Red Spot has persisted for some 300 years?

The Voyager missions to Jupiter have provided scientists with their first clues to the structure of the atmosphere. It is not known whether Jupiter has a surface, so temperatures must be given in terms of pressures. Preliminary results indicate that over the South Equatorial Belt a warm temperature inversion layer occurs at about 35 millibars. Below this a tropopause occurs at a pressure level of 100 millibars and temperature of $113°K$ ($-256°F$). At still lower altitudes the temperature has risen to $150°K$ ($-189°F$) at a pressure of 600 millibars.

Lightning and auroras have been detected on the night side of Jupiter by Voyager. The auroras occur in at least three layers about 700 km (435 mi), 1,400 km (879 mi), and 2,300 km (1,430 mi) above the cloud tops. They are brighter than those on earth and vary on time scales less than a minute.

Like everything else on Jupiter, the lightning bolts are impressive. They are comparable in strength to the superbolts observed near the earth's cloud tops, about 10 billion joules (3,000 kilowatt-hours) of energy. The bolts do not appear to be localized but occur uniformly over the dark side. The lightning also occurs in clusters of bolts.

Jupiter's great bulk and distance from the sun guarantee that Jupiter has probably retained its original atmosphere. Its low density supports the contention that Jupiter's chemical composition is similar to the sun's and should contain mostly hydrogen and helium. Ground-based observations have revealed the presence of hydrogen, methane, ammonia, ethane, acetylene, and phosphine. Infrared observations of Jupiter by the Voyager 1 spacecraft have added deuterated methane (one of the hydrogen atoms in ordinary methane has been replaced by

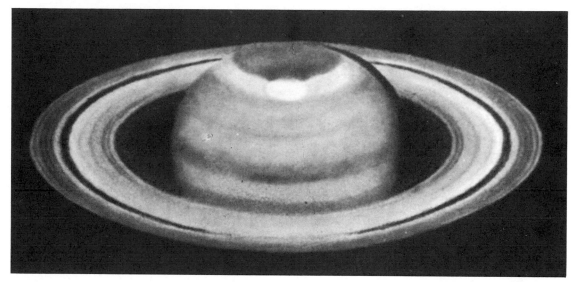

a deuterium atom, heavy hydrogen), water, and germanium hydride. Helium was also found to constitute 11 percent of the atmosphere. The clouds and belts visible above Jupiter probably are frozen ammonia crystals. Below these clouds, a slightly more massive cloud of ammonium hydrosulfide particles may exist on top of a layer of water ice crystals.

Aesthetic Saturn

Saturn's light is yellower than that of the sun. Yellow and green colors predominate in Saturn's atmosphere. Belts band it, too. They are parallel to its equator and much less distinct than Jupiter's. The belts also change in form and appearance. Rare white spots may indicate eruptions or storms at lower levels on the planet.

Methane, ammonia, hydrogen, and ethane have been identified in Saturn's atmosphere, and it must also contain large quantities of helium, with perhaps nitrogen, neon, and other inert gases in small amounts. Again, the visible clouds must be frozen crystals of ammonia in turbulent rotation with the planet, with perhaps a cooler zone of lighter gases above them. Like the sun, both Saturn and Jupiter have differential speeds of rotation of their equatorial atmosphere and the atmosphere at high latitudes.

Saturn clearly reveals its dark belts and lighter zones (north at top) and its outer, middle, and inner or "crepe" rings in a drawing made using the 61-cm (24-inch) Pic-du-Midi telescope on April 27, 1960. One of the rare white spots appears in Saturn's atmosphere at 60° north. White spots were recorded before—in 1876, 1903, and 1933. By May 5 the spot had faded, forming a bright regular zone around Saturn at this latitude.

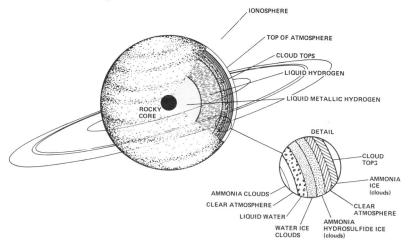

A model of Saturn's atmosphere has layers of ammonia and water on top of liquid hydrogen. Saturn's atmosphere is believed to be similar to the atmosphere of Jupiter.

Saturn appears reluctant to reveal the secrets of its atmosphere. As the Voyager 1 spacecraft approached Saturn in November 1980, scientists were expecting to see more and more detail in the Saturnian atmosphere, just as Jupiter revealed its atmospheric secrets to the approaching Voyager 1 and Voyager 2 spacecraft. Although a large oval feature 10,000 km (6,200 mi) long was detected in August 1980, Saturn, for the most part, covered its secrets in a thick haze.

Not until closest approach in mid-November did scientists learn details in the atmosphere –and these details were not scaled-down versions of those discovered for Jupiter as anticipated. On Jupiter, the boundary between belts and zones is a turbulent region with strong winds; on Saturn, however, features suggestive of such turbulence are seen in the middle of the zones with no evidence of strong winds at a belt-zone boundary. Also, the belt-zone banding extends to higher latitudes on Saturn than on Jupiter. Once again, it has been pointed out to scientists that each planet in the solar system is truly unique!

When viewed with binoculars or a small telescope, Saturn looks lopsided; small wonder that the early observers of the planet drew its shape in many different ways. Finally, it became clear that Saturn's odd protuberances were delicate rings encircling it in the plane of its equator. Observers have marveled ever since at their geometric beauty. While Saturn has a diameter of 120,000 km (about 75,000 mi), the A ring, the outer of the three rings easily distinguishable from earth, ranges far out around the planet, with a maximum diameter of 271,200 km (168,500 mi). The middle B ring is the brightest and densest, while the inner C ring or "crepe" ring is rather difficult to distinguish and, like the A ring, is so tenuous that bright stars can be seen through it. The existence of a fourth ring, the D ring, stretching from inside the C ring to at least half the distance to the top of Saturn's atmosphere, was announced in 1969. Voyager 1 confirmed this ring's existence. Pioneer 11 (Pioneer Saturn) discovered another ring, the F ring, in 1979. Two other rings, E and G, also exist.

Since the rings are lettered by their order of discovery and not by their position relative to Saturn, an imaginary trip from beyond the rings to Saturn's cloud tops is instructive. The first ring encountered in our trip inward is the very tenuous E ring. This ring begins 300,000 km (186,000 mi) or 5 Saturn radii (5R) from the center of Saturn. (The radius of Saturn is 60,000 km or 37,280 mi). Since this ring stretches to 3.35R, the satellites Tethys and Enceladus revolve about Saturn within the E ring. The very narrow G ring is the next ring encountered at 2.80R. This is followed by the F ring at 2.32R. Voyager 1 has shown this ring to be less than 100 km (62 mi) wide. Apparently, Saturn's fourteenth and fifteenth satellites, just outside and inside the F ring, are responsible for keeping this ring narrow. The cameras of Voyager 1 also revealed the F ring to consist of at least 3 individual rings, two of which are braided. Furthermore, the F ring is clumpy. One segment, 200 km (124 mi) long, has more material than the adjacent parts of the ring. Unusual gravitational effects are occurring within this ring.

The F ring is separated from the A ring by the Pioneer Division, a 3,600-km (2,240-mi) gap. Next come the A, B, and C rings at 1.97, 1.53, and 1.21 Saturn radii. These 3 rings are visible from the earth even with a relatively small telescope. Although these rings appear

118

smoother through the largest telescopes on earth, the cameras of Voyager 1 have shown them to consist of a large number of individual rings. One scientist counted at least 360 separate rings on a low-resolution photograph. The actual total may number more than 1,000 ringlets. Other surprises revealed by Voyager 1 were the existence of radial, fingerlike features in the B ring. These features, which theoretically should not exist, revolve about Saturn just as spokes revolve about the center of a wheel. Photographs of the C ring also reveal a ringlet that is not concentric with Saturn. It is 60 km (37 mi) closer to Saturn on one side of the planet than on the other. Even Cassini's Division, the 3,500-km (2,200-mi) wide gap separating the A and B rings has been found not to be empty as previously believed. At least 20 ringlets have been discovered in this presumably "empty" region. Fortunately, Voyager 1 did not travel through Cassini's Division as once suggested. The last of the major rings, the D ring, stretches from the inner edge of the C ring to at least halfway to Saturn's cloud tops.

The rings are very thin, certainly no more than 1.5 km (0.9 mi) thick. In 1965, and at about 15-year intervals, Saturn's rings are oriented exactly edge-on toward the earth; relatively paper thin, they then disappear completely for a day or two, unresolvable from the earth. Radar observations indicate that the ring particles are ice with diameters between 4 and 30 cm (1.5 and 12 inches). These particles represent the smaller sized ring material, since the Pioneer Saturn data revealed that 50 meters (165 ft) is the characteristic size for ring material.

Uranus and Neptune: Two Different Worlds

At 2,870 million km (1,783 million mi) from the sun, Uranus is not an easy object to study. In a sizable telescope, however, it shows a small blue-green disk. Very dim bands can be picked out parallel to its equator when Uranus's equatorial plane is directed toward the earth, but when its polar axis is so oriented the bands are not visible.

Spectroscopic observations of Uranus have demonstrated the presence of methane and hydrogen in its atmosphere, but at its prevailing temperature of about 58°K (−355°F) any ammonia must have been frozen out entirely. Its major gases are probably hydrogen and helium, as with the other gas giants.

Since Neptune and Uranus are approximately the same size and farther from the sun than Jupiter and Saturn, it was generally believed that the atmospheres of Neptune and Uranus would be similar. Spectroscopic observations of hydrogen and methane in both planets supported this belief. But recent evidence indicates otherwise. Ethane has been detected in Neptune's atmosphere, but not in that of Uranus. Infrared observations confirm also a substantial inversion layer in the stratosphere of Neptune. The temperature steadily decreases with altitude until high in the stratosphere at the inversion layer the temperature suddenly rises. Such an inversion layer was suggested from the data obtained during Neptune's occultation of the star BD-17°4388 in 1968. The heating of ozone by sunlight is responsible for the inversion in the earth's atmosphere, but the cause is not known for Neptune. Other infrared data indicate that the temperature of Neptune (55°K or −360°F) is greater than that expected for a planet at Neptune's distance. Neptune, like Jupiter and Saturn, has an internal heat source.

119

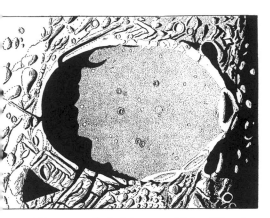

Plato, a walled plain some 96 km (60 mi) in diameter, situated in the mountainous area between the Mare Imbrium and the Mare Frigoris toward the north of the moon. This careful drawing, showing a number of the tiny crater pits within the very smooth and level plain, was made by British selenographer H. P. Wilkins on April 3, 1952, using the 53-cm (33-inch) Meudon, France, refractor.

Uranus, on the other hand, behaves as expected for a planet of its size and location in the solar system.

Differences definitely occur between Neptune and Uranus. Are these differences real or just the results of the unusual orientation of Uranus's rotation axis? Voyager 2's flyby of Uranus or careful monitoring of seasonal variations of Uranus from earth may help provide the answer.

Clues to the true nature of Pluto are difficult to obtain due to its small size and great distance from the sun. The discovery of its satellite helped to refine some of the basic data about Pluto. It is now known to be smaller than earth's moon. In 1979 frozen methane ice was detected spectroscopically on Pluto. This means that the temperature must be cooler than 40°K (−390°F).

Lunar Atmosphere Revisited

The controversy over the presence or absence of an atmosphere on the moon has exhibited the all-too-human proclivity to adopt extreme points of view and to dabble in theories that go far beyond what is actually observed. It has been habitual for most astronomers and other scientists with lunar interests to think of the moon as utterly devoid of activity or atmosphere—a dead place. American astronomer Fred L. Whipple has vividly expressed this point of view: "The moon's surface . . . is a sublime desolation. The lunar plains are more barren than rocky deserts. The lunar mountains are more austere than terrestrial peaks above the timber line. . . . There is no weather on the moon. Where there is no air there can be no clouds, no rains, no sound. Within a dark lunar cave there would be eternal silence and inaction excepting possibly moonquakes. A spider web across a dim recess in such a cave would remain perfect and unchanged for a million years." The only question remaining is: Whence came the spider?

On the opposite side of the fence are those scientists, most prominently those who have devoted lifetimes to patient observation of the moon, who report that they have seen changes taking place on the moon and even definite indications that it has an atmosphere, however slight.

Observers often tell of mists or clouds near craters on the moon, and the walled plain of Plato, just above Mare Imbrium, has been notorious for this. Now and then a colored spot or glow is seen in a crater area and is interpreted as emanating from the crater itself. If this indicates volcanic activity, this could be at least one source for gases on the moon. The crater Alphonsus may have emitted gases in 1958, and possibly again in 1959. A number of clouds or mists were said to have appeared within this crater, which is in the south-central portion of the moon, and in 1963 there were similar appearances in and near the crater Aristarchus, near the northwestern limb. The moon may well emit quite a number of such atmospheric blobs of residual gases, quickly diffused. Whether or not they form any very tenuous general atmosphere before they are swept away or escape from the moon's low gravitational field is another matter.

Radar echoes picked up by radio telescopes from signals bounced from the moon have shown unexpected drops in intensity, which implies that some of their strength was absorbed by passage through ionized gas. The ionized layers in the earth's atmosphere may have done some of the absorbing, and a slight lunar atmosphere may have absorbed the rest, but we know too little about the ionosphere to rely very heavily on speculations of this sort.

Radio astronomy has also turned up some definite evidence that there is a lunar atmosphere. The discovery was related to the fact that an atmosphere refracts radio waves in much the same way as it refracts light. In 1956 the moon occulted radio sources in the constellation Ophiuchus. Again in 1959 the moon occulted radio sources in the Crab Nebula. Observations of these two events showed refractions of radio waves that could only be caused by a lunar atmosphere. The atmosphere responsible is estimated to be only about one ten-trillionth (10^{-13}) as dense as the earth's. It might prove to be a bit denser if argon could be measured by this method—which it probably was not. In any case, however tenuous it may be, the atmosphere is unquestionably there, and a long-standing debate is settled, leaving the field wide open for speculation about how this atmosphere was generated.

With only 0.0125 (1/80) of the earth's mass and 0.17 (1/6) the earth's gravitational potential on its surface, the moon cannot have retained very much of its original atmosphere, if it had one, or of any atmosphere that may have evolved in the course of its development. Furthermore, a goodly proportion of its gases would congeal during the moon's night, when the temperature plummets to about 102°K (−275°F).

After Surveyor unmanned craft and Apollo astronauts landed on and studied the moon, most of these questions of a lunar atmosphere were answered. There is no water on the lunar surface, very little water in lunar rocks, and no permafrost, or frozen water, has been indicated below the surface. No signs of recent volcanic activity have been found in the few spots sampled. Instruments taken to the moon by Apollo 17 astronauts found a very, very thin atmosphere. Hydrogen, helium, neon, and argon were positively identified. Limits were placed on how much oxygen and carbon dioxide could be in the atmosphere, but their presence is uncertain.

There are several possible sources for a slight lunar atmosphere. One is the production of some relatively heavy argon gas by the radioactive decay of potassium in the rocks at or close to the lunar surface. Most of the minute amount of argon in the terrestrial atmosphere was probably produced in this way. Another possible source is the outgassing from volcanic or subsurface bubbles or domes of gas—too many gassy mists have been seen to discount this possibility. The gases would probably include sulfur dioxide, hydrogen, carbon dioxide, and possibly water vapor, constituents of volcanic gas. Another more likely source is the solar wind. This wind constantly bombards the moon. There is probably a precarious balance between the moon's atmosphere and the solar wind. The wind not only strips some of the atmosphere off the moon but also adds to it. The abundances of all the positively identified elements, with the exception of argon-40, are consistent with the solar wind as the source. Undoubtedly the argon-40 has been produced by the decay of potassium.

It is relatively safe to say that the moon has no atmosphere of its own. If the solar wind did not exist, neither would the minute lunar atmosphere. At several Apollo landing sites, the total nighttime abundance was 200,000 particles in every cubic centimeter. For comparison, there are approximately 10^{19} (ten billion billion) particles per cubic centimeter near the earth's surface. Exhausts from the lunar landers added more gases to the atmosphere at their respective sites than had previously existed there. Many of these Apollo gases freeze out and fall to the surface or are blown out into interplanetary space by the powerful solar wind.

Atmospheres of Other Satellites

Few of the 43 or more satellites in the solar system have atmospheres, but the exceptions are notable.

In its orbit of Saturn, Titan is the largest satellite in the solar system. Larger than Mercury and Pluto, it should be capable of retaining any atmosphere. In 1944 G. P. Kuiper of the University of Chicago discovered methane gas on Titan. This was followed years later by the discovery of molecular hydrogen. Ground-based astronomers believed that methane and hydrogen exist in equal amounts in Titan's atmosphere. Furthermore, it was thought that Titan's atmosphere may be similar to earth's primordial atmosphere. Some scientists believed that life, albeit primitive life, might exist on Titan. This belief was supported by Titan's reddish appearance; in fact, as seen from earth, Titan is as red as Mars. The hydrogen and methane in the atmosphere cannot account for its reddish color, nor is it likely that the surface gives Titan its color. Many organic components on earth have red coloring. Among the suggestions for the origin of Titan's atmosphere is volcanic and outgassing from the surface. Electrical discharges (lightning) and/ or ultraviolet radiation can break down the outgassed water and ammonia into large amounts of hydrogen and can produce organic molecules (and hence life), as suggested by Titan's red color.

Preliminary results from Voyager 1, however, indicate that this may not be the case. Titan's atmosphere is almost pure nitrogen; the methane previously detected comprises only a small percentage of Titan's atmosphere. Traces of hydrogen cyanide have also been detected. The maximum atmospheric pressure (presumably at the surface) is 1,500 millibars, half again greater than the earth's surface pressure. Given the size of Titan, this implies that the atmosphere is 5 times more dense than the earth's. The temperature at the 1,500 millibar level of the atmosphere is approximately 92°K (−294°F), close to the tem-

This image of Io's extended sodium cloud was taken on February 19, 1977, with the 61-cm (24-inch) telescope at the Table Mountain Observatory of the Jet Propulsion Laboratory. A picture of Jupiter (north is up), the orbital geometry, and Io's disk (white dot) are also included. The sodium cloud is highly elongated, with more sodium preceding Io in its orbit than trailing it.

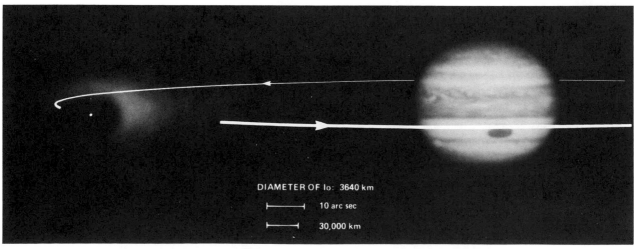

DIAMETER OF Io: 3640 km

10 arc sec

30,000 km

perature where methane can exist as a solid, liquid, or gas. This may "lock" Titan to its current temperature since any excess energy would not go to heating the satellite, but rather to changing the methane from one state to another. "Smog" also exists in Titan's atmosphere. Particles, with a diameter of about 0.20 millionth of a meter (0.000008 in.), form distinct layers in the upper atmosphere except at the north and south poles of Titan. At the North Pole the layers combine to form one thick layer, while the South Pole appears to be free of such a layer. It is not known whether this difference is permanent or represents a seasonal variation.

In 1975 William K. Hartmann wrote, "Io displays some of the most bizarre phenomena found in the solar system." The reddish polar cap, the yellowish equatorial regions, the 10-to-15-minute brightening of Io as it comes out of Jupiter's shadow, and the correlation between radio bursts from Jupiter and the relative positions of Io, Jupiter, and earth are all reasons for his statements. Little did he realize that his words were prophetic. On March 8, 1979, a photograph taken by Voyager 1 revealed at least 2 volcanoes erupting on the surface of Io! Subsequent photographs have revealed at least 8 active volcanoes.

The volcanoes account for at least some of Io's thin atmosphere, which stretches about 1,000 km (620 mi) above its surface, where the atmospheric pressure is about one ten-billionth that of the earth's. Prior to the Voyager missions it had been suggested that Io's surface may be covered by deposits of salt, rich in sodium and sulfur. Energetic particles in Jupiter's extensive magnetosphere constantly bombard Io. These particles can release the sodium from the salts and add it to Io's atmosphere. Potassium and sulfur have also been observed in Io's atmosphere, but no water. The sulfur from the volcanoes can account for the coloration of Io and the sulfur in the atmosphere.

Is there really a boundary to Io's atmosphere? In 1973 an extensive sodium cloud was discovered enveloping Io. In addition to reaching 30,000 km (18,640 mi) above Io, the cloud has been observed to extend some 200,000 km (124,000 mi) back along Io's orbit. This discovery was followed by that of a cloud of ionized sulfur straddling Io's orbit. This cloud appears to be more extensive than the sodium cloud. Its inner edge is some 245,000 km (152,000 mi) from Jupiter's center, while the outer edge is 560,000 km (348,000 mi). The sodium and ionized sulfur seem to form a doughnut or torus around Jupiter through which Io passes. Perhaps astronomers should not have been so surprised when Voyager 1 discovered a ring, less than 30 km (19 mi) thick, 58,100 km (36,000 mi) above Jupiter's equator.

Chapter X
Surface of
the Moon

"... As when by night the Glass of
Galileo ... observes
Imagin'd Lands and Regions in the
Moon."

Milton

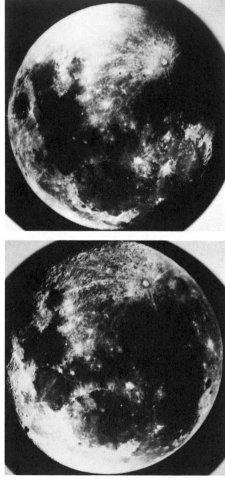

Change in the appearance of the moon in
a 4-day interval from just before full
moon (above) to just after full moon
(below), revealing the prominent features
apparent in this phase with a 38-cm (15-
inch) refractor. The bright and dark areas
are sharply contrasted, and some of the
larger craters and their ray systems stand
out. North is at the bottom in these two
photographs.

Despite centuries of dedicated attention by countless observers, professional and amateur, and despite the observations of astronauts and the analysis of lunar rocks by countless scientists on earth, many features of the lunar surface are still open to dispute and speculation. Before space vehicles or astronauts landed on the moon, a leading lunar authority, Harold C. Urey, urged "... the realization that the moon is very different from the earth and that naïve analogies are useless. The surface of the moon will not be like that of earth. The surface origin is quite different. ..."

The best existing photographs of the moon from earth give resolutions of about 0.4 to 0.5 second of arc. This means that objects much smaller than 0.6 to 0.8 km (2,000 to 2,600 ft) in at least one dimension could not be distinguished. Direct observation of the moon with a telescope is somewhat better. A visual resolution nearly 4 times greater than the photographic has been claimed, so that objects only 150 to 300 meters (500 to 1,000 ft) in size can be picked out. Reports from the 5-meter (200-inch) telescope are that craterlets only 73 meters (240 ft) across and 4.5-meter (15-ft) clefts or cracks can be seen.

Then the Ranger series of spacecraft took photographs up to the last second as they neared impact with the lunar surface. Suddenly craters 1 foot to 3 feet in diameter were visible! Surveyor soft-landing space vehicles settled on the ancient surface and took pictures all around them, even scooping trenches in the surface. Lunar craters of all sizes as well as rocks and soil appeared in photographs Surveyor sent back to earth, including the first pictures of earth photographed from the moon!

Finally astronauts took that last "giant step" and loped about on the lunar surface, picking up rocks, then hopped on the lunar "buggy" or Rover to explore the moon. We will trace this whole development here.

Lunar Topography

When the moon sails high in a clear sky, the naked eye easily distinguishes its bright areas from its principal dark regions. The dark areas, which reflect on the average only 5 to 10 percent of the sunlight falling on them, seem to predominate, particularly across the middle of the moon and to the north and west. The bright areas, seen primarily in the southern and eastern parts and far to the north around the lunar North Pole, reflect up to 20 to 30 percent of the light they receive from the sun.

The moon's main features near full are displayed in the small photographs made with the 38-cm (15-inch) refractor of the Dominion Observatory in Ottawa. The sun's light probes directly into some of the large craters, which become brilliant spots on the moon at this phase, and the ray systems around them are most striking.

The major lunar features apparent at the first and last quarters appear in the two photographs (pages 126–127) forming a general map of the moon, made with the 0.9-meter (36-inch) refractor of the Lick Observatory. Many of the most significant features are named in the table (pages 128–129) and can be located easily on the photographs by means of the coordinates. Except for a few tiny points, all of the lunar features referred to in this chapter can be found on this map. In these photographs, north is at the top, south at the bottom, east is to the right, and west is to the left, following normal cartographic (or, in this case, what is called "astronautical") convention, just as prominent features of the moon are seen in the sky. By tradition, and for convenience, astronomers follow another convention, showing the moon (and other celestial objects) with directions reversed—north at the bottom and south at the top.

The dark areas, called "maria" (the Latin for seas), are relatively flat, with very gradual slopes. They seem to have quite a different composition and origin than the bright areas, as do the related "sinuses" or gulfs off the seas, and "paludes" or smaller dark areas that look like marshes at first sight. If the moon is seen with binoculars or in a small telescope, it appears to have a leaden, pewter, or silver color—duller when the sun is low, brighter and even scintillating when it is high above the surface features. The bright areas resolve into rough, mountainous, or broken regions and into pockmarks or holes called craters.

A number of great mountain ranges cut across the moon and some regions are jumbled mountainous and hilly areas. The Apennine Mountains slash down at an angle from northeast to southwest just above the center of the moon's disk near a rather dark spot called the Sinus Medii, or Central Bay. The Apennines tower up to 5,500 meters (18,000 ft) above the Mare Imbrium (Sea of Rains), the vast plain to their northwest. The Caucasian Mountains (reaching 5,800 meters or 19,000 ft) and the Alps (3,700 meters or 12,000 ft) lie still farther north.

The moon's Southern Hemisphere is very mountainous and cratered. Near its South Pole are the Leibnitz Mountains, with peaks up to 6,000 meters (19,600 ft). Although this is 3,000 meters (10,000 ft) short of Mount Everest's height and about comparable to the height of Kilimanjaro in Africa or of Mount Logan in the Yukon Territory, Canada, the second highest peak in North America, the moon is so much smaller than the earth that its great mountains are at least relatively higher than ours.

The variety of types and sizes of moon craters has given birth to a multitude of terms to distinguish them. The larger ones are called walled plains, ringed plains, and mountain rings; then come crater plains, craters, and craterlets; the crater pits and crater cones are smaller still. "Crater" is often used in a general sense for all these ringed or basin shapes and does not imply a volcanic origin. In a more technical sense it is reserved for the smaller rings, perhaps 6 to 20 km (4 to 12 mi) in diameter, often with a cone or central peak rising within them and usually sunken well into the surrounding surface. It has been estimated that from 200,000 to 1 million craters of all types can be seen on the visible surface of the moon with large telescopes. No matter how close one looks at the lunar surface, craters are detected. Microcraters ranging in size from 1 micrometer (one-millionth of a meter or about four hundred-thousandths of an inch) to more than 1 cm (a little less than 0.5 inch) pit the lunar rocks.

Sixty-four km (40 mi) wide, with walls rising over 3,700 meters (12,000 ft), the great crater Copernicus, perhaps the most striking of all, stands all by itself northwest of the moon's midpoint. It is conspicuous for its multitude of rays, long, whitish streamers that radiate out from and around craters like the points of a star. These rays, promi-

A general map of the moon (pages 126–127) in the normal cartographic convention. As on any map of the earth, and as the moon is seen in the sky, north is at the top, south at the bottom, east to the right, and west to the left. The grid is arbitrary, with x-coordinate numbers running horizontally toward the right, and y-coordinate numbers vertically toward the top from the left-hand corner. (Note that the two photographs, and consequently the x coordinates, overlap somewhat in the middle.) The x and y coordinates for 204 features are given in the table (pages 128–129). To find a given feature whose name is known obtain its x and y coordinate numbers from the table, locate its y number on the grid vertically, and move the eye or place a ruler across the map horizontally until the x number is reached, the feature being located where lines from the x and y numbers cross. To identify a feature as seen on the map, obtain its x and y numbers by placing a ruler vertically and horizontally, respectively, from it to the grid at the edge, and use these numbers to find the name of the feature in the table. The two half-moon photographs were taken in a series by J. H. Moore and J. F. Chappell (1937–38) with the 91-cm (36-inch) refractor of the Lick Observatory.

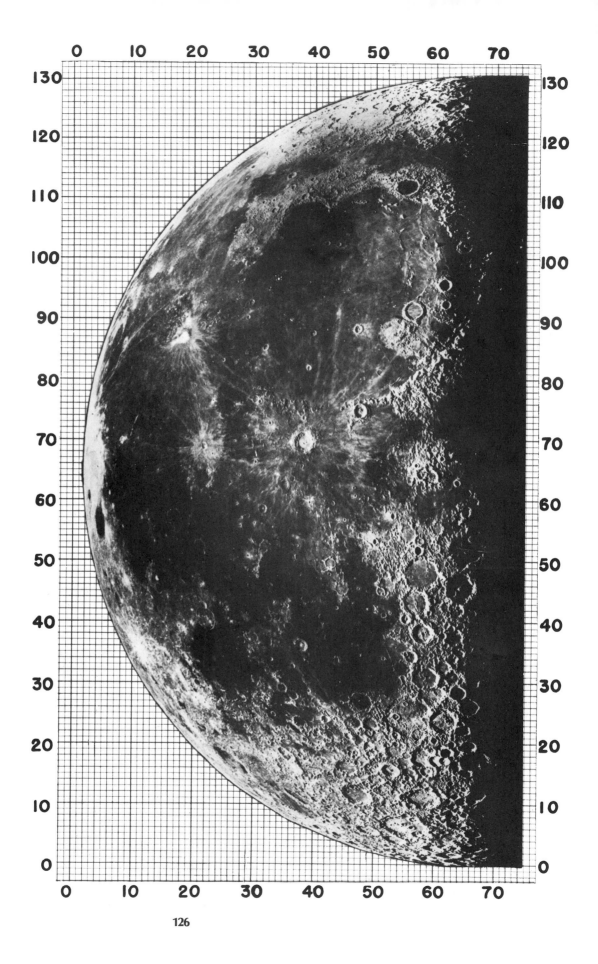

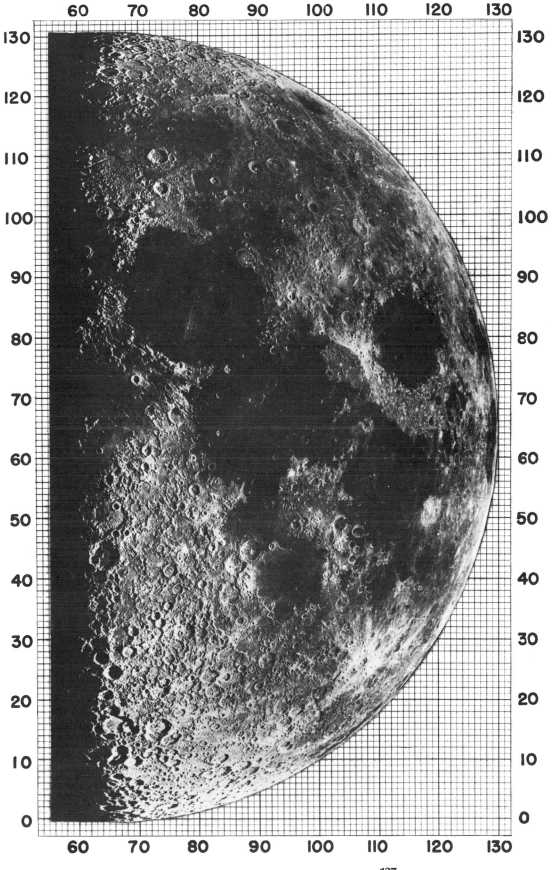

Name of feature	x	y	Name of feature	x	y	Name of feature	x	y
Abenezra	73	34	Euler	32	85	Mare Imbrium	40	95
Abulfeda	74	42	Fabricius	95	17	Mare Marginis	127	80
Agrippa	72	61	Flammarion	55	55	Mare Nectaris	95	40
Albategnius	64	46	Flamsteed	17	55	Mare Nubium	47	36
Aliacensis	65	25	Fracastorius	94	35	Mare Serenitatis	78	88
Almanon	75	39	Fra Mauro	40	51	Mare Smythii	129	62
Alphonsus	56	43	Furnerius	110	25	Mare Spumans	122	63
Alpine Valley	63	109	Gärtner	81	117	Mare Tranquillitatis	90	68
Alps, mountains	63	110	Gassendi	22	40	Mare Undarum	122	69
Altai Scarp	83	32	Geber	75	36	Mare Vaporum	65	72
Anaxagoras	59	124	Geminus	108	95	Marius	16	74
Anaximander	43	122	Godin	72	59	Maurolycus	73	15
Apennine Mountains	58	80	Grimaldi	4	56	Menelaus	77	75
Arago	83	64	Guericke	44	46	Mercurius	104	109
Archimedes	55	91	Gutenberg	104	49	Mersenius	17	37
Ariadaeus	80	64	Haemus Mountains	70	80	Messala	107	98
Aristarchus	18	87	Hell	53	25	Messier	109	57
Aristillus	61	96	Hercules	90	108	Metius	97	18
Aristoteles	74	110	Herodotus	17	87	Meton	69	125
Arzachel	57	38	Herschel	57	52	Milichius	28	70
Atlas	73	108	Herschel, Caroline	33	97	Moretus	63	2
Autolycus	61	92	Herschel, John	44	120	Mösting	53	57
Azophi	74	33	Hesiodus	45	27	Newton	60	0
Bailly	45	4	Hind	68	48	Oceanus Procellarum	10	95–45
Ball	53	21	Hippalus	32	33	Olbers	3	71
Barrow	66	124	Hipparchus	65	52	"Oval Rays"	44	66
Beaumont	91	38	Hortensius	30	66	Palus Nebularum	60	99
Bessarion	23	76	Huygens, Mount	57	81	Palus Putredinis	60	88
Bessel	78	82	Hyginus	66	65	Palus Somnii	105	76
Birt	51	34	Jansen	90	74	Parry	42	50
Bond, W. C.	64	120	Janssen	92	16	Petavius	114	34
Bonpland	41	49	Julius Caesar	76	67	Phocylides	32	11
Brayley	24	83	Kepler	22	69	Picard	113	76
Bullialdus	38	36	Kepler A	23	68	Piccolomini	91	27
Bürg	83	106	Lacaille	61	33	Pickering, W. H.	108	57
Byrgius	12	36	Lambert	39	88	Pico, Mount	54	107
Carpathian Mountains	35	75	Landsberg	31	59	Pitatus	47	27
Cassini	65	105	Langrenus	119	51	Pitiscus	81	13
"Cassini's Bright Spot"	57	24	Laplace, Prom.	42	108	Piton, Mount	59	102
Catharina	85	38	Leibnitz Mountains	75	0	Plato	54	112
Caucasian Mountains	68	98	Le Monnier	91	88	Playfair	69	31
Censorinus	95	57	Licetus	67	11	Plinius	85	75
Clavius	55	6	Lick	112	74	Posidonius	88	94
Cleomedes	110	90	Linné	72	88	Proclus	107	78
Conon	62	81	Longomontanus	46	12	Ptolemaeus	56	48
Copernicus	37	70	Lyot	58	49	Purbach	58	31
Cuvier	69	9	Macrobius	105	83	Pyrenees Mountains	102	43
Cyrillus	86	43	Mädler	92	45	Pythagoras	40	122
D'Alembert Mountains	3	54	Maginus	58	11	Pytheas	39	82
Delambre	79	55	Manilius	70	73	Rabbi Levi	82	21
Deslandres	56	24	Mare Australe	105	15	Ramsden	33	25
Dionysius	79	60	Mare Cognitum	35	48	Regiomontanus	59	28
Doppelmayer	24	29	Mare Crisium	115	80	Reinhold	35	62
Endymion	95	115	Mare Foecunditatis	112	55	Rheita	100	21
Eratosthenes	47	75	Mare Frigoris	30–85	116	Rheita Valley	99	18
Euclides	29	50	Mare Humboldtianum	99	118	Riccioli	3	60
Eudoxus	74	105	Mare Humorum	25	34	Rook Mountains	20	22

Name of feature	x	y	Name of feature	x	y	Name of feature	x	y
Rosse	96	38	Stadius	44	70	Timocharis	46	88
Scheiner	50	6	Stevinus	107	26	Tobias Mayer	31	77
Schickard	26	17	Strabo	88	120	Triesnecker	64	61
Schiller	37	11	Straight Range	47	109	Tycho	52	16
Schröter's Valley	17	88	Straight Wall	52	34	Vitello	28	28
Seleucus	8	86	Taruntius	108	66	Walter	60	24
Sinus Aestuum	50	72	Taurus Mountains	100	95	Wargentin	27	15
Sinus Iridum	37	108	Teneriffe Range	51	109	Werner	63	28
"Sinus Iridum Highlands"	40	110	Thales	86	120	Wrottesley	112	34
Sinus Medii	58	60	Thebit	55	40	Yerkes	109	77
Sinus Roris	26	107	Theophilus	88	45	Zach	66	5

nent near full moon, are the results of material thrown out at the time the parent crater was created. Tycho in the south-central region has the most pronounced system of rays on the moon. Hundreds of them radiate out to great distances and are separated from Tycho itself by a dark ring around it. Tycho is believed to have been one of the last great features produced on the moon. Whatever its origin, the explosion that created it must have been enormous. One of its rays can be traced across the Mare Serenitatis in the moon's northeastern region, and out to the limb, where it disappears onto the far side.

A prominent crater system just south of the midpoint of the moon consists of the craters Ptolemaeus, Alphonsus, and Arzachel, lying close together on the north-south arc. Ptolemaeus is a great walled plain 150 km (90 mi) across, with a very dark, gray interior full of detail that has been a focus of interest. The 117-km (70-mi)-wide Alphonsus has walls up to 2,000 meters (6,600 ft), a strange series of dark spots or streaks near the rim on its floor, and frequent signs of activity in its interior. Arzachel, the smallest of the three, has a central peak and much interior detail.

Far to the north of the Mare Imbrium, just below the moon's North Pole, is another object of much speculation, the great walled plain of Plato, 101 km (60 mi) in diameter with walls rising 2,400 meters (7,900 ft). Mists, vapors, or obscuring gases sometimes seem to veil Plato's floor and have been reported at the same time in the United States and in England. Bright flashes have been seen at Plato, and from time to time light and dark spots or streaks appear in it. One astronomer has described Plato as "one of the most continuously active volcanic regions on the moon"; others deny that anything unusual ever takes place there.

Numerous "domes" have been discovered on the moon's surface. Domes may be somewhat like bulges or uplifts caused by lava beneath the earth's surface, representing arrested stages of volcanism. Sometimes circular, though usually irregular in shape, and sloping or bulging up by perhaps 210 to 300 meters (700 to 1,000 ft), these domes may run 2.4 to 3.2 km (1.5 to 2 mi) in diameter. There are occasional larger ones, as wide as 80 km (50 mi), which may have been volcanic shields, uplifts due to bubbles in the lava of the plains that did not burst through.

A great many clefts, sometimes called rills or rilles—many of them may be lunar faults—meander along the surface of the moon. They may be 1.6 to 3.0 km (1 to 2 mi) or more in width, sometimes narrow-

The western border of the
Mare Tranquillitatis,
photographed at the coudé
focus of the 3-meter (120-
inch) Lick reflector (north at
top). Craterlets dot the
surface of the mare, the crater
Julius Caesar rises to the west
with crater pits scattered on
its floor, and to the south the
Ariadaeus Rill, a distinctive
valley cleft more than 240 km
(150 mi) long, runs almost
east and west.

er. Some are fairly straight, others crooked or curved; they may extend
for tens or even hundreds of kilometers, occasionally cutting through
hills or the walls of craters. The great Cleft of Hyginus, for example,
lying just to the northeast of the moon's midpoint, cuts through the
small crater pit called Hyginus. This cleft runs a rather jagged course,
and patient scrutiny has revealed several small branches that are lesser
clefts, or cracks. Parts of the cleft are composed of crater chains.

The moon's maria probably never contained any water, nor were in
any other respect like the seas or oceans of the earth. A century ago, a
few astronomers did think that the maria might actually be the dried-
up beds of ancient oceans, their dark color due to sediments that had
collected on their floors, from the time when the moon had liquids on
its surface and an atmosphere above it. This has always been a minor-
ity view. No evidence for water on the moon has been found by any of
the Ranger, Surveyor, and Apollo missions of the United States or the
Luna and Lunokhod missions of Russia.

The major lunar seas that are immediately distinguishable include
the Mare Crisium (Sea of Crises), the dark, rather elliptical area on the
east-central side of the moon above the larger and broader Mare Foecunditatis (Sea of Fertility). The Mare Crisium is one of the few isolated seas on the moon; it is surrounded by mountains and unconnected

with other seas. Probably the most beautiful of the moon's seas in the telescope, its 169,000-square-km (66,000-square-mi) area is visible to the naked eye as a small, dark, oval spot. Some observers report that it has a greenish tint, with many fine white streaks and bright spots on its surface. It is near the eastern limb of the moon.

The large dark sea just northeast of the moon's midpoint has been named Mare Serenitatis (Sea of Serenity), and between it and the Mare Foecunditatis lies the large Mare Tranquillitatis (Sea of Tranquility). To the west of the moon's central meridian are the Mare Imbrium (Sea of Rains) to the north, and to the south the Mare Nubium (Sea of Clouds). The Sea of Rains is a large, dark area measuring some 1,200 km (750 mi) from east to west and 1,100 km (690 mi) from north to south. The great smooth area extending far north and south and almost to the moon's western limb is known as Oceanus Procellarum (Ocean of Storms). Its area is estimated as some 5 million square km (2 million square mi).

An isolated portion of Mare Nubium within which Ranger impacted has been named Mare Cognitum (Known Sea), since Ranger photographed parts of it.

Surface Temperatures

Temperatures on the moon's surface have been measured since 1868, and today the very sensitive thermocouples used in scans of the moon's surface show detailed fluctuations in its temperature with changes in the angle of the sun as it passes from east to west in the moon's day. The temperature contour map shows isotherms (lines of equal temperature) on the moon in its first quarter as the whole surface was scanned over a period of 3 hours. The center of the moon, Sinus Medii,

Map of the first-quarter lunar surface temperatures by isotherms of equal temperature on a simultaneous photograph of the moon. Temperatures are shown here in Celsius degrees. A portion of the Mare Crisium north of the subsolar point seems to show a hotter region, as it did also in other thermal maps (north at top).

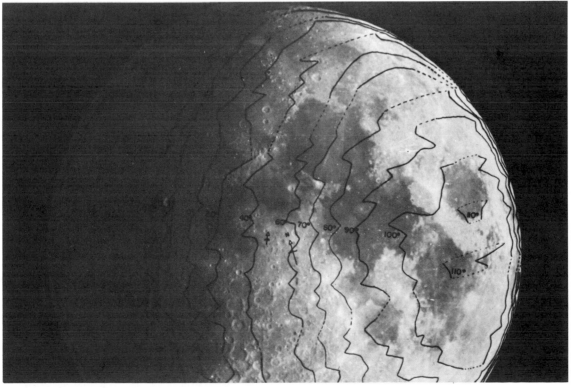

is indicated. Where the sun is fully up, above the eastern part of the disk, the temperature is 230°F (110°C), 18° above the boiling point of water, while it ranges down to the boiling point at the next isotherm line marked. From there, the temperature drops off rather fast, reaching a thoroughly comfortable 68°F (20°C) at this phase just past the moon's center. Then it plummets in the moon's darkness to −140°F (−96°C). The temperatures shown on the contour map are in Celsius.

While the temperature at the moon's midnight point has not been established precisely, a number of measurements have placed it at −247°F (−155°C). When the earth's shadow covers the moon in lunar eclipses, the temperature goes down very rapidly. The moon's surface, however, seems to be a good insulator, and the temperature well below it should not vary a great deal between lunar day and night. With subsurface protection, not only from the sun's heat but also from its much more dangerous particles and gamma rays, human or other forms of life could be maintained very safely and comfortably.

Lunar Maps

Sometime before 1603, William Gilbert, the British discoverer of the earth's magnetism, drew the first known map of the moon, simply from naked-eye viewing. In 1609 (Galileo) and 1610 (Harriot), the first rough telescopic maps of the moon were made. For 3½ centuries thereafter, more and more accurate and detailed lunar maps were prepared.

Only in the past few years have complete maps of the moon been made, covering the far side, the near side, and the poles. These maps are based on photographs made from unmanned spacecraft and by astronauts in orbit.

Determination of the exact position of any point on the moon's surface must be made from the lunar coordinates of latitude (beta or β) and longitude (lambda or λ). On the moon, latitudes (north and south) are determined from the lunar equator, and longitudes (east and west) from the principal meridian perpendicular to the equator. The inclination of the moon's equator to the ecliptic has been found to be about 1 degree, 32 minutes, 40 seconds. The principal meridian is the meridian plane cutting the moon through the point at which the radius vector (or straight line) joining the centers of the earth and the moon is situated at the time of the passage of the moon through perigee or apogee.

The dead center of the moon's disk in the Sinus Medii, where the equator and central meridian intersect, is not marked by any prominent surface feature. The small but unmistakable crater Mösting A nearby, on the western slopes of a rather dark plain called Flammarion, has been selected as the basic reference point. (See the topographic lunar map of the United States Army Corps of Engineers.) Located to the southwest of the central point, its walls rise 2,100 meters (7,000 ft) above the depressed bowl of its interior, and 500 meters (1,600 ft) above the surrounding area, making it an easily identifiable landmark. From this reference point, a group of five to nine other reference points are determined, and the whole system is then used to determine the positions of all the other objects being mapped.

Artists have customarily portrayed the lunar craters, ridges, and mountains as dramatically sharp and rough. While it is true that shad-

132

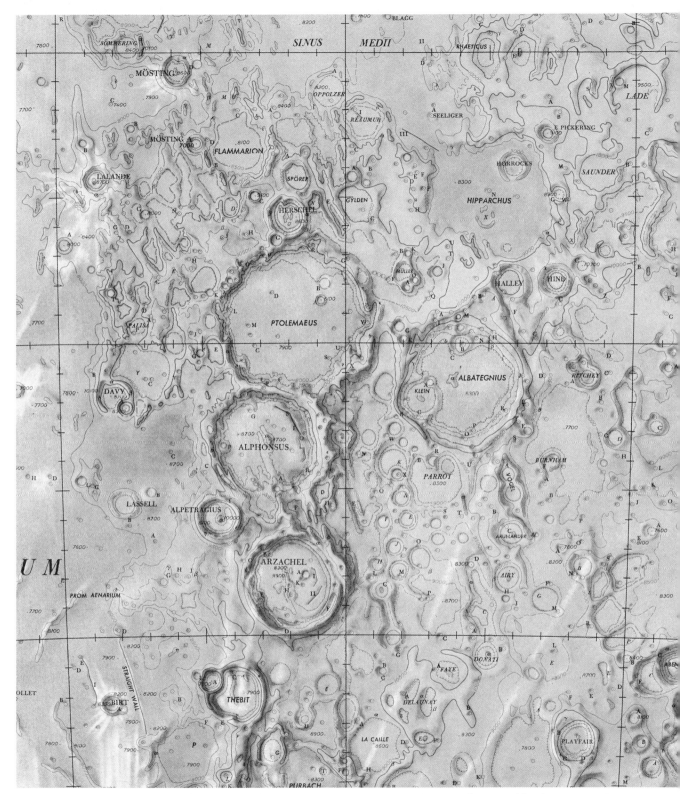

Section of topographic lunar map showing
Flammarion, Mösting, and Mösting A
southwest of the Sinus Medii, and below
them the line of Ptolemaeus, Alphonsus,
and Arzachel. Scale 1:2,500,000; contour
intervals 1,000 meters (3,280 ft) and 500
meters (1,640 ft) (north to top and east to
right).

133

A generation of hard-landing Rangers, spacecraft that returned photographs to earth as they plummeted into the moon, gave much new information about its surface. On March 24, 1965, Ranger IX hit its target in the crater Alphonsus, identified in the earth-made photograph (right). Strange cracks, rills, and dark markings have been observed in Alphonsus, and scientists wondered if it might emit gases, since red glows have been reported in the crater. The central peak rises a sheer 1,005 meters (3,300 ft) from the crater floor.

The pictures below and on page 135 were made during Ranger's fall to the moon, the first at a distance of 1,240 km (775 mi), the last at about 0.8 km (0.5 mi). The white circle in each picture corresponds to that in the next, each picture being a closer view of a small part of the view of the prior picture.

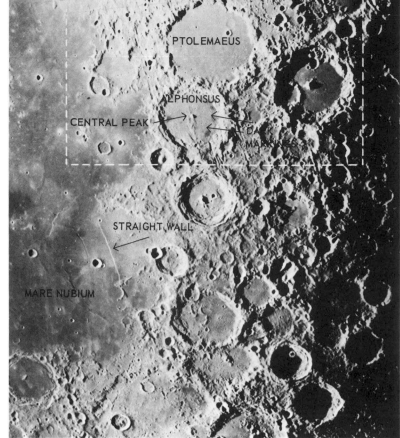

A. Alphonsus (left) from 1,240 km (775 mi), with its central peak, rills, and dark spots on crater floor. Albategnius crater on the right.

B. Alphonsus from 413 km (258 mi) with many more rills and craters now visible. Alpetragius crater (bottom left) has been called an egg in nest.

ows thrown by the sun on the moon's surface often give this impression, modern contour research, using microdensitometer tracings of lunar shadows, has proved that most of the lunar craters and mountains are undulating rather than jagged. The heights of crater walls are usually very small in comparison with their widths.

Most slopes or hills on the moon are not inclined more than a few degrees, and very few slopes run at angles of 10° or more from the horizontal. The typical vista on the moon, then, is of a normally flat, only occasionally gently undulating or rolling surface, somewhat like the Great Plains of the West, unrelieved by sharp mountains and promontories.

Some observers have noted various hues and shades of color here and there on the moon, such as the greenish hue of portions of Mare Crisium. In the main, however, the surface appears to run through monotonous shades of gray. While other colors may often have been due to chromatic aberrations in optical systems, the existence of significant color contrasts on the lunar surface has been demonstrated by spectrophotometry of a number of areas. In general, the brighter areas studied appeared to be redder than others, and color contrasts were found even within the monotonous-looking Mare Nubium.

Contacts with the Moon

The first known direct human contact with the moon was the impact of the Soviet lunar probe Luna 2 at 5:02:24 P.M., Eastern Daylight Saving Time, on September 13, 1959. According to reports in America, Luna fell into the area of Palus Putredinis (Marsh of Decay) in the north-central region of the moon. The Marsh of Decay is an offshoot of the Mare Imbrium and the Sinus Aestuum (Bay of Billows), just north of the Apennine Mountains. The Russians have located the impact point a little farther north and east, on the eastern wall of the crater Autolycus.

Ranger 4, of the American moon-probe series, launched from Cape Canaveral, Florida, with an Atlas-Agena B rocket, was scheduled to place a 330-kilogram (727-pound) capsule with instruments on the lunar surface. It covered the distance to the moon in about 64 hours and is believed to have crashed on April 26, 1962, on the far side—just around the limb of the visible moon. The second stage of the Agena B rocket passed by the moon and into solar orbit.

On July 31, 1964, Ranger 7, which had functioned smoothly throughout its flight, plummeted to impact in the Mare Nubium near the crater Guericke in the south-central quadrant of the moon. Starting at a height of about 1,760 km (1,100 mi) above the moon, it transmitted some 4,300 television pictures back to earth, the last made at an altitude of about 300 meters (1,000 ft) above the surface, revealing details with a resolution of 1 foot to 3 feet. While some areas were heavily pitted with secondary craters, apparently caused by debris shot out when crater Tycho was produced, other areas appeared to be relatively smooth and uncluttered, covered with what was interpreted to be crunchy dust of an undetermined depth. It was estimated that the photographic resolution was some 2,000 times better than in the best photographs ever achieved through the earth's atmosphere.

Another significant lunar first was the taking of photographs of the far side of the moon in October 1959, by the Soviet spacecraft Luna 3.

C. Central peak from 93 km (58 mi). Rills running up from peak's shadow and at right appear in picture D in much more detail.

D. From 19 km (12 mi) up. Crater at left on Alphonsus' floor is 2.4 km (1.5 mi) across; rills are chains of craters with sunken surface between.

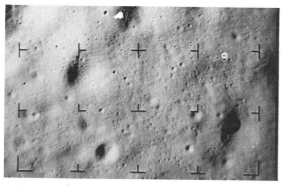

E. At 7.2 km (4.5 mi), Ranger nears its target. Many more craters can be seen, down to 12.2 meters (40 ft) in diameter, but no signs of volcanism.

F. At less than 0.8 km (0.5 mi), 0.9-meter (3-ft) craters are visible; Ranger IX crashed down at white circle (top) next to a 7.6-meter (25-ft) crater.

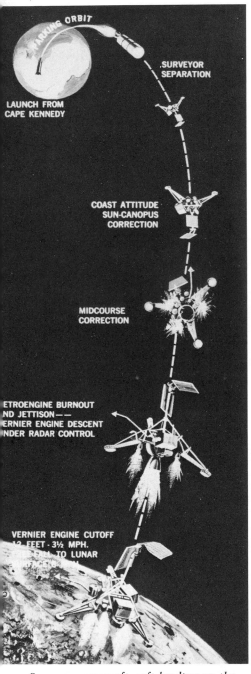

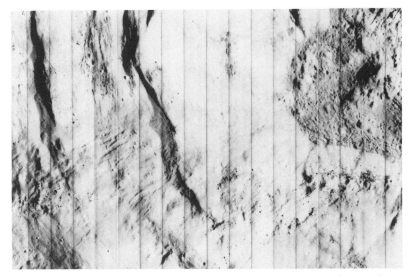

Aristarchus is one of the brightest craters on the moon, located toward the northwest. Astronomers have watched it from earth because many red glows have been reported in and around the crater. Then Lunar Orbiter V took the photograph of the southern wall of the crater, showing much erosion, and its floor (top right) seamed with tiny craters. Whether all the holes are impact craters or some are cinder cones of volcanic action, recent or in the past, may not be decided until astronauts land at Aristarchus and explore it. Lunar Orbiters followed Surveyors with many such photographs from as close as 48 km (30 mi).

Surveyor spacecraft, soft-landing on the moon from 1966 to 1968, studied the surface to aid the selection of sites for Apollo manned landings and to reveal more than Rangers about lunar-surface composition and load capacity.

After a series of hard-landing Soviet and American craft, many soft-landing Luna and Surveyor craft, balancing on their rocket jets, settled on the lunar surface. They panned their directed TV cameras around and furnished on-the-spot close-ups of the lunar soil, the strewn rocks and boulders, and the large and small craters pocking the landscape.

Then artificial lunar satellites called Lunar Orbiters spanned the moon in highly eccentric orbits, coming as close as 48 km (30 mi) above the surface, to provide detailed photographs of areas of the moon from which the most favorable and instructive landing sites could be selected.

Men then came to the moon, first circling the moon in close orbits, and then on July 20, 1969, descending to the surface in the LEM. With the close of the Apollo series of flights, a half-dozen lunar areas had been sampled.

From all these photographic and direct contacts with the moon came a wealth of information. The jumbled peaks of vast mountain ranges could be observed from nearby. Astronauts walked, dug, and rode over lunar seas or maria. Small and large craters were examined, and wrinkled ridges and bright rays were studied, as well as groups of domes scattered on the moon's surface.

Astronauts of the Apollo 15 mission in 1971 explored the edge of the Hadley Rill, one of the long, meandering valleys of the moon. Faults and cracks where the lunar surface had broken and shifted look like those on earth, and dikes of lava had forced their way through the cracks. Selenology rapidly became a science like the geology of the earth, as solid knowledge began to replace speculation.

Early fears of spacecraft and astronauts sinking deep within fine lu-

Rocky landscape with craters (left) pictured by Surveyor VII was probably formed from debris of impact that blasted out Tycho. Rolling hills and ridges to horizon, 12.8 km (8 mi) distant at center, look like parts of eastern United States. Rocky crater in foreground was gouged by block ejected from another crater. Rock in foreground is 1.8 meters (6 ft) across, with 3.7-meter (12-ft) shadow. Plenty of material for moon colonists to play "duck on the rock," but dangerous in space suits!

White circle in center identifies rock in closeup from Surveyor (right photograph). Many of these rocks fragmented in crater are 30 cm (1 ft) or more across. Most lunar rocks are basaltic (maria) or anorthositic (highlands).

Lunar Orbiter V made this photograph of the Alpine Valley in the Alps Mountains in the north-central region of the moon. From earth, astronomers thought perhaps this slash through the mountains had been carved by a meteorite coming in at a low angle. But it turns out to be a wide irregular valley with a rill wiggling down its center, its cause still unknown.

Astronauts began to explore the moon directly with the Apollo 11 mission. Here the Lunar Expeditionary Module (LEM) returns with 2 astronauts from the moon's surface to rendezvous with the astronaut in the Command Module, who took this photograph through its porthole. The return to earth (top) completed this first landing mission.

Apollo 15 astronaut with Lunar Rover (below) looks down the winding Hadley Rill.

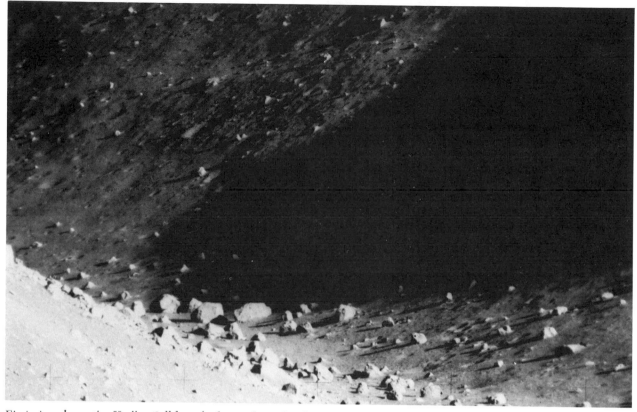

*First view down the Hadley Rill by telephoto (above) by the astronaut
shown in last photo reveals rocky sides but no signs of flow along the
bottom, though faint horizontal layering. Mount Hadley telephoto (below)
shows blocky horizontal layers that prove development of lunar crust here
was complex, with many layers forming one above the other.*

nar dust soon evaporated. The lunar soil, a layer from 4 to 10 meters (13 to 30 ft) deep, was similar in texture to soil on earth. Lunar soil was made up of fragments of rocks and dust broken and churned by meteoritic impacts. Most of the soil was basaltic, a kind of igneous rock that has been heated and melted. Beneath the soil, a layered rock crust 65 km (40 mi) thick was revealed by study of seismic waves from the impact of spacecraft and the rare moonquakes. The upper 25 km (15 mi) of crust is largely basaltic rock. Beneath this comes a 40-km (25-mi) layer of anorthositic rock—older, but still igneous rock. Under the crust the lunar mantle stretches down for 1,000 km (620 mi). The mantle is rigid and stable, probably consisting of pyroxene-rich material. On July 17, 1972, a large meteorite (weighing about a ton) impacted on the far side of the moon. The impact triggered seismic waves that were recorded by Apollo seismic stations. Surprisingly, no direct sheer-wave arrivals were detected. This has led scientists to believe that the moon has a partially molten core with a radius of about 500 km (300 mi).

Lunar Seas

Despite similarities between the cratered surfaces of Mercury and the moon, the vast dark seas on the moon and its hundreds of thousands of visible craters seem to be uniquely lunar. With their limited earth-based photographs of the moon, scientists did their best to explain them, but to tie down an explanation in so distant a place as the moon proved well nigh impossible.

Two theories developed. In one theory the maria had a volcanic origin. It was believed that most of the moon's surface features could be explained completely in terms of internal, volcanic processes. The other theory explained everything on the moon in terms of the impact of meteoroids and asteroids, on the assumption that the moon is an entirely inert and inactive body, without any apparent erosive forces because it almost entirely lacks an atmosphere. These impacting bodies, according to theory, produced both the seas as they now exist and the thousands of craters, which look as if some giant had poked the end of a blunt stick into the soft or plastic surface of the moon over and over again.

The volcanic hypothesis assumes that the maria were produced by huge lava flows early in the moon's history, when it was still very hot or had become hot, or when it had recently crusted over; that it then became hotter still, perhaps from radioactive elements under its surface, or was possibly disrupted by such a titanic event as capture by the earth, and great floods of lava or molten rock poured forth to create the seas. On the other hand, the impact hypothesis envisages a tremendous meteoroid or small asteroid up to 160 to 320 km (100 to 200 mi) in diameter arriving at the surface of the moon, gouging out huge gashes as it came in, striking with great shock waves, and producing heat. With this, lava was released from below the surface. The lava may have already existed or been melted by the heat and streamed out at the impact time or later, when the dome produced by the impact cracked and subsided. Those who support the impact theory have pointed in particular to the Mare Imbrium in the northwestern region of the moon, around which the ranges of the Apennines, the Caucasians, and the Alps curve in a full three-quarter arc of a circle, presumably raised as part of the quantities of debris shot forth by the impact of an asteroid. This highly dramatic explanation for Mare Imbrium has been developed in great and convincing detail. But does it apply to all of the large seas on the moon?

As happens so often, the truth appears to be a combination of both theories. The maria appeared first as basins formed by the impact of huge meteoroids or asteroids on the lunar surface. Later as the moon heated, lava flowed from the interior, flooding these impact basins, creating the maria seen today. Supporting this theory are the lunar samples returned by the first Apollo crew ever to land on the moon. The analysis of these samples showed that the materials in Mare Tranquillitatis are of subsurface volcanic origin. Furthermore, photographs from all the Apollo missions reveal that the lava flows occurred at repeated times. A flow cooled and solidified before another occurred.

The far side of the moon has provided the evidence for the impact portion of the theory. Basins and craters exist on the lunar far side, but no large maria. Apparently, the far side did not experience the extensive lava flooding seen on the near side. The ringed basin Mare Orientale is the best example of the impact origin of the basins. These rings delineate the basin. The inner ring is some 480 km (300 mi) in diameter, while the outer ring is 900 km (560 mi) across. Beyond the outer ring, known as Montes Cordillera, features radial to the basin are evident.

Prior to the Apollo missions it was generally believed that the moon had formed cold with the falling together of the condensing materials of the original nebula of gas and dust making up the solar system, and that the moon remained cold. A new picture has developed from the Apollo missions.

Some 4.6 billion years ago the moon formed by the accretion of small chunks of material. Very early in its history, in its first 200 mil-

The Mare Orientale basin as viewed by Lunar Orbiter IV. These circular scarps surround the inner basin, which is partially filled with mare material. The outermost scarp, the Cordillera Mountains, is almost 900 km (560 mi) in diameter. The middle ring is known as the Rook Mountains. These mountains, along with the Cordillera Mountains, rise more than 3 km (2 mi) above the lunar surface and are among the highest mountain chains on the moon. The sharpness of the mountain rings and the texture of the basin floor have led scientists to conclude that Mare Orientale is the youngest of the moon's large circular basins.

lion years, the lunar surface was heated either by the continued influx of material from beyond the moon and/or radioactive decay. Chemical differentiation of the lunar minerals occurred. In the melted state the lighter elements rose to the surface, forming a quickly hardening crust. As the crust cooled between 4.4 and 4.1 billion years ago, interplanetary material still bombarded the lunar surface. Many of the craters in the lunar highlands were formed at this time. The material below the lunar surface was still molten.

Between 4.1 and 3.9 billion years ago the large basins that later became the maria were formed by impact of large meteoroids. Lava flowed out from below the crust. At this time KREEP material was brought to the surface. This material, containing large amounts of potassium (K), rare earth elements (REE), and phosphorus (P), resembles terrestrial basalts. The crust again cooled, but radioactive decay reheated some areas. The basins filled with lava during this reheating, forming the maria. The lava flowed off and on for some 900 million years, from 3.9 to 3 billion years ago. The filling in of the maria marked the end of any major lunar activity. All that remained was the further cratering of the surface, a process that continues today but infrequently.

This picture is painted with broad strokes, and much detail needs to be supplied. The mystery of the mascons remains. These large mass concentrations were discovered under the maria by changes in the paths followed by the Lunar Orbiters. Too large to be the remains of asteroids that hit the moon, it is believed that the mascons indicate pools of melted heavier materials that sank to the bottom of the basins when the mare material was still molten.

Lunar Craters

Robert S. Richardson, an American astronomer, comments, "The chief difficulty in writing about the origin of the lunar craters is the appalling number of hypotheses that have been advanced to explain them. Apparently everybody who has looked at the moon has had a try at it. Some of these explanations sound like plain crank ideas. Others are undeniably ingenious. But today there is only one that seems acceptable to us." He refers to the meteoroid-impact hypothesis. On the other hand, varied volcanic explanations of the origin of lunar craters have been developed, and many scientists, particularly some in the Soviet Union, have elaborated on the volcanic theory.

It is generally believed today that both impact and volcanic craters exist on the moon. The Mare Orientale basin provides an example of each. The crater Maunder is believed to represent a meteoroid-impact crater, while the crater Kopff is believed to represent a crater of volcanic origin. Both craters are found inside the inner ring of Mare Orientale.

Volcanically produced craters usually have a polygonal form, although some are nearly circular. The inner and outer walls of the crater have nearly equal slopes. Dark, smooth ejecta surround these shallow craters. The ejecta are distributed fairly uniformly, since no extensive ray systems are known to exist about these craters.

The impact craters are usually circular. The slope of the interior wall is steeper than that of the outer wall. Furthermore, unlike the volcanic craters, the interior wall is terraced in the large craters. The ejecta blanket is lighter than the surroundings, shows radial and dune-

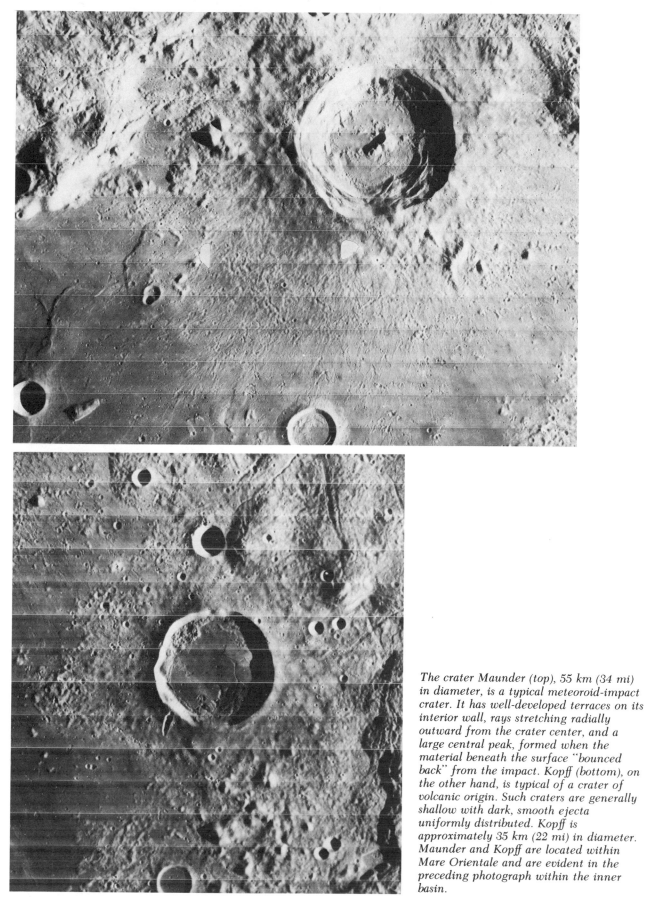

The crater Maunder (top), 55 km (34 mi) in diameter, is a typical meteoroid-impact crater. It has well-developed terraces on its interior wall, rays stretching radially outward from the crater center, and a large central peak, formed when the material beneath the surface "bounced back" from the impact. Kopff (bottom), on the other hand, is typical of a crater of volcanic origin. Such craters are generally shallow with dark, smooth ejecta uniformly distributed. Kopff is approximately 35 km (22 mi) in diameter. Maunder and Kopff are located within Mare Orientale and are evident in the preceding photograph within the inner basin.

The crater Giordano Bruno (arrow) may have been formed on the night of June 18, A.D. 1178. Medieval accounts report that "a flaming torch sprang up" from the moon. Bruno, 19 km (12 mi) in diameter, has a well-developed ray system that is characteristic of a young impact crater. Calculations show that on the night in question Bruno was 370 km (230 mi) beyond the limb of the moon. The English monks may have seen debris thrown high into the lunar sky and illuminated by the sun.

like structure, and stretches to at least one crater diameter beyond the crest of the crater rim. Rays, stretching radially outward from the crater beyond the ejecta blanket, are formed by ballistic debris from the impact site. The meteoroid-impact craters are also unusually deep and, if large, have a central peak that probably formed when the rock beneath the surface bounced back like a rubber band. It should be noted that it is easy to distinguish between the two types of craters when they are young, as in the case of Maunder and Kopff. The older the craters the more difficult it is to place them in proper niches.

On the night of June 18, A.D. 1178, some English monks reported that "a flaming torch sprang up" from the moon, "spewing out, over a considerable distance, fire, hot coals, and sparks." Furthermore, "the body of the moon which was below writhed, as it were, in anxiety" and "throbbed like a wounded snake." Improbable as this sounds, it is possible that the monks may have witnessed the formation of the crater Giordano Bruno. This crater is about 19 km (12 mi) in diameter and has a well-developed ray system. Calculations reveal that on the evening in question, the moon was a thin crescent in the sky, only 1.6 days past new moon. Bruno was 370 km (230 mi) beyond the limb of the moon. Based on the description, the monks may have seen debris thrown out from impact illuminated high in the lunar sky imposed upon the unlit portion of the moon. The impact should have caused the moon to wobble or oscillate in various directions. All of this should have disappeared except for a slight back-and-forth wobble.

Among the instruments left on the moon are corner-cube reflectors, which send light back along the direction it entered the reflector. The earth–moon distance can be accurately determined by beaming laser beams to the moon so that they reflect from these reflectors back to the earth. The data indicate that a wobble, like that predicted, exists in the motion of the moon. The existence of the wobble does not prove that it was caused by meteoroid impact, but it does suggest that this outrageous tale may be true!

Changes on the Moon?

Diametrically opposed views exist on whether any changes at all have occurred on the lunar surface during the period over which it has been observed with telescopes.

Proponents of the meteoroid-impact theory of lunar-crater formation are pronounced skeptics when it comes to any reports, past or present, of changes on the moon that might have been internally caused. It is true that changes were reported much more often in the past than nowadays. Before detailed maps of the moon had been drawn, it was quite natural to interpret an observed variation as an appearance of a new object or as a disappearance of a familiar one, when in reality it may have been only a changed reflection of light from an object due to the angle of the sun at the time of observation. Nonetheless, most selenographers who have devoted a great deal of time to the moon say they have seen activity or obscuration there. Proponents of the volcanic theory of lunar-crater origin are, of course, looking for evidence of continuing activity to buttress their theories. Any evidence for changes must be thoroughly evaluated.

There are numerous reports of veils, mists, and small clouds on the moon, which obscured known features in such craters as Aristarchus and Plato. So many of these reports have come in, in some instances confirmed by independent observers, that it is difficult to shrug them off as due to poor seeing, inferior instruments, inaccurate drawings, illusions, or memory lapses. Something akin to the escape of gas or the vaporization of solid gases or solids does seem to occur on the moon, though very rarely, despite the belief that volcanic processes ceased on the moon 3 billion years ago and have not resumed one iota since. A relatively few years ago 1 such event was recorded on a spectrogram— or at least was so interpreted by the astronomer who obtained it.

The event in question took place on November 3, 1958, in the crater Alphonsus, located just south of Ptolemaeus and to the west of the central meridian. Three famous dark spots, along the floor of the crater near the edge, which can be distinguished even with small telescopes, have aroused a great deal of interest. But the story begins two years earlier when, on October 26, 1956, Dinsmore Alter, using the 152-centimeter (60-inch) Mount Wilson reflector, took photographs of the Alphonsus area and the adjoining craters of Ptolemaeus and Arzachel. Some plates were made without a filter, in violet-blue light, and others were made with infrared filters. There was considerably less contrast and more blurring in the blue light than in the red. Alter believed that this was in the portion of the photographs showing the crater Alphonsus, not throughout the blue photographs. He said that the fissures in the eastern half of the crater appeared in these photographs to be much more blurred than those in the adjoining crater of Arzachel and took this to mean that a temporary emission of gas had occurred in the eastern part of Alphonsus.

Following up on the reports of the Alter photographs, N. A. Kozyrev, of the Pulkovo Observatory in Leningrad, U.S.S.R., began making spectrograms of the lunar surface near the terminator in the fall of 1958, using the 127-centimeter (50-inch) reflector of the Crimean Astrophysical Observatory. He made a special point of obtaining spectrograms of the interior of the crater Alphonsus. While taking the second of 3 30-minute spectrograms of the area on November 3, 1958, he noted that the central peak in the crater suddenly appeared brighter and whiter than usual and then dropped to normal intensity. At this point a third spectrogram was taken, and this, as well as the first spectrogram taken an hour earlier, showed a normal spectrum. The second spectrogram, however, showed lines that were not normal for Alphonsus, which Kozyrev interpreted as a band indicating diatomic mole-

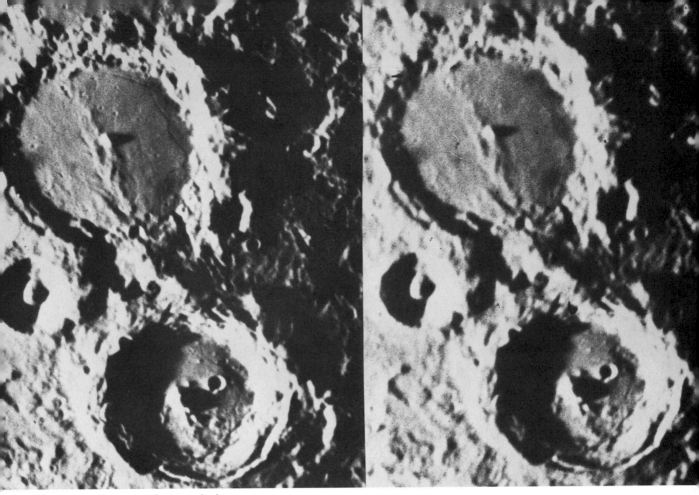

The crater Alphonsus photographed in infrared (left) and blue-violet (right) light on October 26, 1956, with the 1.5-meter (60-inch) Mount Wilson reflector, showing possible obscuration of the floor of Alphonsus at the upper right in the blue-violet light. The rill clearly visible in the infrared near the edge of the floor of Alphonsus is barely discernible in the blue-violet, particularly toward the top (north to top and east to right).

cules of carbon (C_2) and representing an emission of volcanic gases containing carbon from the crater. From the timing of the spectrograms, Kozyrev estimated that this process could not have lasted for more than an hour.

While there has been disagreement about the interpretation of Kozyrev's spectrogram, particularly whether its bands manifest the presence of carbon or not, it is now generally agreed that a small residual gaseous emission must have occurred in Alphonsus on November 3. Kozyrev reported another similar occurrence on October 23, 1959, but the spectrogram does not show such striking bands as the earlier one and it is questioned whether any emission took place at that date.

The number of discoveries of activities on the moon may be as much a function of the amount of time large instruments are trained on it as a measure of actual events occurring there, for in recent years reports of lunar events have multiplied. On the evening of October 29, 1963, James Greenacre and Edward Barr were using the 61-cm (24-inch) refractor of the Lowell Observatory at Flagstaff, Arizona, in the lunar mapping program of the United States Air Force, and saw three colored spots in the vicinity of the crater Aristarchus, toward the limb of the moon northwest of Copernicus. Light ruby-red or reddish-orange in color, two of these spots (one covering an area of about 2.4 by 8 km [1.5 by 5 mi] over a domelike structure and the other about 2.4 km [1.5 mi] in diameter on a hilltop) appeared near the Cobra Head widening of Schröter's Valley, and a pinkish streak about 2.4 by 18 km (1.5 by 11 mi) extended along the inner rim of Aristarchus itself. Within 25 minutes the spots had all disappeared.

On November 27, 1963, the same observers and others saw a larger light-ruby-red streak. This one was about 2.4 by 19 km (1.5 by 12 mi) in size, appeared in almost exactly the same place on the rim of Aristarchus, and lasted for 45 minutes. They notified two colleagues at the Perkins Observatory at Flagstaff, who checked the area in their 175-cm (69-inch) reflector and verified the observation, so the streak must have occurred.

These color flashes and red patches glimpsed on the moon have been explained in many ways. Perhaps the rising sun heats minerals that then luminesce; perhaps moonquakes uncover granite that flashes as its minerals, irradiated for aeons by the solar radiations, are exposed and warmed. The best explanation may derive from the moonquakes reported by instruments left on the moon by Apollo astronauts. Most quakes occur at times when the moon is most pulled by tidal gravitational forces from the earth. Gases trapped under the surface may be released by quakes and raise clouds of electrically charged dust that sparkle and glow.

In 1955 Soviet astronomer Kozyrev had noted a peculiarity in a spectrum he made of Aristarchus, which he interpreted as a luminescent glow. Again in 1961, working with the 127-centimeter (50-inch) reflector of the Crimean Astrophysical Observatory, spectra he made of the central part of the crater on November 26 and 28, and two on December 3, showed emission lines that he identified as those of molecular hydrogen gas, which he believed must have escaped from the moon's interior.

Aristarchus is also the region with the greatest degree of radioactive radon activity. The Apollo 15 command-service module carried an alpha-particle instrument to detect such areas. Scientists believe that the highly radioactive radon results from the gases trapped beneath the surface outgassed in Aristarchus.

Lunar Surface Composition

Full moonlight is much too brilliant for visual comfort when it is gathered in the optical system of a telescope, yet here on earth we see an average of only some 7 percent of the light that falls on the moon from the sun. The moon's overall reflectivity is very low. What kinds of materials would absorb so much of the light falling on them? For many decades, astronomers tried to answer this question. Speculation about the material of the moon's surface has run riot. Only since the Apollo, Luna, and Lunokhod missions has the composition of the moon's surface been truly determined.

The data not only indicate that the lunar surface is different (but not too different) from the earth's surface, but also that differences occur among the different parts of the moon. Mare materials compose about a fifth of the lunar surface. Basalts are the major components of all lunar maria. Basalt is a type of lava common in volcanic areas of the earth. In fact, the compositions of Mare Tranquillitatis and Sinus Medii are similar to that of the basalts of the Columbia River Plateau in the northwestern United States. Variations in grain size and crystalline structure occur among various lunar sites.

The highland materials make up the remaining four fifths of the lunar surface and are more complex. They consist mostly of rock known as anorthosites. These are igneous rocks poor in iron and magnesium

147

but rich in aluminum and calcium silicates. By comparison, the mare basalts are rich in iron and titanium. KREEP basalts and breccias are also found in the lunar highlands. Breccias are rocks and mineral fragments cemented together, in this case by heat.

Small glasses are found abundantly scattered throughout the lunar soil. They exhibit a variety of shapes—ellipsoids, teardrops, dumbbells, rods, and spheres, with the latter most common. The spheres are typically 0.1 mm (about .004 inch) in diameter. Most are the result of melting during meteoroid impact.

Lunar rocks differ from their terrestrial counterparts in several ways. Lunar rocks contain more titanium, uranium, iron, and heavy elements, but lack the volatile elements. These elements have low boiling points and accordingly would vaporize at relatively low temperatures. Since the lunar material was heated to high temperatures in its infancy, these elements are not present. Finally, the lunar samples are dry; no water was found in any of them.

One conclusion from the various core samples taken by the Apollo astronauts is that the surface is made up of many layers. For example, the Apollo 15 deep core tube, 242 cm (about 8 ft) long, contained 42 different layers, ranging from a few millimeters to 13 cm (5 inches) in thickness. Each layer, however, is well mixed.

The term "gardening" has been used to describe the process occurring on the lunar surface. The surface is continuously gardened by the impact of meteoroids, micrometeoroids, and the solar wind particles. Each impact turns over some surface material like a gardener on earth. The material may be old or new, so it all is blended together. Each layer built up depends on the number of incident particles. One researcher has pointed out, however, that the surface is "turned over not in the manner of a terrestrial gardener digging with a spade, but more like a heavily bombarded battlefield."

With an eye on design of landing craft capable of coping with lunar surface conditions, Krafft Ehricke conceived the surface as consisting of a soft layer, perhaps up to 30 to 60 cm (1 to 2 ft) thick, resembling sun-baked, cracked mud. The bombardment of cosmic rays, solar flares, micrometeoroids, and cislunar dust would have produced fine particles on the surface over a million years, he believed. These particles would tend to adhere to one another in the absence of an atmosphere, be baked together and cracked by further bombardment, and be riddled with small meteoroid impacts. Such material would smooth out the surface over small pits and cracks but would not cover larger fissures, pits, and clefts. With the exception of the fissures and cracks, Ehricke's idea of the surface came closest to the reality that was discovered, perhaps, but most of the other theories were "in the ball park" too. Fortunately, the loose dust to great depths did not engulf the astronauts and their vehicles.

As experience on the lunar surface soon proved, astronauts sank only a matter of inches into the dust, beneath which was a fairly well compacted soil. This could bear the weight of the astronauts and their buggy as they trudged and drove across it. Unmanned Soviet vehicles also trundled over the surface with ease.

The soil of basaltic rocks and glassy spheres has been churned over millions of years into the consistency of a well-plowed field. The footprints of no other visitors to the moon from space have been found. If they are there, they will wait for aeons.

No matter how large the terrestrial telescope, the unhappy fact is that no fine details at all can be seen on any of the planets, even the closest ones. With a rare resolution of one second of arc, the estimated smallest spots visible photographically on Mars at opposition (with the earth nearly on a straight line between Mars and the sun) are from 290 to 400 km (180 to 250 mi) across. On Venus at inferior conjunction, the spots distinguishable photographically are about 240 km (150 mi) across. Visually, under exceptionally favorable seeing conditions, the smallest spots discernible on Mars are 30 to 40 km (18 to 25 mi) across, and about 26 km (16 mi) across on Venus (at a resolution of 0.1 second of arc). Thus only large-scale conformations can be seen on the planetary surfaces—merged patterns reminiscent of the way objects on the far horizon look from on top of a mountain.

It is hard to imagine the state of planetary astronomy today without the use of spacecraft. The canals of Mars have given way to immense volcanoes and deep canyons. Venus's impenetrable cloud cover has grudgingly been penetrated by sophisticated instruments to reveal a rocky surface. Dull, uninteresting Mercury, at first glance, now appears to be a mirror image of the moon, heavily cratered and barren.

The amount of information available is simply astounding. Consider the following example worked out by American astronomer Carl Sagan. In the time of Christian Huyghens (1629–95), the first to recognize the rings of Saturn, approximately 10 bits summed up man's entire knowledge of the surface of Mars. A bit represents a piece of information. It is analogous to a dot in a newspaper photograph. By itself it is relatively insignificant, but when placed beside others, a picture forms. The more dots or bits in the photograph, the more detail visible.

By the time of Mars's opposition in 1877, the number of bits rose to perhaps a few thousands. The introduction of photography to astronomy increased the number further, but still slowly. Twenty-two photographs were taken of a limited area of the Martian surface as Mariner 4 flew by the ruddy planet in 1965. But these 22 photographs contained about 5 million bits of information, an amount approximately equal to all the prior photographs taken of Mars. The Mariner 6 and Mariner 7 flybys in 1969 increased the bit total 100 times. Mariner 9, orbiting Mars in 1971 and 1972, increased the number of bits by an additional factor of 100. The Viking missions to Mars in 1976 have increased the number even farther. The Viking 1 Lander continued to send data through 1980. The number of bits available today is truly astronomical.

The studies of early astronomers served their purpose. Despite some seemingly inane theories, many showed remarkable insight, culling truths from meager data. Many of our ideas may seem inane years hence.

Mercury: Not Another Moon

Mercury so closely precedes or follows the sun in the sky that Mercury is a very elusive object to study from the earth and is often lost entirely in the sun's glare. Under the best seeing conditions, with powerful telescopes, astronomers have been able to observe on the Mercurian disk some faint shadings or markings that appear to be fairly permanent, though shifting somewhat with its large librations.

Italian astronomer Giovanni V. Schiaparelli, who had directed at-

Chapter XI
Planetary Surfaces

"... or if they list to try Conjecture,
   he his Fabric of the Heav'ns
Hast left to their disputes, perhaps
   to move
His laughter at their quaint Opinions wide ..."

                          Milton

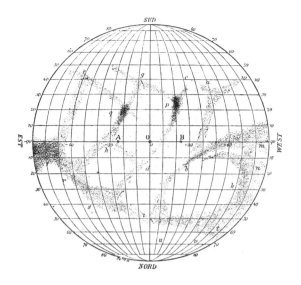

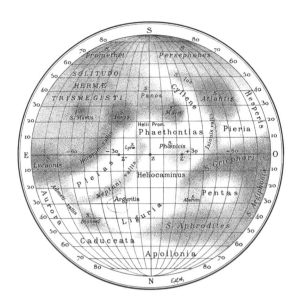

Above left: Map of the faint markings of Mercury, drawn by the Italian astronomer Schiaparelli on a planisphere of the planet (north at bottom and west at right, according to astronomical convention).
Above right: E. M. Antoniadi's map of the markings on Mercury with the names he assigned to some of the more prominent light areas and dark areas, based on his observations from 1924 to 1929, with the 0.8-meter (32-inch) refractor at Meudon Observatory, France.

tention to the Martian *canali* or "channels" in the 1870s, observed Mercury carefully with a small telescope during the 1880s. He reported what seemed to be permanent spots and linear markings on Mercury's surface. He reproduced these on the simple planisphere, or representation of a sphere on a plane, given here.

Schiaparelli also shook up the astronomical world with the announcement that Mercury rotated only once in a revolution of the sun (88 days), keeping the same face toward it except for slight veerings, or librations, as the planet moved in its orbit. A similar phenomenon is exhibited by the earth's moon. Earlier astronomers had thought the rotation of Mercury was close to 24 hours, though they indicated slight variations in the turning. Apparently their preconceptions were father to the thought that the planet had spun full around in 24 hours, returning to nearly the same position, and so presenting the same face to the observer.

One of the most careful Mercurian maps was made up by E. M. Antoniadi, a French astronomer, who used an 81-cm (32-inch) refractor at Meudon Observatory in France in daytime observations of Mercury from 1924 to 1929. Rather quaint Latin names are shown on this map for some of the features of Mercury. He called a gray or dark area "wilderness." (The "S" stands for *solitudo*, the Latin word for wilderness.) "Prom." is an abbreviation of the Latin *promontorium*, a high point of land or rock, or a headland projecting into a sea. Antoniadi also believed that he observed changes in some of the markings.

The suggestion was made that the dark markings on Mercury might represent large-scale maria, or outpourings of lava, similar to the maria on the moon and possibly produced by impacts of meteoroids. Ralph B. Baldwin, who developed the impact theory of the lunar maria and craters in detail, wrote, "Through the telescope Mercury appears very much like a blurred vision of the moon seen with the naked eye. The dark Mercurian areas look much like lunar maria. On both Mercury and the moon, the dark markings are most prominent at the full phase. Within the limits of observation Mercury seems to be a slightly enlarged version of the moon."

Other observations led astronomers to believe that the moon and Mercury were identical. Polarization curves of the integrated light

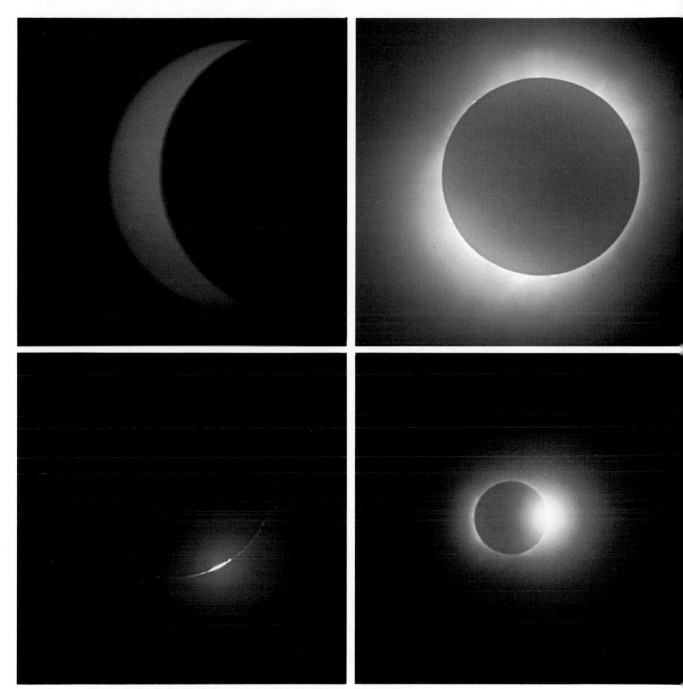

On February 26, 1979, a total solar eclipse occurred over the northwestern
United States and central Canada. As the moon passes in front of the sun,
more and more of the sun becomes covered (top left). At totality (top right)
prominences appear as red tongue-like flames sticking out from the limb
of the sun into the corona, the pearly-white halo about the sun. At the
beginning and end of totality, small portions of the sun peek around the
mountains and through the valleys of the moon creating the phenomenon
called Bailey's Beads (bottom left). Usually one brightens to form the brilliant
diamond ring effect (bottom right).

Full Earth as photographed by the Apollo 17 crew on their way to the moon.

The Grand Canyon of the Colorado as seen by Landsat in October 1979.

Jupiter and three of its Galilean satellites as photographed by Voyager 1 on February 5, 1979 from a distance of 28.4 million km (17.5 million mi). Europa is the bright image to the right; Io, to the left of Europa, is seen superimposed in Jupiter's disk. Callisto is barely visible at the bottom left of the photograph.

The Galilean satellites of Jupiter as recorded by the cameras of Voyager 1. Clockwise from top left, they are Io, Europa, Callisto, and Ganymede.

In this view of the unilluminated side of Saturn's rings, the regions with the least amount of ring material appear the brightest since sunlight passes through easily. The whitest stripe near the middle of the photograph is Cassini's division, normally seen as a dark gap in Saturn's rings.

This montage of the Saturnian system was prepared from photographs recorded by the Voyager 1 spacecraft during its Saturn encounter in November 1980. The large satellite in the left foreground is Dione, followed counterclockwise by Tethys, Mimas, Titan, Rhea, and Enceladus.

from Mercury were intermediate between those of the waxing and waning moon when Mercury was at greatest elongation (when the line from Mercury to the sun forms a 90° angle with that from the sun to the earth). But when Mercury swung closer to inferior conjunction with the earth (on a line between the sun and the earth), Mercury's polarization curves were almost indistinguishable from those of the moon. Sometimes the polarization of light from small regions of Mercury showed wide variations. These might indicate the presence of a local or temporary atmosphere, dust veils, or some other events. Polarization studies seemed to indicate that in an over-all way the surface of Mercury might be very like the moon's.

Then radar observations of Mercury were made by scientists in Russia and at the Goldstone tracking station of the Jet Propulsion Laboratory in the Mohave Desert, where a 26-meter (85-ft) parabolic antenna was used both for transmitting and for receiving the signals. Both teams used strong transmitting power (100 kilowatts or more) in order to receive identifiable echoes back from the tiny, distant planet. The Russians reported that Mercury and the moon appeared to have similar reflection characteristics. The Goldstone scientists obtained striking confirmation of the length of the astronomical unit as determined from the earlier radar-echo studies of Venus. Radar bouncing from Mercury is similar to the echo from a dime at a distance of 16,000 km (10,000 mi). They also concluded that Mercury's surface is much rougher than that of Mars and perhaps twice as rough as that of Venus, more like that of the moon. Later studies revealed the presence of several big, rough surface areas and one smooth area on Mercury.

Radar also provided the first hint that Mercury and the moon may be different. The markings on Mercury indicated that the day and the year are equally long for any Mercurians. But radar observations in the mid-1960s indicated that Mercury actually rotates rather faster on its axis, once in 59 days, about two thirds of its 88-day-long period of revolution of the sun. Apparently the markings on Mercury are so dim, and the rotation so slow, that its 59-day rotation could be mistaken for periods of 88 days or of 24 hours.

In 1974 and 1975 the Mariner 10 spacecraft flew by Mercury 3 times. It took over 2,700 pictures, covering approximately 50 percent of the surface. The smallest recognizable feature is about 100 meters (330 ft).

The pictures revealed that Mercury is similar to the moon. Craters are everywhere. They range in size from the smallest recognizable feature (100 meters or 330 ft) to immense basins 1,000 km (620 mi) across. Unlike the moon, however, the surface of Mercury is marked by noticeable plains, relatively smooth areas between the craters and basins. These plains are level. When compared to the heavily cratered terrain, relatively few craters have scarred the surfaces of the intercrater plains. They probably are among the youngest features on Mercury.

The intercrater plains are probably the most common type of terrain on Mercury. They are found between the large craters that comprise the third type of Mercurian landscape, the heavily cratered terrain. The intercrater plains are level or gently rolling surfaces pockmarked by numerous craters in the 5-to-10-km (3-to-6-mi) range. These craters are probably secondary-impact craters—that is, they

151

This mosaic of Mercury was made from a series of photographs from a distance of approximately 60,000 km (37,300 mi) on March 29, 1974, 2 hours after Mariner 10 made its closest approach to Mercury. This hemisphere of Mercury is dominated by smooth plains and resembles portions of the lunar maria regions. Several craters with ray systems are evident. North is at the top; the equator crosses about two thirds down the disk from the top of this photograph.

This high-resolution photograph of Mercury was taken by Mariner 10 from a height of 5,900 km (3,700 mi) on March 29, 1974, and covers an area 50 by 40 km (31 by 25 mi). Craters of all sizes dominate this scene just as they do in some lunar photographs. Craters as small as 150 meters (500 ft) across can be recognized in this photograph.

Craters appear within craters. A new crater with a diameter of 12 km (7.5 mi) is seen in the center of an older crater basin.

formed as a result of the impact of an object nearby, which either bounced or caused other material to blast out and form additional craters.

The heavily cratered terrain is distinguished by clusters of closely packed overlapping craters, with diameters from about 30 km (19 mi) to several kilometers. A careful examination of the Southern Hemisphere of Mercury shown in the photograph reveals these main types of terrain.

The craters of Mercury are similar to the impact craters of the moon, with terraced inner walls, ejecta, and central peaks. The youngest craters have extensive ray systems, in some cases stretching more than a thousand kilometers. As on the moon, there is a gradation between the youngest and the oldest craters. The youngest have the sharpest features. The craters age by erosion and by meteoroid bombardment, just like those on the moon.

Another major difference between the moon and Mercury is the presence of lobate scarps, scalloped cliffs running for hundreds of kilometers with heights from a few hundred meters to 3 km (2 mi). They are evident throughout the region covered by Mariner 10. These scarps appear to be the results of a decrease in Mercury's radius by about 2 km (about 1.25 mi).

The Southern Hemisphere of Mercury, seen in this mosaic of about 300 photographs taken by Mariner 10, shows the different types of terrain present on Mercury: the rayed craters, the heavily cratered terrain, and the intercrater plains. Mercury's equator nearly coincides with the upper horizon in this mosaic, while the South Pole is in the large crater along the terminator at bottom center.

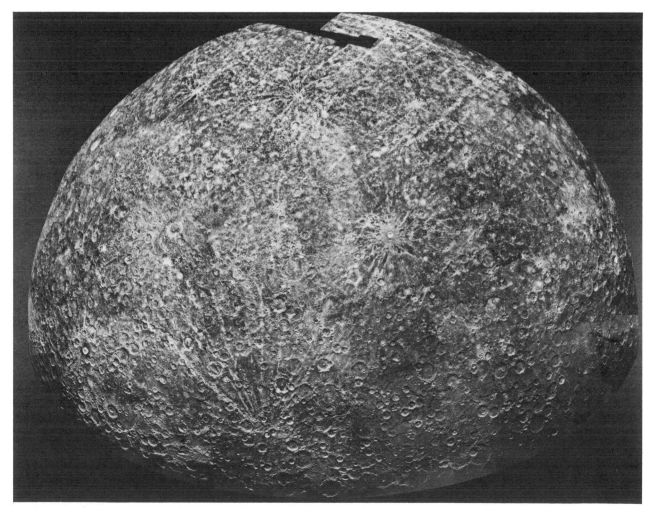

153

A major difference between the moon and Mercury is the presence of lobate scarps, or scalloped cliffs, on Mercury. Such a scarp, more than 300 km (185 mi) long, runs diagonally from upper left to lower right in this photograph of Mercury. Mariner 10 snapped this picture from a distance of 64,500 km (40,000 mi) on September 21, 1974.

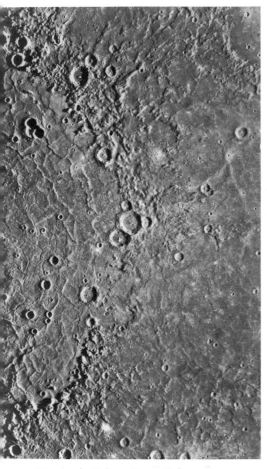

Mercury's Caloris Basin (left center) is similar to the Imbrium Basin on the moon. A 1,300-km (800-mi) diameter ring of mountains with heights to 2 km (6,500 ft) marks the outer edge of this basin. Numerous valleys and ridges stretch beyond the basin. The inner basin is filled by plains that are highly ridged and fractured unlike the Imbrium Basin.

The history of the surface of Mercury parallels that of the moon. Mercury's beginning is similar to that of other planets. Mercury formed out of the solar nebula, getting larger as it accreted material. No recognizable volcanic, tectonic, or atmospheric modification of the large old craters has occurred. But Mercury's magnetic field implies that an iron core is embedded in the interior. In turn, the chemical differentiation into an iron core-silicate crust must have occurred early. The surface needed a degree of rigidity to withstand the intense meteoroid bombardment that followed.

The bombardment marks the second stage in the history of Mercury. It is not clear whether this bombardment occurred at the end of the accreting stage or whether it is a distinct, separate event. In any event, the heavily cratered terrain formed on top of the intercrater plains. The shrinking of Mercury also occurred about this time, forming the lobate scarps.

Toward the end of the heavy bombardment, the third major event occurred: the formation of the Caloris Basin. This feature is some 1,300 km (800 mi) in diameter and resembles the Imbrium Basin on the moon. The Caloris Basin is ringed by mountains and has an extensive system of valleys and ridges reaching out from it. Unlike the Imbrium Basin, the Caloris Basin has a large number of fractures and ridges in its floor.

Exactly opposite the Caloris Basin on the other side of Mercury are hills 5 to 10 km (3 to 6 mi) wide and between 0.1 and 1.8 km (330 ft and 1.1 mi) high, and large, straight valleys running at right angles to each other. This terrain is unique to Mercury and probably is related to the formation of the Caloris Basin.

Shortly after the Caloris Basin formation, the fourth stage began. The smooth plains formed, probably by volcanism. The stage resembles the filling in of the lunar maria.

The final stage, which continues, is the impact by additional bodies from interplanetary space. These impacts have produced the craters visible in the smooth plains as well as the younger craters with their well-defined ray systems. No other activity is occurring.

What of the features observed by Schiaparelli, Antoniadi, and others? The Mariner 10 photographs revealed that the features identified by Antoniadi could not be related to any geological formation on Mer-

154

cury. It is not clear what the early visual observers were actually seeing, especially since they named features under the assumption that Mercury always kept the same face to the sun.

Detailed studies of the surface of Mercury, Venus, and Mars are presenting astronomers with a new and unusual problem: What do you name the newly discovered features? Comets are usually named after the discoverer, while the discoverer of an asteroid is free to name it, provided the name hasn't been used before.

Astronomers have reserved the craters of Mercury for honoring contributors to the arts and humanities. Examples are the craters Homer, Milton, Cervantes, Titian, Rodin, Handel, and Bach. There are two exceptions: Kuiper is a crater named after G. P. Kuiper, a prominent planetary scientist and member of the team responsible for the Mariner 10 photographs, who died shortly before Mariner 10's encounter with Mercury. The second exception is the small crater Hun Kal. For mapping Mercury, astronomers have agreed that the twentieth meridian of longitude of Mercury passes through the center of this crater. Hun Kal is the Mayan word for twenty.

Craters on the moon are now named after scientists. Those on Mars are named after individuals who have contributed either to the scientific study of Mars or its lore, to interpretation of Martian phenomena, or to basic discoveries of significance to the exploration of Mars.

Venus's Unseen Surface

Just before the turn of the century, Percival Lowell's report and drawings of what he claimed were fairly permanent markings on Venus created an uproar. In some of his drawings, the darker markings look like the spokes of a wheel radiating out from a hub in the center of Venus, but without a rim around the edge of its disk. In the midst of all the hubbub about the existence of artificially created canals on Mars, a smaller rhubarb developed about whether the spokes tended to prove the existence of intelligent life on Venus. Perhaps, some speculated, this almost geometrical design on the face of Venus was another rational system of roadways or canals or some other planetary construction program.

To Lowell's credit, however, he himself did not interpret the Venusian wagon wheel as evidence of intelligence. He described these radial markings as akin to crow's feet. "In addition to some of more ordi-

The radial markings of Venus as drawn in 1896 and 1897 by Percival Lowell. Below the series of drawings he noted "Rotation 225 days."

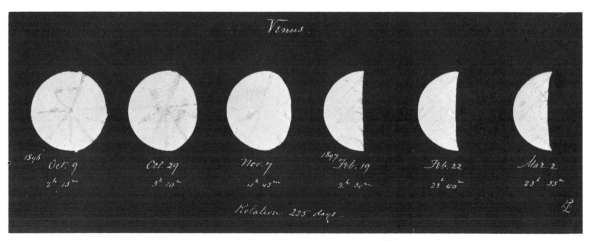

nary character," he wrote, "were a set of spokelike streaks which started with the planet's periphery and ran inwards to a point not very distant from the center. The spokes started well-defined and broad at the edge, dwindling and growing fainter as they proceeded, requiring the best of definition for their following to their central hub." While he believed the markings to be on Venus's surface, not in its atmosphere, he noted a number of times that he did not consider these streaks on Venus to be anything but natural, like those on Mercury. Other astronomers did not rush to confirm Lowell's charts of Venus.

The radial markings drawn by Percival Lowell are now generally accepted as possible on occasion. Even more remarkable is the fact that he explained them with detailed wind-convection diagrams. In this instance, too much of Lowell's work, showing both accurate observation and remarkable insight, had been thrown out like the baby with the bath water.

The thick clouds of Venus prevent astronomers from viewing its surface. Nor are cameras aboard orbiting spacecraft capable of penetrating Venus's dense cover. Fortunately, the relatively new radar astronomy has provided a "picture" of the Venusian surface. The image is formed by analyzing the time, the frequency, and the power of the radar echo bouncing off the surface of Venus. The radar signal, beamed either from the earth or from an orbiter, is capable of making the two-way trip through the Cytherean clouds.

The Venusian radar images reveal similarities to the earth, Mars, the moon, and Mercury. There are volcanic features, circular depressions, and rift valleys reminiscent of the East African Rift on earth.

The circular features are believed to be ancient impact craters. They have rim-width-to-floor-diameter ratios and a size-to-number-of-features relationship that is characteristic of large degraded craters on other terrestrial planets and on the moon. This further indicates that regions of Venus, as on Mercury, Mars, and the moon, have been modified little since their formation. Other features, however, indicate that some regions have been modified. These features are volcanoes, mountainous terrain, and canyons.

Two types of volcanoes exist on Venus. The first type is similar to the Tharsis volcanoes on Mars and are isolated, huge structures. One

A large trough system (T), some 1,400 km (870 mi) long, 150 km (90 mi) wide, and approximately 2 km (1 mi) deep, is seen in this radar image of Venus obtained with the antenna at the Goldstone tracking station of the Jet Propulsion Laboratory. This system has been compared to the Valles Marineris on Mars and the East African Rift on earth. Also visible is a large plateau (P) marked with several isolated peaks (arrows). This image of Venus covers approximately 2,300 by 1,400 km (1,430 by 880 mi).

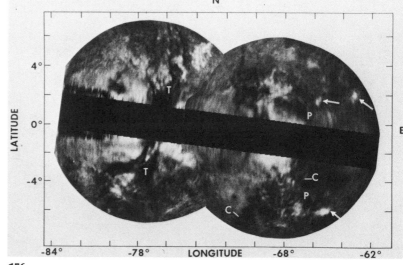

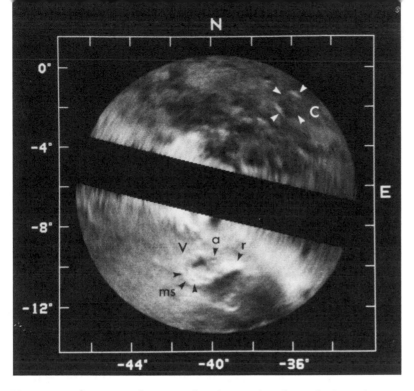

A craterlike form (C) is seen in this radar image of Venus. The feature V has been interpreted as volcanic terrain similar to the Tharsis volcanoes on Mars. A large ridge (r), rim (ms), and a smaller satellite crater (a) are identified. This image represents a region 1,400 km (870 mi) across.

Venusian volcano is at least 400 km (250 mi) wide at the base (it may stretch to about 800 km or 500 mi) and may be 10 km (6 mi) high. The second type is similar to the San Francisco Peaks near Flagstaff, Arizona. This cluster of peaks, with heights of about 3,600 meters (12,000 ft), are believed to be the remnants of an ancient volcano that towered some 7,900 meters (26,000 ft) above the desert. Such peaks are rarely seen on Mars, Mercury, or the moon. A Venusian region approximately 1 km (0.6 mi) higher than the surrounding plain and encompassing about 300 square km (120 square mi) contains a cluster of at least 15 peaks.

The radar images also suggest that tectonic activity has occurred or is occurring on Venus. A region of parallel hills and valleys near the Venusian equator may have been formed by the collision of two plates like the European Alps or the Tibetan Himalayas. Other scientists disagree. They believe that this terrain was formed by an extension similar to that which formed the basin-and-range topography of the western United States. The boundary between the hills and valley and the surrounding plain is sharp and linear, suggesting a pronounced scarp. The hills actually range in size from smallish hills to small mountains with heights between a few hundred meters and 2 km (1.2 mi).

Indications of extensive tectonic activity are 2 large canyons or rifts. One was detected from the earth, while the other was detected by the Pioneer Venus Orbiter. The first measures at least 1,400 by 150 by 2 km (870 by 90 by 1 mi). The second, found as part of the radar mapping of Venus from the Pioneer Venus Orbiter, stretches for at least 1,400 km (870 mi). In places the canyon may be as wide as 280 km (170 mi) and 4.6 km (2.9 mi) deep. Gently rolling plains exist on either side of the canyons.

Ultimately the Pioneer Venus Orbiter will provide radar mapping of a large portion of Venus's surface. The orbit is fixed in space, but Venus rotates slowly beneath it so that the orbit moves relative to Venus approximately 1.5 degrees a day. This will permit the radar equipment to obtain profiles of the planet's surface. Other discoveries of the

Venus's surface as seen by Venera 9 on October 22, 1975 (top). Stones several tens of centimeters in size are evident. The sharp edges on the stones surprised some scientists who believed that strong erosive forces would have smoothed the rocks. Part of the spacecraft can be seen in the foreground, while the horizon is visible in the upper right corner.

On October 25, 1975, Venera 10 took this photograph of Venus's surface (bottom). Located in a different part of Venus, this landing site is probably older than the rocky desert seen by Venera 9. The rocks have smooth edges and are covered by a dark, fine-grained soil. The horizon can be seen in the upper right of the picture, and part of the spacecraft is visible in the foreground.

radar equipment are a group of impact craters some 600 to 700 km (370 to 430 mi) across and only 500 to 700 meters (1,600 to 2,300 ft) deep. Two of these craters have central peaks, characteristic of impact craters on the moon and Mercury. These observations confirm the ground-based observations of similar features on Venus.

Only two photographs have been taken of the surface of Venus. They were made by the Russian spacecraft Venera 9 and 10 in 1975. Both vehicles soft-landed on the surface and operated briefly before succumbing to the intense surface heat and pressure.

Rocky desert is seen in the two panoramas. The Venera 9 photograph revealed a heap of stones several tens of centimeters in size, with sharp edges. These sharp edges surprised some scientists, who believed that the rocks should be smoothed out by erosion from winds in the thick atmosphere.

Other scientists were surprised by the smooth rocks seen in the Venera 10 panorama, since they don't believe there are erosive forces, including wind, acting on Venus. The stony landscape in the photograph may possibly be a scree on the slope of a hill. The Venera 10 photograph reveals a smooth surface with only slight stony elevations. The rocks have smoother edges and are covered with a darker, fine-grained soil. This landing site is probably a plain or plateau older than that seen in the Venera 9 photograph.

The photographs support radar images of large expanses on Venus with moderate or high reflectivity suggestive of bouldery surfaces. The radar images and the Venera photographs appeared to have laid to rest the old idea of a Venus with vegetation and vast petroleum oceans.

Martian Kaleidoscope

When people study telescopic photographs of Mars for the first time, or even view it through a sizable telescope, their reaction is often a mixture of frustration and disappointment. Can this smudged little orb, slightly ocher-hued, a white polar cap its only outstanding feature, with the fuzzy edge of its dim disk almost merging with the blackness of space around it, be the much-vaunted Red Planet? How can anything at all have been learned about such a vaguely outlined, dusky wad of stuff so far away in space?

As the planet is viewed intensely for a long time and, with concentration, a few details are picked out, admiration grows for the observers who have produced maps of Mars like that shown.

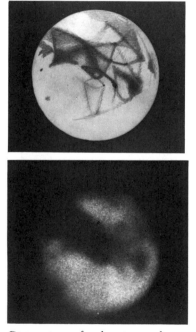

Comparison of a drawing and a photograph made at the same time during the opposition of Mars in 1926.

The chart showing the major light and dark markings on Mars was developed between the years 1941 and 1952 by G. de Mottoni of the French Pic-du-Midi Observatory, on a Mercator projection, based on composites derived from hundreds of photographs of Mars. It was officially adopted by the International Astronomical Union at its 1958 meeting.

This map shows a surprising amount of detail on Mars, perhaps more than could be distinguished on the earth, because of our more clouded atmosphere, if similar-sized Martian telescopes were aimed in this direction. Astronomers who concentrate on Mars are more familiar with its markings than most of us are with the shapes and positions of the continents and major islands on globes of the earth.

A careful comparison of this map with the more modern version shows that the bright and dark areas on the earlier maps are actually there, although they change mysteriously in size and shape over the years. With telescopic viewing, the bright areas were called "deserts" and the dark areas "vegetation," but Mariner Mars flights have changed these ideas. Mariner 9 has shown that Mars is more rugged for its size than the earth, with an overall elevation difference of 26 km (16 mi).

The International Astronomical Union has the task of naming the features on the various planets and satellites in the solar system. In the case of Mars it attempted to retain as much as possible the names given to the Martian features by the early observers as well as adding new ones.

Fourteen classes of features are recognized on Mars. Approximately 6,000 craters with diameters greater than 20 km (12 mi) are known. Craters larger than about 100 km (62 mi) have been named after individuals who in some manner were associated with the study or lore of the ruddy planet. Other recognized features are: a chain or line of craters (catena), canyon (chasma), ridge (dorsum), long, shallow depression or ditch (fossa), a complex of intersecting valleys (labyrinthus), mesa (mensa), mountain (mons), irregular or complex crater with scalloped edges (patera), plain (planitia), plateau (planum), hill (tholus), valley (vallis), and extensive plain (vastitas).

Once the general appearance of Mars was revealed by Mariner spacecraft, attempts were made to correlate the bright and dark areas seen by earth-based observers with features seen in the photographs. Some believed that the dark areas are low areas on Mars, just as they are on the moon. Others argued that the bright areas are lower than the dark areas. Current evidence indicates that there is no correspondence between the satellite and earth-based observations. Some of the highest and some of the lowest areas on Mars appear equally bright.

The Northern Hemisphere and the Southern Hemisphere of Mars differ from each other. It is as if two separate contractors made Mars, the southern contractor specializing in craters and relatively flat terrain, and the northern contractor in extensive lava flows and huge volcanoes. When it came time to piece the two hemispheres together they didn't quite agree, so now a huge canyon, Valles Marineris, separates them.

The differences between the Northern Hemisphere and the Southern Hemisphere reflect the different geologic processes that have occurred on Mars. The southern represents the older surface. Probably

NOMENCLATURE MARTIENNE SELON L'U.A.I. - I.A.U. NAMED MARTIAN MARKINGS

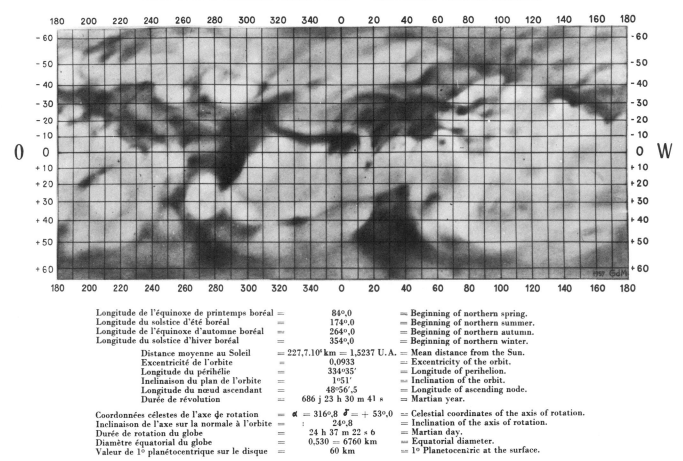

Longitude de l'équinoxe de printemps boréal	=	84°,0	= Beginning of northern spring.
Longitude du solstice d'été boréal	=	174°,0	= Beginning of northern summer.
Longitude de l'équinoxe d'automne boréal	=	264°,0	= Beginning of northern autumn.
Longitude du solstice d'hiver boréal	=	354°,0	= Beginning of northern winter.

Distance moyenne au Soleil	=	227,7.10⁶ km = 1,5237 U.A.	= Mean distance from the Sun.
Excentricité de l'orbite	=	0,0933	= Excentricity of the orbit.
Longitude du périhélie	=	334°35'	= Longitude of perihelion.
Inclinaison du plan de l'orbite	=	1°51'	= Inclination of the orbit.
Longitude du nœud ascendant	=	48°56',5	= Longitude of ascending node.
Durée de révolution	=	686 j 23 h 30 m 41 s	= Martian year.

Coordonnées célestes de l'axe de rotation	=	α = 316°,8 δ = + 53°,0	= Celestial coordinates of the axis of rotation.
Inclinaison de l'axe sur la normale à l'orbite	=	24°,8	= Inclination of the axis of rotation.
Durée de rotation du globe	=	24 h 37 m 22 s 6	= Martian day.
Diamètre équatorial du globe	=	0,530 = 6760 km	= Equatorial diameter.
Valeur de 1° planétocentrique sur le disque	=	60 km	= 1° Planetocentric at the surface.

Les petits détails sont désignés par leurs coordonnées planétographiques.
Small features are designated by their planetographic coordinates.

Les grandes régions sont désignées par un nom dont voici la liste et les coordonnées.
Main markings are designated by names according to the following record and coordinates.

Acidalium M. (30°, + 45°)
Aeolis (215°, — 5°)
Aeria (310°, + 10°)
Aetheria (230°, + 40°)
Aethiopis (230°, + 10°)
Amazonis (140°, 0°)
Amenthes (250°, + 5°)
Aonius S. (105°, — 45°)
Arabia (330°, + 20°)
Araxes (115°, — 25°)
Arcadia (100°, + 45°)
Argyre (25°, — 45°)
Arnon (335°, + 48°)
Aurorae S. (50°, — 15°)
Ausonia (250°, — 40°)
Australe M. (40°, — 60°)
Baltia (50°, + 60°)
Boreum M. (90°, + 50°)
Boreosyrtis (290°, + 55°)
Candor (75°, + 3°)
Casius (260°, + 40°)
Cebrenia (210°, + 50°)
Cecropia (320°, + 60°)
Ceraunius (95°, + 20°)
Cerberus (205°, + 15°)
Chalce (0°, — 50°)
Chersonesus (260°, — 50°)
Chronium M. (210°, — 58°)
Chryse (30°, + 10°)
Chrysokeras (110°, — 50°)
Cimmerium M. (220°, — 20°)
Claritas (110°, — 35°)

Copais Palus (280, + 55°)
Coprates (65°, — 15°)
Cyclopia (230°, — 5°)
Cydonia (0°, + 40°)
Deltoton S. (305°, — 4°)
Deucalionis R. (340°, — 15°)
Deuteronilus (0°, + 35°)
Diacria (180°, + 50°)
Dioscuria (320°, + 50°)
Edom (345°, 0°)
Electris (190°, — 45°)
Elysium (210°, + 25°)
Eridania (220°, — 45°)
Erythraeum M. (40°, — 25°)
Eunostos (220°, + 22°)
Euphrates (335°, + 20°)
Gehon (0°, + 15°)
Hadriacum M. (270°, — 40°)
Hellas (290°, — 40°)
Hellespontica Depressio (340° — 6°)
Hellespontus (325°, — 50°)
Hesperia (240°, — 20°)
Hiddekel (345°, + 15°)
Hyperboreus L. (60°, + 75°)
Iapigia (295°, — 20°)
Icaria (130°, — 40°)
Isidis R. (275°, + 20°)
Ismenius L. (330°, + 40°)
Jamuna (40°, + 10°)
Juventae Fons (63°, — 5°)
Laestrigon (200°, 0°)
Lemuria (200°, + 70°)

Libya (270°, 0°)
Lunae Palus (65°, + 15°)
Margaritifer S. (25°, — 10°)
Memnonia (150°, — 20°)
Meroe (285°, + 35°)
Meridianii S. (0°, — 5°)
Moab (350°, + 20°)
Moeris L. (270°, + 8°)
Nectar (72°, — 28°)
Neith R. (270°, + 35°)
Nepenthes (260°, + 20°)
Nereidum Fr. (55°, — 45°)
Niliacus L. (30°, + 30°)
Nilokeras (55°, + 30°)
Nilosyrtis (290°, + 42°)
Nix Olympica (130°, + 20°)
Noachis (330°, — 45°)
Ogygis R. (65°, — 45°)
Olympia (200°, + 80°)
Ophir (65°, — 10°)
Ortygia (0°, + 60°)
Oxia Palus (18°, + 8°)
Oxus (10°, + 20°)
Panchaia (200°, + 60°)
Pendorae Fretum (340°, — 25°)
Phaethontis (155°, — 50°)
Phison (320°, + 20°)
Phlegra (190°, + 30°)
Phoenicis L. (110°, — 12°)
Phrixi R. (70°, — 40°)
Promethei S. (280°, — 65°)
Propontis (185°, + 45°)

Protei R. (50°, — 23°)
Protonilus (315°, + 42°)
Pyrrhae R. (38°, — 15°)
Sabaeus S. (340°, — 8°)
Scandia (150°, + 60°)
Serpentis M. (320°, — 30°)
Sinaï (70°, — 20°)
Sirenum M. (155°, — 30°)
Sithonius L. (245°, + 45°)
Solis L. (90°, — 28°)
Styx (200°, + 30°)
Syria (100°, — 20°)
Syrtis Major (290°, + 10)
Tanaïs (70°, + 50°)
Tempe (70°, + 40°)
Thaumasia (85°, — 35°)
Thoth (255°, + 30°)
Thyle I (180°, — 70°)
Thyle II (230°, — 70°)
Thymiamata (10°, + 10°)
Tithonius L. (85°, — 5°)
Tractus Albus (80°, + 30°)
Trinacria (268°, — 25°)
Trivium Charontis (198, + 20)
Tyrrhenum M. (255°, — 20°)
Uchronia (260°, + 70°)
Umbra (290°, + 50°)
Utopia (250°, + 50°)
Vulcani Pelagus (15, — 35)
Xanthe (50°, + 10°)
Yaonis R. (320°, — 40°)
Zephyria (195°, 0°)

Map of the principal formations of Mars for the years 1941 to 1952, drawn by G. de Mottoni on the Mercator projection, with a system of coordinates based on position measurements by Henri Camichel (north at bottom, west at right, according to astronomical convention). Data on the planet, its orbit, rotation, and the seasons are given, as well as the coordinates of the named features adopted at the 1958 meetings of the International Astronomical Union. This map should be compared with the following one of Mars, which is based on the Mariner results from Mars.

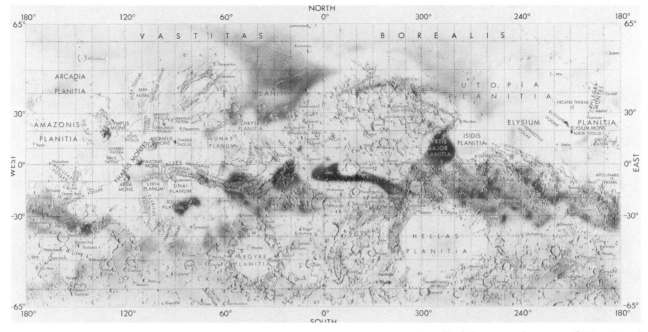

An albedo/topographic map of Mars based on Mariner spacecraft data and showing the new Martian nomenclature of the International Astronomical Union. In order to compare this map with the previous one, note that north is at the top and west is to the left. A careful comparison of the two maps identifies several of the topographic features of Mars with the albedo features seen from the earth.

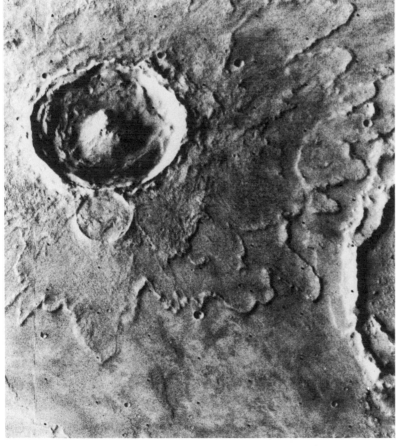

The crater Yuty, 18 km (11 mi) in diameter, is a typical impact crater. It has the central peak characteristic of impact features; the flows emanating from the crater are layers of broken rocks thrown out of the crater by the shock following impact. The ridges at the leading edge of the flows are similar to those of great avalanches on earth. Viking 1 photographed this feature from a distance of 1,877 km (1,165 mi).

Mars as seen by Viking from a distance of 560,000 km (348,000 mi) on June 17, 1976, shows the 4 giant Martian volcanoes. Olympus Mons, the largest, is the single feature near the top. The row of three girding the middle are (left to right) Arsia Mons, Pavonis Mons, and Ascraeus Mons. The white, circular feature at the bottom is the impact basin Argyre Planitia.

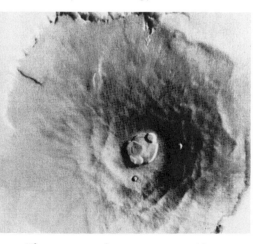

The gigantic volcanic mountain Olympus Mons rises 21 km (13 mi) above its base, which measures 700 km (435 mi) across. The summit crater is some 80 km (50 mi) wide. Olympus Mons is the largest of the Martian volcanoes.

numerous Martian craters were formed by impact, just as the moon, Mercury, and to a lesser extent the earth were scarred early in their evolution. The southern basins Hellas Planitia, Argyre Planitia, and the northern Isidis Planitia have rim structure and resemble Mare Imbrium on the moon, suggesting an impact origin.

The cratering must also have occurred in the Northern Hemisphere, but volcanic activity undoubtedly obliterated them. The volcanoes of Mars occur in one region of the Northern Hemisphere and completely dominate the landscape. The three volcanoes of the Tharsis Montes and the nearby Olympus Mons sit on a crustal bulge some 6 km (4 mi) above the adjacent plain. The elevated region extends some 4,000 km (2,500 mi) north to south and 3,000 km (1,900 mi) east to west. When compared to earth the dimensions of this area are continental.

Arsia Mons, Pavoris Mons, and Ascraeus Mons, which form the Tharsis Montes, and Olympus Mons are shield volcanoes. These features are large cones with gentle slopes that are formed by successive flows of highly fluid basaltic lavas. A terrestrial example is Mauna Loa on the island of Hawaii. The island of Hawaii itself is made of several shield volcanoes; it has a diameter of 200 km (120 mi) and rises 9 km (6 mi) above the ocean floor. The largest of the Martian volcanoes, Olympus Mons, is 700 km (430 mi) across and rises 21 km (13 mi) above its base. The height of this giant above the surrounding plain is 2½ times the height of Mount Everest, earth's tallest mountain, above sea level! The caldera at the top of the cone is 80 km (50 mi) in diameter, which means it would hold the state of Rhode Island.

The Valles Marineris is an enormous canyon system that dwarfs the Grand Canyon of the Colorado. The Valles Marineris runs some 4,500 km (2,800 mi) east to west along the equator of Mars and varies in width between 150 and 700 km (90 and 430 mi). Depths range between 2 and 7 km (1 and 4 mi). The length of this canyon measures about a quarter of the distance around Mars.

Valles Marineris is actually a series of canyons pieced together to form one mammoth system. The age of the canyon is not certain. It crosses upland plains with moderate to heavy cratering as well as beginning near the elevated region containing Tharsis Montes. Little cratering is evident in the valley floor, but this just may result from events occurring within the valley. Landslides are an example of such altering processes.

The origin of this extensive canyon may never be known. It is fairly definite that no single process produced it. The western end undoubtedly has been influenced by the processes that formed the massive volcanoes. The eastern end was also the result of tectonic activity, but erosion due to wind or water masks evidence for tectonics.

The polar ice caps have always been in the limelight of studies of the Martian surface. Percival Lowell believed that the ice caps were composed of water ice that melted as spring and summer arrived. Later evidence indicated that the winter cap was frozen carbon dioxide, or dry ice. Early in the Viking missions it was learned that the residual northern ice cap, the ice left in the summer, is exclusively water ice. By analogy the residual southern cap should also be water ice. But this is not the case. The two ice caps of Mars are different. Another mystery has been added to the long list of mysteries of Mars: The southern polar ice cap is dominated, winter and summer, by dry ice, while the residual northern polar ice cap is water ice.

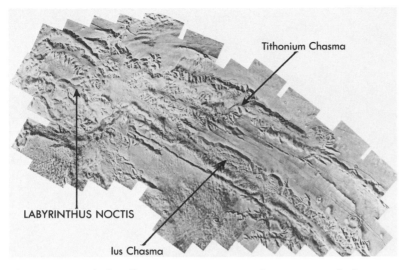

The western end of Valles Marineris is seen in this mosaic made from more than 100 photographs taken with the cameras of Viking Orbiter 1 in August 1976. The two canyons, Tithonium Chasma and Ius Chasma, extend to the east from Labyrinthus Noctis. Faults, tributary systems from flowing water, and landslides can be recognized.

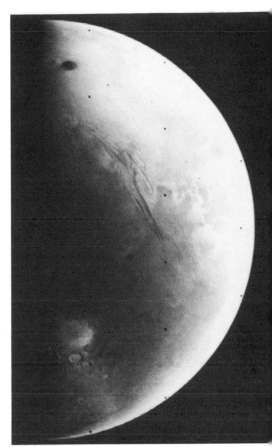

The complete extent of the Valles Marineris is seen running from upper left to lower right across the middle of the Martian disk. This "Grand Canyon" stretches about a quarter of the distance around Mars, measuring 4,500 km (2,800 mi) in length; it varies in width between 150 and 700 km (90 and 430 mi), and in depth between 2 and 7 km (1 and 4 mi). On earth this canyon system would extend from Los Angeles to New York. The dark circular feature at the top is the volcano Ascraeus Mons; Argyre Planitia is the bright circular feature at the bottom. This photograph was taken by Viking 1 on June 18, 1976, 1 day before it went into orbit around Mars.

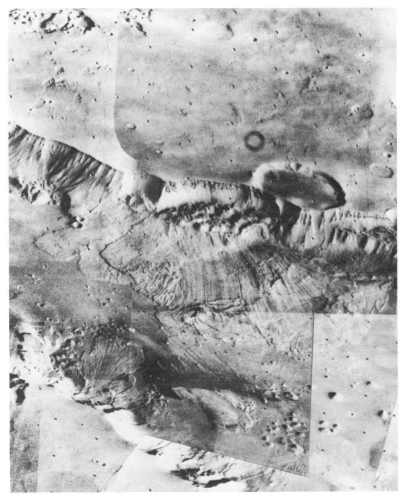

This view across the Valles Marineris shows the results of landslides, both on the near and far canyon walls. The linear markings show the direction of material flow. On the far wall, a landslide appears to have occurred on top of an earlier slide.

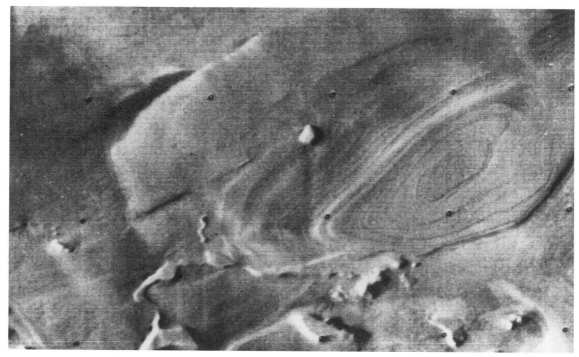

Mariner 9 photographed what may be an oval glacier near Mars's South Pole. The light layers may be frozen carbon dioxide and water ice between dark layers of dust or volcanic ash. Beneath these are jagged pits and grooves of an older deposit.

The discovery of water ice in the northern polar ice cap was greeted with satisfaction by many scientists. There is considerable evidence that many of the numerous channels seen in the Mariner and Viking photographs could have been formed only by flowing water. But the outstanding question is: Where is all the water? Liquid water cannot exist under the conditions now prevailing on Mars. Nor can the amount of water in the residual northern polar ice cap account for all the channels.

Viking data indicate that channels were formed at different times under different conditions. Broad channels at the edge of southern highlands near Chryse Planitia probably originated when permafrost (subsurface water ice) was melted by geothermal heat. The water breaks through at the base of a hill, flooding the valley and forming the broad channels. Other channels resemble terrestrial river systems.

"Islands" in a channel within the Ares Valley have been etched out by water and wind. Markings on the channel show the direction of the water flow. Water has not been present for some time, as indicated by the number of impact craters peppering the islands and the channel floor.

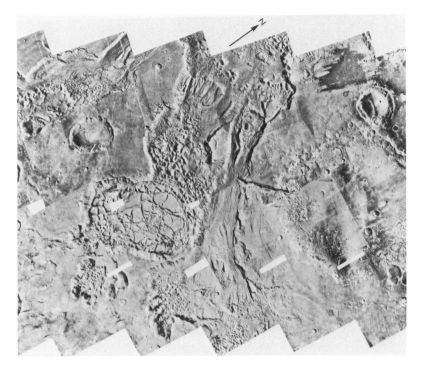

Numerous collapse features associated with outwash channels are evident in this photomosaic of the eastern end of Valles Marineris. One channel splits the photograph in half. Scientists believe that many collapse features form when subterranean ice melts. As the water drains away in the channels (here in the northerly direction), the unsupported surface collapses.

These filamentary channels often originate at the rims of craters, then flow onto lowland plains or crater floors, where they end abruptly. Scientists are divided whether or not these channels are formed by Martian rainfalls, but they do seem to have been formed during at least two separate times.

A third type of channel consists of stubby, sinuous channels with many tributaries. These originate from melted permafrost in box canyons. Due to their common occurrence over a broad area, it is unlikely that the permafrost was melted by local geothermal heating. A general climatic warming has been suggested for the formation of these channels.

No one denies the existence of the channels. The mystery today is what happened to the water. Many believe that thick layers of permafrost lie beneath the Martian surface, but they have yet to be discovered. A recent report claims that liquid water may exist a few centimeters below the surface in Salis Planum and in a plain west of Hellas Planitia. Greater amounts of water vapor are observed over these two areas than over other regions of Mars. Furthermore, infrared detectors have shown that these two regions undergo daily and seasonal temperature variations. The variations are large enough to melt ice in the soil. On the basis of this report, these two regions will undergo closer scrutiny in the future.

Two spacecraft have landed on Mars. Viking 1 landed in Chryse Planitia at 22° North, 48° West on July 20, 1976, Viking 2 in Utopia Planitia at 44° North, 226° West on September 3, 1976. Photographs taken by the Viking Landers reveal a variety of rocks among fine-grained material. The site of Viking Lander 1 has rocks ranging from a few centimeters to almost 2 meters (6.5 ft) across strewn about an undulating surface. The rocks are of a basaltic igneous type, the majority angular with coarsely pitted surfaces. In several places, bedrock is visible as well as sand drifts. The drifts range from large complexes of

*The Martian landscape at the
site of the Viking 1 Lander.
The reddish surface is covered
by various size boulders and
rocks. To the right of the
meteorology boom are
trenches (bottom right) dug by
the Lander. Materials from
these trenches were analyzed
for chemical composition and
for evidence of Martian life.*

*Utopia Planitia as viewed by Viking
Lander 2 on May 18, 1979, reveals not
only the rocky terrain but also shows a
thin coating of water ice on the rocks and
soil. Although ice and clouds indicate that
water exists on Mars, it is present only in
very small amounts.*

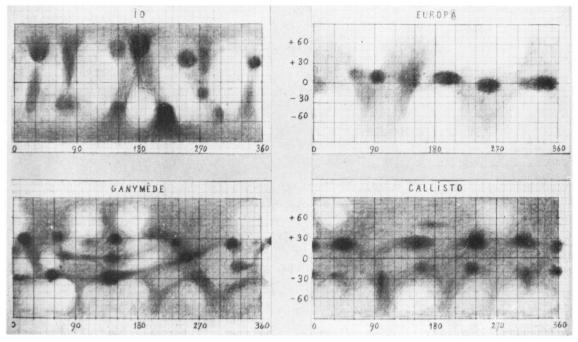

about 10 meters (33 ft) to smaller individual drifts approximately 1 to 3 meters (3 to 10 ft) in size and even smaller (about 10 cm or 4 inches) leeward of rocks. Apparently this area has been formed by the chemical and mechanical erosion of the upper few meters of a volcanic flow of basalt. Water appears to have played a major role in this landscape.

In contrast, the Utopia site of Viking Lander 2 is generally flat and exhibits no bedrock or large sand drifts. The rocks are all similar, unlike the varieties seen at Chryse. The boulders are evenly distributed and may represent the ejecta of the crater Mie nearby. At both landing sites the Martian surface has been found to be firmer than that of the moon.

In the words of one scientist, "Mars is a toughie." Despite the tremendous wealth of data from the Mariner and Viking missions, Mars has its secrets well hidden. Numerous changes occur: Dust storms come and go, altering the landscape; a slight "slumping" of the surface has been observed; landslides may have occurred recently in the Valles Marineris; the ice caps change with the seasons, while the residual caps show that a layering has occurred over long periods of time. Any theory for the evolution of Mars may never be able to account adequately for all its observed features.

Planisphere drawings of Jupiter's satellites: Io (Jupiter I), the diameter of which is a little larger than that of the earth's moon; Europa (Jupiter II), the markings of which concentrate along the equator rather than well above and below it, as on Io; Ganymede (Jupiter III), larger than the planet Mercury; and Callisto (Jupiter IV), slightly smaller than the moon in size. The drawings are after Bernard Lyot, with the contrast exaggerated, using the 61-cm (24-inch) refractor at Pic-du-Midi Observatory. Now that the Voyager 1 and Voyager 2 spacecraft have viewed these satellites from close up, drawings like the above retain only historical interest; it is difficult to correlate the photographs with the drawings.

Surfaces of the Outer Planets and Their Satellites

The atmospheres of the outer planets contain large quantities of methane and ammonia gases, as well as hydrogen, helium, nitrogen, and neon in quantities proportional to those in the sun.

Radio emissions of Jupiter and Saturn have been under study since 1955. Jupiter has an ionosphere and a strong magnetic field, varying from 3 to 14 gauss. It also has well-developed Van Allen belts, containing radiation of much greater intensity than that banding the earth. Some radio emissions appear to originate deep below the visible atmosphere of Jupiter. The nature of its lower atmosphere and distinguishable surface, if any, have been the objects of great speculation.

Voyager 2 provided this close-up view of Europa on July 9, 1979. Europa is believed to have a mantle of ice some 100 km (62 mi) thick. The dark features are cracks in the icy surface that have filled in with dark material from below. Unlike Ganymede and Callisto, Europa has few craters on its surface.

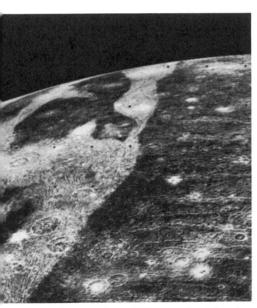

This close-up view of Ganymede, taken by Voyager 2 from a distance of 137,600 km (86,000 mi) on July 8, 1979, shows some of its dark, heavily cratered terrain. The origin of the light, linear features striping the dark region is unknown. They resemble the outer rings of the large, impact-produced ring structure observed on Callisto, but they may also be internally produced fractures.

No models for Jupiter and Saturn, as well as for Uranus and Neptune, are made with solid globes. Most models envision layers of various crystals and ices forming these planets. It is not even definite whether the gas giants have rocky cores, although some models have such centers.

Russian and American scientists reported in 1963 that faint radar echoes had been returned from Jupiter. The data from the Soviet experiment have not been announced. The American report from the Goldstone radar station of the Jet Propulsion Laboratory interpreted the radar signals received back from Jupiter as indicating that a part of Jupiter's surface (or whatever level the waves were reflected from) is smoother than those of Mars and Venus.

The surfaces of the Galilean satellites of Jupiter—Io, Europa, Ganymede, and Callisto—were also observed from the earth. Like Mercury, Venus, and Mars, drawings were made of their surfaces. As in the previous instances, the examples given in the figure bear little resemblance to reality. The Voyager photographs have shown the surfaces of these satellites to be cratered, cracked, and in the case of Io, marked with active volcanoes. For the most part Ganymede, Europa, and Callisto have icy mantles, which have cracked the surface due to the various stresses placed on it. Furthermore, impact craters are present. Similar remarks apply to Rhea, Dione, Tethys, Enceladus, and Mimas. These satellites of Saturn have been shown by the cameras of Voyager to be icy bodies, covered by numerous impact craters, sinuous valleys, and light streaks, analogous to, but not identical to, lunar rays. Io has the youngest surface of all. Many of the features observed on the other Galilean satellites have been obliterated on Io by the magma spewing out of its active volcanoes.

"The human understanding," Francis Bacon wrote nearly 350 years ago, "supposes all other things to be . . . similar to those few things by which it is surrounded." It is this characteristic fallibility of the human mind that down through the ages has, as Bacon put it, "colored and infected" man's beliefs about the possibility of life on other planets. It was Bacon's own revolutionary proposals for the scientific method of inquiry that in time enabled men to approach this question free of myth, superstition, and "the authority of former conclusions."

What is this "life" that may or may not flourish on other planets in our system or in the universe at large? In simplest biological terms, life means the existence of organisms that absorb materials from the environment, process them to supply energy, and return the waste products to the environment. By these means organisms both sustain themselves and grow. Attaining greater complexity, they are able to disperse or move about, they reproduce themselves, and, finally, they react and adapt to their environment or remold it. Taken together, these characteristics roughly differentiate inanimate matter from living organisms ranging in size from the inconceivably tiny virus to the whale.

Living organisms are literally spread over the face of the earth. They crowd the oceans, teem in and on the soil of the continents, and permeate the air. Life's density and omnipresence have radically altered the earth's environment. A conspicuous example of this process is the availability of that necessary element for animal respiration, oxygen, produced almost entirely by living plants.

Evidence of Life in Meteorites?

Time and again in recent years certain light, crumbly meteorites called carbonaceous chondrites have challenged scientific thought about life in the universe. Principally composed of silicates with lumps or globules of carbon and tiny spherical chondrules scattered through them, they constitute only 2 to 3 percent of known meteoritic falls. Scientists examining some fragments of these meteorites have found what they thought were living or fossilized organisms in the form of spores, viruses, or bacteria.

In 1857 German chemist Friedrich Wöhler extracted a small amount of organic material from a carbonaceous meteorite that had fallen that year near Kaba, Hungary. On analysis this proved to be a solid, high-molecular hydrocarbon, a compound of carbon and hydrogen that was closely associated with life as we know it. Similar hydrocarbons were found in the Orgueil meteorite, a carbonaceous chondrite that fell in France in 1864.

It became a question of whether or not these hydrocarbons were in themselves a sure indication of life, because some complex hydrocarbons of the types found in these meteorites had been synthesized from inorganic materials.

In 1961 Bartholomew Nagy of Fordham University and a number of colleagues reported that chemical analysis of the carbonaceous remains of four meteorites revealed the presence of chemical compounds normally associated only with life on earth. They had studied meteorites from Alais and Montauban in France, Tonk in India, and Tanganyika in eastern Africa, using mass-spectrographic analysis, chromatographic methods of identification, and ultraviolet and in-

Chapter XII
Native Life on Other Planets and Their Satellites

"Dream not of other Worlds, what Creatures there
Live, in what state, condition or degree."

Milton

Orgueil carbonaceous chondrite meteorite, weighing 2 kilograms (4.5 pounds), which fell on May 14, 1864, at Montauban, France. Containing much insoluble, black carbonaceous material (presumably a complex polymer of high molecular weight), this is one of the meteorites from which many organic molecules have been extracted. (The ruler at left reads in centimeters [1 cm = 0.39 inch].)

frared spectroscopy. They not only discovered evidence of very complex hydrocarbons in the carbonaceous material, such as cholesterol and butyric acid found in butter, but also data indicating that liquid water may have been a part of a somewhat alkaline environment on the parent body of the meteorites. Perhaps even more significant was the conclusion that the meteorites contained many saturated hydrocarbons and aromatic compounds similar to those in sediments on earth normally associated with remains of life. Support for the existence of water in these objects is found in the recent suggestion by scientists that magnetite is formed in carbonaceous meteorites during low-temperature mineralization of the parent body. The latter process involves water.

This report was followed by another from Nagy and his coworkers that was even more startling. Certain microscopic "organized elements" had been found in some of these meteorites that could only be identified, they believed, as the fossil remains of once-living, one-celled organisms.

Elements that looked like collapsed spore membranes, as well as two microscopic bodies with an umbrella or mushroom form, which looked like fossils of living things, were found in samples of the Orgueil meteorite by Robert Ross of the British Museum of Natural History. Harold C. Urey, who was very much interested in these investigations, wrote, "If it can be shown that these hydrocarbons and the 'organized elements' are the residue of living organisms indigenous to the carbonaceous chondrites, this would be the most interesting and indeed astounding fact of all scientific study in recent years."

In 1963 Edward Anders and colleagues at the University of Chicago processed and stained various microscopic materials just as Nagy had, and reported the positive identification of one type of organized element as ragweed pollen, which must be contamination.

Notions of evidence of extraterrestrial life in meteorites received another blow when it was discovered that a part of the Orgueil meteorite showed definite signs of contamination with materials from living earth organisms, perhaps intentionally. Definite "organized elements," beyond contamination, could not be proved in other meteorites. The evidence seemed to have fallen apart. Paul B. Hamilton of the Alfred I. duPont Institute was prompted to say: "What appears to be the pitter-patter of heavenly feet is probably instead the print of an earthly thumb."

Then, however, complex molecules were discovered in interstellar space. Since such molecules are precursors on earth in the formation of many biochemicals, three of the carbonaceous chondrites were examined with more sensitive methods. All of these carbonaceous chondrites—the Orgueil, the Murray, and the Murchison—turned out to have hydrocarbon and amino-acid molecules in them, some identical with those found in living protein, some unknown in it. Also, while protein has amino acids of a "D" structure, the acids in the meteorites showed an "L" structure in half the molecules, similar to those produced in laboratories under conditions like those of the primitive atmosphere.

The investigators concluded that these molecules seemed, then, to have been formed before the meteorites reached earth, occurring in meteorites as well as in interstellar space. In addition, the types of ami-

170

no acids as well as the distribution of the D and L forms in the Murray and Murchison meteorites forced the investigators to conclude that naturally occurring chemical processes, not life processes, produced the amino acids in these two carbonaceous chondrites. These results should not be construed as negative evidence against the existence of extraterrestrial life. Rather they provide an impetus for the search for extraterrestrial life, as they show organic chemistry has a place in interstellar space.

Origin and Conditions of Life

In the everyday world of the earth some 4 billion human beings are spread across every continent, thriving within hundreds of different complex social structures. Within, each one of us has extremely intricate, beautifully organized systems of specialized organs, tissues, and cells, all functioning together to preserve life, to adjust to environmental change, and to bring forth the generations to come. Around us are countless other species of living things, some adapted to land and some to air or water, blanketing the whole surface of the earth.

Life has penetrated to the utmost extremes of temperature, humidity, and pressure found on the earth. Life burgeons most luxuriantly in the consistently warmer climates of the tropics, yet it can adapt to dry deserts, to the frigid Arctic and Antarctic, to mountaintops with eternal ice and snow and tenuous atmosphere, and to the beds of oceans, despite the massive pressure of water piled high above.

The total weight of living substance on the earth has been estimated at as much as a ten-thousandth of the weight of the earth's crust. The most striking impression from a broad view of life is that once it has come into existence it develops and spreads indomitably, in spite of extreme conditions around it. It is tough and resilient, not easy to destroy. Those responsible for the complete sterilization of spacecraft to land on the moon or planets will testify to this.

Such is the great flowering of life over the earth on the levels immediately observable. When we turn to the eyepiece of a microscope, we enter a whole new world fully as complex, teeming with thousands of unicellular and multicellular organisms in every drop of water or particle of soil. The live weight of microscopic organisms in an acre of soil to the plow depth of 15 to 18 cm (6 to 7 inches) has been estimated at over 2,000 kilograms (4,400 pounds). This includes 910 kilograms (2,000 pounds) of molds, 455 kilograms (1,000 pounds) of bacteria, and another 455 kilograms (1,000 pounds) of branching unicellular organisms (actinomycetes). In addition, there are an estimated 90 kilograms (200 pounds) of protozoa, 45 kilograms (100 pounds) of algae, and 45 kilograms (100 pounds) of yeasts. Viruses are present in great numbers, but their weight is insignificant.

In view of the complexity of even the simplest organisms, the products of billions of years of evolution, and our ignorance of the details of most of the processes going on in them, to ask how life began seems highly presumptuous. But the accumulation of discoveries about a few organic processes and the trends revealed in evolution have brought us perhaps to that stage where tentative answers to such questions may be possible.

It is known, for example, that photosynthesis (the process by which plants with chlorophyll utilize the energy of the sun's rays with water and carbon dioxide to manufacture more complex compounds and give off oxygen) appeared relatively late in the evolution of life. With photosynthesis, free oxygen became available for animal respiration systems, providing vast effective energies previously lacking in organic substances. Earlier life probably developed without oxygen, utilizing energy from the transformation of simpler compounds. Many non-oxygen-using (anaerobic) forms of life exist today, as well as other forms that use oxygen when available but fall back on anaerobic metabolic processes when it is not.

Investigators have obtained many organic compounds by synthesis from inorganic materials. By passing electrical discharges through gaseous mixtures of methane, hydrogen, ammonia, and water vapor, or by irradiating them with ultraviolet light, they have produced compounds as complex as amino acids, the building blocks of protein molecules and eventually of all living things. Hydrogen, methane, ammonia, and water, and their interaction products, such as hydrocarbons and aldehydes, may well have composed the primitive atmosphere of the earth. Under primitive earth conditions there probably was lightning, which would have provided the electrical discharges, and (without ozone) plenty of ultraviolet light from the sun, so this may have been the way in which the basic constituents of life on our planet were formed.

Some very complex organic molecules, components of nucleic acids, have already been produced by further combination of these amino acids. Adenosine triphosphate (ATP), a very complex molecule used for the chemical storage and release of energy in cells and made by animals in the metabolic process and by plants by photosynthesis, has been produced in a California laboratory by directing ultraviolet light on a solution of compounds thought to resemble the composition of the earth's ocean about 4 billion years ago.

It is surmised that after such complex materials had developed in the nutrient broth of the oceans the next stage in the origin of life was the pulling together of very simple molecules analogous to coacervate droplets or of more complex proteinlike molecules, which form simple precellular models somewhat resembling bacterial cells. In either case, a selective relationship between the droplets and their environment was set up, and metabolic processes adaptive for the continuance of the organized droplets begun. But it must be emphasized that investigations of this type have just started and that knowledge of these processes is extremely limited and speculation rampant.

What conditions are necessary for the formation of the substances from which life might derive and grow? A good supply of simple hydrocarbons and water is considered basic. For chemical transformations to go on, the water would have to be, at least on occasion, in a liquid state, neither ice nor vapor all the time. Some electrical discharges, ultraviolet light, or heat would have to be present to produce high free-energy compounds like the amino acids. And there would have to be sources of the many other elements that play a role in all living things, such as nitrogen, phosphorus, calcium, and sodium.

At first thought, these may not appear to be very limiting conditions for the origin of life, but upon examination they prove to be quite restrictive. For one thing, they seem to imply that life could begin only in water, at or near the surface of a body large enough to retain a con-

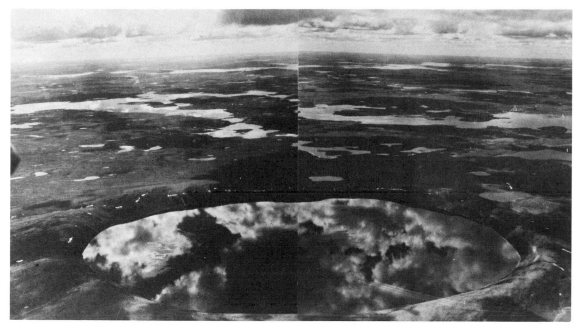

Conditions conducive to life at New Quebec (Chubb) Meteor Crater, 3.2 km (2 mi) in diameter, and filled with a lake 240 meters (800 ft) deep, situated on the Ungava Peninsula, 208 km (130 mi) south of Hudson Strait, Quebec. The bodies of water in the lake and in the distance and the atmosphere with its clouds reflected in the lake and stretching to the horizon represent environmental conditions on earth favorable to the development of life as we know it.

siderable enveloping atmosphere. While pockets of water might exist under the surface of a body, electrical or ultraviolet energy sources would not normally be present there, and it is difficult to think of energy sources that might take their place. It has recently been proved, however, that the amino acids and other organic compounds can be produced by heating nutrient solutions at from 150° to 200°C (300° to 400°F), temperatures consistent with the thermal history of the earth at or beneath the surface.

The occasional need for water in a liquid state is another very restrictive condition. While it has not been proved that thin films of water on the surface of rocks or particles of soil would be enough (nor to the contrary, that water must be present in great quantities in seas and oceans), the water must enter into many of the chemical reactions and form a component in many of the compounds involved in living substance, as a liquid, not as a vapor or ice. And here the temperature range, though dependent on pressure and the concentration of solutions, is quite limited and seems to require a rather substantial atmosphere, as does the requirement for fairly permanent bodies of water. While the necessity for an atmosphere is a moot point, it is hard to conceive of adequate substitutes for it, such as vast caverns or nearly covered areas containing pools of water, which might not be too transient.

With water and hydrocarbons, it is possible to conceive how a variety of the kinds of life with which we are familiar could develop; with some other medium and basic building compounds, we might find it difficult to recognize the result as life.

Lunar Life

Many features of the moon have been seized upon in the past as indicators of life or even of intelligence there. William of Occam (1285?–1349) warned against this kind of speculation. "Beings ought not to be multiplied," he said, "except out of necessity" in the attempt to ac-

173

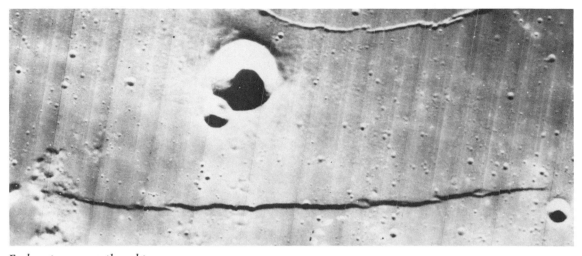

Early astronomers thought that the moon's Straight Wall was made by intelligent moon men. The Lunar Orbiter photograph here shows the wall to be a natural fault scarp 120 km (75 mi) long and 265 meters (870 ft) high. Much more solid evidence would be necessary to prove the existence of extraterrestrial life.

count for phenomena. This dictum became known as "Occam's Razor," a handy instrument for cutting theories down to the bone—that is, to the simplest explanation that covers the facts.

Geometrical forms of all sorts, thought to be representative of intelligence, were discovered on the moon in the early days of observation. One such formation, known as Mädler's Square, was described in the 1830s by the famous selenographers Johann Heinrich Mädler and William Beer, who used a 9.5-cm (3.75-inch) refractor in their mapping of the moon. North of the Mare Frigoris, near the North Pole of the moon, they drew a strongly marked square that looked artificial.

Before long all of these early beliefs were discounted. Telescopes with greater resolution proved that the forms were natural and irregular, not strictly geometrical. Larger instruments show that Mädler's formation consists of very irregular ridges, walls, craterlets, rings, and hills that do not constitute a precise square. Many of the walled plains or ring mountains on the moon appear to have a roughly polygonal (hexagonal) shape, but this is recognized as a natural geological phenomenon; sun-dried and caked mud flats on the earth crack into such forms.

But what of all the radial bands, spots, and linear markings that some observers, even in recent years, have taken as signs of vegetation or some other form of life growing and spreading during the lunar day? Here we should also wield Occam's Razor. Some physical markings undoubtedly extend or broaden as the angle of the sun's rays varies with the lunar dawn or evening. Others may be gases escaping infrequently from beneath the surface as it is warmed by the sun, or as the tugging tidal forces of the earth affect the moon. Still others may be the rare volcanic disturbances and emissions that are reportedly seen in particular locations. And some might be selective effects on certain materials of the solar radiation beating down on the moon's surface.

What actual possibility is there that some form of life may have originated and developed on the moon? It has no lasting atmosphere. Any oxygen, carbon dioxide, or nitrogen would be quickly dissipated into space. No one claims that water as a liquid stands anywhere on the surface of the moon, although it has been suggested that under the upper insulating surface of the moon there may be a heavy layer of ice, or pockets of ice or water, particularly near the moon's poles, where the temperatures would not rise as high during the lunar day as around its equatorial zone. But the moon is hot underground.

The first Ranger and Surveyor vehicles that impacted or soft-landed on the moon were sterilized very thoroughly so as not to contaminate the lunar surface. If spacecraft were not sterilized and earthlike organisms turned up on the moon or another planet, who could say whether it was extraterrestrial life or not?

The lunar rocks and soil returned to earth by Apollo astronauts were kept under sterile conditions as far as possible. So, too, were the astronauts until it was quite certain that exposure to the lunar environment had given them no unearthly organisms that might contaminate the earth. But neither astronauts nor soil have shown any evidence of such organisms. The last of the Apollo astronauts were not even quarantined for a period, as were the early astronaut crews.

Samples of lunar soil and rock particles were sent to many crews of scientists to study for any evidence of lunar life. No evidence appeared under microscopes of any fossil life long since vanished. No living organisms grew from lunar dust placed in three hundred life-nurturing cultures. Except for possible contamination, no complex molecules associated with protein, like amino acids, were found. There was surprisingly little carbon on the moon, to say nothing of even its simple compounds, hydrocarbons. Evidence that the rocket engine jets helped form such hydrocarbons in the lunar soil when the Lunar Module landed was the best that could be obtained from these explorations.

A typical report concluded, "The principal components of the various spectra were contaminant gases and traces of low molecular-weight hydrocarbons which had absorbed onto the surface of the lunar sample during handling and exposure to the (earth's) atmosphere."

In the sampling done so far, then, no primitive life forms have been found on the moon, and the lunar conditions do not offer any hope that they will be found in the future. Water seems almost nonexistent on the moon, although traces can be baked from its rocks at very high temperatures. The lunar atmosphere is only local and transient. Meteoroids blasting into the moon would more likely carry life in them than would the lunar rocks themselves.

Life on Mercury or Venus

What of life on little Mercury, circling so close to the flaring sun? Mercury is so difficult to observe from earth-based observatories even under the most favorable conditions that no fine markings can be seen on its surface. Indistinct features have been noted and used to determine (incorrectly) the rotation period. Some observers have claimed to have seen a shifting haze condition. No direct evidence for life on Mercury was ever observed, although it was populated in the customary way— by imaginations working overtime.

The Mariner flybys of Mercury surprisingly revealed that an extremely tenuous atmosphere surrounds this tiny planet. The atmosphere, consisting of argon, neon, and helium, is less than 0.1 percent of the earth's. No trace of life-sustaining water was detected.

Mariner's cameras revealed Mercury's surface to be similar to that of earth's moon: meteor-impact craters superimposed upon maria. Conditions on Mercury essentially preclude the existence of life there.

The almost nonexistent atmosphere is no barrier to the copious amounts of solar radiation falling on its harsh landscape. Even if life could survive the bombardment of harmful ultraviolet radiation, it would be subjected to an enormous range in temperature. The average daytime temperature is 350°C (600°F), while the nighttime temperature is some 500°C (932°F) cooler! This range is over 10 times that which life on earth experiences. Few believe that life, as we know it, can survive on Mercury.

Venus has often been called our "sister" planet, because of its many similarities to earth. It is only a little smaller and less dense than the earth and its cloud cover has been obvious since telescopes were turned toward it. Many imaginative ideas have been formed about the conditions on Venus's surface under its clouds. The occasional "ashen light" of its dark side has been interpreted as dim glimpses of fires set by primitive Venusians as they burn the dense jungle for farming! And when at one time it was suggested that Venus's clouds might be hydrocarbons, it was imagined that a petroleum ocean covered Venus. But all these imaginings and any hopes of eventually discovering native life on Venus have gone glimmering in recent years.

The ubiquitous cloud cover of Venus is also responsible for surface conditions that probably prohibit the existence of any life on Venus. The ultraviolet light from the sun passes through the Cytherean cloud cover and heats the surface. In turn, the surface emits infrared radiation that cannot pass back into space. A greenhouse on earth operates in the same manner; however, a greenhouse has glass in place of clouds. This "greenhouse effect" is so effective on Venus that it raises the surface temperature to nearly 500°C (932°F). Also, the atmospheric pressure is nearly 90 times that of the earth.

The Cytherean atmosphere is mostly carbon dioxide, with traces of water vapor, oxygen, nitrogen, hydrogen chloride, hydrogen sulfide, argon, and carbon monoxide. Although the presence of water vapor is encouraging for the existence of life, other conditions are not so favorable. Sulfuric acid, hydrochloric acid, and hydrofluoric acid, all extremely corrosive, have been detected in the clouds of Venus. This atmospheric composition, the high surface temperature, and the high atmospheric pressure combine to make Venus an unlikely habitat for life.

Martian Life?

More than any other planet, Mars has captured man's imagination. Edgar Rice Burroughs populated Mars with red, yellow, green, and white races. H. G. Wells wrote of warlike Martians who invade earth. Were these flights of fancy or was there evidence that supported their writings?

From the earth Mars is often wreathed in white clouds, yellow clouds or veils, and unusual blue clouds or haze. Astronomers can sometimes pick out numerous details on its surface, particularly when the planet is in close opposition. Consequently, they have been able to map the relations between the bright regions and the dark markings and to determine changes in the intensity and extent of both.

Mars is an active planet. Its tawny bright areas, usually known as "desert" regions, sometimes become lighter, or new bright areas develop. Some dark areas or markings, often called "vegetation," appear

Mars photographed in its spring and summer, showing melting of the south (top) snow cap and striking seasonal development of dark markings in the tropics. Note the doubling of dark bands across the center. The Martian dates given are analogous to calendar dates in our Northern Hemisphere.

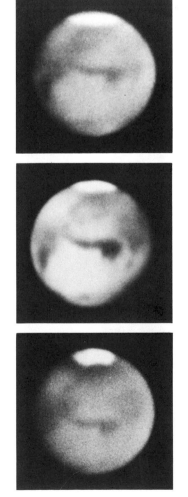

April 7

April 29

May 10

and disappear over the years or increase or decrease in size. The "canals" appear to extend out from the dark areas and sometimes pass through them. They manifest the same kind of coloring, ranging from shades of light gray to dark gray, and often cross bright areas to meet in blotches or "oases" of the same dark markings.

Even more mysteriously, the shade of the dark markings turns deeper progressively from the poles with the round of Martian spring and summer, the darkening passing at a rate of up to 40 to 48 km (25 to 30 mi) a day down to and below the equator.

It was this seasonal variation that led Percival Lowell to believe that Mars was indeed the habitat of intelligent life. As spring developed in one hemisphere the polar ice cap, assumed to be water ice, began to melt. The Martians, in desperate need of water, had built enormous canals to transport this life-sustaining liquid to the temperate zones. As the water flowed through the canals, vegetation grew along them. As seen from the earth, this vegetation appeared as dark areas. As spring turned to summer, larger areas turned dark with lush vegetation, just as the earth's desert regions are reclaimed with water. As fall approaches the dark areas brighten, suggesting that the crops have been harvested and the water supply is diminished. In the dead of winter many dark areas have totally disappeared. The polar cap has reached its greatest extent and is awaiting the spring thaw.

Although it later became evident that Percival Lowell was over-enthusiastic with regard to Martian life forms, a favorable explanation of the Martian dark markings remained—that in large measure they were caused by living organisms. Mars is large enough to have held its water and lighter gases for some time. The resulting reducing atmosphere and small surface bodies of water could have been conducive to the development of life during a primitive period through which Mars passed more quickly than the earth. Now Mars may have reached a state of equilibrium in which the water vapor emitted from its interior equals that being dissociated in its atmosphere and escaping as hydrogen from its exosphere, or it may simply be in the final stage of losing the last of its original supply of water. If, in addition, the planet was warmer than it is now, so that its water was not frozen most of the time, the primary conditions for the development of simple forms of life could have been fulfilled.

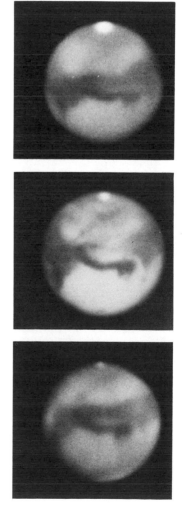

June 29

July 10

July 31

The first good look at Mars in the full range of the infrared region of the spectrum was made in 1963 with a 92-cm (36-inch) telescope carried 24 km (15 mi) up over Texas above most of the earth's atmosphere in a Stratoscope balloon. The analysis of the infrared data obtained in 5 scans of Mars indicated that any water vapor and carbon dioxide in Mars's atmosphere were in very small quantities, marginal for supporting the existence of any but the most primitive forms of life as it is known on the earth. In the same year, another study of the near-infrared spectra of Mars made with the 2.5-meter (100-inch) reflector at Mount Wilson Observatory led to similar conclusions. Only very weak lines of water vapor were observed, and they seemed strongest over the Martian poles.

Life on Mars could never have been on any such scale as that on earth. For one thing, Mars never evolved the quantities of free oxygen in its atmosphere that photosynthesis in living things produced on earth. The respiratory processes of Martian organisms probably would not involve oxygen directly, so they would be quite different from those on earth.

The most direct evidence that some form of life might exist on Mars was found with the results of American astronomer, William M. Sinton. He observed what he called absorption bands in infrared scans of the dark markings on Mars obtained with the 5-meter (200-inch) Hale telescope. These were interpreted as evidence of carbon-hydrogen compounds in the markings, perhaps aldehydes. Even if Sinton's identification were correct, it was still possible that such compounds were produced by chemical means, as they have been on earth, without the mediation of living organisms.

The strength of Sinton's evidence was diminished by the report of a group of scientists at the University of California, who checked the spectra of many substances, including varied samples of pure organic chemicals, polymers, biological specimens, pure inorganic compounds, and samples of minerals to see whether they could identify what had caused three notable bands in Sinton's infrared spectra. They found the resolution of the spectra taken by Sinton quite low and pointed out that they may well have included considerable Martian bright areas as well as dark markings. They found reason to doubt that these were purely absorption spectra, but thought they might combine absorption and reflection spectra in a manner resulting in difficulties of interpretation. Their study practically eliminated the interpretation of the spectra as carbohydrates, such as sugars and starches, or even as cellulose, a major substance in plants, but it left open the possibility of free aldehydes, possibly even acetaldehyde, which might be the result of anaerobic metabolic processes.

Lichens were found to give a band similar to one of Sinton's bands, while the smooth, waxy leaf of the lily *Agapanthus*, and that of the prickly-pear cactus, give spectra somewhat like Sinton's. Thus a relationship to organic materials was found. But a number of inorganic carbonates also gave spectra similar to 2 of Sinton's bands, though the third band might only have been produced inorganically by lead carbonate, not likely to be widespread on the Martian surface. No other inorganic samples showed much promise.

All of these possibilities were so inherently dubious that the group concluded, "At present we know of no satisfactory explanation of the Martian bands. Observations of the planet with improved spectral and spatial resolution, in conjunction with radiometric temperature measurements, could possibly define the problem sufficiently to enable a solution to be found."

The United States spacecraft Mariner 9 provided additional evidence that some form of life might exist on Mars. Data from Mariner 9 indicated an atmosphere consisting largely of carbon dioxide, but with small amounts of water vapor. The temperatures at the Martian poles are cold enough to freeze the carbon dioxide so that the polar caps were believed to be mostly dry ice. However, in the Martian spring and summer the caps diminish rapidly in size. Mariner 9 recorded more water vapor over the North Pole in these seasons, probably since the residual northern polar cap is known to be water ice. Mariner 9 photographs also showed glacial features on the caps that probably have come from water. Other photographs of the planetary surface revealed branching stream systems and valleys that look as if they had been worn by water at some time in the past.

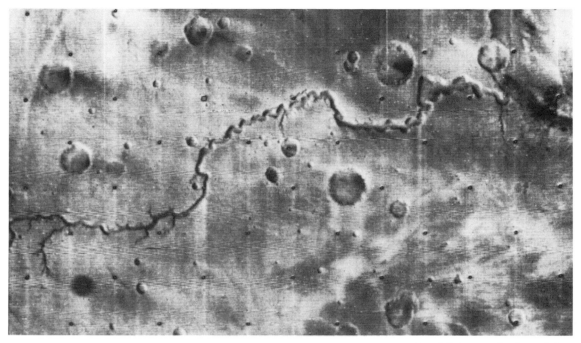

The Viking 1 and Viking 2 missions to Mars were the culmination of 15 years' work by the National Aeronautics and Space Administration of the United States. Viking's primary mission was to determine whether life existed on Mars. Each Viking consisted of a lander and an orbiter. Photographs from the orbiters were used to make the final decision on the landing site for each of the landers.

The Viking landers analyzed the Martian atmosphere on their way to the surface. The results were encouraging for life, since the necessary elements are present even though in the wrong proportions for human life. Near the surface the atmosphere is found to be about 95 percent carbon dioxide, 2.5 percent nitrogen, 1.5 percent argon, and traces of oxygen, carbon monoxide, neon, krypton, and xenon. One important ingredient, water vapor, is essentially missing. The greatest amount of water vapor is found near the edge of the northern polar ice

In addition to clouds and fog, valleys, like that pictured here, may have been formed by flowing water on Mars. This long valley is some 400 km (250 mi) long and 5 km (3 mi) wide and is reminiscent of terrestrial rivers. No branching "tributaries" like this are found in the rills on the moon.

A schematic of the landing of the Viking spacecraft on Mars. Periapsis and apoapsis are the closest and farthest points, respectively, in the orbit of the spacecraft about Mars.

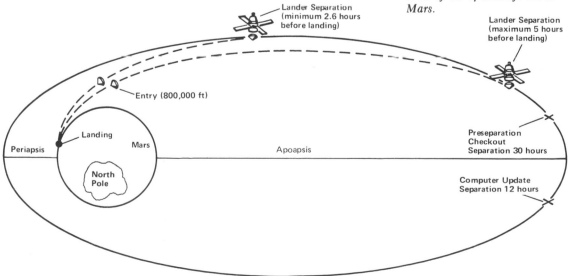

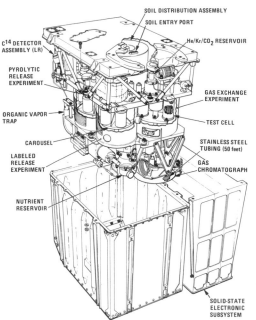

SOIL DISTRIBUTION ASSEMBLY
SOIL ENTRY PORT
He/Kr/CO$_2$ RESERVOIR
C^{14} DETECTOR ASSEMBLY (LR)
PYROLYTIC RELEASE EXPERIMENT
GAS EXCHANGE EXPERIMENT
ORGANIC VAPOR TRAP
TEST CELL
CAROUSEL
STAINLESS STEEL TUBING (50 feet)
LABELED RELEASE EXPERIMENT
GAS CHROMATOGRAPH
NUTRIENT RESERVOIR
SOLID-STATE ELECTRONIC SUBSYSTEM

The biological laboratory aboard the Viking Landers weighs 15 kilograms (33 pounds) and would fit easily into the interior of a microwave oven. And yet it is a sophisticated scientific laboratory. Soil samples were inserted into the assembly and searched for evidence of Martian life. The experimental results cannot directly prove that life exists on Mars.

cap, but even the amount found there is small. Mars is an exceedingly dry place.

Each of the Viking landers had 5 instruments available to search for Martian life: cameras to view the landscape for any large artifacts, a gas chromatograph and mass spectrometer to analyze the surface for organic material and a gas-exchange experiment, a labeled-release experiment, and a pyrolytic-release experiment to detect metabolic activities of soil microorganisms.

The results from the Viking landers have not been conclusive. One series of experiments seemed to give positive results, while 2 others were negative. The general consensus among scientists is that the processes observed are not associated with any life processes but represent some new, unusual chemistry. There is no doubt that further exploration of Mars is highly desirable.

If life does not now exist on Mars, at least at 2 locations, how about in the future? The atmosphere contains the necessary ingredients for life. Some scientists believe that Mars may still be developing its atmosphere. In the future it may become more earthlike. The key is water. Evidence exists that water once flowed freely on the surface of Mars. Where is it now? Is it trapped in the polar ice caps, or is it frozen somewhere below the surface? Has it left the planet entirely? This remains a great Martian mystery that begs to be solved.

What about the dark markings observed for so many years on Mars? These appear to be related to dust driven by the violent winds blowing across the Martian surface. The winds cover and uncover various features, causing the surface variations detected in the past.

The words of Marcia Smith aptly summarize the question of life on Mars: "It seems clear that the scenarios painted by Percival Lowell and H. G. Wells are far from the truth, but we still do not know what the truth is."

The Outer Planets and Planetary Satellites

As in the case of Venus, astronomers are unable to penetrate the cloud cover of Jupiter. Evidence appears contradictory on the existence of Jovian life. On the positive side Jupiter's internal heat source would provide sufficient energy for any organisms, while ammonia, hydrogen, methane, and water, all necessary for life, have been observed in its atmosphere. On the other hand, the atmosphere is highly convective. Any organisms that could survive in favorable climes would be destroyed as they are carried along into regions where high temperatures and high pressures would destroy them.

Saturn is thought to resemble Jupiter, but since Saturn is farther from the sun it is colder. Because of these cooler temperatures it is not likely that Saturn harbors any life. The remaining three planets, Uranus, Neptune, and Pluto, are even more remote from the sun. Accordingly, they are even cooler and less likely to support life.

How about the satellites of planets? The majority of the satellites are too small to hold an atmosphere conducive to life. The earth's moon is a cold, forbidding place devoid of any significant atmosphere. The moons of Uranus and Neptune have no atmosphere and are probably too cold for life to exist there. The Galilean satellites of Jupiter, and Titan, a satellite of Saturn, are often mentioned in connection with life. The Voyager spacecraft have shown the former to be rather inhospitable. Callisto, Europa, and Ganymede have little if no atmosphere but may have large amounts of water below their surfaces. Io does have an atmosphere, consisting of sodium, potassium, and sulfur. Considerable volcanic activity exists on Io and might bury any possible living organisms under molten magma. On the other hand, a warm environment exists near these volcanoes and could provide a suitable habitat for life.

Titan, with a diameter of 5,120 km (3,175 mi), has a dense atmosphere of methane and nitrogen. Its surface temperature may be as low as −181°C (−299°F) and its atmospheric pressure may be one and a half times that of the atmospheric pressure at the surface of the earth. Titan's surface itself may be covered by methane ice, and any precipitation like rain or snow may consist of methane rather than water. Furthermore, the possibility of volcanoes or some other heat sources which would provide liquid pools on Titan's surface is vanishingly slim.

Only in the few locations on the moon where the astronauts walked and at the 2 Viking lander sites on Mars have the existence of life definitely been ruled out. On other planets life probably does not exist. The strongest possibilities (and even these are remote) for life in the solar system are Jupiter and Titan. If life does exist it is probably of a lower form. Astronomers would be shocked to discover cities and advanced cultures elsewhere in the solar system.

Life in the Universe

It is nearly a certainty that the phenomenon called life is not unique to our solar system. According to even the most conservative estimates, there are at least 100,000 stars in the Milky Way Galaxy alone that provide an environment favoring the germination and support of living organisms. In the universe at large, estimates of the probabilities that stars will have life-supporting planetary systems vary all the way from 10 to 20 percent of all stars to 1 in a million.

What tests must a star pass if it is to qualify for this life-supporting role? Many astronomers believe that binary- and multiple-star systems can be eliminated at the outset. They argue that planets in such systems would have orbits so complex as to introduce enormous variability in the amounts of radiation they would receive from their stars. However, it has recently been shown that it is possible to have stable planetary orbits within the necessary habitable zones, provided the planet closely orbits one of the members of the system or orbits the binary system at a distance.

Whether the planets belong to a single star or a close binary, they must have nearly circular, not too eccentric orbits, since dependable, fairly constant amounts of radiation are a must if life is to be maintained. Furthermore, the star must be neither too young nor too old, neither too large nor too small. If too young, it may be very large or not have given birth to planets; if too old, it may be expanding and intensely hot, burning its progeny to a crisp, or too small and cold to provide enough heat. Finally, the masses of its planets must be within certain limits—not as great, for example, as those of our own "gas giants" Jupiter and Saturn—if they are to have atmospheres hospitable to life, and not be likely to become stars in their own right. The ideal location to search for life would be on a planet with a mass somewhere be-

Two photographs of Barnard's star (arrow), taken 11 months apart (July 31, 1938, and June 24, 1939), with the 61-cm (24-inch) Sproul Observatory refractor. In making the combined print, the second plate was shifted slightly with respect to the first. It is quite apparent that Barnard's star has moved against the background of other, virtually fixed stars; its large rate of motion (10.3 seconds of arc per year) can actually be detected on photographs taken 1 night apart.

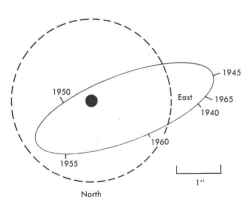

The inferred orbit of the invisible companion relative to the visible component of Barnard's star. The dashed circle indicates the greatest size of the latter's image on the plates taken with the 61-cm (24-inch) refractor at Sproul Observatory.

tween that of Mercury and Neptune, with liquid water, orbiting a star with a mass somewhere between 0.75 and 1.25 times the mass of the sun.

Lest this question of life elsewhere in the universe seem to be speculation of the wildest sort, some actual astronomical observations may support the theory that there are planetary systems other than our own. Astronomers at Swarthmore College's Sproul Observatory have found a wobble in the motion of Barnard's star, a star only 6 light-years or about 60 trillion km (36 trillion mi) from our solar system. The star itself shows a great motion in comparison with the relatively fixed stars in our sky nearby. The star's wobble can be most simply explained as a perturbation caused by an unseen companion. This companion could be a small, dark neighboring star. More probably, it can be classed as a planet, some 1.5 times as massive as Jupiter, or 500 times as massive as the earth. The Sproul Observatory astronomers have deduced from their observations that this invisible body moves in an elliptical, highly eccentric (0.6) orbit about Barnard's star, like that diagrammed. They estimate that its reflected light must make it about the thirtieth magnitude, much too dim to be seen in a telescope on earth or even from an orbiting earth satellite, and that it is probably too far from its primary star for the nurture of life. Further analysis of the wobble had implied that at least 2 dark bodies may orbit the star, rather than a single body. This begins to look more like a planetary system!

Earlier, Sproul Observatory astronomers had directed their attention to 2 other stars, the motion of which showed evidence of the presence of invisible companions. These were Lalande 21185, at a distance of 8.12 light-years, and 61 Cygni, 11.08 light-years away. The companions of both stars may have masses about 0.01 (1/100) that of the sun, placing them on the borderline between extremely large planets and very small stars.

George Gatewood of the Allegheny Observatory questions whether these planetary systems are real. He has been unable to obtain either the same results as the Sproul astronomers, or corroborative data. Doubt is also expressed whether a planet really orbits Epsilon Eridani, a star 10.76 light-years from the sun. An additional system, CD-43°4305, 16.9 light-years from the sun, requires additional study.

It will be a long, long time before space probes can be launched toward stars near our own. Meanwhile, the best approach to the question of life elsewhere in the universe is radio or optical surveillance of possible emissions from other stars that could represent attempts to communicate. A practical trial surveillance has already been made, to work out procedures and solve the problems entailed.

In 1960–61, the 26-meter (85-ft) radio telescope of the National Radio Astronomy Observatory at Green Bank, West Virginia, followed the radio emissions from 2 nearby stars of the same type as our sun, Tau Ceti, 11.77 light-years away, and Epsilon Eridani, 10.76 light-years distant. The trial was called Project Ozma, after the queen of the fictional land of Oz, a very distant and inaccessible place inhabited by strange beings. For receiving signals the 21-cm wavelength (1,420 MegaHertz frequency) was used. This is the wavelength of hydrogen emissions, the most commonplace of radio radiations in space, and thus a likely medium for communications. It also has the virtue of

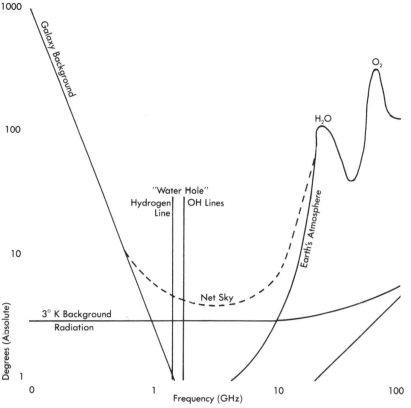

The "water hole" represents a band in the radio spectrum where there is little background noise and where neutral hydrogen and the hydroxyl radical radiate. Since water, a combination of hydrogen and oxygen, is essential for life on earth, a number of scientists have suggested that the "water hole" is a region to search for intelligent signals from extraterrestrial life.

passing freely through atmospheres like that of the earth. No indications of any attempts to communicate were discovered.

Since this pioneering study several additional searches for extraterrestrial signals have been made, both in the United States and in the U.S.S.R. All searches to date have been unsuccessful.

Not all searches have been made at the 21-cm line of hydrogen. Nor is there unanimous agreement about what frequency is the most likely to be the carrier of extraterrestrial signals. Sentimental favorites are those frequencies found in the "water hole," bounded on one side by the hydrogen emission and on the other by emissions of the hydroxyl radical. The combination of the hydroxyl radical (OH) with hydrogen (H) forms water (H_2O), which gives this particular spectral region its fanciful name. Just as terrestrial life in the wild revolves around the water hole, so do some radio astronomers believe that the "water hole" is the most likely region for interstellar communication. Other frequencies have been suggested, however, among them the formaldehyde emission line.

Although man has not yet received any radio signals from intelligent life in outer space, he has made several feeble attempts to communicate with extraterrestrial civilizations. The Pioneer 10 and 11 spacecraft have on board a 152-by-229-mm (6-by-9-inch) plaque shown in the figure, which pictorially describes the place of origin, the time of launch, and some information about the crafts' designers to anyone who would find these crafts.

The Voyager 1 and 2 spacecraft will also leave the solar system and travel into interstellar space. Rather than plaques, each Voyager carries a long-playing copper record along with a needle and playing

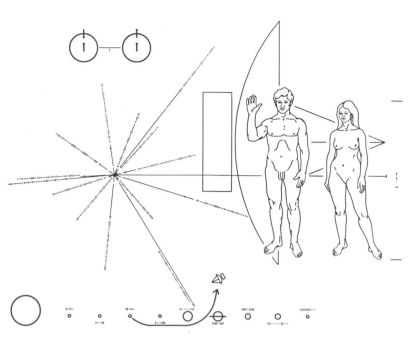

The Pioneer 10 spacecraft will be the first human artifact to leave the solar system. It passed Jupiter in 1973 and is currently traveling through the farther reaches of the solar system. Attached to this spacecraft is a plaque with a pictorial message that would tell other cultures the sun's location in space from 14 pulsars (left center), our appearance (right) to the scale of the Pioneer, and our place in the solar system (bottom).

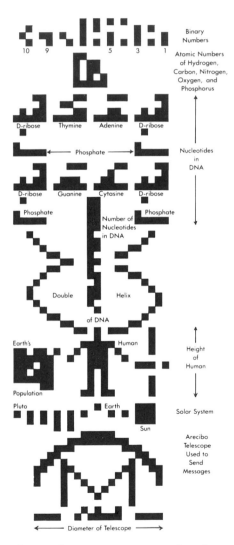

The Arecibo message transmitted to the cluster of stars in Hercules known as Messier 13 consisted of 1,679 bits of information. These data can be converted into a picture that attempts to tell the recipients about earth.

instructions. The record contains 115 electronically transcribed photographs of the earth, messages of greeting in 55 different languages, as well as sounds of earth and its inhabitants. The complete contents give a fairly representative sampling of humanity.

On November 6, 1974, a radio message was beamed by radio astronomers to the Great Cluster in Hercules, a group of some half million stars also known as Messier 13. The message, consisting of 1,610 bits or pieces of information, starts by teaching the recipient how to count from 1 to 10 in binary, since most of the message is in binary code. Then the atomic numbers of hydrogen, carbon, nitrogen, oxygen, and phosphorus, constituents of terrestrial life, are given. This is followed by information on the DNA molecule, the number of inhabitants on the earth, the solar system, and the instrument used to send the message. If any civilization in Messier 13 should ever decode the message and send a reply, mankind should receive the answer in 48,000 years, due to the immense distance between the sun and the cluster, 24,000 light-years.

It is generally agreed that all these messages are intended more for the inhabitants of earth than for any extraterrestrial civilization. The senders hoped that the messages would unite the world and truly make man aware that the earth is just one small part of the universe.

Chapter XIII

Rockets and Space Vehicles

"And here an engine fit for my proceeding."
        Shakespeare

With the advent in the heavens of tiny, beeping Sputnik 1, the old earth's first artificial satellite placed in orbit by the Soviet Union on October 4, 1957, man finally achieved what had been theoretically possible since Isaac Newton formulated the laws of celestial mechanics in the seventeenth century.

In 1961, President John F. Kennedy announced ambitious plans to land men on the moon by 1970. By December 31, 1969, four American astronauts had landed on the moon via the Apollo 11 and 12 missions. After the first two decades of the space age (1977), 9 manned flights have been to the moon, and 12 American astronauts have walked on the moon's surface. A total of 2,146 spacecraft had been placed in orbit, of which 69 had been lunar missions and 40 planetary. Soviet spacecraft had totaled 1,211, American 827, 12 other nations 73, and 3 consortiums 35. Sixty-two manned space flights had been launched. American astronauts had spent 22,278 hours in space and Soviet cosmonauts 15,866. Knowledge had flooded in about the sun, the moon, other planets, and most of all the earth itself from an entirely new environment: space.

All of this has been made possible by a piece of equipment called a rocket. What are rockets? What gives them such awesome power?

Types of Rockets

Rockets are vehicles carrying a load propelled by a reaction to the gasses produced by the combustion of their self-contained fuel and oxidant systems. Already many families of rockets, and generations within these families, have been designed, built, and tested for different space transport missions. Perhaps the simplest type are the sounding rockets, which "sound" or probe the atmosphere; they usually consist of a series of stages or sections and carry an instrument package as a payload. They are designed to shoot straight up as high as 3,200 km (2,000 mi) or more above the earth, conduct their observations, and return under the pull of gravity, often ejecting their instrument package to drop by parachute. But these are only midgets compared with their younger brothers.

The missile, a rocket structure designed for military use, is sent into a trajectory like a shell; the missile carries a warhead armed with a nuclear or other device to a target. Missiles may be shot from the surface of the earth to impact on the surface, or from air to air, or air to surface, and so on; they vary greatly in complexity, range, and destructiveness of the warhead they carry. The IRBMs are intermediate-range ballistic missiles; ICBMs are intercontinental ballistic missiles. The space-launch vehicle or space carrier is another kind of rocket designed to go out into space with its complement of engines, other stages, and payload. Often the engines used in missiles and in space carriers are interchangeable.

Rocket engines or motors are called rockets in a more restricted sense, though they are simply one section—the propulsion stage—of the whole rocket. The rocket engine consists basically of fuel compartments and a combustion and thrust chamber with an escape nozzle and much auxiliary equipment. The rocket engine that lifts a vehicle off the ground—that is—the first-stage engine, is the rocket booster, constituting one section of the complete rocket. Sustainer engines are intermediate-vehicle stages or are used to assist the booster engine; the

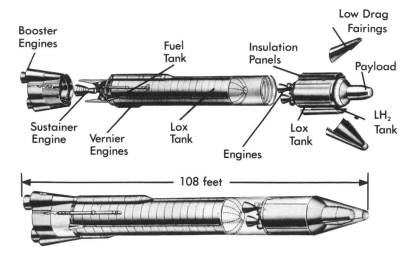

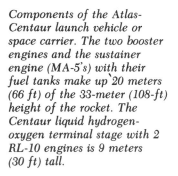

Components of the Atlas-Centaur launch vehicle or space carrier. The two booster engines and the sustainer engine (MA-5's) with their fuel tanks make up 20 meters (66 ft) of the 33-meter (108-ft) height of the rocket. The Centaur liquid hydrogen-oxygen terminal stage with 2 RL-10 engines is 9 meters (30 ft) tall.

terminal-stage engine is the final powered stage, designed to give an accurate final velocity and direction to the remainder of the rocket, placing the payload truly in orbit or on its course out into space. Booster, sustainer, and final-stage engines must be differently designed for their specialized functions. The Atlas-Centaur stages are shown. This rocket has been used for many launches by the United States and will be retired when the Space Shuttle becomes fully operational in the 1980s.

Other stages or sections of rockets may consist of intermediate auxiliary instrument and equipment compartments, guidance, control, and service sections, and the payload. The payload carries the items for accomplishing the mission or objectives of the rocket. The payload may consist of a warhead or some other type of package in a missile, and of some kind of satellite, space vehicle, or spacecraft in a space-carrier rocket. Usually the terms "space vehicle" and "spacecraft," instead of referring to the entire rocket system, are used in this way for only the unmanned and manned payloads, respectively.

An artificial satellite is a payload injected into orbit around the earth or some other large body like the moon or planets. A space probe is a payload injected into an orbit with velocity sufficient to escape the earth's gravity, instrumented for observations and experiments in space. An artificial planet or planetary satellite is a payload that has been placed in orbit of the sun, aping the natural planets. A spaceship is a sizable spacecraft designed to carry a number of human beings on lengthy trips into space. A space station or platform is a large, manned satellite of the earth or another body providing a base for scientific observations, the final release of space probes, and the refueling of spaceships, or a platform for assembling and launching satellites or missiles.

Rocket Principles

The whole rocket assembly of 2 to 4 towering stages topped by a payload lifts ponderously as it is finally unleashed from its launching pad, quivers up slowly foot after foot, and then slides swiftly up and away, disappearing in a twinkling into the blue and beyond. The launching of an Atlas-Centaur rocket from Cape Canaveral, Florida, is shown. The sound effects accompanying such a magnificent spectacle are just as striking—a vast, rolling, booming noise. All this apparent straining power comes from the rocket-booster engine, which has been billowing masses of flame on its pad. These lengthen into a diamond-brilliant shaft of extremely hot gases trailing behind the rocket as it shoots up toward space. How does all this happen?

In burning or combustion, oxygen combines with the material or fuel being burned, whatever it may be, forming oxides and gases in combination with the material. Combustion goes on at varying rates. In a rocket engine, very rapid but not quite explosive combustion occurs. Rocket fuel is injected into the combustion chamber of a liquid-propellant engine, as is the oxidant or oxidizer, which consists of some material very rich in oxygen, or of pure gaseous or liquid oxygen. The fuel and oxidizer are ignited, or they spontaneously ignite in what are called hypergolic mixtures, and a jet of hot and expanding gases resulting from their combination roars out of the exhaust nozzles.

What makes the rocket engine drive the whole heavy mass of the ship into space? If the gases produced in the combustion chamber were contained within its strong casing, and not released, they would simply push, or apply their force, outward in all directions equally, and nothing would happen. According to Newton's first law of motion, a body at rest remains at rest, and a body in motion remains in uniform motion, unless it is acted on by some external force. But Newton's third law of motion states that there is an equal and opposite reaction for every action of a force; thus, if there is a hole in the chamber, and the gases are allowed to escape through that hole, as the air does from the neck of a balloon, they push out forcefully, producing a great equal force in the opposite direction, thrusting back against the rocket. Similarly, if a youngster kneels on a knee in his wagon and pushes backward with a foot against the ground, the wagon will move forward. And, finally, following the second law of motion, any body acted on by a force is accelerated in the direction of the force in direct proportion to the mass of the body. In the case of the rocket, the force is the counterthrust provided by the escaping gases, and the acceleration is determined by the total mass of all stages of the rocket.

Rocket Systems

Rocket launch vehicles are wracked by tremendous strains of expansion, contraction, and extreme or zero g's. In view of the conflicting forces within and without during a launching it is remarkable that most rockets somehow hold together.

Rocket engines may burn either solid or liquid fuels. The basic, simple elements of solid-propellant rocket engines are diagrammed; they are similar to the powder-packed rockets used for patriotic celebrations. After ignition, the solid propellant is burned directly in the tube that contains it and forces its way, at high temperatures and pressures, out through the convergent-divergent exhaust nozzle.

Atlas-Centaur lifts off Pad 36 at Cape Kennedy on November 27, 1963, on a flight that placed the whole 4,630-kilogram (10,200-pound) Centaur stage (top) into earth orbit after separation from the Atlas stage (below "United States" on the rocket). The Atlas-Centaur has been the workhorse of the National Aeronautics and Space Administration, lifting many payloads into orbit. It will be retired from service when the Space Shuttle becomes operational.

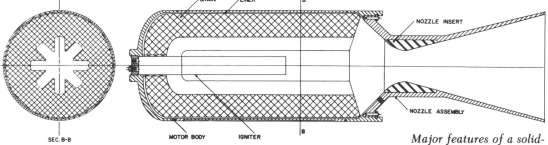

Major features of a solid-propellant rocket engine.

For certain functions, solid-propellant rockets possess great advantages. The solid propellants are much easier and safer to store than liquid propellants. Solid-propellant engines can be ready to ignite at any moment; long countdowns are needed for liquid-propellant engines, for filling their tanks with the highly dangerous and corrosive fluids, often at exceedingly low temperatures.

Liquid-propellant rocket engines require large tanks to store the oxidizer and the fuel, usually separately, and a source of power to run turbine pumps that force the oxidizer and fuel into the combustion chamber under pressure. Valves must be designed to carry extremely cold liquids, such as liquid oxygen (boiling point, $-218°C$ or $-361°$ F) or liquid hydrogen (boiling point, $-252.7°C$ or $-422.9°F$), without locking up, and to open and shut almost instantaneously. So much piping is required that liquid-propellant systems have been called a plumber's nightmare.

The simplified diagrams show different oxidizer and fuel-flow systems for a liquid-propellant engine using liquid oxygen and liquid hydrogen. In the pump-fed system (left), the liquid hydrogen absorbs heat as it cools the combustion chamber by circulating through its casing. In what is called a topping cycle, the heated hydrogen is then injected into the combustion chamber by the turbine; control is obtained by the turning of the turbine valve to regulate the thrust in the chamber and the turning of the mixture valve to maintain the proper mixture ratio of oxygen and hydrogen. In the simpler, but less flexible pressure-fed system (right), the propellant-tank pressures force the hydrogen and oxygen into the combustion chamber, the hydrogen cooling the chamber walls by circulating in its casing on the way. The regulation of pressure in the supply tanks controls the combustion-chamber pressure and mixture ratio.

Such solid fuels as synthetic rubber and other complex organic molecules called polymers may be used, while liquid fuels often employed include ammonia (NH_3), hydrazine (NH_2NH_2), aniline, hydrogen (H_2), and the fuels gasoline or kerosene. Ammonium perchlorate (NH_4ClO_4) is one of the most important solid oxidants, while the major liquid oxidizers are hydrogen peroxide (H_2O_2), nitric acid (HNO_3), and oxygen (O_2). Any of these provide pure oxygen directly, or loosely combined

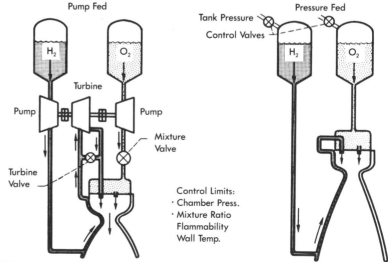

Pump-fed (left) and pressure-fed (right) flow systems for a liquid-propellant rocket engine using liquid oxygen and liquid hydrogen.

oxygen, which then rapidly combines with and oxidizes the fuel. Fluorine is also being used as an oxidant, since, like oxygen, it combines very actively with many substances. Its mixture with other oxidants may increase the efficiency of the propellants by as much as 30 to 60 percent without raising the combustion temperature too high.

Liquid oxygen-hydrogen rocket engines provide many advantages in terms of high specific impulse and exhaust velocities. After extensive development, they became operational in the Centaur and Saturn launch vehicles. The fluorine-liquid hydrogen combination is also receiving attention. Other so-called exotic mixtures are under development, such as diborane-oxygen difluoride and beryllium-oxygen-hydrogen combinations, which might provide very high energies if they prove to be manageable. Hybrid propellants, crosses between liquid and solid propellants, are being developed. Such a propellant might have an unoxidized solid-fuel core and a liquid oxidizer, or a liquid fuel and a solid oxidizer.

Somewhat like an umbrella on the end of your finger, rockets must balance delicately as they rise slowly from their launching pads; they may be affected by gusts of wind at low speeds, and are carried through a variety of atmospheric conditions and movements into what must be very precise trajectories. The accurate and split-second guidance and control of rockets has become a field of specialization in itself, dominated by transistors, computers, and a variety of special sensing instruments. Rockets can be steered in several ways: by rudders or jet vanes of such substances as graphite or tungsten in, or at the perimeter of, the engine exhaust gases; by the gimbaling of the whole combustion chamber of the rocket or the exhaust nozzle—that is, swiveling it around a circle of small arc, directing its thrust in various directions to the center of gravity of the vehicle; by the firing of small auxiliary (vernier) rockets at the sides of all engines to apply angular thrusts in the desired directions; or by the injection of gases into the side of the combustion chambers or exhaust nozzles to deflect the main flow of exhaust gases and thus redirect the counterthrust. But who is to control these steering methods, and how?

Remote-control guidance by radio from control stations on earth is one answer to this question. The rocket or missile transmits data to the control station on its position and flight, and such data may be received from tracking stations; these are coordinated by computer to compare the actual course with the programmed one. Then the necessary corrections are calculated in a split second by computer and transmitted by radio to the rocket to keep it on its precise course. In the instrumentation and control sections of the rockets, accelerometers indicate their positions very accurately, while fast-spinning gyroscopes maintain a constant position to which reference can be made in reporting and correcting the flight of the rockets.

If rockets are to be guided by radio, they must be within radio contact of some control station. This can lead to difficulties, since rockets pitch over after the immediate blastoff and may quickly be far distant from the control station; or they must be injected into escape trajectories from parking orbits at precise times, when they may not be conveniently near a control station. So self-contained inertial-guidance systems have entered the rocket picture more and more. The rocket has its optimum course programmed into its own computer. In a split second, a check is made through data from sensors affected by accelerometers, which show how the rocket is heading and accelerating. In the computer in the instrument section of the rocket this is compared with its program, the computer determines the necessary corrections, and these are sent out to control fuel flow and exhaust direction in the rocket engine and to bring the whole vehicle squarely back into its predetermined trajectory.

Space Payloads

Both the United States and the Soviet Union made remarkable leaps ahead during the 1960s in their rocket launch-vehicle programs. Thrust doubled and tripled and went on doubling and tripling. The high-energy propellant composed of liquid oxygen and liquid hydrogen came into use—hardly imaginable a few years before, since these gases were thought too dangerous to handle together. The payoff came with the much larger payloads carried into space and placed in orbit of the earth or sent to the moon, Venus, Mars, and beyond.

On May 15, 1958, the U.S.S.R. placed Sputnik 3 in earth orbit; it weighed, with a cylindrical case, an estimated total of 3,200 kilograms (7,000 pounds), 1,330 kilograms (2,932 pounds) of which were payload. On January 2, 1959, they sent off Luna 1, now in solar orbit; its reported weight, given escape velocity, was over 1.5 tons (1,475 kilograms or 3,245 pounds). They announced another vast step ahead with Sputnik 4, launched into earth orbit on May 15, 1960, and weighing 5 tons (4,545 kilograms or 10,000 pounds). Their Venus probe, launched on February 12, 1961, weighed 645 kilograms (1,419 pounds), and was injected into escape from Sputnik 8, which had been placed in a parking orbit and weighed 6,489 kilograms (14,275 pounds or 7 tons), perhaps including the weight of the probe. The Vostok space vehicles, carrying Soviet cosmonauts in low earth orbits, have all weighed in at about 4,545 kilograms (10,000 pounds or 5 tons). Later, Soyuz-manned space vehicles have weighed about 7 tons. The Soviet unmanned lunar space flights have consisted of vehicle payloads of from 3 to 7 tons. On the other hand, some Soviet research satellites, like the Proton craft, which was placed in orbit of the earth, have weighed from 17 to 20 tons. The Soviet unmanned lunar landers weigh about 2 tons, scooping up lunar soil and returning it to earth or carrying crawling lunar rovers to study the moon's surface. The Salyut space stations of the Soviet Union weigh about 18,500 kilograms or close to 20 tons.

With its Atlas-Centaur and then its Titan rockets, American launch vehicles forged ahead very rapidly. When the Saturn 1 was launched into orbit on January 29, 1964, weighing over 9,100 kilograms (20,000 pounds) (17,100 kilograms or 37,700 pounds including the second stage placed in orbit), the United States gained the lead over the Soviet Union in launch-vehicle power.

As the Saturn V launch vehicle was developed and tested, the United States was ready to meet the requirements for sending astronauts to the moon. The 5 huge engines of Saturn V's first stage produced a total thrust of 7.65 million pounds. The 5 second-stage rocket engines yielded up to 1.1 million pounds of thrust. The single-engine third stage generated up to 200,000 pounds of thrust at first burn and the same on a second burn. The total height of this great rocket with spacecraft atop was 110 meters (362 ft). Suddenly, 110 tons could be

The launch of the Viking spacecraft was the first successful operational flight of a Titan-Centaur rocket. The Centaur upper stage sits atop the Titan booster, which features 2 solid-rocket motors strapped on to a liquid-propellant core rocket. After expending their fuel, the 2 boosters strapped onto the remainder of the rocket fall away as the bulk of the rocket continues on its way into orbit or beyond.

The mighty Saturn V is poised over Pad A, Launch Complex 39, during the launch of Apollo 16 on April 16, 1972. The Saturn V was designed for the sole purpose of carrying astronauts to the moon and back. The 5-first-stage engines produce a thrust of 7.65 million pounds.

placed by Saturn V in a low earth orbit, and 45 to 55 tons sent into an escape orbit from earth, carrying men for the first time toward the moon!

The giant Saturn V holds a record for placing the greatest payload into orbit, the Skylab Orbital Workshop, weighing 74,817 kilograms (164,597 pounds). This mammoth satellite was truly a first step for the United States in the development of a space station. Measuring 36 meters (117 ft) in length, it provided 350 cubic meters (12,190 cubic ft) of habitable working space for 3 astronauts. Three separate crews visited Skylab for periods of 28, 59, and 84 days. Not only were many scientific experiments carried out by the astronauts, but they also served as experiments: These missions provided many clues as to how man could work and survive in space. The astronauts were poked, prodded, measured, and weighed almost daily in between their chores of photographing the earth and the sun. These missions were huge successes. Not only were 182,842 photographs of the sun and 40,286 photographs of the earth taken, but also the missions showed that man can survive extended periods of weightlessness.

Skylab will remain the heaviest satellite launched for some time. The United States will rely heavily for the next 2 decades on the Space

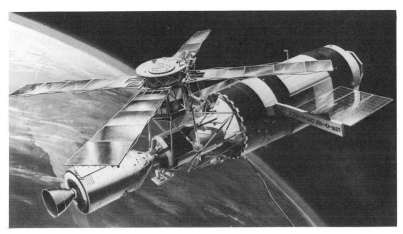

This artist's conception shows an Apollo spacecraft docked to the Skylab Orbital Workshop. Skylab was the heaviest payload ever put into earth orbit. Three separate crews visited Skylab for periods of 28, 59, and 84 days; Skylab was the first step in the development of a true space station where astronauts and scientists can live and work.

Shuttle. This reusable spacecraft is capable of lifting 29,500 kilograms (32.5 tons) into earth orbit. The Soviet Union appears to be developing a space station, but it will undoubtedly be assembled in space.

Forecasters believe that chemical propulsion will remain the main power drive of spacecraft for the foreseeable future. To get heavier payloads into space, variants of existing launch vehicles will be used. It is predicted that either an upgraded version of the Space Shuttle or the Rhombus/Nexus class of vehicles will be capable of lifting payloads of 180,000 kilograms (400,000 pounds) into earth orbit by the year 2000.

Nuclear and Electric Propulsion

Since the inception of intensive development of rocket propulsion in the United States, atomic nuclear reactions have been investigated as a source for power. Terrific punch is packed into small space with nuclear energy. Very sizable specific impulses (indicating efficiency) of 750 to 1,000 seconds, and eventually 1,500 seconds, may be derived from the use of nuclear-power propulsion systems, as compared with a probable top of 400 to 500 seconds of specific impulse derivable from chemical propellants, whether solid or liquid. By this index, nuclear power offers 2 to 3 times as efficient a performance as chemical propulsion. Then, too, the long periods of time over which nuclear power can be available or stored without great deterioration make it a requisite for lengthy space journeys. Beyond the direct application of nuclear power lies its development for the so-called electric-propulsion engines, which may yield such extreme specific impulses as 3,000 to 10,000 seconds. Nuclear power is for space, not initial blastoff.

Nuclear reactions can perform 2 functions in space; first, the generation of electricity for auxiliary uses on rockets or spacecraft, providing a lightweight, long-term nuclear source of electric power; second, the nuclear production of power for actual propulsion. Great progress has been made in its first space application, using fissioning radioisotopes to generate electricity by means of thermocouples, as in what is called the Snap program, with a generator that employs polonium 210 or plutonium 238 as a heat source. A circuit is composed of 2 different metals in a thermoelectric converter or a thermocouple; this circuit develops a voltage when a metal is heated, directly converting the heat into electrical energy. The radioactive isotopes produce the heat for this reaction, but they are not useful for the generation of large amounts of power since they are heavy, weighing 454 kilograms (1,000 pounds) or more per kilowatt. These radioisotope thermoelectric generators (RTGs) have been successfully used to provide power for the Apollo Lunar Surface Experiments Package (ALSEP) and the Pioneer 10 and 11 and Voyager 1 and 2 spacecraft.

Another promising source for small supplies of electricity in space has been through gathering solar power. Earth satellites have guaranteed sunlight half of the time, when they are above the sunlit hemisphere of the earth, while space probes receive sunlight all the time on that side facing the sun. The ordinary satellite generates some electricity for "housekeeping" purposes and for charging its batteries through its silicon (or the more radiation-resistant cadmium-sulfide) cells exposed in blocks on broad surfaces to the sun's radiation. The solar cell is a form of photovoltaic cell, absorbing photons of light from the sun on its boron-treated surface. The photons release free electrons, leav-

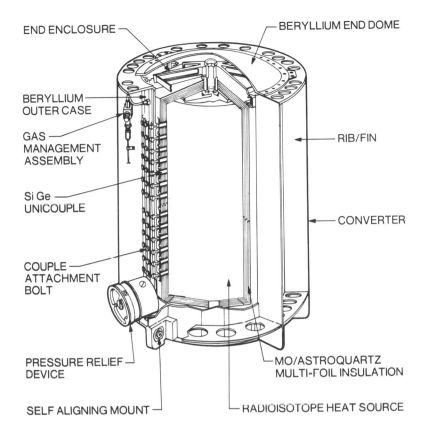

END ENCLOSURE

BERYLLIUM END DOME

BERYLLIUM OUTER CASE

GAS MANAGEMENT ASSEMBLY

Si Ge UNICOUPLE

COUPLE ATTACHMENT BOLT

RIB/FIN

CONVERTER

PRESSURE RELIEF DEVICE

SELF ALIGNING MOUNT

MO/ASTROQUARTZ MULTI-FOIL INSULATION

RADIOISOTOPE HEAT SOURCE

Cross section of a radioisotope thermoelectric generator (RTG) used on the Voyager spacecraft. Three such RTGs provided the electrical requirements during the long missions of these spacecraft. These units convert to electricity the heat released by the decay of radioactive plutonium-238.

ing electron vacancies or holes. As the electron density builds up, some of the free electrons can move through the boron film into an external circuit, thus producing electric power.

Several new solar-powered systems are designed to use the direct heat from the sun, concentrate it, and produce power in turbogenerator systems, rather than through solar cells or a nuclear reactor. In another system, the sunlight is focused by a mirror on a cavity that contains a hydrogen heat exchanger. Here liquid hydrogen is heated and then directly exhausted for propulsion.

A rather unusual application of solar power is the use of solar sails. Just as terrestrial winds fill the sails of ships at sea, so can sunlight fill the sails of spacecraft and propel them on a voyage across interplanetary space. The pressure of sunlight is very small, however. It will be necessary to make the sails very large in order to achieve any reasonable acceleration. Solar sails may prove especially useful for missions that would require a large amount of energy, such as moving out of the ecliptic plane. In the spirit of exploration, an American scientist has suggested that the first three spacecraft to use solar sails should be named the *Niña*, the *Pinta*, and the *Santa Maria*.

A great deal of research and development has been devoted to the use of nuclear power to propel spacecraft themselves. A nuclear-reactor core is used to heat a light propellant gas, such as liquid hydrogen, to high temperatures within a pressure chamber; then the hydrogen is ejected at very high velocities through an exhaust nozzle. Radiation protection without excessive weight, the prevention of uncontrolled explosions, and deterioration in the reactor core due to great heat and vibration are among the problems that make design difficult.

In a solid-core, heat-transfer nuclear-propulsion engine, the reactor is located forward of the exhaust nozzle. Nuclear-fission energy is produced within the solid materials of which the reactor core is composed. The propellant gas, hydrogen, is stored in the liquid state in a tank, pumped through the nozzle walls for cooling purposes, and also passed through the reflector regions around the reactor and any other parts of the engine that require cooling. On leaving the reflector, the already gasified hydrogen flows through the passages of the reactor core, where it is heated to as high a temperature as the core materials will stand, perhaps up to 3,300° C (6,000° F). The high-temperature, high-velocity hydrogen blows down and is exhausted through a convergent-divergent nozzle to produce the thrust. In comparison with chemical-propellant engines, such nuclear engines offer a tenfold weight reduction, most valuable for space flight.

Beyond such nuclear engines lies another family of electric-propulsion rocket engines being investigated as the eventual answer for efficient propulsion for periods of months or years in space. All of these will use nuclear reactors or radioactive fission in some form as a source of power. When controlled nuclear-fusion reactors (fusing hydrogen atoms to produce helium with the release of tremendous quantities of energy) are eventually constructed, they should have an immediate application in space to furnish this power, and they might in time be used as propulsion engines.

Arcjet systems, in which the propellant gas is heated to high temperatures in an electric arc and then ejected, appear to have the capacity for 50 to 60 percent power efficiency and may eventually have specific impulses of from about 1,100 seconds up to 1,500 or 2,000 seconds. Such systems offer ready applications to satellite-orbit adjustment, attitude control, orbit-to-orbit transfer, and perhaps lunar-ferry functions, or to power communications-satellite or spacecraft operations.

A most unusual type of electric-propulsion engine, called electrostatic, produces electricity of high voltages by electrostatic means in space. In such a system, a radioisotope film (polonium 210) on the inner sphere emits charged particles, which build up a charge on the metal foil of the large collector sphere. This generates a potential difference between the concentric emitter and collector spheres, produc-

A design for a solid-core, heat-transfer nuclear propulsion unit (left) and some of the control problem areas and operational limits with such propulsion engines (right).

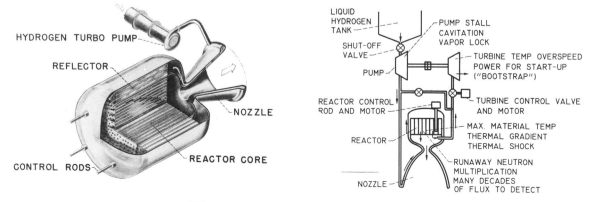

HYDROGEN TURBO PUMP
REFLECTOR
NOZZLE
CONTROL RODS
REACTOR CORE

LIQUID HYDROGEN TANK
SHUT-OFF VALVE
PUMP
PUMP STALL CAVITATION VAPOR LOCK
TURBINE TEMP OVERSPEED POWER FOR START-UP ("BOOTSTRAP")
REACTOR CONTROL ROD AND MOTOR
TURBINE CONTROL VALVE AND MOTOR
REACTOR
MAX. MATERIAL TEMP THERMAL GRADIENT THERMAL SHOCK
RUNAWAY NEUTRON MULTIPLICATION MANY DECADES OF FLUX TO DETECT
NOZZLE

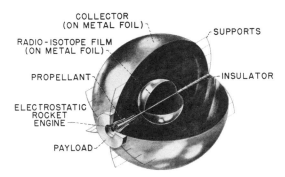

COLLECTOR
(ON METAL FOIL)

SUPPORTS

RADIO-ISOTOPE FILM
(ON METAL FOIL)

PROPELLANT

INSULATOR

ELECTROSTATIC
ROCKET
ENGINE

PAYLOAD

Theoretical design of a 500-kilowatt electrostatic propulsion system with a direct nuclear electrogenerator using radioisotope film.

ing the electric current. This power is then used either in a contact-ionization engine, in which a stream of neutral cesium ions furnishes the jet driving out from the exhaust nozzles, or in a bombardment type of engine producing mercury-ion driving jets. The cesium-ion engine promises to be very efficient and long-lived, furnishing 5,000 seconds of specific impulse, if not more. In the contact-ionization type the liquefied cesium (melting point, 28° C or 83° F) is passed through a porous disk of tungsten, tantalum, or niobium metal, becoming a jet or beam of cesium ions in the electric field. These ions are accelerated to tremendous velocities, neutralized to become cesium atoms, and then shot out of the exhaust nozzle to provide the thrust.

Heavy-particle or colloid engines produce various kinds of colloidal particles, as small as a hundred-millionth inch in diameter, which are electrically charged, accelerated, and passed out in a fast-moving jet stream, as in the cesium engine. Experiments have been performed with droplets of aluminum chloride, glycerol, low-melting metal alloys, and oils.

Electromagnetic propulsion engines couple a strong magnetic field to currents flowing in a gas plasma (a hot, ionized gas) in such a way as to accelerate the plasma, using it then as the driving jet. One type is called a photon engine, driven with photons or light-energy particles. In another device, a pulsed, plasma-pinch accelerator causes a ring of hot plasma to contract and at the same time to be deflected by curved electrodes so that the plasma is ejected in a jet-beam drive along the axis of the spacecraft. In still another design, plasma pulses are ejected by pulse currents through heavy single-turn coils. These electric engines may prove to be most efficient in the intermediate range of specific impulse.

All these electric-propulsion engines involve thrusts that are limited to a few pounds. This restricts them to operations in space, since they do not have the great power needed to boost loads into orbit. Their small thrusts acting over extended periods can produce high velocities, and they can be engineered for extremely high specific impulses over very long operating periods, with great flexibility in starting, stopping, and applying thrust.

Many of these systems require considerable development and lie on the frontier of technology. The solar-sail concept should be available in the early 1980s. The majority of the remaining systems will not be available until the 1990s or later. Although many problems lie ahead, they are not insurmountable. After all, it was only 66 short years from the time man made his first powered flight in an airplane to his first walk on the moon!

Chapter XIV

Artificial Satellites and Space Probes

"I see a great round wonder rolling through space."

Whitman

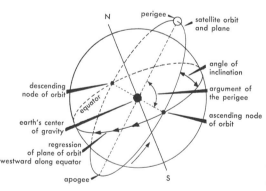

Features of artificial earth-satellite orbits. The angle of inclination is the angle that the plane of the satellite's orbit makes with the plane of the earth's equator. The regression of the plane of the satellite's orbit westward along the equator is caused by the earth's equatorial bulge. The apogee is the point where the satellite is most distant from the earth, the perigee is its point of closest approach, and the argument of the perigee is the angle that a line from the perigee to the earth's center of gravity makes with the point where the plane of the orbit cuts the plane of the earth's equator.

In a few short years the science of launch vehicles was mastered, and the earth has been "deflated" to a small globe that can be girdled in less than 90 minutes. Traditional standards of speed, size, and distance have been shattered—by the 59,000-pound thrust that rocketed the experimental X-15 up to 6,600 km (4,105 mi) an hour, by the earth-orbiting manned flights that more than quadrupled this speed, and by the manned and unmanned space flights that have bettered 40,000 km (25,000 mi) an hour.

Earth-Satellite Orbits

The terms that astronomers use for elements of the moon's orbit, such as apogee, perigee, and the argument of the perigee, are applied as well to the orbits of artificial earth satellites. These orbits must be circular or elliptical. If they were parabolic or hyperbolic, the space vehicle would not remain near the earth. One complete revolution of a satellite traces out a flat plane that can be conceived as cutting through the earth. When the satellite's orbit is circular—that is, at all points approximately the same distance from the earth's surface—then the center of the orbit coincides with the center of mass (or center of gravity) of the earth, and the radius of the orbit from this center is everywhere the same length. When the orbit is elliptical, one of the focuses of the ellipse must coincide with the earth's center of mass, or an orbit will not be established. A satellite in an equatorial orbit moves in the plane of the earth's equator, cuts the earth's center of mass with its plane, and has one focus there. In an inclined orbit, the plane is tilted from the equator. When this so-called angle of inclination from the equator is 90°, the satellite is in a polar orbit and crosses both poles. An orbit of the earth cannot be established along a parallel at the latitude of, let us say, Buenos Aires or New York, since its focus would not coincide with the earth's center of gravity.

When a satellite is launched, the angle of inclination of its orbit to the equator is often announced, together with the apogee and perigee heights of the orbit. Although the perigee and apogee heights above the earth's center of mass are used in calculating earth orbits, news reports usually give apogee and perigee heights above the earth's surface, since these are the figures that interest most people. The argument of the perigee may be announced sometimes, particularly in technical publications, since it serves to determine the orientation of the orbit. Not usually reported is the line of nodes of the orbit, which is the line made by the plane of the orbit cutting the plane of the earth's equator. The ascending node is the point where the orbit crosses the equator moving northward; the descending node is the point on the opposite side of the earth where the orbit crosses the equator going southward.

To take advantage of the speed of the earth's rotation, satellites are normally launched in an easterly direction. When they are launched into polar orbits, their booster thrust must provide the whole orbital velocity. Polar orbits have certain advantages. In time, because the earth is rotating beneath it, the satellite will pass over its entire surface. In addition, as in an equatorial orbit, the satellite can be observed once in each revolution by a single tracking station, in this case at one of the poles. Though a satellite in an orbit with an inclination of 65° to the equator will in time cover most of the land masses of the earth ex-

196

cept the polar areas, there must be a line of tracking stations from north to south to keep it under fairly constant observation.

Injection into Orbit

In the simplest case, to maintain a circular orbit at a given altitude above the earth's surface, a satellite must have a specific velocity if it is not to fall toward the earth or move away from it. A balance must be maintained between the gravitational pull of the earth and the centrifugal force imparted by the thrust. The satellite's height, velocity, and period of revolution all fit together for its particular orbit. Thus for a satellite in a circular orbit at increasing heights above the earth's surface, the velocity decreases and the period increases. A height of 1,680 km (1,044 mi) determines a 2-hour orbit, a height of 35,853 km (22,283 mi) puts the satellite in the 24-hour synchronous orbit, and so on. The speed required for a circular orbit diminishes with greater height. The closer to the earth a satellite is, the faster it must spin around the earth to maintain its orbit against the greater pull of gravity.

Satellites are lofted by their launching vehicles to their desired heights, where they must be accurately oriented in relation to the surface of the earth and then "injected" into orbit—that is, given the final exactly measured burst of speed by the last-stage rocket engine, which shoots them precisely into the planned orbit. If satellites are not injected in this manner and do not attain orbital velocity, they will behave as ballistic missiles do and fall back to earth. This is what happened to Alan Shepard and Virgil Grissom in their intentionally suborbital Mercury flights.

The two significant factors that establish a satellite in the desired orbit on injection, then, are the exact direction in which it is pointed and its exact velocity. When the velocity given to the satellite or spacecraft is correct for its altitude above the earth's surface, and when the angle at which that velocity is directed is precisely at right angles (90°) to the line straight down from it to the earth's center of mass, the satellite will be injected into a circular orbit. When the injection angle to the line between the earth's center of gravity and the satellite is greater than 90°, that center becomes the primary focus of an elliptical orbit, with the perigee of the satellite's orbit ahead of the point of injection, naturally, since the satellite will be closer to the earth at perigee. An

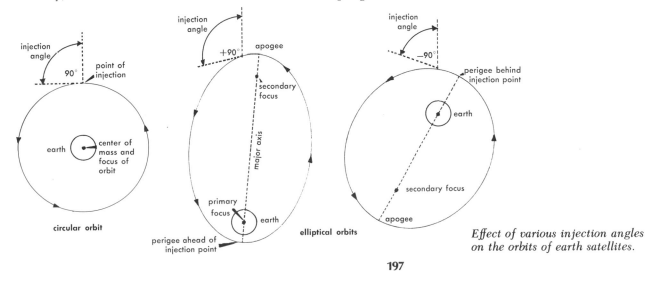

Effect of various injection angles on the orbits of earth satellites.

197

elliptical orbit also results when the angle of injection is less than 90°, with the perigee behind the point of injection into the orbit.

If a satellite at 322 km (200 mi) above the earth's surface is injected into orbit at precisely 7.71 km (4.79 mi) a second, and also if the thrust is exerted at a precise 90° angle to the earth's center of mass, the satellite will go into a 322-km (200-mi) circular orbit. If the velocity is increased by as much as 1 percent, then the orbit becomes elliptical, with the same perigee height (322 km or 200 mi) but with an apogee height of 596.6 km (370.8 mi). If the velocity is decreased by 1 percent (about 0.08 km or 0.05 mi a second), the perigee becomes the apogee, and the satellite will approach within 59.7 km (37.1 mi) of the earth, right into the atmosphere, and will burn up as it plummets toward earth.

Thus the apogee and perigee of an elliptical orbit are radically affected by minute changes in velocity, and the satellite will not orbit at all if the velocity is 1.25 percent below that required for a circular orbit. Similarly, with an error in the injection angle of 1°, for an injection elevation of 322 km (200 mi), the perigee elevation would become about 270 km (170 mi) and the apogee about 620 km (385 mi). Calculations made to correct orbits must take into account the fact that corrections produce new orbits, not simply shifts in directions or heights, with the new orbital injection point at the location where the correction was initiated. This is only one of the complications that make the rendezvous of 2 satellites in orbit such a tricky proposition.

Re-entry

The orbit of an artificial earth satellite gradually decays and shortens. It is slowed down by atmospheric drag, the amount of which depends largely on the satellite's height above the earth. Revolution by revolution, it loses its original orbital velocity and begins to re-enter the atmosphere. The apogee height is lessened and moves back closer and closer to the earth; the perigee height remains nearly constant until the last few revolutions. The satellite loses some velocity each time it passes through the lowest portion of its orbit about the perigee, so it cannot speed quite as far out to apogee as it did on the previous revolution, and the apogee approaches nearer to the earth. The perigee moves very slightly lower, and the major axis of the ellipse of the orbit turns a little in each successive revolution.

The satellite tends to lose velocity faster and faster, because, as its apogee shortens, its ellipse loses more and more of its eccentricity, approaching a circular orbit and passing through more atmosphere each time it goes through perigee. When the ellipse finally degenerates into a circle, the atmosphere is dragging continuously on the satellite. The perigee height becomes the apogee height, and the two switch back and forth as the satellite spirals in through the atmosphere.

Without properly designed re-entry configuration and materials, the satellite burns up like a great meteorite entering the earth's atmosphere. The recovery of unmanned-satellite instrument payloads without damage on re-entry and the safe return of men in spacecraft through the earth's atmosphere have posed complex engineering problems.

The problem is that the craft must lose all of the energy of motion that has been imparted to it by the enormous energy of combustion of the rocket engines, which lifted it by reaction from its launching pad and injected it into orbit. In the drag of the atmosphere, this energy of motion is turned back into heat energy. Temperatures rapidly shoot up to 1,100° to 1,650°C (2,000° to 3,000°F) on the outer shell of the craft, as if it had been placed in an electric-arc furnace. The heating becomes even more intense at the more than 40,000-km (25,000-mi)-an-hour velocities of craft that have escaped the earth's gravity and are returning to it, as from a trip to the moon. This speed could be reduced somewhat by using forward-firing retrorockets before the craft re-enters the atmosphere, which would place the craft in a slower orbit around the earth.

In the case of an Apollo mission to the moon, the returning command rocket had a heat shield made of a stainless-steel honeycomb filled with ablative material 1.5 to 7 cm (0.7 to 2.7 inches) thick, depending on the expected heat loads. In ablation the heat is carried off by melting, vaporization, or sublimation of the surface material.

The command module also had a degree of maneuverability. As it re-entered the earth's atmosphere its 12 reaction-control jets oriented the spacecraft properly. Atmospheric forces helped to stabilize the command module so that the heat shield encountered the atmosphere first and the upper conical edge was nearly parallel to the flight path. This flight angle provided aerodynamic lift, allowing the pilot to adjust the entry path horizontally and vertically.

The heat-protection system of the Space Shuttle orbiter consists of interior insulation, thermal window panes, thermal seals, a high-temperature structure, and reusable surface tiles. The nose and leading edges of the wings will experience the highest temperatures, about 1,650°C (3,000°F). These parts of the Shuttle are made from reinforced carbon-carbon. The temperatures of the underside of the Shuttle are expected to remain below 1,250°C (2,300°F), and it is covered with 15-cm (6-inch)-square silica tiles. The tail section and the sides and top of the forward fuselage should experience temperatures less than 650°C (1,200°F) and are made of 20-cm (8-inch)-square silica tiles. These tiles differ from those on the underside only in size and the surface coating applied before launch. The remainder of the spacecraft is covered with a coated Nomex felt. Temperatures should be less than 370°C (700°F) in these areas.

Manned Orbital Flights

Two typical American satellite orbits are diagrammed against a representation of the earth as a globe, in what is called by mapmakers an oblique orthographic view. One satellite is represented (left) as launched into an inclined orbit from Cape Canaveral, Florida, into the Atlantic Missile Range (AMR), at an inclination of 34° south of the equator, while the other is represented as sent into a polar orbit from Point Arguello or Vandenberg Air Force Base, California, into the Pacific Missile Range (PMR), with an inclination of 90° to the equator. In the other diagram (right), the so-called flat Mercator projection map of the earth shows the satellite launched from the Kennedy Space Center in what is called a sine curve, which is like a stretched-out wave, because the vertical meridian lines in this projection have been given a constant parallel distance from each other, though actually, as shown in the left-hand diagram, the distance between them narrows to

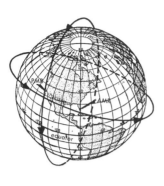

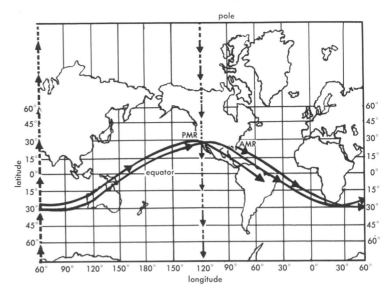

A satellite orbit around the globe (left) at 34° inclination south of the equator from the Atlantic Missile Range (AMR) and another orbit at 90° inclination to the equator from the Pacific Missile Range (PMR). (Right) The same orbits against a Mercator projection of the earth, showing the effects of this projection on the flat, plane orbits. The wavy line from AMR (right) represents the orbit inclined 34°; the earth has rotated from west to east with each revolution of the satellite in orbit, so the orbital track against the earth moves toward the west with each orbit, though actually the orbital plane has not moved. The satellite orbit remains stationary and the earth rotates within it. The dashed line from PMR represents the polar orbit, with the track passing the South Pole, then coming up across the Indian Ocean and across the U.S.S.R. to pass over the North Pole and return down across Canada and the United States. The earth rotates inside this orbit in the same way, so with each revolution the orbital track would move westward, completing its swing around the earth in 24 hours.

zero at the earth's poles. The plane of the satellite orbit actually cuts through the earth's center of gravity and has to be represented on the Mercator projection as a curve, but the satellite is not actually curving in orbit. It is moving in a great circle of the earth in the plane of its orbit as shown in the left-hand diagram. Similarly, the two vertical dashed lines indicate the polar orbit on the Mercator projection, but it is actually one great circle as shown in the oblique orthographic view.

A satellite cannot be launched at an angle of inclination to the equator that is less than the latitude (north or south) of its point of injection into orbit, for then the plane of orbit would not pass through the earth's center of mass, which thus would not form one of the focuses of the orbit, as it must. However, a rocket can be launched from a launching site at a smaller angle of inclination and then turned into the correct angle to achieve an orbit (when it is close to orbital velocity or at the injection point). Because of its shape, this is called a "dog-leg" trajectory or "dog-legging" the satellite into orbit. It has not often been attempted because it takes extra thrust to change the direction of motion of the satellite in this manner, and every pound of thrust has been at a premium in the early flights. On November 1, 1963, the Russians announced the launching of a craft called Polyot 1 (Flight 1), which they claimed went through several dog-leg maneuvers, changing the inclination of its orbit before settling into its final path. On April 12, 1964, it was reported they had done it again—the Polyot maneuverable satellite became a series.

The periods of manned orbits of the earth are around 90 minutes for a complete revolution. The United States craft used an inclination near 30° south of the equator, running from Cape Canaveral in a southeasterly direction toward Africa, across the South Atlantic Ocean. The exceptions were the 4 Skylab missions, which were launched at a 50° angle to the equator. This inclination allowed greater photographic coverage of the earth.

The Vostok and Voskhod spacecraft of the Soviet Union all orbited at an inclination of 65° north from the equator. The Soyuz spacecraft orbit at 52° inclinations. These inclinations must be most convenient from their launch location, keeping their craft over Soviet territory as they move up into orbit toward the northeast. The Soviet manned-spacecraft launch site is located in the southern U.S.S.R., near Baikonur in the Kazakh S.S.R., some 355 km (220 mi) northeast of the Aral Sea. Soviet cosmonauts often land from orbit in this flat, desert country.

There has been one cooperative manned mission between the United States and the Soviet Union: the Apollo-Soyuz Test Project. On July 15, 1975, Soyuz 19 and Apollo 18 were launched from their respective spaceports. After rendezvous the two spacecraft docked on July 17. Crews were exchanged, demonstrating that a common system works for the two different craft. After undocking the two crews conducted various scientific and engineering experiments both jointly and independently. On July 21, Soyuz 19 safely returned to earth, while Apollo 18 returned on July 24.

Few scientists have been in space. The astronauts and cosmonauts have usually been pilots and engineers. The Space Shuttle will change this. It is expected that a maximum of only 3 g's during launch and 1.5 g's during re-entry will be experienced by the passengers and crew. These accelerations are about one third those of previous manned flights. Coupled with a standard sea-level atmosphere, these accelerations are tolerable, enabling scientists to conduct their own experiments.

The number of people lofted into space at a time will also increase with the Space Shuttle. The pioneering Mercury and Vostok spacecraft had barely enough room for 1 person. The Gemini and Voskhod spacecraft carried crews of 2, although 3 cosmonauts did cram into Voskhod 1. The Soyuz spacecraft also carry crews of 2. The Space Shuttle orbiter will normally carry up to 7 crew members and passengers. In emergency situations 10 people can be placed on board. With the Space Shuttle and the Soviet Salyut space stations a new era is dawning in space. Space is no longer reserved for a few specialists but is being opened to the average terrestrial citizen.

The Space Shuttle has ushered in a new era in manned space flight for the United States. Shown here coupled to a Boeing 747 during flight tests, the Space Shuttle Orbiter enables scientists to make space flights routinely and to conduct their own experiments in space.

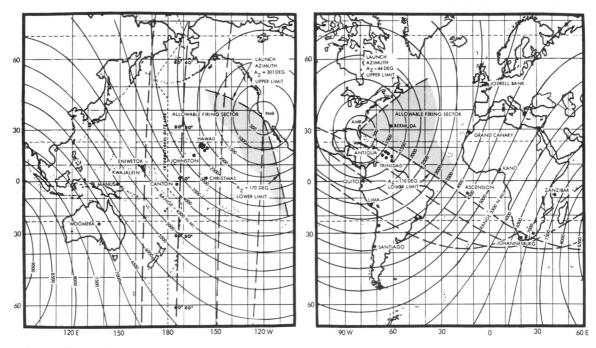

The Pacific Missile Range (left) and the Atlantic Missile Range (right). Arcs indicate the distance in nautical miles (1 nautical mi = 1.15 statute mi) from the Cape Canaveral and California launching sites, the shaded area shows the possible launching sectors, and dots indicate the placement of the major tracking stations. Azimuth angles (A$_z$) shown are measured as from the north point of the horizon (0°) eastward or clockwise through 360°. Dashed lines are typical ground tracks of satellite orbits, plotted against this Mercator projection map.

Missile Ranges and Tracking Networks

The United States has 3 principal missile ranges from which missiles and space carriers can be launched: (1) the Atlantic Missile Range (AMR) at Cape Canaveral and Merritt Island on the east coast of Florida, about 80 km (50 mi) directly east of Orlando and 96 km (60 mi) south of Daytona Beach; (2) the Pacific Missile Range (PMR), which is headquartered at Point Mugu, California, about 40 km (25 mi) northwest along the coast from the Los Angeles area, and which has launching complexes at Point Arguello and Vandenberg Air Force Base, about 160 km (100 mi) farther up the coast; and (3) the Wallops Island (Virginia) Station, on the Atlantic side of the Delmarva Peninsula, about 65 km (40 mi) south of Salisbury, Maryland.

The charts show the safe launching sectors, typical ground tracks of launchings, and the principal tracking stations supporting the Atlantic and Pacific missile ranges. The American manned space program is carried on from the Atlantic Missile Range; military missiles and satellites are launched primarily at the Pacific Missile Range. With southeast launchings from Kennedy Space Center at Cape Canaveral, rockets can be tracked largely from island-based stations in the Caribbean Sea and the South Atlantic and need not pass over land (at the southern tip of Africa) until well into orbit. The Kennedy Space Center was expanded to Merritt Island to the northwest to allow plenty of room for the huge Titan and Saturn launch vehicles as America's space program burgeoned.

As demonstrated in the chart, the Pacific Missile Range is ideal for polar-orbit launchings. It has the whole open stretch of the South Pacific Ocean, Antarctica, and the Indian Ocean for launchings. Missile launchings can also be made out over a series of tracking stations to the southwest in the Pacific, from which antimissile missiles can be shot up for test interception of the missiles. The landing areas for the Gemini and the Apollo manned vehicles were located in the wide expanses of the Pacific to give room for orbital shifts.

202

Artificial Satellites and Space Probes

Complex facilities on the earth accomplish the tracking of missiles and space vehicles by radio and radar, eye, and telescope. Some facilities receive data from the vehicles by means of telemetry. Telemetry encompasses instrument data-sensing on the craft, coding of the data and their translation into radio signals sent back to earth, and guidance and control of the craft by transmitted radio signals. The Minitrack Network, with over a dozen stations placed around the globe, receives radio signals from unmanned satellites. The Manned Space Flight Tracking Network consists of another dozen or more complex ground stations placed along the band covered by manned orbits. These stations maintain contact with the spacecraft by means of radar, radio-listening devices, radio-telemetry equipment that can control the craft, and direct radio communication with astronauts.

The Deep Space Instrumentation Network follows and guides lunar and interplanetary probes and spacecraft from four large radio antennas at Goldstone (near Mohave), California, and near Woomera and Canberra, Australia, and Johannesburg, South Africa. The stations are equipped to receive telemetry data from the spacecraft and to transmit commands to them. The Jodrell Bank radio telescope of the University of Manchester, near Macclesfield, England, has also assisted in tracking spacecraft and space probes.

An Optical Tracking Network at 12 locations around the world uses precision telescopic tracking cameras to locate satellites accurately when they are visible and to determine their orbits; information on the rough positions to be used by this network is sometimes provided by organized groups of observers.

The American Space Surveillance System (Spasur) is a radar network of 7 alternating transmitting and receiving stations along the Thirty-third North Parallel in the United States from the East Coast to the West Coast. They bounce radio signals from passing satellites, receive their echoes, accurately locate their positions, and predict their orbits.

The 64-meter (210-ft) antenna at Goldstone, California. Four such antennas form the Deep Space Instrumentation Network that tracks interplanetary spacecraft, sends commands to them, and receives telemetry data from them. The other 3 antennas are in Johannesburg, South Africa, and Woomera and Canberra, Australia.

Space-Age Astronomy

The payloads boosted into orbit by powerful rocket-launching vehicles carry a wide range of instrumentation into space. Each sounding rocket payload, each satellite, and each space probe contains instruments for one or more investigations and experiments. Perhaps the most fruitful observations so far have been the weather and communications studies and the studies of the earth itself; these have gathered more knowledge about its shape, gravitational and magnetic fields, and atmosphere. Other satellite series have already furnished data about interplanetary space, the planets, the sun, and the stars.

Aircraft have also provided platforms from which astronomical observations have been made, especially in the infrared part of the spectrum. A LearJet 24B aircraft carried the first airborne telescope. It was a 30-cm (12-inch) telescope mounted in the side of the airplane for open-port observations. Seventy minutes of observations were typically made at altitudes of 13,700 to 15,000 meters (45,000 to 50,000 ft).

Probably the most sophisticated aircraft-mounted telescope is the Kuiper Airborne Observatory, operated by the National Aeronautics and Space Administration. This observatory has an 0.9-meter (36-inch) telescope mounted in a modified C-141, a military transport jet. The telescope is stabilized about 3 axes and is controlled by a sophisticated computer system to maintain accurate tracking.

High-altitude (or stratospheric) balloons, sounding rockets, and satellites are releasing astronomers and astrophysicists from the exasperating limiting conditions of the earth's atmosphere. Telescope-carrying balloons like the Stratoscope series (1957, 1959, and 1963) are above 96 percent of the earth's atmosphere at their observational height of about 24,000 meters (80,000 ft).

The Stratoscope balloons used 30-cm (12-inch) telescopes in their early flights and a 0.9-meter (36-inch) mirror in 1963. Stratoscope I made observations of the sun with a resolution of about 0.5 second of arc; later observations reached a resolution of about 0.3 second of arc. This is probably close to the limit, because the sun heats the mirror and the thin atmosphere in and around the telescope structure, resulting in some turbulence. Valuable solar data can be obtained at these resolutions, however. On the night side of the earth, without interference from the sun, the telescopes do better. The Stratoscope balloon telescopes have been used to study the fine cloud structure of Venus (small "white dots" have been noted by some observers), analyze Mars's atmosphere and any detectable fine surface features, and investigate the atmosphere of Jupiter, the detailed structure of Saturn's rings, the optical diameter of Pluto, and the internal structure of galaxies and nebulas.

Other balloons carrying telescopes from 15 cm (6 inches) to 1 meter (39 inches) have been used to study the center of the Milky Way Galaxy, to survey the entire sky as well as the Milky Way in far infrared wavelengths, and to map the structure of huge, cold clouds of gases in space.

Sounding rockets penetrate much higher than balloons, but since the rockets turn right around and come back, their observations of celestial phenomena are like snapshots as compared with the series of photographs or spectrograms that can be made from the balloons.

Even with their limited flight times, sounding rockets have provided useful data. An example is the all-sky survey made at 4 infrared wavelengths by the U. S. Air Force Geophysical Laboratory. Ninety percent of the sky was covered at least once at a particular wavelength, and 60 percent of the sky was covered at least twice at the same wavelength with a 16.5-cm (6.5-inch) telescope in 11 rocket flights. Each flight had about 300 seconds of observation time. To conduct a similar survey from the surface of the earth with a 1.5-meter (60-inch) telescope would require about a year of constant observation.

The first series of satellites devoted exclusively to astronomical studies are the Orbiting Solar Observatories (OSO), recording a broad spectrum of the radiation of the sun. The OSO 1 was launched on March 7, 1962, from Cape Canaveral by a 3-stage Delta rocket launch vehicle. The space observatory carried 3 solar x-ray experiments, a gamma-ray experiment, and a micrometeoritic dust-particle experiment. The majority of its instruments were concentrated on a whole series of observations of the sun, the causes of sunspots and solar flares, and solar radiations. The OSO 1 was highly successful. From March 7 until August 2, 1963, it transmitted nearly 1,000 hours of valuable data on the sun, opening up the solar ultraviolet and x-ray radiations to detailed study. The far ultraviolet spectrum was found to vary, its intensity increasing during solar flares. Some 75 flares and subflares were also measured. Flare information is sought to learn more about these storms on the sun and perhaps to be able to predict them, so that lunar or interplanetary space flight could be scheduled accordingly. OSO 8 was launched on June 21, 1975, and continued the work of its predecessors.

Another series of satellites are the Orbiting Astronomical Observatories (OAO), to distinguish them from the solar observatories. The body of these satellites is octagonal, measuring some 2 meters (7 ft) wide and 3 meters (10 ft) high, with 4 large panels of solar cells mounted on the sides. A sunshade at the top of the satellite prevents sunlight from directly entering the experimental core. Designed for more and more accurate astronomical observations in space, these satellites have a precision attitude-control system programmed from earth, and are instrumented to study the regions in the electromagnetic spectrum in space above and below the slot of the visible spectrum used by optical telescopes on earth.

The OAO series of satellites were among the most sophisticated of their time and were very expensive. Unfortunately, the batteries of the first of the series failed after a day in orbit, while the third of the series, OAO-C, never achieved orbit. OAO 2 and OAO 3 have more than justified the expense of the program, not only providing a wealth of data but also serving as test instruments for future technology.

OAO 3, launched on August 21, 1972, was named Copernicus in honor of the five-hundredth anniversary of the birth of the father of modern astronomy. It carried an 80-cm (32-inch) telescope for ultraviolet observations of hot, young stars and the interstellar gas. X-ray sources are also being observed.

OAO 2, launched on December 7, 1968, carried a 40-cm (16-inch) telescope, four 30-cm (12-inch) telescopes, and six 20-cm (8-inch) telescopes. These conducted ultraviolet observations of stars, galaxies, and the interstellar gas, and measured for the first time the amount of ozone and oxygen in the earth's upper atmosphere. Designed to operate for only a year, OAO 2 was turned off nearly 4 years later, when Copernicus was launched.

In the first year of operation, the Smithsonian Astrophysical Observatory experiment package aboard OAO 2 took more than 6,000 photographs of 2,300 sections of the sky, each measuring 2° on a side. These photographs have provided information on 17,000 stars.

The University of Wisconsin experiment package aboard OAO 2 has made more than 2,000 separate observations of nearly 600 objects. The value of the OAO satellites is evident when compared to the fact that it required about 40 sounding-rocket flights over a 15-year period to obtain 3 hours of ultraviolet data on some 150 stars.

Other astronomy satellites have also been launched. Uhuru (Explorer 42) discovered many x-ray sources. This satellite was followed by other satellites conducting observations in the x-ray region of the spectrum. Among these are the Astronomical Netherlands Satellite (ANS), Ariel 5 launched for the United Kingdom, COS B launched for the European Space Agency, and the High Energy Astronomy Observatory (HEAO) series of satellites. HEAO 1 and HEAO 3 have conducted a survey of the entire sky for x-ray sources, while HEAO 2 is studying in more detail selected x-ray sources found earlier. A complete listing of satellites used exclusively for astronomical research or conducting some research in astronomy is given in Table 7.

What about the future? Two orbiting observatories are planned: the Space Telescope and the Infrared Astronomical Satellite (IRAS). Scheduled for polar-orbit launch early in the 1980s, IRAS is a cooperative effort among the United States, the Netherlands, and the United Kingdom. IRAS houses a 60-cm (24-inch) telescope supercooled to only 2° above absolute zero (−271°C). The cooling of the telescope adds greater sensitivity. If the telescope operates as expected, it would be capable of detecting an object with a diameter of 6 cm (a little more than 2 inches)—for example, a baseball—with a temperature of 20° C (68° F) located 3,000 km (1,860 mi) away. Cool stars and regions where stars are forming should be detectable anywhere within the Milky Way Galaxy. Any spiral galaxy like the Milky Way should be detectable out to a distance of 200 million light-years. At 1 wavelength of operation about 1,000 infrared sources are currently known. Upon completion of an all-sky survey at this wavelength by IRAS, this number is expected to be about 1 million.

The Space Telescope (ST) is an outgrowth of the Orbiting Astronomical Observatory program and is scheduled to be launched by the Space Shuttle in 1984. It is unusual in that it will be capable of being retrieved from orbit and refurbished. This makes the Space Telescope similar to earth-based telescopes. As technology advances, equipment attached to the telescope can be improved, an option not possible with the Orbiting Astronomical Observatory. A full range of experiments, from determining accurate distances of nearby stars to cosmological studies, is planned for the Space Telescope. The majority of these studies will be conducted in the ultraviolet and infrared regions of the spectrum.

Other astronomical research will be conducted on Spacelab missions. Spacelab is a combination of experimental pallets and a manned module that fits into the cargo hold of the Space Shuttle orbiter.

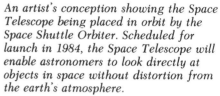

An artist's conception showing the Space Telescope being placed in orbit by the Space Shuttle Orbiter. Scheduled for launch in 1984, the Space Telescope will enable astronomers to look directly at objects in space without distortion from the earth's atmosphere.

Spacelab is being built for the National Aeronautics and Space Administration by the European Space Agency. Experiments can be changed on Spacelab, since it will return to earth each time with the orbiter. Different missions will have different objectives. The Spacelab 2 mission scheduled for the early 1980s will be the first devoted primarily to astrophysics. Among experiments planned are a cosmic-ray experiment to determine precisely the composition and energy spectra of particles with energies between 50 billion and 2 trillion electron volts, the distribution of x-ray-emitting material in clusters of galaxies, the absolute abundance of helium in the sun, and to survey the entire sky for extended (not starlike) objects with a small infrared telescope. This last experiment is intended to complement the survey of the Infrared Astronomical Satellite.

The establishment of a full-fledged astronomical observatory on the surface of the moon may lie somewhere in the distant future. This possibility has stirred lively discussions; too many unknowns are involved for a decision as yet. The moon offers certain advantages as a site for large telescopes and other astronomical equipment, with a firm base for mounting them, slower motion, and protection under the lunar surface for observers from space radiation and meteoroids. However, free dust on the moon's surface would be very harmful, the temperature variation with lunar day and night would be extreme, and lunar gravity, though slight, would require structures heavier than a space station to provide rigid equipment. The type of bearings on which the telescope would have to turn might give trouble in the near vacuum of the moon.

Lunar and Interplanetary Probes

The citizens of Europe had new worlds opened to them in the first part of the sixteenth century. Following Columbus's discovery (or rediscovery) of America in 1492, European interest in the New World was high. Magellan's circumnavigation of the earth from 1519 to 1521 was the first step in placing a limit on the size of the earth.

We are now living in a similar age of exploration. However, it is not the earth that is being explored but its home in space, the solar system. In 1959 we got our first glimpse of the far side of the moon. In 1969 astronauts walked on the lunar surface. All the planets from Mercury to Saturn have been visited by spacecraft. If the Voyager 1 and 2 missions proceed as scheduled, Voyager 2 will visit Uranus in 1986 and Neptune in 1989. That would leave only tiny Pluto isolated on the fringes of the solar system. Table 8 lists the facts of selected missions to the moon, and Table 9 gives similar information for the trips to the planets.

Basic facts related to space flight to the moon and planets include their gravity fields and speeds. The surface gravities of these bodies are all-important features. The earth produces 1 g (1 gravity) on the average at its surface (a free-fall acceleration of 980 cm [32 ft] per second per second). The gravitational forces of the moon and other planets are often calculated in relation to the earth's gravity taken as 1, so they represent g's of gravity in relation to the earth's 1 g. The force of gravity on Mercury is only about ⅓ that of the earth, Venus has nearly $\frac{9}{10}$ of our gravity, and Mars about ⅖; the moon's gravity is only about ⅙ that on earth. It takes little effort to walk or run on the surface of the moon.

A space probe or spacecraft must have a certain escape velocity if it is to pass beyond the predominant influence of the gravitational field of the body from which it is launched into the predominant influence of another gravitational field. Escape velocity from the earth's gravitational field in a hyperbolic orbit is about 11 km (about 7 mi) a second, which is 670 km (420 mi) a minute or an astounding 40,320 km (25,200 mi) an hour. Escape velocity is substantially less from the other inner planets and only 2.4 km (1.5 mi) a second from the moon. Because of the great masses of the outer planets (except for Pluto), their escape velocities are tremendous—a staggering 60 km (37.3 mi) a second for Jupiter and 36 km (22.4 mi) a second for Saturn. Aside from the extremely poisonous, perhaps cold, and very dense natures of the atmospheres of the gas giants, their escape velocities are the main reason why manned landings on only their satellites might be attempted.

The average speed at which the earth and other planets move in their orbits of the sun is a most significant vital factor in planning flights to them. Venus and Mercury, closer to the sun, move faster than the earth's 29.8 km (18.6 mi) a second and have shorter years; the moon's speed in earth orbit is slower, of course, as is that of Mars and the outer planets. A space probe directed toward the moon can disregard the velocity that the moon also has in tagging along with the earth around the sun, but the speed of the earth in relation to the other planets is a vital factor in choosing the most efficient orbits toward them. Fortunately, electronic computers are now available to make most of the necessary and formidable calculations.

Opposition and conjunction refer to certain relative positions of the planets, the sun, and other bodies in the solar system and are important in determining the shortest routes between planets. At inferior conjunction with the earth a body lies directly on a line between the

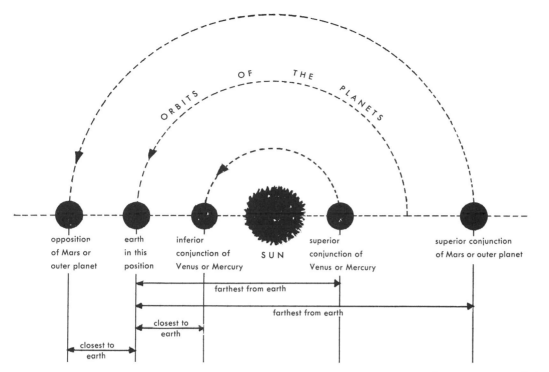

earth and the sun (disregarding inclination to the ecliptic), while in superior conjunction the sun is directly on the line between the earth
and the other body. Only the planets Mercury and Venus, some of the
asteroids with small orbits, like Adonis, Apollo, Hermes, and Icarus,
and a few of the comets actually can reach inferior conjunction, in
which they approach closest to the earth. In superior conjunction,
which any of the planets can attain, they lie beyond the sun from the
earth, at their greatest distance from our planet. At opposition, a position of the planets farther from the sun than the earth, the earth lies on
the line between the outer planet and the sun. The outer planets, as
does Mars, come closest to the earth at opposition.

The closest and the remotest distances from the earth of the other
planets in conjunction or opposition, as the case may be, affect space
flight. However, the closest distances are for the most favorable positions, and often at conjunction or opposition the planets do not come so
near. Mars, for example, never comes closer than 55 million km (34
million mi) from the earth, and on an average opposition is 77 million
km (48 million mi) away. The outer planets lie at distances roughly 10
times or more farther from the earth than Mars at their closest
approaches.

The times of transit to the other planets by the most economical trajectory in terms of fuel use can be precisely calculated. These routes
are ellipses intersecting the path of both planets and are called Hohmann transfer routes or transits for the scientist Walter Hohmann,
who first worked them out in detail in the 1920s. Such periods of
travel as 146 days for a flight to Venus and 237 days for one to Mars
are necessary for the minimum energy expenditure, so that the greatest possible payload can be lifted into escape velocity. These periods
can be shortened considerably if spacecraft are placed in parabolic or
hyperbolic orbits at higher than escape velocities.

The Mariner 10, Pioneer 11, and Voyager 1 and 2 missions repre-

*Relative positions of the earth, the sun,
and the other planets when they are in
conjunction and in opposition to the
earth, looking down on the solar system
from above. (Distances and sizes are not to
scale.)*

209

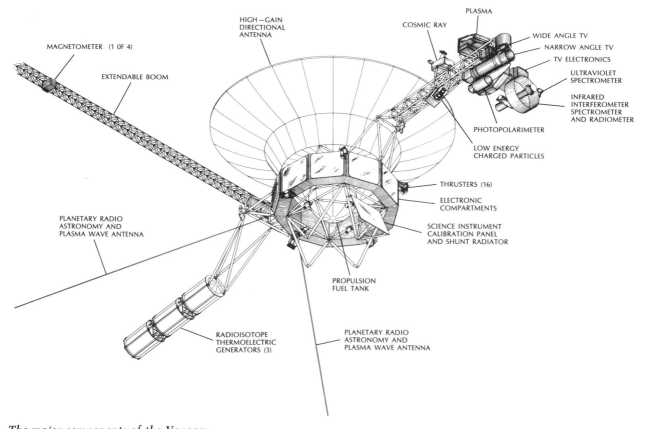

MAGNETOMETER (1 OF 4)

EXTENDABLE BOOM

HIGH – GAIN
DIRECTIONAL
ANTENNA

COSMIC RAY

PLASMA

WIDE ANGLE TV

NARROW ANGLE TV

TV ELECTRONICS

ULTRAVIOLET
SPECTROMETER

INFRARED
INTERFEROMETER
SPECTROMETER
AND RADIOMETER

PHOTOPOLARIMETER

LOW ENERGY
CHARGED PARTICLES

PLANETARY RADIO
ASTRONOMY AND
PLASMA WAVE ANTENNA

THRUSTERS (16)

ELECTRONIC
COMPARTMENTS

SCIENCE INSTRUMENT
CALIBRATION PANEL
AND SHUNT RADIATOR

PROPULSION
FUEL TANK

RADIOISOTOPE
THERMOELECTRIC
GENERATORS (3)

PLANETARY RADIO
ASTRONOMY AND
PLASMA WAVE ANTENNA

The major components of the Voyager
spacecraft are identified in this drawing.
The Voyager missions to Jupiter have
proven to be very successful. The 2
Voyager spacecraft have followed the trail
of Pioneer 11 (Pioneer Saturn) to historic
encounters with Saturn.

sent steps forward in interplanetary travel. The gravitational pull on any spacecraft increases as it approaches a planet. These forces not only increase the speed of the spacecraft; its course can also be changed. If the spacecraft is sent toward a planet with the right speed and direction, the gravitational assist will "kick" the spacecraft into the right direction and give it the proper speed for an encounter with another planet. Such gravitational assists have been used in the missions given above. The travel times to Saturn by the Voyager 1 and 2 spacecraft were halved as a result of their visit to Jupiter first. If these missions proceed as planned, Voyager 2, flung by Saturn, will rendezvous with Uranus in 1986. Uranus, in turn, will assist Voyager 2 to a Neptune encounter in 1989.

The figure shows the gravitational-assist technique as applied to Pioneer 11. Pioneer 11 was launched in a direct ascent from the Kennedy Space Center on April 6, 1973, by a 3-stage Atlas-Centaur vehicle. Only 11 hours passed before it crossed the moon's orbit. On April 11, 1973, a small course correction was made that aimed Pioneer 11 to the right of Jupiter as seen from the earth and would allow Pioneer 11 to come within 20,000 km (12,400 mi) of Jupiter's cloud tops. More importantly, it gave scientists the option of later redirecting the spacecraft to Saturn.

On April 19, 1974, the thrusters aboard Pioneer 11 added another 63.7 meters (210.2 ft) a second to its velocity. Not only did this direct Pioneer 11 to come 3 times closer to Jupiter at the time of closest approach than Pioneer 10, but it also meant that Pioneer 11 was accelerated by Jupiter to a velocity 55 times that of the muzzle velocity of a high-speed rifle bullet, an astounding 173,000 km (108,000 mi) an hour. This velocity carried Pioneer 11 some 2.4 billion km (1.5 billion mi) across the solar system to Saturn.

Pioneer 11 approached Jupiter from below Jupiter's South Pole. This meant that Pioneer 11 would be within Jupiter's intense radiation belts for the least amount of time. It also was directed to fly by Jupiter against the direction of Jupiter's rotation. Approaching from the illuminated side, Pioneer 11 zoomed around the dark side, completed its circuit of Jupiter, and was redirected to Saturn. Pioneer 11 successfully made its closest approach to Jupiter on December 2, 1974. Renamed Pioneer Saturn after its Jupiter encounter, it coasted to its historic rendezvous with Saturn on September 1, 1979.

Manned Space Flights

Before manned expeditions could be sent to land on the moon, many unmanned hard-landing, soft-landing, and lunar-orbiting vehicles had to make preliminary investigations of lunar conditions. These craft had to provide the basic information about the moon's surface before manned landing vehicles could be designed and engineered with full assurance. A start in this direction was made by Luna 3, launched from the U.S.S.R. on October 4, 1959. In its initial orbit it approached the moon at a distance of about 6,100 km (3,800 mi) from its surface and from the south. It swung past to about 64,000 km (40,000 mi) from the moon, where it made the first photograph of the far side on October 7. The moon's gravitational attraction deflected Luna 3 northward into another plane, and it came back around the earth in an elongated orbit with a period of 16.2 days, a perigee of 40,638 km (25,252 mi), and an apogee of 468,925 km (291,376 mi). This orbit decayed, and the vehicle burned up in the earth's atmosphere on April 20, 1960.

A total of 11 spacecraft hard-landed on the moon, among them the Ranger craft that sent back sharp photographs of the lunar surface as they fell faster and faster toward impact. Then came a group of soft-landing craft, like the American Surveyors and Soviet Lunas, which were slowed by their rockets as they approached the moon and landed gently in a cushion of rocket flame. These research craft dug, tested, and photographed right on the lunar surface.

Finally, a series of Lunar Orbiters circled the moon at distances ranging from hundreds of miles down to fifty miles from the surface, mapping both the moon's near side and its far side. The amazingly clear close-up photographs transmitted were studied for the selection of the landing sites that would offer the best samples of the lunar surface. In the meantime, unmanned and manned Apollo spacecraft were

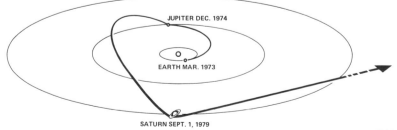

The gravitational assist technique enabled the Pioneer 11 (Pioneer Saturn) spacecraft to recross the solar system to its historic encounter with Saturn in September 1979.

211

All the key steps in an Apollo manned mission to the moon and return to earth, described by number in the text. The moon moves along in its orbit of the earth, from west to east, as the mission is accomplished.

being tested and flown in earth orbits. A listing of selected lunar missions is given in Table 8.

On December 21, 1968, 3 astronauts in Apollo 8 went into earth orbit and then became the first human beings to go into "escape orbit" of the earth as they blasted toward the moon. After 10 lunar orbits they returned to earth. Apollo 9 tested the manned lunar module in earth orbit in March 1969. With Apollo 10, in May 1969, when 2 astronauts came within 16 km (10 mi) of the moon in the lunar module, preparations were completed for a manned lunar landing with Apollo 11.

The paths followed around the earth and moon in the Apollo 11 and later manned missions to the moon are shown in the chart. The numbered positions show 15 key steps in Apollo expeditions: (1) Lift-off from the Kennedy Space Center; (2) earth-orbit checkout; (3) injection into orbit toward the moon; (4) turnaround of command, service, and lunar modules; (5) midcourse correction of orbit; (6) retrofiring to slow Apollo for lunar orbit; (7) elliptical lunar orbit; (8) separation of lunar module with 2 astronauts aboard; (9) landing on the moon; (10) LM ascending and docking; (11) ascent stage of LM left in orbit; (12) injection on homeward orbit; (13) course correction for precise re-entry angle; (14) service module jettisoned; and (15) chutes lower command module to Pacific splashdown.

Nine manned Apollo missions to the moon were achieved with 6 manned landings. Each thoroughly studied another type of lunar surface and landscape, with the exception of Apollo 13, disabled by the blowout of an oxygen container in midflight. The astronauts on this mission rounded the moon and brought their ship back to earth, fortunately without mishap, despite the danger.

Each Apollo crew left instruments on the moon to report long-term conditions and changes back to earth, and brought back with them more and more precious lunar rocks and soils for study. A great deal has been learned by scientists about the moon today and its history back to its time of formation 4.6 billion years ago with the rest of the solar system.

Although the Apollo lunar exploration has now lapsed, it is small wonder that our attention is directed elsewhere, and scientists have enough data to try to fit together into an overall picture of the earth-moon system for a long time to come. Sometime in the future, people will revisit the moon in order to begin to use it for purposes for which it is best fitted, as we come to understand it and learn much more about the great variety of human reactions under low-gravity and weightless conditions.

In the meantime, space observations will be continued in manned space stations and observatories like the Skylabs, Spacelabs, and Salyuts orbiting the earth. Human observers have a valid function in such space vehicles, as well as do the unmanned satellites. But both launch vehicles and their spacecraft will require extensive development in the future before the manned exploration of another planet such as Mars will be feasible.

Chapter XV
Man in Space

"The long, long anchorage we leave."
Whitman

In May 1927, Charles A. Lindbergh winged solo across the Atlantic from Roosevelt Field, Long Island, nonstop to Le Bourget Airport near Paris. In his stubby *Spirit of St. Louis*, which reflected the most advanced aeronautical design of the day, he flew at times as low as 3 meters (10 ft) above the waves and once climbed to an altitude of 3.2 km (2 mi) to avoid clouds. His 5,800-km (3,600-mi) record journey lasted 33 hours, 30 minutes, at an average speed of 177 km (110 mi) an hour. Thirty-six years later, in May 1963, it took Gordon Cooper 30 minutes longer to orbit the earth 22 times in his Mercury capsule *Faith 7*. He covered a distance of some 965,400 km (600,000 mi) at 28,200 km (17,550 mi) an hour, at heights ranging from 160 to 267 km (100 to 166 mi) above the earth's surface. In roughly the same time he had flown over 80 times higher and over 160 times faster and farther than Lindbergh. An astronaut blasting off for the moon must speed at over 40,200 km (25,000 mi) an hour.

Whether or not man will be tough enough in both body and spirit to endure lengthy space flights is an open question. The more we learn about space, the more man's chances for surviving it appear to shrink. The discovery of high-energy radiations in the earth's magnetosphere and their increasing great intensity at greater heights seemed to dash man's hopes of survival in space—until these radiations were found to be localized in the doughnut of the Van Allen belts that ring the earth. Gherman Titov's nausea after 6 hours of weightlessness in the second Soviet manned flight prompted gloomy talk of a natural period after which vertigo might occur in other astronauts. When other men flew weightless for more than 6 hours without difficulty, this hurdle toward full space flight had been cleared.

The human body is made up of many systems that must function smoothly together to maintain an adequate adjustment to an alien environment. These are the musculoskeletal, cardiovascular, sensory, nervous, endocrine, respiratory, digestive, and excretory systems. The most important factors in space flight are acceleration, atmosphere, gravitational and magnetic fields, and particle and electromagnetic radiations. Numerous critical interactions between the human systems and these environmental factors will take place—the effect of acceleration on respiration and movement, the effect of weightlessness on the sensory and cardiovascular systems, and the bathing of the whole body in radiations, to name a few.

Noise and Vibration

Enclosed in their snugly fitting space suits and lying on cushioned couches shaped to their own contours, astronauts are never safer than while they wait for the end of the countdown and the liftoff of the rocket. Even if the highly explosive liquefied gases being pumped into the fuel tanks of the booster blew up, they would be yanked out of danger by the small rocket in the escape tower above. But as soon as the rocket booster is ignited, rapidly builds up roaring thrust on the pad, and is released to hover and shoot upward, bearing them with it, astronauts face many dangers, particularly in the first 5 minutes of flight. Among the most potent of these are noise and vibrations.

A fearful, thunderous noise radiates around the rocket booster as it reaches full thrust. It is a snarling, growling, roaring monster. The rocket and spacecraft are enveloped in resounding waves of noise

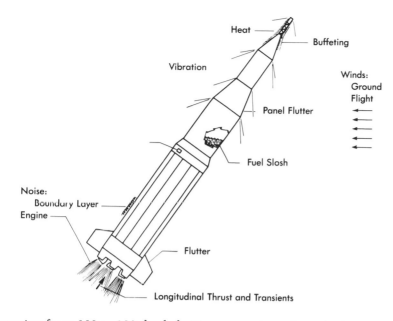

Heat

Buffeting

Vibration

Winds:
Ground
Flight
←
←
←
←
←

Panel Flutter

Fuel Slosh

Noise:
Boundary Layer
Engine

Flutter

Longitudinal Thrust and Transients

Launch-vehicle problem areas.

ranging from 100 to 180 decibels. For comparison, the noise intensity of heavy traffic is about 80 decibels and the roar of a jet engine can touch 140 decibels, the level that may cause ear pain. The noise levels reached by various booster systems range so high that breakage of equipment has resulted frequently at great distances from the launching site. The Saturn rocket booster makes a grumbling, roaring, shattering noise from near at hand. The National Aeronautics and Space Administration has bought up land far around Cape Canaveral, not only to provide more space for launching complexes but also to lessen the risk to people and things from the noise or explosions. As the rocket gains speed, the air begins to whistle past the nose cone or space cabin and builds up acoustic pressures at the boundary layer, the area of greatest friction between the shell of the rocket and the air. This is added to the tremendous noise produced by the rocket engines.

Men can tolerate noise in the range of audible frequencies at the 100-decibel level for up to 8 hours, at 120 decibels for about 5 minutes, and at 135 decibels for only about 10 seconds; 150 decibels and above may cause severe damage to the inner ear, pain, and nausea.

Special acoustic insulation may be required for space flights of the future. Space cabins might absorb up to 30 decibels of the noise and space suits and helmets about the same, but such absorption would be in the range of frequencies above 30 cycles per second. Below 20 cycles a second, sound is not audible but is felt as vibration, and in the larger rocket systems most of the sound may be subaudible, ranging from about 10 to 20 cycles per second. Below 0.5 cycle per second, vibrations are felt simply as single jolts. It is believed that the chorus of noises in space cabins can be kept below dangerous levels, but the problem could cause failure of manned flights within the first 2 minutes.

The many vibrations running up the length of rocket systems as they are launched have a variety of sources. Among these are the shocks of engine ignition, pulsations in the engine thrust, the chugging of fast-spinning turbines, the effects of control forces and fuel sloshing in the tanks as the rocket veers, slightly unbalanced spinning compo-

215

nents, and the shocks of engine burnout and the release of initial stages of the rocket. The human body can absorb or pass vibrations of high frequency without harm, but vibrations below 100 to 200 cycles per second can be extremely damaging. Body systems, particularly in the abdominal area, may begin to vibrate in sympathetic resonance with the waves penetrating them, and this can shake and tear soft tissues apart, causing irreparable damage. After some 6 to 12 seconds of vibrations at 10 cycles per second, under an acceleration of 3 to 10 g, men experience severe chest pain, which may be followed by weakness and collapse if the vibration exposure continues.

Astronauts have said they get quite a jolting during the first minutes of their ride, partly from the buildup of high g's flattening them back against their couches and partly from the hammering up through the whole system of the rocket. Designers must provide adequate structural strength in the thin skins of rocket sections to absorb this hammering without damage and to prevent as much of the vibration as possible, without adding too much weight. The problem of eliminating vibration has sometimes slowed the development of larger rocket-engine systems.

As if the noise and jolting of launch were not enough, as the rocket accelerates up through the dense lower atmosphere it must pass through turbulent air currents. These buffet against the tall, slender shell of the rocket system and may cause fluttering of fins or thin panels. Rising through cross winds can produce severe shearing forces that tend to bend and twist the column this way and that, and the boundary-layer noise and vibration become more severe. Finally, the rocket spire is so long that it inevitably sways and bends lengthwise as it is buffeted and the force of the rocket propulsion varies. Astronauts reported that they can feel the rocket swaying behind them; somewhat like observers standing atop a tall building swaying in a wind, they feel their capsule weaving about at the peak of the rocket as it accelerates.

Too much of this swaying, buffeting, and longitudinal vibration has torn rockets and missiles apart. But the noise and buffeting decrease quickly as the rocket penetrates into the thinner upper atmosphere, and the vibrations and swaying are gone as soon as the capsule goes into orbit.

Acceleration and Deceleration

Extreme noise and vibration have not caused nearly as much trouble as have the high g's built up as rocket vehicles accelerate or decelerate to and from their earth-orbiting velocities of nearly 29,000 km (18,000 mi) an hour. Greater velocity is required for orbits toward the moon or toward other planets—the escape velocities of 40,200 km (25,000 mi) an hour or more away from the earth must be reached, and later lost again when the vehicles re-enter the earth's atmosphere. For earth orbits, the gravities jamming against the astronauts run up to 6 to 8 g's on launching and re-entering—that is, the astronaut weighs about 7 times more than his normal weight at sea level as he accelerates up through the atmosphere. While the g's need not mount forever with launching into an orbit toward the moon or a planet, because lower acceleration developed for a slightly longer period will produce the same velocity as higher acceleration for a shorter time, or a space vehicle launched from parking orbit already has a good share of its required velocity, the astronauts must face and endure up to 10 g's on any direct flights from and direct returns to earth.

The giant test centrifuges in which astronauts are whirled around, at the end of long arms, in cabins simulating those designed for space, first proved that astronauts can absorb such high acceleration and deceleration punishment for short periods of time. The human body is so resilient that it can take this mauling and drubbing without any permanent damage, though as the g's pile up the astronaut feels the effects strongly in his stomach and eyeballs and has difficulty in moving his arms and legs, and eventually in breathing.

Men totally immersed in water can absorb acceleration best, although space suits to restrain the body organs have been found adequate to meet the g's encountered, and the complexities of water immersion have not been necessary. It was soon discovered that the position of the astronaut's body is the key to the ability to absorb high g's. If the body is aligned head to foot with the direction of the acceleration, the blood is squeezed toward the head or feet as if by a hydraulic ram; this is the worst position. So the astronauts are seated across the rocket diameter. Extended across their capsules in this position they face in the direction of flight on ascent ("eyeballs in" is the graphic expression for the resultant pressure), and with their backs to the direction of flight on descent, again pressed back into their couches. High gravities are not as tolerable in the "eyeballs out" position.

Practice makes astronauts more familiar with high-g conditions and enables them to continue to function fairly efficiently, using their fingers and even talking clearly under 6 to 8 g's, although the experience is far from pleasant. When astronaut Gordon Cooper was faced with the breakdown of his automatic attitude-control system for re-entry into the atmosphere, he was able to fire his retrorockets at the end of his Mercury flight and then hold his bucking capsule in the proper position as it slowed down rapidly, operating so effectively that he landed within 6 km (4 mi) of the aircraft carrier U.S.S. *Kearsage*.

Weightlessness

We are thoroughly accustomed to the 1-g condition here on earth—the gravitational force with which the massive sphere pulls at our bodies. This force acts in such a way that on a spring scale we have our given weight, and in free fall near the surface of the earth we would experience an acceleration of 980 cm (32 ft) per second per second. But strange things happen to the effects of gravity under the conditions of space flight.

When an express elevator accelerates upward very rapidly, its passengers feel that they weigh a little more, being thrust down with greater force against the floor of the elevator. When they accelerate downward very fast, the floor of the elevator seems to drop out from under them and they feel light and airy. Going up, they are experiencing hypergravity (gravity conditions greater than 1 g); going down, hypogravity (gravity conditions less than 1 g). At the microgravity or 0 g of a space vehicle in earth orbit, the astronaut feels no weight at all, the sensations of actual weight of limbs and muscles are lacking, and he seems simply to float or be suspended just where he is.

The human body is equipped with a number of little-understood sensory receptors acted on mainly by gravity, the so-called gravireceptors. The nonauditory labyrinths of the middle ear contain otoliths, tiny calcium-carbonate granules surrounded by nerve endings. Linear accelerations in any direction can be detected by the pressure of the otoliths against the nerves. The semicircular canals, located in the same labyrinths, register angular accelerations of the head, and the sense of balance derives from their functioning. Mechanoreceptors report localized pressures, tensions, and accelerations, such as Merkel's corpuscles in the skin, and the nerve networks around the hair follicles. Within the body, proprioceptors immediately under the skin and in muscular and connective tissues supply the sensations of the position and posture of the body.

Weightlessness, it was predicted, would knock out the astronaut's sense of balance and position and sooner or later produce nausea, loss of body sense, disorientation, and inability to function. While this would be known as spacesickness, rather than seasickness or airsickness, it was thought it would involve the same symptoms and be just as incapacitating.

Most of the fears arising from the oddity of weightlessness appeared to be ill founded as the American astronauts in the Mercury and Gemini flights experienced weightlessness. While it took them a few seconds to get their bearings as they were injected into orbit and weightlessness, and to place their craft in relation to the earth, they were not disoriented. They found weightlessness pleasant, even exhilarating. They did not experience nystagmus, the involuntary eye movements associated with motion sickness or vertigo. They found that they maintained their postural sense and could write, take photographs through the ports, operate many types of delicate equipment and instruments, and control the attitude of their craft—in short, could carry on habitual activities without difficulty. When the body is properly restrained, the speed and accuracy of hand motions appear to be almost the same during 0 g as during normal g.

In August 1961 the first case of spacesickness occurred. Soviet cosmonaut Gherman Titov became dizzy and almost nauseated after

In space, weight disappears. Everything must be securely fastened or it will float away. A piece of paper no longer drops to the floor as on earth, but curls and floats as shown here. Alan L. Bean, commander on Skylab 3, is checking data while the teleprinter tape hangs "up" rather than "down."

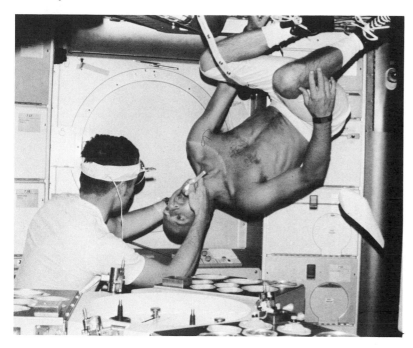

Weightlessness can have its advantages. Astronaut Charles Conrad, Jr., Skylab 2 commander, has floated upside down under weightless conditions into a convenient position for an oral physical examination by Joseph P. Kerwin. Note the floating piece of paper on the right. The extended Skylab missions have proved that man can adapt to space, at least for missions lasting a few months.

about 6 hours of weightlessness. (Physicians have warned astronauts to avoid vomiting while weightless, since it might cause suffocation. The American astronauts, and perhaps also the Russian cosmonauts, have carried drugs to prevent such an eventuality.) While Titov's vertigo became worse when he turned his head or observed fast-moving objects, and may have involved the organs of balance of the middle ear, it was apparently controllable, and he continued on in his flight to a total of over 25 hours, able to sleep and carry out his assigned tasks.

American astronauts experienced symptoms of spacesickness during Apollo and Skylab missions. Fortunately, though, the symptoms disappear after 2 to 5 days in space and do not affect the astronauts' performance during extended missions.

When first released from the long hours of their confinement, astronauts have exhibited varying degrees of blood pooling in the major body cavities, such as the abdomen and legs, a reaction known as orthostatic hypotension. This depletes the brain circulation and is reflected in difficulty in standing upright and walking steadily. It appears to be caused by a combination of diminished blood volume, which many astronauts have shown, reduced blood pressure, and changes in the sympathetic nervous system that reduce the tone or elasticity of blood vessels. The condition lasts only a few hours, however, and regular vigorous exercise in the capsule during flight may well prevent it entirely.

No way has yet been found to overcome the diminished blood volume and accompanying loss in sodium and potassium levels in the blood, however. Apparently gravity has something to do with maintaining blood volume in the body. Under long weightlessness, calcium, phosphorus, and nitrogen are lost from bones. These losses are comparable to those of patients confined to total bed rest on earth. The Skylab missions, the longest of which was 84 days, indicate that remedial measures may be necessary to replace the calcium, but in 1980 two Soviet cosmonauts stayed 185 days in space without weight loss.

Artificial gravity may yet have to be produced in space vessels if adverse and uncontrollable physiological reactions occur during extended periods of weightlessness. Weight could be created in a number of ways. A space station with a sizable diameter might be rotated on a central axis, a miniature earth, to reproduce part or all of normal gravity at its perimeter. Or a spacecraft might be made to revolve around its propulsion engine, to which it could be connected by a cable or pole, to produce artificial gravity. Systems like this would be very complex, however, and would require equipment that would add an enormous amount of weight. Preliminary experiments have uncovered many design problems in rotating spacecraft around a short radius.

Basic physiochemical reactions may yet prove to be limiting factors in space flight under weightless conditions, until ways can be discovered to counteract them directly in the body or with artificial gravity. Gravity on the moon is about one sixth that on earth, on the planet Mars it is only a quarter, and in orbit it is 0. What effects these gradations in reduced gravities might have on human growth and the maintenance of health and energy cannot now be foretold, but they offer exciting experimental conditions. Space stations or lunar or Martian installations could offer laboratory environments most fruitful for comparison with the ways our bodies react here on earth under 1 g.

Life-support Systems

Nuclear-powered submarines have provided examples of many men living together in a completely closed environment for long periods of time. While much has been learned about human requirements and reactions under these circumstances, a submarine is not a space capsule, unfortunately, and nothing comparable to a submarine in size and weight could be launched into space. Weight, whether in equipment, stored provisions, or air, must be cut to an absolute minimum in space flight.

The creation of small, light, closed life-support systems for spacecraft flights to the moon and beyond, and for short-term life support in space suits under the conditions of interplanetary space of the surface of the moon, has been the objective of much research. One of the most clear-cut results to date has been the conclusion that for periods of some weeks, and possibly months, storage of the necessities of life and its waste products will be adequate, and recycling from waste back to necessities will not be required. The power of the mighty Saturn rocket made it possible for large quantities of consumables to be launched into space with Skylab, even though individual crews did restock supplies. On the 185-day mission (man's longest) of Leonid Popov and Valery Ryumin, the Soviet cosmonauts aboard the Salyut 6 space station, supplies were often received from unmanned Progress spacecraft. For long missions away from earth such resupply will not be possible and some wastes must be regenerated. The more regeneration the better, of course—if body evaporation and wastes can be reprocessed in part to potable water, the spacecraft will have to carry less extra weight.

On earth, it has been customary to say man's basic needs are food, clothing, and shelter. Those who climb or fly to great heights soon find that an atmosphere of a certain consistency is another basic necessity. Atmosphere is the main thing lacking in space. In addition, the equiv-

220

alents of food, clothing, and shelter in space are very different from those on earth; when life must be maintained in a tiny, light container, the design of the life-support system becomes a veritable nightmare.

The atmosphere in space cabins, for instance, must be kept above a minimum pressure, below which oxygen would not be transferred properly to the blood in the lungs; but if the pressure is too high, carbon dioxide will not be adequately vented from the lungs in breathing. The air must be kept in motion to allow perspiration to evaporate from the skin. The air must contain enough oxygen to fill the astronaut's needs without extra exertion; but experiments have indicated that too great a proportion of oxygen over weeks of time can have detrimental effects.

The American Mercury astronauts were provided with a pure oxygen atmosphere at a pressure of 0.35 kilogram per square cm (5 pounds per square inch or about a third of that at sea level) and worked easily in it. The Russian Vostok cosmonauts were given an atmospheric mixture of oxygen and nitrogen, more like our normal terrestrial air. The oxygen in American space capsules was mixed with some helium during the critical first phase of flight, after the disastrous fire in a grounded Apollo capsule that killed 3 astronauts. For the extended Skylab missions, the crew breathed a mixture of 74 percent oxygen and 26 percent nitrogen at 0.35 kilogram per square cm (5 pounds per square inch). This marked the first time such a mixture was used by the American astronauts.

Oxygen can be carried as a compressed gas or as a liquid at low temperatures in bottles. It can also be generated from oxygen-rich chemicals such as potassium or sodium superoxides, sodium chlorate, or hydrogen peroxide. The superoxides have the advantage of removing carbon dioxide, odors, water vapor, and bacteria from the atmosphere. Oxygen can also be made by the electrolysis of water into its components or by the decomposition of carbon dioxide exhaled in breathing. Plant photosynthesis also creates oxygen. But producing oxygen by these methods demands complex, heavy systems or uses too much electricity to be feasible for short space trips.

While American astronauts have sometimes had trouble adjusting the temperatures within their space suits and cabins to the ideal range, this was because of mechanical malfunctioning of the air-conditioning systems, and not because there were any inherent environmental extremes in space that could not be overcome. The old fears about the near-absolute-zero chill of the vacuum in space have evaporated. The sun is a reliable source of heat, which the thinly dispersed particles in space cannot carry away rapidly from the space vessel. The heat exchange between the spacecraft and space can be adjusted by the absorptive, radiative, and reflective character of the skin of the craft so that a fairly normal temperature range can be maintained, and temperature can be regulated within the craft by air conditioning to suit the needs of the astronauts. A greater problem is radiation of the heat produced in the vehicle's systems into space fast enough to maintain a normal operating temperature without requiring too much radiative equipment.

Astronauts can eat and drink (and even be merry) in space and can perform all of their normal bodily functions; they have simply had to learn to do so under weightless conditions. Water and food are carried

Astronauts Charles Conrad, Jr. (background), and Joseph P. Kerwin (foreground) show the type of space suit worn by Skylab astronauts for extravehicular activity. An umbilical cord connects the astronauts to the mother ship and provides the life-sustaining oxygen.

in squeeze tubes or canisters because, if loosely carried, bits of food and droplets of water float helter-skelter about space cabins. Water poured into the air in a cabin simply forms a globule wherever it is released. Astronauts can eat cubed, desiccated foods or cookies with ease as long as they keep their mouths shut. Muscles of the mouth, throat, and esophagus deliver the food and drink efficiently to the stomach despite the weightlessness. A fairly normal, tasty diet can be predicted for the astronauts of the future, although they won't be grilling steaks in celestial barbecue pits.

The average daily requirements on a strict regimen for an astronaut in a space cabin total about 3.6 kilograms (8 pounds). This includes about 2.21 kilograms (4.8 pounds) of water, 0.9 kilogram (1.9 pounds) of oxygen, and 0.5 kilogram (1.2 pounds) of solids—foods and minerals. The atmosphere can be carried in pressure bottles, and the food and water in containers. The waste output of the astronauts is balanced with this at about 3.6 kilograms (8 pounds)—2.5 kilograms (5.6 pounds) of water a day, 1 kilogram (2.2 pounds) of carbon dioxide, and 0.05 kilogram (0.1 pound) of solid waste, urea, and minerals. The excess water vapor from breathing and perspiring can be wrung out of the capsule's atmosphere by the conditioning system. Exhaled carbon dioxide can be filtered from the air with an absorptive compound like lithium hydroxide, a pound of which can absorb about 0.34 kilogram (0.75 pound) of carbon dioxide before it is saturated. This can be stored, as can body wastes, until the return of the spacecraft to earth. For some years and maybe decades, human needs in space flight can be taken care of quite adequately in this manner. As more power becomes available and greater weight can be carried, more recycling from human output to input items can be effected.

Completely closed and fully recycled life-support systems should not be needed until there are long-term space stations, or spacecraft fly beyond the moon toward the planet Mars, toward an asteroid, or past the planets Mars and Venus and back to earth. These self-sufficient systems might use plants or algae, which could recycle the wastes, produce fresh oxygen, use up carbon dioxide, and in the process create food. A similar system would be necessary for astronauts proposing to dig in and live on the moon for extended periods, although there the problem of the weight of equipment would not be as serious as it would be for spacecraft. Unmanned craft could land equipment in separate loads on the moon; some input raw materials might be discovered on the moon itself.

Effective Human Action in Space

There is concern that essential physiological rhythms might be disturbed or destroyed by weightlessness or by the lack of the normal magnetic and gravitational fields experienced continually at the earth's surface. Can the effective energy for a normal day's work be maintained by a human being under space conditions? Will the lack of familiar day and night cycles tend to disrupt the astronauts' sleep, rest, and work cycles? Will the confinement and resultant need for tedious, energy-consuming exercise diminish the effectiveness of human beings in space?

On the short trips that have been made in near space, astronauts have tended to follow their natural day-night cycles on earth with little difficulty. Astronaut Gordon Cooper, who had a habit of catnapping, was able to refresh himself in the same way in his *Faith* 7 Mercury capsule, sleeping on 13 different occasions for a total of 4 hours, 9 minutes in his 34-hour journey. Astronauts on longer flights have slept as long as 8 hours at a stretch. The long Skylab missions showed that man can obtain adequate sleep in space over long time periods and during regularly scheduled 8-hour sleep periods.

The long-term psychological effects are another matter. Without

The space suits worn by the Apollo astronauts on the moon had to be self-contained units. Oxygen is contained in the backpack seen behind the helmet of Apollo 12 astronaut Alan L. Bean. The reflection of Charles Conrad, Jr., is seen in the visor of Bean.

223

frequent communication with others, aviators on lengthy missions at high altitudes have occasionally reported what is known as the "break-off phenomenon"—that is, they began to feel detached from the earth and from human beings, to lose sight of their objectives, and to indulge in unrealistic feelings and actions. Flight up in space might well give rise to more acute breakoff, even to a desire never to come back. For this reason among others, the long flights in prospect are planned for 2 or more astronauts together. In the relatively brief flights to date, astronauts traveling alone have not reported this psychological reaction.

Of greater concern is the so-called sensory deprivation. In space there promises to be much less input into the sensory receptors, partly because of the weightless condition and the limited environment in which the astronauts must remain. In sensory-deprivation experiments subjects have become unrealistic, turned within themselves, and grown prone to hallucinations. The work load of the astronaut, however, is such that he can occupy every minute of his waking time fruitfully. The astronauts were wise to insist that the Mercury craft be equipped with a porthole and a periscope. To see the earth rolling beneath them, the awesome sunsets, and the brilliance of stars in the black sky above must surely have compensated for whatever slight sensory deprivation the capsule environment imposed. In long-term confinement in a capsule, however, the sensory factor might prove critical.

Harsh and long-endured stress has its inevitable effects on the human system. The battle fatigue of war has often led to lasting mental deterioration, inability to face obstacles with aplomb, and sometimes complete breakdown. While individual tolerances range widely, the continuation of stress over a long period will eventually crush almost anyone's strength, efficiency, and spirit. Reactions to great stress are manifold: forgetfulness, failure to notice changes in one's surroundings, slowness or lack of ability to analyze problems and make decisions, lack of balanced coordination, erroneous estimates of speed and distance, carelessness, and improper operation of controls or reading of instruments. A single lapse of this kind could spell death to an astronaut.

With the wide individual differences in the capacity to withstand stress, astronauts can be selected who have proved their greater-than-normal endurance. Battle conditions have shown the remarkable ability of some men to live through ever-present threats to life for weeks at a time. And the more nearly the space environment is made to approach normal, everyday conditions, the longer the astronauts will be able to endure the strains they face.

Probably the best way to ward off the effects of continued stress is by sending groups of astronauts, 2 or 3 at the beginning, into space to allow adequate rest and sleep periods and to maintain normal communication with each other and with the earth. The inclusion of women to maintain a more normal atmosphere has been suggested for more extended flights and would probably be a must on the long flights to other planets in the solar system. The first space flight of a woman, Valentina Tereshkova, a 75-hour journey, indicates that the Russians may be planning that men and women will enter space together.

As soon as two or more human beings get together, to be sure, particularly in a confined space, complex social interactions come into play. Petty irritations and repeated frustrations develop. One of the group may try to dominate the others, openly or indirectly, or to vent hostility on them. One of the group may become a scapegoat for the aggressions of the others and may rebel at this role. The possibilities of trouble are endless. Nonetheless, with a completely planned schedule of operations, properly allocated functions, and a high morale deriving from the overall objectives, there is little doubt that 2 or more astronauts will carry off space flights together much more efficiently than could a man alone.

In the flights to come, unforeseen psychological reactions are bound to occur, but thus far physiological and psychological limitations (in theory, at least) do not raise insuperable obstacles. Man is an adaptable and extremely tough creature. It appears that he can take it.

But what of the external obstacles and hazards that space may have in store for us? What are the chances that meteoroids might blow out a spacecraft, or that penetrating radiations in space might sometimes be too strong for human beings to survive?

Meteoroids and Dust

Interplanetary space is almost entirely empty. Its emptiness surpasses by a good margin that of the emptiest vacuums obtainable in laboratories here on earth. In recent years, with liquid-hydrogen systems, vacuums of ten-trillionth torr have been approached (a torr is the feather pressure necessary to support a column of mercury 0.1 cm [0.04 inch] high). The pressure from the thin gas in interplanetary space is estimated to be on the order of ten-quadrillionth torr, on the other hand.

Despite the great emptiness, a variety of bodies and radiations crisscross interplanetary space: the solar wind, consisting of high-velocity protons, electrons, and neutrons ejected from the sun; solar radiation and cosmic rays from interstellar space; interplanetary dust and gases; and asteroids, meteoroids and meteoric dust, and comets or their remains.

The solid bodies—the asteroids, large and small, the meteoroid streams, the cometary particles, and smaller meteoroid grains—hurtling at tremendous velocities through space could be terribly destructive to spacecraft. The larger comets and the asteroids, the orbits of which are known with fair accuracy, and the identified meteoroid streams can be avoided, it is true, by launching at appropriate times or simply by steering clear of them. Before the Mars 1 spacecraft failed far out on its probe toward Mars, it had passed through a previously unidentified meteoroid stream about 37 million km (23 million mi) from the earth, according to Soviet reports. Given adequate instrumentation, the approximate position and movement of such a stream could be mapped.

Various estimates have been made of the probability that spacecraft will be damaged or holed by meteoroids or solid grains in space. One authority has stated that a 0.25-cm (0.1-inch) stainless-steel hull of a space vehicle 0.9 meter (1 yard) in diameter is likely to be penetrated by a sporadic meteoroid only once in 1,450 years, while if the hull is 1.25 cm (0.5 inch), penetration would occur only once in every 180,000 years. Another estimate indicates a penetration by sporadic or shower meteoroids every 110 days for a hull 0.25-cm (0.1-inch) thick

Astronaut Neil Armstrong, first man on the moon, photographed by Edwin Aldrin, his companion, setting up the experiment to test the composition of the solar wind, with the Lunar Expeditionary Module in the background.

The Apollo 15 lunar station shows the Lunar Module Falcon *on the left and the Lunar Roving Vehicle on the right with astronaut James B. Irwin. The Lunar Roving Vehicle gave the astronauts increased mobility, enabling them to explore larger areas of the moon.*

of a craft 46 meters (50 yards) in diameter, or every 300 years if the hull is 2.5 cm (1 inch) thick.

Data on meteoroids come from 3 sources. The least accurate source consists of earth-based photographic and radar observations. Instruments aboard spacecraft have provided a large amount of data on meteoroids ranging in mass from 1 microgram (1 millionth gram) to 1 gram. The seismic instruments left on the moon by the Apollo astronauts are believed to be 100 percent efficient for reporting meteoroids with masses greater than 10 kilograms.

The results from space indicate that the most common meteoroid in space is a mixture of dust bound together by frozen gases rather than the stones and stony irons striking the surface of the earth after their fiery trip through earth's atmosphere. A study of meteoroid impact on space colonies indicates that a 0.3-gram meteoroid would strike such a facility 1,000 meters (3,280 ft) long and 200 meters (650 ft) in diameter once every 3 years. But the damage from such a collision is so minimal that risk to human life aboard such a vehicle stemming from meteoroid strikes is very low compared to the daily risks due to accident and natural disaster.

226

The asteroid belt may not pose the problem originally thought. On July 15, 1972, Pioneer 10 was the first spacecraft to enter the asteroid belt. It had been estimated that Pioneer 10 could be seriously damaged in a collision with any particle larger than 0.05 cm (0.02 inch). However, the probe successfully traversed the asteroid belt, as have its successors Pioneer 11, Voyager 1, and Voyager 2.

Pioneer 11 registered 20 penetrations of its gas-cell instrument. Of these 20, only 7 hits actually occurred in the asteroid belt. Most of the particles recorded by the asteroid-meteoroid telescope aboard Pioneers 10 and 11 ranged in size between 0.1 and 1 millimeter (0.004 and 0.04 inch) in diameter and in mass between 1 millionth and 1 thousandth gram. Although Pioneer 10 did detect particles as large as 20 cm (8 inches), the asteroid belt no longer poses a grave threat to space travel.

The rate of erosion of spacecraft shells by meteoroid dust and small solid grains does not seem to pose much of a problem for space flight. The erosion rate has been estimated, by studying meteorites that have landed on the earth, at an upper limit of 2 to 3 micrometers (8 to 12 hundred-millionths inch) per year or less. At this rate, even telescope mirrors exposed for several years in space should escape serious damage. But larger grains and bodies in space are another story, and ways must be found to protect spacecraft against their impact.

What is the best way to shield a spacecraft from solid particles? A very thick wall, which would really protect, adds too much weight. Meteoroid bumpers have been proposed, employing the device of making the wall of the spacecraft or an outer wall beyond it double, so that the outside skin would absorb most of the heat and blast of the impact of a particle, without holing the inner shell. Another device would be to locate the larger approaching bodies or streams by radar and to avoid those approaching too close by propulsion into a different course. This would not be feasible until spacecraft design and propulsive power had advanced beyond their current state. Still, it is heartening that space probe and meteoritic studies to date suggest that encountering solid particles much larger than fine dust in space will be a rare event.

Space Radiations

Out beyond the earth's effectively shielding atmosphere, radiations are another serious threat to manned space flight. The discovery of the Van Allen belts, extending up to 64,000 km (40,000 mi) above the earth's surface in the magnetosphere, for a time fostered the belief that they might prevent or greatly hinder manned exploration of space, since their radiation levels were intense, with unknown upper limits. Some people even theorized that the Van Allen radiation might be a manifestation of the sun's corona, which would become more and more intense nearer the sun. It has since been discovered that the Van Allen belts have an outer limit within the earth's magnetosphere, since this particle radiation is trapped in the earth's magnetic field.

Earth satellites and spacecraft over 480 to 800 km (300 to 500 mi) above the earth's surface are exposed to much more intense radiation than were the astronauts in orbits 160 to 320 km (100 to 200 mi) high. The major types of dangerous radiation include primary cosmic rays, protons and electrons in the Van Allen belts, and the low- and high-energy protons and electrons from solar flares. Doses might run anywhere from a fraction of a rad a day up to thousands of rads an hour. (A rad in living tissue is about equivalent to a dose of 1 roentgen.) For comparison, in the United States a maximum permissible dose rate of 0.3 roentgen per 3 months has been set for radiation workers, or up to 12 roentgens a year. For industrial safety it is generally assumed that a person can take without serious effects a single exposure of about 25 rads of hard (short wavelength) x-rays or gamma rays, or several exposures adding up to 15 rads a year. The normal radiation level from stray radiations from the earth and the atmosphere, which we all receive, is about 0.001 rad a day, or 0.38 rad a year.

The rem, another and more practical standard unit from the viewpoint of space flight, takes into account the type of radiation particle, its energy, the dose rate, and the size of the absorbing target, such as a person, in defining the "roentgen equivalent for mammal or man." This is the dose in rads multiplied by a factor of relative biological effectiveness (RBE), which depends on the variables named above. The RBE may be about 2 for the Van Allen belts, and about 10 for solar-flare radiation, based on the nature of the complex radiations in them. For comparison, the RBE is 1 for x- and gamma radiation, 2 to 5 for slow or thermal neutrons, 10 for fast neutrons, 8 to 10 for protons (hydrogen nuclei), and 15 to 20 for alpha particles (larger helium nuclei).

What are the effects of different levels of doses of radiation on man? A dose of about 20 rads is likely to cause nausea; 100 rads of hard x- or gamma rays may well cause vomiting, which might suffocate an astronaut in a weightless condition. Even though medication can be carried to control nausea and vomiting, doses of 150 rads of radiation would probably be about the limit of exposure, because of the increasing probability of serious disease or death beyond this limit.

The primary cosmic rays, despite their tremendous energies, are not concentrated enough in space to cause very serious effects. The Apollo astronauts, who flew through the Van Allen radiation belts on their lunar missions, received average doses of 0.16 rad to 1.14 rads, well below the limits set for the Apollo missions. The Skylab 4 crewmen experienced the greatest exposure to radiations for American astronauts, 86 millirads a day. This totals about 7 rads for their 84-day mission—about one half the "permissible" annual dose of 15 rads that presumably can be absorbed without ill effects. While cosmic rays can produce genetic changes, so can many other types of radiation to which we are all exposed daily here on earth.

In or above the Van Allen zones, the radiation field inside the cabin of a spacecraft will consist of a mixture of many types of radiation—primary and secondary cosmic rays, gamma and x-rays, electrons, nucleons, fast and slow neutrons, high-energy protons, alpha particles, and mesons, as well as radio-frequency waves and microwaves. The composition and intensity of the radiation at any point will be the result of the radiation around the spacecraft, its shielding, and the total interior radiation from within the craft itself.

Solar Flares

Stormy weather in space consists of solar-flare outbursts of radiation, of the magnetic fields they sweep along with them, and of fast solar particles that find their way through these fields. The intensity of solar x-radiation, probably produced mainly in the sun's inner corona, runs in cycles related to the cycles of dark blotches on the sun, called sunspots, and a lot of x-radiation is released with solar flares.

Solar flares are the greatest known danger to men in space. They could inflict tremendous doses of radiation. The problem is complicated by the fact that while most major flares occur at times of sunspot maxima, some have taken place well down in the 11-year sunspot cycle. Flares emit particles of various energies in a range of intensities. It has been estimated that about 9 flares of low-energy particles at a low intensity occur per year, and that the probability of encountering such a flare in a 1-week space flight is about 16 out of 100; only 3 flares of low-energy particles and very high intensity may occur in a year, with a probability of about 6 chances out of 100 of meeting such a flare. Flares of high-energy particles of high intensity occur only once in 4 years, so the chance of meeting such a flare in a 1-week flight would be 3 in 1,000. In a week's flight to or around the moon and back to the earth (about 35 to 70 hours one way), there are, then, about 20 chances out of 100 that a hazardous solar flare might develop and spray its radiation through the spacecraft. The protons largely composing the flares are flung across space with such monumental energy that it would be much simpler at least to avoid the worst ones than to try to shield spacecraft against them.

Solar flares occur in or near sunspot fields on the sun, flare up very abruptly, and then gradually decay and subside, usually in less than an hour, though they may last as long as 10 to 20 hours. They move out from the sun at velocities of about 1,120 km (700 mi) a second or even faster.

The solar flares are at a statistical minimum during the periods of a "quiet" sun, about midway in the 10-to-11-year periods of sunspot maxima. During quiet periods there is little likelihood of intense solar flares. Then their frequency builds up in 3 to 5 years to the next sunspot maxima. Still, the danger of the occurrence of a great flare is not too great for short periods in space. Many Apollo astronauts accomplished trips to the moon and returned to earth without being overexposed to radiations during the 1969 to 1970 high period.

The Skylab missions were flown near the time of solar minimum. Although several flares did occur, the radiation doses received by the crewmen were below the detectability limit of the dosimeters on board. The particles emitted in the flares were of low energy and intensity and the crew were naturally shielded by the earth's magnetic field.

In the long run, it is believed that large solar flares will probably be predictable far enough ahead so that a 2-day trip between the earth and the moon can be made in comparative safety, particularly after a maximum sunspot period. Once on the moon, adequate protection can be obtained by tunneling under its surface. But what of flares that may appear suddenly around the limb of the rotating sun? And what of flights to the inner planets, which will take at least 3 to 6 months? Some kind of shielding against the solar-flare radiation likely to be met on such a trip is a must.

Shielding

Passive shielding, simply a protective body that will absorb the radiation, and active shielding, setting up strong magnetic fields about a spacecraft, are both under study. Oddly enough, the lighter elements provide more adequate passive shielding per unit of mass than do the heavier elements. Carbon, nitrogen, and oxygen are quite effective; hydrogen would be best. Any of these might be incorporated into some metallic or plastic material to produce a passive shield.

The great weight is one objection, but not the only one, to passive shielding. It would cut down the primary radiation, but would produce secondary radiation of such particles as protons, gamma rays, and neutrons as they strike the shielding material itself, and these would add to the dosage received within the spacecraft. The shield weights required for moderate solar flares have been put at several tons at least, and this on a spacecraft on which every ounce has to be justified. For extreme solar flares, tens or hundreds of tons would be needed for the primary radiation alone, forgetting about the secondary radiation that would be produced. Passive shielding thus involves many serious problems, and much research will have to be done to devise its most effective form.

Small heavy inner capsules into which astronauts could crawl when solar flares were reported might reduce the requirements for outer shielding for the spacecraft as a whole, as well as the secondary radiation it would produce. It is also possible that selective shielding of the spleen, a vital, blood-forming organ greatly affected by radiation, might enable astronauts to live through heavy flares. Experimental animal studies of drugs that might reduce the effects of heavy radiation are under way, but as yet no effective compound has been found without dangerous side effects. So far it is a case of the cure being as bad as the disease.

In considering the use of active shielding, which requires a magnetic field about a spacecraft strong enough to deflect most, if not all, of the incoming radiation, the effects of intense magnetic fields on human beings must be taken into account.

Reports of scientists who are often in strong magnetic fields in their laboratory work indicate in a preliminary way that man can tolerate fields up to 20,000 gauss without sensations for at least short periods of time, and that no cumulative effects are apparent from exposures of fields up to 5,000 gauss for total periods of 3 days a year. Taste sensations have been experienced in strong magnetic fields by some people with metallic fillings in their teeth. This kind of evidence, however, does not cover situations in which people might live in strong magnetic fields for many hours or days at a time. In all probability, active magnetic shielding would be used only when intense radiation threatened.

What would be the effect of magnetic fields lower than normal? Little or nothing is known in this area. The human reaction over long periods of time to living in very weak magnetic fields, or almost none at all (as in interplanetary space or on the surface of the moon), is an important possible hazard and must be investigated. One expert suggests that very weak magnetic fields might change biological rhythms or the perception of space and time. This is a variable in the space environment that will have to be studied closely as men venture into it. However, reports from persons working in conditions of very low magnetic fields, as in "degaussing" coils in ordnance work, do not indicate that there are specific detrimental effects on their health.

230

Man in Space

High-intensity magnetic fields built up by superconducting coils might provide active shielding for spacecraft, without the great weights necessary for passive shields. In entirely warding off the primary radiation, these magnetic fields would also prevent the formation of the secondary radiation produced in the passive shields. Hard, superconducting solenoid coils made of such materials as niobium-tin or niobium-zirconium alloys might be necessary to withstand the effects of the high magnetic fields they produced. Nonsuperconducting magnetic coils would not effect any great saving in weight over the passive shielding and would require great amounts of power and volumes of coolants. The magnetic fields produced would deflect both negatively charged particles like electrons and positively charged particles like protons.

Active protection might also be obtained by electrostatic shielding—that is, a positively charged outer spherical shell to deflect the positively charged particle radiation such as protons. This, however, has the weakness of actually accelerating negative electron radiation toward it, which would produce secondary x-radiation. The addition of a negatively charged sphere within the outer one would overcome this reaction, but it presents knotty design problems.

All these techniques—the passive, the active magnetic, and the electrostatic shielding—are under study. What will turn out to be the most effective space-radiation shielding is unpredictable. But some very strong shielding against solar-flare radiation is certainly in order if men are to venture safely on lengthy space flights. Men have successfully broken the bonds holding us to our home planet, earth, on expeditions circling the earth and traveling to the moon and back. Can astronauts adjust to prolonged weightlessness or the weak gravitation of the moon, an asteroid, or Mars? Can adequate protection from space radiations be fashioned? How will extra-strong or weak magnetic fields affect people? Undoubtedly the answers to these and many other questions will be worked out during the 1980s and following decades. Man's future in the solar system offers many challenging goals to be achieved.

Table 1. Features of the Orbits, Size, and Rotation of the Planets[a]

Characteristics		Mercury	Venus	Earth	Mars	Jupiter	Saturn	Uranus	Neptune	Pluto
Mean distance from sun	(km)	57,910,000	108,200,000	149,597,870	227,940,000	778,320,000	1,427,000,000	2,869,600,000	4,496,600,000	5,900,100,000
	(mi)	35,984,000	67,236,000	92,958,000	141,640,000	483,640,000	886,710,000	1,783,100,000	2,794,100,000	3,666,300,000
	(a.u.)[b]	0.3871	0.7233	1.0000	1.5237	5.2028	9.5388	19.1819	30.0578	39.44
Perihelion distance[c]	(km)	46,001,000	107,470,000	147,095,000	206,650,000	740,610,000	1,347,600,000	2,734,000,000	4,458,000,000	4,425,100,000
	(mi)	28,585,000	66,783,000	91,404,000	128,410,000	460,200,000	837,360,000	1,698,900,000	2,770,100,000	2,750,200,000
Aphelion distance[d]	(km)	69,817,000	108,940,000	152,100,000	249,230,000	816,040,000	1,506,400,000	3,005,100,000	4,535,100,000	7,375,100,000
	(mi)	43,383,000	67,696,000	94,512,000	154,870,000	507,070,000	936,050,000	1,867,300,000	2,818,000,000	4,583,650,000
Orbital eccentricity[e]		0.20563	0.00679	0.01672	0.09338	0.04845	0.05565	0.04724	0.00858	0.250
Mean orbital velocity	(km/sec)	47.89	35.03	29.79	24.13	13.06	9.64	6.81	5.43	4.74
	(mi/sec)	29.8	21.8	18.5	15.0	8.1	6.0	4.2	3.4	2.9
Length of year[f] (sidereal period of revolution in tropical earth years)		0.24085	0.61521	1.00004	1.88089	11.86223	29.4577	84.0139	164.793	247.7
Length of year (earth days)		87.969	224.70	365.26	686.98	4332.59	10,759.22	30,685.4	60,189	90,465
Diameter at equator	(km)	4,850	12,140	12,756	6,790	143,200	120,000	51,800	49,500	2,700[j]
	(mi)	3,013	7,543	7,926	4,219	88,980	74,560	32,190	30,760	1,680[j]
Mean radius	(earth=1)	0.380	0.950	1.000	0.532	11.23	9.41	4.067	3.887	0.21[j]
Oblateness[g]		0.0	0.0	0.0034	0.009	0.060	0.108	0.030	0.026	?
Volume	(earth=1)	0.054	0.88	1.00	0.149	1316	755	67	57	0.01?
Mass	(earth=1)	0.0554	0.815	1.00	0.1075	317.89	95.2	14.6	17.2	0.0026[j]
Density	(earth=1)	0.98	0.94	1.00	0.72	0.24	0.13	0.24	0.30	0.27[j]
Mean density	(water=1)	5.4	5.2	5.52	3.95	1.314	.704	1.21	1.66	1.5[j]
Inclination of equator to orbit[h]		28°	3°	23°27'	23°59'	3°05'	26°44'	97°55'	28°48'	?
Sidereal rotation period[h]	days	59	244							6
	hours		7	23	24	9	10	15.6[i]	15	9
	minutes		12	56	37	50	39		48	17
	seconds			4.1	22.6	30	24			

a. Data from C. W. Allen, *Astrophysical Quantities*, 3d ed. London: Athlone Press of the University of London (1973); R. L. Newburn, Jr., and S. Gulkis, "A Survey of the Outer Planets Jupiter, Saturn, Uranus, Neptune, Pluto, and Their Satellites," *Space Science Reviews*, 3 (1973), 179–271; David W. Hughes, *Nature*, 274 (1978), 309; D. M. Huntin, *Nature*, 276 (1978), 16.

b. 1 a.u.=the mean distance from the earth to the sun. It is equal to 149,597,870 km (92,958,000 mi).

c. Perihelion distance is the minimum distance between the planet and the sun.

d. Aphelion distance is the maximum distance between the planet and the sun.

e. The eccentricity defines the shape of the orbit. A circle has an eccentricity of 0.

f. The sidereal period of revolution is the period calculated from a position of alignment of the body with the sun and any given star through the revolution and back to the same position.

g. Oblateness, an index of the degree of flattening of the planetary disk, is the equatorial diameter minus the polar diameter of the planet, divided by the equatorial diameter.

h. The sidereal period of rotation is the period calculated from a position of alignment of the body with the sun and any given star through a rotation and back to the same position again. Venus's direction of rotation is from east to west, retrograde to that of the other planets in a period greater than that of its revolution.

i. Questions still remain about the rotation period of Uranus. Estimates range from just under 11 hours to 24 hours. The value quoted here is from R. A. Brown and R. M. Goody, "The Rotation of Uranus," *The Astrophysical Journal*, 217 (1977), 680–87.

j. This value is still uncertain and is based on the motion of Pluto's satellite about the parent body.

Table 2. Satellites of the Solar System [a]

Planet (Primary)	Satellite	Year of Discovery	Discoverer	Approximate Mean Distance from Primary's Center km	mi	Approximate Diameter km	mi	Sidereal Period[b] of Revolution (days	hrs.	min.)
Mercury	none									
Venus	none									
Earth	Moon			385,000	239,000	3476	2160	27	7	43
Mars	Phobos	1877	A. Hall	9,400	5,840	27x21x19[c]	17x13x12[c]	0	7	39
	Deimos	1877	A. Hall	23,500	14,600	15x12x11[c]	9x7.5x7[c]	1	6	18
Jupiter	Io	1610	Galileo	421,600	261,970	3,640	2,262	1	18	28
	Europa	1610	Galileo	670,900	416,900	3,130	1,945	3	13	14
	Ganymede	1610	Galileo	1,070,000	664,900	5,280	3,280	7	3	43
	Callisto	1610	Galileo	1,880,000	1,168,000	4,840	3,007	16	16	32
	Amalthea	1892	E. E. Barnard	181,300	112,700	265x140[d]	165x87[d]	0	11	57
	Himalia[e]	1904	C. D. Perrine	11,476,000	7,130,800	120	75	251		
	Elara[f]	1905	C. D. Perrine	11,737,000	7,293,000	40	25	260		
	Pasiphae[g]	1908	P. J. Melotte	23,500,000	14,600,000	12	7	739	(retrograde)	
	Sinope[h]	1914	S. B. Nicholson	23,700,000	14,700,000	14	9	758	(retrograde)	
	Lysithea[i]	1938	S. B. Nicholson	11,900,000	7,394,000	14	9	264		
	Carme[j]	1938	S. B. Nicholson	22,600,000	14,000,000	14	9	692	(retrograde)	
	Ananke	1951	S. B. Nicholson	21,200,000	13,200,000	12	7	631	(retrograde)	
	Leda	1974	C. Kowal	11,145,000	6,925,000	8	5	240		
	1979J1	1979	G. E. Danielson D. Jewitt	129,400	80,500	30 to 40	18 to 25	0	7	8
	1979J2	1980	S. Synnott	322,600	200,450	70 to 80	44 to 50	0	16	11.4
	1979J3	1980	S. Synnott	127,950	79,970	40	25	0	7	4.5
Saturn	Mimas	1789	F. W. Herschel	185,000	115,000	390	242	0	22	37
	Enceladus	1789	F. W. Herschel	238,000	148,000	500	310	1	8	53
	Tethys	1684	G. D. Cassini	295,000	183,000	1,050	652	1	21	18
	Dione	1684	G. D. Cassini	377,400	234,000	1,120	696	2	17	41
	Rhea	1672	G. D. Cassini	527,000	327,000	1,530	950	4	12	25
	Titan	1655	C. Huyghens	1,222,000	759,300	5,720	3,550	15	22	41
	Hyperion	1848	G. P. & W. C. Bond	1,481,000	920,000	310	193	21	6	38
	Iapetus	1671	G. D. Cassini	3,560,000	2,185,000	1,440	895	79	7	56
	Phoebe	1898	W. H. Pickering	12,950,000	8,046,700	140	87	550	11	(retrograde)
	1980S1[k]	1966 and 1980	A. Dollfus and B. Smith, et al.	151,450	94,100	140	87	Outside G ring		
	1980S3[k]	1966 and 1980	A. Dollfus and D. Cruikshank	151,400	94,000	200	124	Outside G ring		
	1980S6	1980	P. Lacques, J. Lecacheux	377,400	234,000	80	50	In Dione's orbit		
	1980S13	1980	B Smith, et al.	289,600	179,000	?				
	1980S26	1980	Voyager	141,700	88,000	250	155	Outside F ring		
	1980S27	1980	Voyager	139,400	86,000	200	124	Inside F ring		
	1980S28	1980	Voyager	138,200	85,000	100	62	Outside A ring		
Uranus	Ariel	1851	W. Lassell	190,900	118,620	1,400	870	2	12	29
	Umbriel	1851	W. Lassell	266,000	165,000	1,000	620	4	3	28
	Titania	1787	F. W. Herschel	436,000	271,000	1,800	1,100	8	16	56
	Oberon	1787	F. W. Herschel	583,400	362,500	1,600	990	13	11	7
	Miranda	1948	G. P. Kuiper	129,800	80,650	400	250	1	9	55
Neptune	Triton	1846	W. Lassell	355,550	220,930	3,770	2,340	5	21	3 (retrograde)
	Nereid	1949	G. P. Kuiper	5,567,000	3,459,000	600	370	359	21	9
Pluto	Charon	1978	J. W. Christy	20,000?	12,000?	850?	530?	6	9	17

Notes to Table 2 will be found on page 234.

Notes to Table 2

a. Based on data from C. W. Allen, *Astrophysical Quantities*, 3d ed. London: Athlone Press of the University of London (1973); R. L. Newburn, Jr., and S. Gulkis, "A Survey of the Outer Planets Jupiter, Saturn, Uranus, Neptune, Pluto, and Their Satellites," *Space Science Reviews*, 3 (1973), 179–271; J. Ververka, J. Elliot, and J. Goguen, "Measuring the Sizes of Saturn's Satellites," *Sky and Telescope*, 50, 6 (1975), 356; D. W. Hughes, "Phobos and Deimos, the Moons of Mars," *Nature*, 267 (1977), 757; D. W. Hughes, "Pluto's Satellite," *Nature*, 274 (1978), 309; D. Morrison et al., "Introducing the Satellites," *Planetary Satellites*, J. A. Burns, ed. Tucson: University of Arizona Press (1977); G. A. Wilkins and A. T. Sinclair, *Proceedings Royal Society London* A, 336 (1974), 85; *Science News*, 114 (1978), 174; Bradford A. Smith et al., "The Jupiter System Through the Eyes of Voyager 1," *Science*, 204 (1979), 951–72.
b. The sidereal period of revolution is the time required for a complete revolution around the primary, from alignment with a given star to alignment with the same star again as seen from the primary.
c. Phobos and Deimos have ellipsoidal shapes. The three longest dimensions are given.
d. The Voyager 1 spacecraft found Amalthea to be an elongated object as indicated here.
e. This is the name adopted by the International Astronomical Union in 1976. It has also been known as Hestia.
f. This is the name adopted by the International Astronomical Union in 1976. It has also been known as Hera.
g. This is the name adopted by the International Astronomical Union in 1976. It has also been known as Poseidon.
h. This is the name adopted by the International Astronomical Union in 1976. It has also been known as Hades.
i. This is the name adopted by the International Astronomical Union in 1976. It has also been known as Demeter.
j. This is the name adopted by the International Astronomical Union in 1976. It has also been known as Pan.
k. Both 1980S1 and 1980S3 may have been observed in 1966 by A. Dollfus, identified as one satellite, and named Janus.

Table 3. Solar Constants, Albedos, and Magnitudes of the Earth, Moon, and Other Planets[a]

Celestial Body	Solar Radiation Available (Solar Constant)[b]	Proportion of Light Reflected (Mean Residual Albedo)[c]	Brightness in Magnitudes	
			Unit Visual Magnitude[d]	Mean Opposition Magnitude[e]
Inner Planets				
Mercury	6.7	0.056	−0.36	—
Venus	1.9	0.72	−4.34	—
Earth	1.00	0.39	−3.9	—
Mars	0.43	0.16	−1.51	− 2.02
Moon	1.00	0.067	+0.23	−12.73
Outer Planets				
Jupiter	0.04	0.70	−9.25	− 2.55
Saturn	0.01	0.75	−8.80	+ 0.75
Uranus	0.0031	0.90	−7.19	+ 5.52
Neptune	0.001	0.82	−6.87	+ 7.84
Pluto	0.0006	0.145	−1.01	+14.90

a. Data based on that in C. W. Allen, *Astrophysical Quantities*, 3d ed. London: Athlone Press of the University of London (1973); R. L. Newburn, Jr., and S. Gulkis, "A Survey of the Outer Planets Jupiter, Saturn, Uranus, Neptune, Pluto, and Their Satellites," *Space Science Reviews*, 3 (1973), 179–271.
b. The solar constant, the amount of solar radiation present immediately above the atmosphere of a planet in a unit area at right angles to the surface, is given in relation to that of the earth taken as 1.00; actually, the solar constant of the earth is about 0.13 kilowatt per square foot.
c. The average proportion of the light reflected by the planet in relation to that impinging on it.
d. Magnitude or brightness at identical unit distances from the earth and the sun.
e. Mean magnitude or brightness at opposition for the planets, when the earth is on a straight line between the sun and the planets; not applicable, therefore, to Mercury and Venus, always nearer the sun than the earth, nor to the earth. The apparent visual magnitude of the planets, their visible brightness as viewed from earth, is given in Chapter Three.

Table 4. Features of Some Asteroids or Minor Planets

Name	Number	Year of Discovery	Diameter km	Diameter mi	Mean Distance from Sun[b] million km	Mean Distance from Sun[b] million mi	Period (Earth Years)	Inclination of Orbit to Ecliptic in Degrees	Eccentricity of Orbit	Features
Ceres[a]	1	1801	1025	640	413.8	257.1	4.602	10.6	0.079	Largest known asteroid and first discovered.
Pallas[a]	2	1802	608	380	414.1	257.3	4.610	34.8	.235	Great inclination to ecliptic.
Juno[a]	3	1804	247	150	399.1	248.0	4.364	13.0	.256	Third asteroid discovered.
Vesta[a]	4	1807	538	340	353.4	219.6	3.628	7.1	.088	Only asteroid rarely visible to unaided eye.
Astraea[a]	5	1845			385.5	239.6	4.136	5.3	.190	First asteroid discovered by an amateur.
Hebe	6	1847	110	68	362.9	225.5	3.778	14.8	.203	
Iris	7	1847	100	62	356.9	221.8	3.680	5.5	.230	
Flora	8	1847			329.3	204.6	3.267	5.9	.156	
Metis	9	1848			357.1	221.9	3.687	5.6	.123	
Hygiea	10	1849	160	100	471.4	292.9	5.591	3.8	.099	
Brucia	323	1891			356.0	221.2	3.68	24.2	.301	First asteroid discovered by photography, by Max Wolf.
Eros	433	1898	14	9	218.1	135.5	1.758	10.8	.223	Used in determining a.u.
Achilles	588	1904			779.4	484.3	11.98	10.3	.148	First of Jupiter's Trojan asteroids discovered.
1973 NA		1973	3	2	357.54	222.1		68.0		Largest inclination to ecliptic.
Chiron (1977 UB)		1977	160–540	100–400	2,048.7	1,273.1	50.68	6.9	.379	Greatest known aphelion distance: 18.9 a.u.
Ra-Shalom	2100	1978	3	2	124.9	77.6	0.758	16		Smallest mean distance from sun.

a. Called the "big four" of the asteroids; diameter measured directly.
b. Mean distance only approximate and varying, because the orbits of asteroids are frequently perturbed by the major planets.

Table 5. Most Prominent Nighttime Meteor Showers[a]

Name of shower	Period of Detectable Meteors	Date of Peak Activity	Visual Hourly Rates[b]	Duration of Peak (days)	Radiant Coordinates (deg.)[c]	
					right ascension	declination
Quadrantids[d]	Jan. 1–4	Jan. 3	35	0.5	231	+50
Corona Australids	March 14–18	March 16	(5)[e]	(5)[e]	245	−48
Virginids	March 5–April 2	March 20	(less than 5)	(20)	190	0
Lyrids	April 19–24	April 21	5	2	272	+32
Eta Aquarids[d]	April 21–May 12	May 4	12	10	336	0
Ophiuchids	June 17–26	June 20	(20)	(10)	260	−20
Capricornids	July 10–Aug. 5	July 25	(20)	(20)	315	−15
Southern Delta Aquarids[d]	July 21–Aug. 15	July 30	20	15	339	−17
Northern Delta Aquarids[d]	July 15–Aug. 18	July 29	10	20	339	0
Pisces Australids	July 15–Aug. 20	July 30	(20)	(20)	340	−30
Alpha Capricornids	July 15–Aug. 20	Aug. 1	5	(25)	309	−10
Southern Iota Aquarids	July 15–Aug. 25	Aug. 5	(10)	(25)	338	−15
Northern Iota Aquarids	July 15–Aug. 25	Aug. 5	(10)	(25)	331	− 6
Perseids[d]	July 25–Aug. 17	Aug. 11	50	5	46	+58
Kappa Cygnids	Aug. 18–22	Aug. 20	(5)	(3)	290	+55
Orionids	Oct. 18–26	Oct. 20	20	5	95	+15
Southern Taurids	Sept. 15–Dec. 15	Nov. 1	(5)	(45)	52	+14
Northern Taurids	Oct. 15–Dec. 1	Nov. 1	(less than 5)	(30)	54	+21
Leonids	Nov. 14–20	Nov. 16	(5)	4	152	+22
Phoenicids	(Dec. 5)[e]	Dec. 5	(50)	(0.5)	15	−55
Geminids[d]	Dec. 7–15	Dec. 13	50	6	113	+32
Ursids	Dec. 17–24	Dec. 22	15	2	217	+80

a. Adapted from D. W. R. McKinley, *Meteor Science and Engineering* (New York: McGraw-Hill Book Company, 1961).
b. Number of meteors observable visually by a single observer at maximum shower activity.
c. +, North of the celestial equator, south of it, −.
d. Among the stronger and more consistent meteor showers.
e. Figures in parentheses less reliable than other figures for duration of the peak activity, visual hourly rates, and period of detectable meteors.

Table 6. Major Terrestrial Meteoritic Craters by Approximate Date of Discovery[a]

Name and/or Location	Number of Craters	Diameter[b] (m)	Diameter[b] (ft)	Date of Discovery	Features
Barringer Meteor Crater, between Winslow and Flagstaff, Arizona	1	1,200	3,937	1891	Created possibly 25,000 years ago by a metallic (iron or stony-iron) meteorite, estimated the equivalent of a 5-megaton nuclear explosion; many meteoritic fragments around main crater; natural coesite first found here.
Odessa, Ector County, Texas	2	160	530	1921	Metallic meteoritic crater; with many small fragments, thousands of years old, since fossil bones of extinct animals found in excavation of crater.
Dalgaranga, Western Australia	1	70	230	1923	Metallic meteoritic crater.
Oesel Island, Baltic Sea, Kaalijarv, Estonia, U.S.S.R.	7	100	327	1927	Small metallic meteoritic fragments found; largest crater filled with a lake.
Tunguska, Central Siberia, U.S.S.R.	10+	50	164	1927 (fell 1908)	Possibly produced by a comet head or cometary materials; no meteorites recovered; trees leveled by fall.
Henbury, Central Australia	13	200x110	660x360	1931	Metallic meteoritic crater; largest may be 2 overlapping smaller craters; irons excavated from smaller craters.
Wabar, Al Hadija, Saudi Arabia	2	100	328	1932	Possibly metallic meteorite; coesite and large amounts of silica glass (impactite) found.
Brenham, Haviland, Kansas	1	17	56	1933	Originally thought a buffalo wallow, then identified as a meteoritic crater; stony-iron meteorites scattered over a wide area.
Campo del Cielo, Gran Chaco, Argentina	many	56	184		Several metallic meteorites of over a ton in weight found.
Box Hole, Central Australia	1	175	575	1937	Metallic meteorite crater; number of iron meteorites found; probably very old.
Sikhote-Alin, north of Vladivostok, Siberia, U.S.S.R.	106	28	92	1947	Metallic meteorite of an estimated 75 tons fragmented in passage, creating many craters; iron meteorites found.
Wolf Creek, northwestern Australia	1	840	2,756	1947	Stony-iron meteorites found.
New Quebec (formerly Chubb) Crater, Ungava Peninsula 208 km (130 mi) south of Hudson Strait, Quebec	1	3.3 km	2 mi	1949	Crater contains lake, observed in aerial photography; may be fossil crater 2 billion years old; no meteorites found.
Brent Meteor Crater, Algonquin Provincial Park, Ontario	1	3.2 km	2 mi	1961 (verified)	A fossil meteor crater, perhaps 600 to 900 million years old; crater walls 915 meters (3,000 ft) high.
Clearwater Lake Craters, 80 km (50 mi) east of Richmond Gulf, east coast of Hudson Bay, Canada	1 / 1	32 km / 22.4 km	20 mi / 14 mi	1963 (verified)	May be fossil craters 2 billion years old; no meteorites found; 2 craters form Clearwater Lake; shattered rocks found.
Holleford Crater, 26 km (16 mi) north of Kingston, Ontario	1	2.34 km	1.46 mi	1963 (verified)	Fossil crater produced perhaps 500 to 600 million years ago; coesite identified, as well as shocked quartz.
Manicouagan, 200 km (125 mi) northwest of Port Cartier on St. Lawrence River, Canada	1	65 km	41 mi	1972 (verified)	Fossil crater produced 200 million years ago; filled with water of Lake Manicouagan.

a. Excludes some craterlike structures found that may be impact craters of great age, or "fossil craters," and sites not yet fully authenticated as meteoritic, even though shatter cones (Sierra Madera, Texas; Vredefort Ring, Transvaal, South Africa) or coesite (Ries Kessel Basin, southern Germany; Ashanti, Lake Bosumtwi, Ghana, Africa) may have been found.

b. Diameter of largest crater given when more than 1 crater is involved.

Table 7. Astronomy Satellites

Spacecraft	Origin	Launched	Remarks
Pioneer 5	U.S.A.	Mar. 11, 1960	In solar orbit; transmitted until June 26, 1960 providing information of solar system to 22.5 million miles from earth.
Solrad 1	U.S.A.	June 22, 1960	Returned solar data until April 1961.
Solrad 3	U.S.A.	June 29, 1961	Returned solar x-ray data until late 1961.
OSO 1	U.S.A.	Mar. 7, 1962	OSO= Orbiting Solar Observatory. In earth orbit; transmitted data on 75 solar flares until Aug. 6, 1963.
Solrad 6	U.S.A.	June 15, 1963	Decayed Aug. 1, 1963; solar radiation experiment.
Solrad 7A	U.S.A.	Jan 11, 1964	Transmitted until August 1966; solar radiation satellite.
OSO 2	U.S.A.	Feb. 3, 1965	Returned solar x-ray, gamma-ray, ultraviolet data until November 1965.
Solrad 7B	U.S.A.	Mar. 9, 1965	Solar radiation satellite.
Explorer 30	U.S.A.	Nov. 18, 1965	Solar radiation satellite; inactive.
Pioneer 6	U.S.A.	Dec. 16, 1965	Solar orbit; returning good data.
Pioneer 7	U.S.A.	Aug. 17, 1966	Solar orbit; 6 solar interplanetary experiments active.
OSO 3	U.S.A.	Mar. 8, 1967	9 experiments; in earth orbit.
OSO 4	U.S.A.	Oct. 18, 1967	Returned first picture of sun in extreme ultraviolet.
Pioneer 8	U.S.A.	Dec. 13, 1967	In solar orbit; 8 experiments, studying solar radiation.
Explorer 38	U.S.A.	July 4, 1968	Radio Astronomy Explorer 1 monitoring radio emissions from cosmic, solar, and earth sources.
Pioneer 9	U.S.A.	Nov. 8, 1968	In solar orbit; 8 experiments, providing data on solar radiation.
OAO 2	U.S.A.	Dec. 7, 1968	OAO= Orbiting Astronomical Observatory; 11 telescopes study stars in ultraviolet, infrared, gamma-ray, and x-ray radiation.
OSO 5	U.S.A.	Jan. 22, 1969	Data on solar radiation.
OSO 6	U.S.A.	Aug. 9, 1969	Advanced solar physics research platform; main new ability is offset raster scan and scan near edge of sun's disk.
Uuru (Explorer 42)	NASA/Italy	Dec. 12, 1970	NASA's Small Astronomy Satellite (SAS-1). Surveyed sky for x-ray sources.
Solrad 10 (Explorer 44)	U.S.A.	July 8, 1971	Continuation of solar radiation series. Monitor x-ray and ultraviolet radiation.
OSO 7	U.S.A.	Sept. 29, 1971	Continued investigations of solar x-rays, gamma rays; orbit decayed July 9, 1974.
Copernicus (OAO 3)	U.S.A.	Aug. 21, 1972	First large telescope (81-cm or 32-inch diameter mirror) to study ultraviolet radiation from stars and other celestial objects.
Explorer 48 (SAS-B)	U.S.A.	Nov. 15, 1972	Small Astronomy Satellite to study gamma-ray radiation.
Skylab 1	U.S.A.	May 14, 1973	Although not strictly an astronomy satellite, the Skylab crews took thousands of photographs of the sun and Comet Kohoutek.
Skylab 2	U.S.A.	May 25, 1973	Charles Conrad, Jr., Dr. Joseph P. Kerwin, and Paul J. Weitz in orbit for 28 days, 49 minutes; took 30,242 pictures with the Apollo Telescope Mount (ATM), a solar observatory.
Explorer 49	U.S.A.	June 10, 1973	Radio Astronomy Explorer B. In lunar orbit, this satellite explored low-frequency radiation from galactic and extragalactic sources as well as from the sun, earth, and Jupiter.
Skylab 3	U.S.A.	July 28, 1973	Alan L. Bean, Dr. Owen K. Garriott, and Jack R. Lousma remained in orbit 59 days, 11 hours, 9 minutes. Took 77,600 pictures with ATM.
Skylab 4	U.S.A.	Nov. 16, 1973	75,000 pictures were taken with the ATM by Gerald P. Carr, Dr. Edward G. Gibson, and William R. Poque. They remained in orbit 84 days, 1 hour, and 16 minutes. Observed Comet Kohoutek.
ANS	Netherlands	Aug. 30, 1974	Astronomical Netherlands Satellite. Measure x-ray and ultraviolet radiation of celestial sources.
Ariel 5	United Kingdom	Oct. 15, 1974	X-ray observatory.
Helios 1	Germany	Dec. 10, 1974	Solar probe; passed within 47 million km (29 million mi) of sun.
Explorer 53 (SAS-C)	U.S.A.	May 7, 1975	X-ray satellite.
OSO-8	U.S.A.	June 21, 1975	Continuation of x-ray and ultraviolet observations of sun.
COS-B	European Space Agency	Aug. 9, 1975	Gamma-ray satellite.
D2-B	France	Sept. 27, 1975	Ultraviolet and gamma-ray satellite.
Helios 2	Germany	Jan. 15, 1976	Passed within 43 million km (27 million mi) of sun.
HEAO 1	U.S.A.	Aug. 12, 1977	High Energy Astronomy Observatory. X-ray survey of the sky.
IUE	NASA/ ESA/U.K.	Jan. 26, 1978	International Ultraviolet Explorer. Carries a 45-cm (18-inch) telescope to study the ultraviolet sky.
Einstein (HEAO 2)	U.S.A.	Nov. 13, 1978	Has 58-cm (23-inch) telescope for studying galactic and extragalactic x-ray sources.

Table 8. Highlights of Modern Lunar Exploration

Spacecraft	Origin	Launch Date	Remarks
Luna 1	U.S.S.R.	Jan. 2, 1959	First successful flyby of moon; now orbiting sun.
Luna 2	U.S.S.R.	Sept. 12, 1959	First spacecraft to impact on moon.
Luna 3	U.S.S.R.	Oct. 4, 1959	First spacecraft to photograph moon's far side.
Ranger 7	U.S.A.	July 28, 1964	Impacted on moon; first Ranger success; returned 4,308 photographs.
Ranger 8	U.S.A.	Feb. 17, 1965	Impacted on moon; returned 7,137 photographs.
Ranger 9	U.S.A.	Mar. 21, 1965	Impacted on moon; 5,814 photographs; landed in Alphonsus.
Luna 5	U.S.S.R.	May 9, 1965	Impacted; attempted first soft landing.
Zond 3	U.S.S.R.	July 18, 1965	Retransmitted photographs during flyby, in solar orbit.
Luna 9	U.S.S.R.	Jan. 31, 1966	Soft landed; returned photographs for 3 days.
Luna 10	U.S.S.R.	Mar. 31, 1966	Lunar orbiter; data until May 30, 1966.
Surveyor 1	U.S.A.	May 30, 1966	Soft landed; 11,150 photographs up to July 13, 1966.
Lunar Orbiter 1	U.S.A.	Aug. 10, 1966	Photographed moon until August 29, 1966; impacted on moon on October 29, 1966.
Luna 11	U.S.S.R.	Aug. 24, 1966	Lunar orbiter; returned data until October 1, 1966.
Luna 12	U.S.S.R.	Oct. 22, 1966	Photographed moon; lunar orbit.
Lunar Orbiter 2	U.S.A.	Nov. 6, 1966	Returned 205 photographs; impacted moon on October 11, 1967.
Luna 13	U.S.S.R.	Dec. 21, 1966	Landed; returned photographs, soil density data.
Lunar Orbiter 3	U.S.A.	Feb. 4, 1967	Returned 182 lunar photographs; impacted on moon on October 9, 1967.
Surveyor 3	U.S.A.	April 17, 1967	Landed on moon; soil samples, photographs until May 3, 1967.
Lunar Orbiter 4	U.S.A.	May 4, 1967	163 photographs; impacted on moon on October 6, 1967.
Lunar Orbiter 5	U.S.A.	Aug. 1, 1967	Impacted on moon on January 31, 1968.
Surveyor 5	U.S.A.	Sept. 8, 1967	Landed on moon; returned 19,000 photographs; soil analysis data.
Surveyor 6	U.S.A.	Nov. 7, 1967	Landed on moon; performed first rocket takeoff from moon.
Surveyor 7	U.S.A.	Jan. 7, 1968	Landed January 10, 1968; last of program; 5 successes in 7 tries.
Luna 14	U.S.S.R.	April 7, 1968	In lunar orbit; studied earth-moon mass relationship, moon's gravitational field.
Zond 5	U.S.S.R.	Sept. 15, 1968	Re-entered on September 21, 1968; first lunar fly around; recovered from Indian Ocean.
Zond 6	U.S.S.R.	Nov. 10, 1968	Re-entered on November 17, 1968. Second unmanned circumlunar flight; landed in U.S.S.R. after double-dip glide re-entry, aerodynamic lift for deceleration.
Apollo 8	U.S.A.	Dec. 21, 1968	Re-entered December 27, 1968; first manned circumlunar flight; astronauts Frank Borman, James A. Lovell, William A. Anders recovered in mid-Pacific after 10 lunar orbits, 147 hours.
Apollo 10	U.S.A.	May 18, 1969	Re-entered May 26, 1969; second manned circumlunar flight; LEM piloted to 9.26 mi of moon on May 22, 1969; astronauts Thomas P. Stafford, John W. Young, and Eugene A. Cernan splashed down after 192.1 hours; first color television from space.
Luna 15	U.S.S.R.	July 13, 1969	Impacted on moon on July 21, 1969; flight time 204 hours, 56 minutes; orbited moon 52 times; orbit altered 2 times, unlike Luna 9 and 13.
Apollo 11	U.S.A.	July 16, 1969	Re-entered July 24, 1969. First manned lunar landing, July 20, 1969; EVA (extra-vehicular activity) performed by Neil A. Armstrong and Edwin E. Aldrin for over 2.5 hours. LEM *Eagle* landed in Sea of Tranquillity, remained 21.6 hours. CM *Columbia* pilot Michael Collins in lunar orbit 59.5 hours; splashdown after 195.31 hours.
Zond 7	U.S.S.R.	Aug. 8, 1969	Re-entered August 14, 1969; third unmanned circumlunar flight; recovered in U.S.S.R.
Apollo 12	U.S.A.	Nov. 14, 1969	Re-entered November 24, 1969. Second manned lunar landing, November 19, 1969; 2 EVAs by Charles Conrad, Jr., Alan L. Bean, November 19 and 20; LEM *Intrepid* landed in Ocean of Storms, stayed 31.6 hours; CM *Yankee Clipper* pilot Richard F. Gordon, Jr., in moon orbit for 89 hours; spashdown after 244.6 hours.
Apollo 13	U.S.A.	April 11, 1970	Recovered April 17, 1970. Failure of spacecraft oxygen tank No. 2 approximately 56 hours into mission caused abort. Astronauts James A. Lovell, John L. Sweigert, and Fred W. Haise took crippled spacecraft around the moon; splashed down in Pacific after 142 hours, 53 minutes in space.
Luna 16	U.S.S.R.	Sept. 12, 1970	Unmanned lunar lander touched down on Sea of Fertility, September 20, 1970; returned to earth on September 24, 1970, with lunar soil samples.
Luna 17	U.S.S.R.	Nov. 10, 1970	Landed on moon, November 17, 1970; unmanned lunar rover (Lunokhod 1).

(continued)

Apollo 14	U.S.A.	Jan. 31, 1971	Recovered February 9, 1971. Landed on moon February 5, 1971, in hilly upland near Fra Mauro crater. Two EVAs made by astronauts Alan B. Shepard, Jr., and Edgar D. Mitchell lasting total of 9.4 hours. CM pilot Stuart A. Roosa conducted lunar orbit experiments.
Apollo 15	U.S.A.	July 26, 1971	First extended lunar mission. Astronauts David R. Scott and James B. Irwin spent 66 hours, 55 minutes on lunar surface. During 3 EVAs totaling 18.6 hours, they traveled 28.2 km (17.5 mi) in the first Lunar Roving Vehicle (LRV). CM pilot Alfred M. Worden conducted lunar orbiting experiments. Crew recovered on August 7, 1971.
Luna 18	U.S.S.R.	Sept. 2, 1971	Orbited moon for 4.5 days before impacting on moon on September 11, 1971.
Luna 19	U.S.S.R.	Sept. 28, 1971	In lunar orbit; lunar photography mission.
Luna 20	U.S.S.R.	Feb. 14, 1972	Returned lunar soil samples.
Apollo 16	U.S.A.	April 16, 1972	Astronauts John W. Young and Charles M. Duke landed on moon April 21 for a 71-hour stay near Descartes. During 3 EVAs lasting 20.2 hours the astronauts drove the LRV 26.7 km (16.6 mi). CM pilot Ken Mattingly conducted lunar orbiter experiments. Astronauts returned to earth April 27, 1972.
Apollo 17	U.S.A.	Dec. 7, 1972	Last of the Apollo missions to the moon. Astronauts Eugene A. Cernan and Harrison H. Schmitt landed on the lunar surface on December 11. CM pilot Ronald E. Evans performed lunar orbiter experiments. Apollo 17 set many records: longest stay on lunar surface, 74 hours, 59 minutes, 38 seconds; longest single EVA in time and distance, 7 hours, 37 minutes, 21 seconds and 19 km (11.8 mi); longest total lunar surface EVA time, 22 hours, 5 minutes, 6 seconds; longest total distance traversed with Rover, 33.8 km (21 mi); longest Apollo mission, 301 hours, 51 minutes; longest time in lunar orbit, 147 hours, 48 minutes; most samples returned to earth, 113.4 kilograms (250 pounds). Crew returned to earth on December 19.
Luna 21	U.S.S.R.	Jan. 8, 1973	Landed on moon on January 16 in crater Lemogneir at eastern edge of Mare Serenitatis. Region explored by unmanned Lunokhod 2.

Table 9. Planetary Probes

Satellite	Origin	Launch Date	Mission
Mariner 2	U.S.A.	Aug. 26, 1962	Venus flyby, now in solar orbit; transmitted data out to 86.7 million km (53.9 million mi).
Mariner 4	U.S.A.	Nov. 28, 1964	Passed 9,844 km (6,118 mi) from Mars on July 14–15, 1965. Returned 22 pictures of Mars showing heavily cratered surface.
Venera 3	U.S.S.R.	Nov. 16, 1965	Impacted on Venus March 1, 1966; failed to return data.
Venera 4	U.S.S.R.	June 12, 1967	Presumed to have impacted on Venus October 18, 1967. Transmission ended during 94-minute descent.
Mariner 5	U.S.A.	June 14, 1967	In solar orbit; 3,990-km (2,480-mi) flyby of Venus on October 19, 1967.
Venera 5	U.S.S.R.	Jan. 5, 1969	Descent capsule entered Venusian atmosphere May 5, 1969; penetrated deeper than Venera 4; aerodynamic and parachute descent; presumed to have impacted.
Venera 6	U.S.S.R.	Jan. 10, 1969	Descent capsule entered Venusian atmosphere May 17, 1969; mission similar to Venera 5, presumed to have impacted.
Mariner 6	U.S.A.	Feb. 24, 1969	In solar orbit; flew over equator of Mars July 31, 1969, at a distance of 3,410 km (2,120 mi); took 75 pictures at 42.3-second intervals.
Mariner 7	U.S.A.	Mar. 27, 1969	In solar orbit; flew over the Southern Hemisphere of Mars on August 5, 1969, at a distance of 3,520 km (2,190 mi); took 126 pictures.
Venera 7	U.S.S.R.	Aug. 17, 1970	Soft-landed on surface of Venus December 15; transmitted data for 23 minutes before intense heat and pressure stopped transmissions.
Mariner 9	U.S.A.	May 30, 1971	Went into Mars orbit November 13, 1971. Returned 7,329 pictures and mapped entire Martian surface.
Pioneer 10	U.S.A.	Mar. 2, 1972	First flyby of Jupiter. Passed within 130,000 km (81,000 mi) of Jupiter's cloud tops December 4, 1973. Pioneer 10 will be the first man-made object to leave the solar system.
Venera 8	U.S.S.R.	Mar. 27, 1972	Landed on Venus July 22. Transmitted data for 50 minutes before the high Venusian temperature destroyed it.
Pioneer 11	U.S.A.	April 5, 1973	On December 2, 1974, Pioneer 11 flew to within 42,760 km (26,575 mi) of Jupiter's cloud tops. Its orbit was altered by Jupiter's gravitational attraction, and it headed 2.4 billion km (1.5 billion mi) across the solar system, where it passed within 21,400 km (13,300 mi) of Saturn's cloud tops on September 1, 1979.
Mars 4	U.S.S.R.	July 21, 1973	Failed to achieve Martian orbit but did return photographs in February 1974.
Mars 5	U.S.S.R.	July 25, 1973	Achieved Mars orbit in February 1974.
Mars 6	U.S.S.R.	Aug. 5, 1973	Landed in March 1974. Transmitted atmospheric data but signals ceased on touchdown.
Mars 7	U.S.S.R.	Aug. 9, 1973	Failed to land.
Mariner 10	U.S.A.	Nov. 3, 1973	Venus flyby February 5, 1974; flew within 750 km (466 mi) of the surface of Mercury March 29, 1974; within 48,000 km (30,000 mi) on September 21, 1974; and within 300 km (186 mi) on March 16, 1975.
Venera 9	U.S.S.R.	June 8, 1975	Operated 53 minutes from surface of Venus. Returned first photograph of Venusian surface.
Venera 10	U.S.S.R.	June 14, 1975	Operated 65 minutes from surface of Venus. Returned photograph of surface.
Viking 1	U.S.A.	Aug. 20, 1975	Reached Mars orbit June 1976; first American soft landing on Mars July 20. Many experiments to search for signs of Martian life.
Viking 2	U.S.A.	Sept. 9, 1975	Landed on Martian surface September 3, 1976. Continued experiments of Viking 1 Orbiter and Lander.
Voyager 2	U.S.A.	Aug. 20, 1977	Close approach of Jupiter July 1, 1979. Approach to Saturn August 1981, then on to Uranus 1986 and Neptune 1989.
Voyager 1	U.S.A.	Sept. 5, 1977	Close encounter with Jupiter March 5, 1979. Returned 15,000 photographs. After Saturn encounter November 1980, leaving solar system.
Pioneer Venus 1	U.S.A.	May 20, 1978	Went into Venus orbit December 4, 1978.
Pioneer Venus 2	U.S.A.	Aug. 8, 1978	Arrived at Venus December 9, 1978. Five separate probes sent into Venus's atmosphere.
Venera 11	U.S.S.R.	Sept. 9, 1978	Transmitted for 95 minutes from surface of Venus December 25, 1978.
Venera 12	U.S.S.R.	Sept. 14, 1978	Transmitted data for 110 minutes from surface of Venus before transmission ended December 21, 1978.

Credits

Dinsmore Alter, *Pictoral Guide to the Moon*, and Lick Observatory, Mt. Hamilton, Calif., pp. 126–27.

Dinsmore Alter, and Hale Observatories, p. 146.

American Museum of Natural History, pp. 94, 169.

Ames Research Center, National Aeronautics and Space Administration (NASA), pp. 29 (bottom), 70, 71, 109, 117 (bottom), 211.

E. M. Antoniadi, *La Planète Mercure et la Rotation des Satellites*, p. 150.

Army Map Service, Corps of Engineers, U.S. Army, p. 133.

Virgil E. Barnes, Director, Research on Tektites, U. of Texas, p. 98.

John H. Baumert, and George A. Stokes, Jr., p. 6 (top).

Carlton Beals, and Royal Canadian Air Force, p. 95.

P. W. Blum, and H. J. Fahr, U. of Bonn, p. 76.

John E. Bortle, and *Sky and Telescope*, p. 102.

Donald A. Bradley, Max A. Woodbury, and Glenn W. Brier, *Science*, p. 65.

Franklyn M. Branley, Mark R. Chartrand III, and Helmut K. Wimmer, *Astronomy*, pp. 46 (bottom), 80.

George Carruthers, U.S. Naval Research Laboratory, and Apollo 16 Astronauts, NASA, p. 67.

Cerro Tololo Inter-American Observatory, p. 11 (top left).

J. Christy, and R. Harrington, U.S. Naval Observatory Photograph, p. 19 (top).

J. Christy, R. Walker, and R. Harrington, U.S. Naval Observatory Photograph, p. 17 (left).

R. S. Dietz, and J. C. Holden, *Journal of Geophysical Research*, p. 46 (top).

A. Dollfus, Observatoire de Paris, Meudon, France, pp. 117 (top), 167.

A. Dollfus, President, Commission for Physical Study of the Planets and Satellites, International Astronomical Union, p. 160.

Dominion Astrophysical Observatory, Victoria, B.C., p. 86 (top).

Dominion Observatory, Ottawa, Canada, p. 124.

John A. Eddy, National Center for Atmospheric Research, p. 63.

Flagstaff Station, U.S. Naval Observatory, p. 38 (top).

R. E. Folinsbee, and L. A. Bayrock, *Journal of the Royal Astronomical Society of Canada*, p. 90.

G. L. Freeland, and R. S. Dietz, National Oceanic and Atmospheric Administration, p. 47.

Ann R. Geoffrion, Marjorie Korner, and William M. Sinton, *Lowell Observatory Bulletin*, p. 131.

Goddard Space Flight Center, NASA, pp. 74, 105.

Goddard Space Flight Center, NASA, and National Space Science Data Center, pp. 141, 143, 144.

Bruce A. Goldberg, Jet Propulsion Laboratory, p. 122.

Hale Observatories, pp. 12, 18 (top), 79, 100.

Hale Observatories and C. Kowal, pp. 16 (right), 18 (bottom).

John W. Harvey, Kitt Peak National Observatory, pp. 77, 101 (bottom).

High Altitude Observatory of the National Center for Atmospheric Research, Courtesy of, p. 14 (top right).

International Geophysics Bulletin, p. 106.

Jet Propulsion Laboratory and California Institute of Technology, pp. 3, 4, 24, 30, 36, 37.

Jet Propulsion Laboratory and NASA, title page, pp. 35, 112–14, 116 (top), 137 (top), 152–54, 161 (bottom), 162–66, 168, 179, 180, 193, 203, 210.

Johnson Space Center, NASA, pp. 218, 219, 222, 223, 226.

Peter van de Kamp, Sproul Observatory, Swarthmore College, p. 182.

William M. Kaula, UCLA, p. 41.

Kitt Peak National Observatory, p. 10.

Robert G. Knollenberg, Particle Measuring Systems, Inc., p. 110.

B. J. Levin, O. Schmidt Institute of Physics of the Earth, Moscow, USSR, p. 27.

Lick Observatory, Mt. Hamilton, Calif., pp. 38 (bottom), 130, 158 (bottom).

Percival Lowell, *The Evolution of Worlds*, p. 155.

Lowell Observatory, pp. 31, 34.

Mikhail Ya. Marov, USSR Academy of Sciences, p. 158.

Martin Marietta Aerospace Corporation, p. 2.

Harold Masursky, U.S. Geological Survey, p. 161 (top).

D. S. Mathewson, M. P. Schwarz, and J. D. Murray, Mount Stromlo and Siding Spring Observatory, p. 11 (bottom).

K. Matthews, G. Neugebauer, and P. Nicholson, California Institute of Technology, p. 16 (left).

Peter M. Millman, National Research Council, Ottawa, Canada, p. 91.

Mount Stromlo and Siding Spring Observatory, Australian National U., pp. 8–9.

National Aeronautics and Space Administration (NASA), pp. 26, 29 (top), 43, 136, 137 (bottom), 138, 139, 174, 186, 187 (top), 188, 190, 191, 194, 195, 201, 207, 212, 215, 225.

NASA and Hale Observatories, p. 134.

NASA and the U.S. Geological Survey, Eros Data Center, p. 88.

National Oceanic and Atmospheric Administration, pp. 44, 60, 62.

Norman F. Ness, Laboratory for Space Sciences, NASA, and *Review of Geophysics*, p. 68.

Seth B. Nicholson (adapted from), No. 381, Astronomical Society of the Pacific, p. 87 (top).

D. W. Parkin, R.A.L. Sullivan, and J. N. Andrews, p. 58.

Bertrand M. Peek, *The Planet Jupiter*, p. 116 (bottom).

Elizabeth Roemer, U.S. Naval Observatory, Flagstaff, Ariz., pp. 87 (bottom), 99, 101, 103.

Royal Canadian Air Force, p. 173.

Sacramento Peak Observatory, Association of Universities for Research in Astronomy, Inc., pp. 14 (top left), 78.

Carl Sagan, and Frank Drake (adapted from), The Arecibo Message of 1974 was sent from the Arecibo Observatory in Puerto Rico. The Arecibo Observatory is operated by Cornell University under contract with the National Science Foundation, p. 184 (bottom).

Carl and Linda Sagan, and Frank Drake, p. 184 (top).

R. Stephen Saunders, and Michael C. Malin, pp. 156, 157.

E. C. Slipher, Lowell Observatory, Flagstaff, Ariz., pp. 176, 177.

Douglas E. Smylie (adapted from), "Earthquakes and the Earth's Wobble," *Science*, vol. 161 (1968), p. 8 (top).

Solar Physics Group of American Science and Engineering, Inc., p. 14 (bottom).

Space Data, Thompson Ramo Woolridge Space Technology Laboratories, Inc., pp. 9, 202.

U.S. Navy and Johns Hopkins U., p. 42.

Raymond E. Wiech, Jr., and Robert F. Strauss, *Fundamentals of Rocket Propulsion*, p. 187 (bottom).

H. P. Wilkins, and Patrick Moore, *The Moon*, p. 120.

World Data Center A for Solar-Terrestrial Physics, Environmental Data Information Services, National Oceanic and Atmospheric Administration, p. 13.

Color photos: p. 1, All photos were taken in Souris, Manitoba, Canada, by the Connecticut College Eclipse Expedition, of which John Baumert was a member; p. 2 (top), Lyndon B. Johnson Space Center and NASA; p. 2 (bottom), NASA and U.S. Geological Survey, Eros Data Center; p. 3, Jet Propulsion Laboratory and NASA; p. 4, NASA.

Index